Landing on a moving deck requires precision flying; this is an SA 365F Dauphin.

MODERN
FIGHTING
HELICOPTERS

Liftoff by a menacing troop of US Army AH-1S Cobras.

A deadly combination: a Royal Navy HAS.2 Lynx armed with Sea Skua missiles.

MODERN FIGHTING HELICOPTERS

Bill Gunston   Mike Spick

Published by
CRESCENT BOOKS
New York

A Salamander Book   Credits

First English edition published by
Salamander Books Ltd.

This 1986 edition is published by
Crescent Books,
distributed by
Crown Publishers, Inc.,
225 Park Avenue South
New York, New York 10003,
United States of America.

ISBN 0-517-61349-2

Editor: Philip de Ste. Croix

Designers: Nick Buzzard and Barry Savage

Colour artwork (aircraft section): Mark Franklin, Terry Hadler,
David Palmer, Tony Payne, Stephen Seymour, Hans Wiborg-Jenssen.

Diagrams: Michael A. Badrocke and TIGA.

Filmset by SX Composing Ltd.

Colour reproduction by York House Graphics Ltd.

Printed in Italy by G. Canale & C SpA, Turin.

The publishers wish to thank wholeheartedly the many companies,
organisations and individuals in the aerospace industry and the armed
forces of various nations who have all been of considerable help in the
preparation of this book. Special thanks are due to Major D. J. Norrie,
HQ Army Air Corps, Netheravon; Major David Patterson, C.O. of 657
Sqn; Commander P. R. P. Madge of FONAC; Lt-Commander G. R. N.
Foster; Christina Gotzhein of MBB; and Debbie Lines of Westland
Helicopters Ltd.

The Authors

Bill Gunston is a former RAF pilot and flying instructor, and he has spent most of his working life accumulating a wealth of information on aerospace technology and history. Since leaving the Service, he has acted as an advisor to several aviation companies and become one of the most internationally respected authors and broadcasters on aviation and scientific subjects. His numerous books include the Salamander titles "The Illustrated Encyclopedia of the World's Modern Military Aircraft", "Modern Fighting Aircraft", "American Warplanes", "The Illustrated Encyclopedia of the World's Rockets and Missiles", "Soviet Air Power" (with Bill Sweetman), "Modern Air Combat" (with Mike Spick), and many of Salamander's successful illustrated guides to aviation subjects. He has also contributed to the authoritative "The Soviet War Machine" and "The US War Machine", by the same company, and carries out regular assignments for technical aviation periodicals. Mr. Gunston is also an assistant compiler of "Jane's All the World's Aircraft" and was formerly technical editor of "Flight International" and technology editor of "Science Journal".

Mike Spick was born in London less than three weeks before the Spitfire made its maiden flight. Educated at Churchers College, Petersfield (a school with a strong naval interest!), he later entered the construction industry and carried out considerable work on RAF airfields. An occasional broadcaster on aviation topics, Mr. Spick's interests include wargaming, which led him to a close study of air warfare, followed by a highly successful first book, "Air Battles in Miniature" (Patrick Stephens). Other books to his credit include the Salamander titles, "Modern Air Combat" (with Bill Gunston), "B-1B Fact File", "F-4 Phantom II Fact File" (with Doug Richardson), "F-14 Fact File", "F/A-18 Fact File", and "Fighter Pilot Tactics" (Patrick Stephens, 1983), which is a historical study of the evolution of tactics. He is currently working on a study of success in air combat.

Below: Photographed during Exercise Bright Star in 1980, a formation of Kiowas, Black Hawks and Cobras are silhouetted above the Egyptian pyramids.

Contents

Below: Symbolic of the new generation of battlefield helicopters, a McDonnell Douglas 530MG Defender and AH-64A overfly desert terrain in Arizona.

Foreword

Many of man's major inventions have materialized in different places but at the same time. At the very beginning of this century there was a great upsurge of interest in France in heavier-than-air machines that could fly, one result of which was that in 1907 two independently built helicopters succeeded in getting daylight under their wheels quite near each other in northern France. But from then on the helicopter was mostly a story of frustration. Not for another 30 years did such people as Dorand, Flettner and Focke develop helicopters that actually worked.

Flettner was certainly the first to get a helicopter into combat service, while in 1944 the 1,000hp Focke-Achgelis Fa 223 was far and away the most capable helicopter in the world. These are today almost forgotten, not least because they happened to be on the side that lost World War 2. It was left to the great Russian emigré Igor Sikorsky, with almost unbelievable determination, to coax from the uncontrollable VS-300 of 1939 something that could fairly be called a useful helicopter. The worth of his achievement is encapsulated in the saying "Before Sikorsky there was no helicopter industry; after him there was."

Today the moguls of TV entertainment have discovered that the aggressive helicopter rivals the dangerously driven car in helping push up audience ratings. Pop stars fly them, and thousands of people to whom time is precious use them as an everyday working tool. This, quite rightly, tends to obscure the fact that the helicopter was one of the most difficult of man's inventions to develop to an acceptable degree of efficiency and safety.

There cannot have been many helicopter designers who have not felt that all helicopters so far have been sadly imperfect

Below: A Royal Navy HAS.2 Sea King of 819 Naval Air Squadron during a simulated search and rescue operation at sea. Primarily an ASW aircraft, the HAS.2 here shows how helicopters can swiftly adapt to fulfil varying roles.

Above: A Boeing Vertol CH-47D Chinook uplifting a 155mm M198 howitzer, a load weighing 15,600lb (7076kg). The ability of such helicopters to move troops and equipment rapidly has added a new dimension to land warfare.

vehicles, flawed in basic ways that are difficult to overcome. Their basic aerodynamics are fine for hovering, but very poor as a way of going from A to B. Many must have felt tantalizingly close to a breakthrough that would get the best of both worlds. At the other end of the scale, the VTOL jet is fine in going from A to B, if necessary at Mach 1, but extremely inefficient when hovering. As a general rule, the bigger the airflow on which a vehicle can work, the less the acceleration that needs to be imparted to each parcel of air in order to obtain lift or propulsion, and the greater the efficiency. Thus, in hovering flight the giant helicopter rotor does better than the thunderous small-diameter jet; but in translational (ie. forwards) flight the rotor travelling almost sideways is nothing like as good as a fixed wing.

It was in an attempt to find a better compromise that, 35 years ago, Bell began designing a tilt-rotor VTOL aircraft. In the hover it was broadly a helicopter, while in translational flight it was an aeroplane with grossly oversized propellers. The history of aviation is liberally sprinkled with prototypes and research aircraft that were built to see if an idea worked, proved that the idea did work and were then thrown away and forgotten. In fact the surviving Bell XV-3 did at least get to the USAF Museum, but that is hardly the place for a harbinger of new technology. About 25 years after the XV-3 stopped flying someone picked up the tilt-rotor again and, for the second time, found it worked. Again, Bell was the chief company involved, and this time the idea has not merely been filed away. Bell and Boeing Vertol are jointly building a related family of tilt-rotor aircraft that promise to start off with almost 1,000 sales to US armed forces alone.

This machine, the V-22 Osprey, has been included in this book for two reasons. One is that it hovers like a helicopter. The other is that its successors are going to knock the stuffing out of the world helicopter market.

In hovering flight a tilt-rotor is inferior to a helicopter, so the world's helicopter builders can breathe a sigh of relief and go on planning helicopters for the anti-tank mission, ASW and SAR for as far ahead as can be seen. But most helicopters use their vertical lift capability only at the start and finish of each flight. By the 1990s we shall begin to see all of these being replaced by tilt-rotors, which will burn a gallon or two more on takeoff and landing but save half the fuel in flying to their destination at over 300mph (482km/h). This will not only save time but also cost.

Of course, if you are trying to save lives then cost per ton-mile is a secondary consideration. During its early years what we today call the SAR (search and rescue) mission was almost the only thing the helicopter was able to accomplish. Throughout the 1920s and 1930s Sikorsky's unceasing vision of the helicopter was spurred by his realization of what it could do for humanity. In his words, "If a man is in need of rescue, an airplane can come in and throw flowers on him, and that's just about all. But a direct-lift aircraft could come in and save his life".

Today we have succeeded in developing powerful helicopters that can save lives in adverse conditions, reconnoitre battlefields through darkness, smoke and winter blizzards, find and destroy the heaviest battle tanks, or hunt down and kill giant submarines. This is exciting, quite apart from being technically interesting, and it is the intention of this book to allow the reader to sample some of the excitement as well as providing comprehensive technical data and analysis. It opens with a 68-page fact-packed review of today's combat helicopter technology. There follow 92 pages devoted to the actual types in use or under development. The next 34 pages analyse the missions they can fly, concluding with what many readers will find essential: a glossary of terms.

Above: Today simulators are widely used to prepare pilots for combat. This is the view from the pilot's cockpit of the Link AH-64 Combat Mission Simulator. It can provide both out-of-the-window and sensor (in-cockpit) imagery.

Below: A pilot of the 38th Aerospace Rescue and Recovery Squadron at the controls of his HH-3E Jolly Green Giant. Search and rescue has been a vital mission throughout the history of helicopter operations.

Helicopter Technology

The point was made in the introduction to the book that the helicopter was one of the most difficult of man's inventions to develop to an acceptable degree of efficiency and safety. It has taken very large and sustained efforts by many thousands of engineers to produce such Rolls-Royces of the vertical-lift world as a comprehensively equipped VIP S-76B, or, in the harsher olive-green world of war, the AH-64A. The former gives you a smooth ride in opulent surroundings; the latter is a flying tank and exudes an aura of capability and survivability.

In fact, any really objective observer would be bound to say "If such machines are the best you can do, you're not very clever." Most helicopters are aurally obtrusive; you can hear them coming when they are still a dot on the horizon. Their method of locomotion is so ridiculous as to be a joke, pulled along by a rotor travelling almost sideways at the top of the machine. One side of the rotor runs into high-speed shock-stall problems near Mach 1 while the other side is partly stalled and partly has reversed airflow crossing the blades from trailing edge to leading edge! As the helicopter is pulled along from the top it tilts nose-down, so it probably has a tailplane pushing down at the back, which in effect increases weight as drag; perhaps one day we shall see a canard helicopter with a foreplane that adds to the lift? Again at the back we find a second rotor that is dragged through the air sideways and, often working in disturbed downwash from the main rotor, pushes sideways to stop the fuselage from spinning round.

Clearly, the fundamental aerodynamics of the helicopter impose severe limitations, but these strange birds can still do things no other vehicles can do. In the Soviet Union, more than anywhere else, helicopters play a central role in all land warfare as an organic part of the overall force structure. Strenuous efforts are being made to help them survive bullets and cannon shells (though SAM warheads are more difficult). Obviously, the modern "stealth" technology is especially relevant to these basically rather fragile flying machines.

In the following 66 pages all the chief facets of the technology of the modern helicopter are examined in some detail: structure and design, propulsion, cockpit technology, visionics and sensors, armament, protective systems, and likely future developments. The longest single section is covered by the ghastly portmanteau word "visionics". Many workers in the field of combat helicopters would agree that anybody can build a helicopter; fitting it with the right kit to enable it to see in the dark, fly at grass-top height in safety, avoid electric cables and other obstacles, see and destroy enemy tanks, operate in foul weather and generally do a useful job is 1,000 times more difficult. As for the question of survival, this also has a section to itself wherein will be found most of the current thinking on how helicopters can avoid being detected, avoid being aimed at if they are detected, avoid being hit if they are aimed at, avoid being shot down if they are hit, and avoid killing the crew if they are shot down.

The fact that, despite so many severe drawbacks, helicopters are eagerly sought in large numbers by air forces, armies and navies all over the world serves to underscore their value. Really they offer only one capability that is not possessed in much greater measure by aeroplanes: the ability to hover. Yet even here the aeroplane can hover, if we wish. The Harrier II not only hovers but can fly with agility, speed, altitude, range and endurance far beyond anything possible with helicopters. McDonnell Douglas have thought of all sorts of totally new missions such aircraft could perform, but they now have a helicopter company and have no wish to compete with themselves.

This introduction to helicopter technology is not intended to "knock" the helicopter. Rather it is a reminder that there is another side to the coin, and for the helicopter's ability to emulate the hummingbird we pay a very high price. Indeed, the word "price" can be taken literally. Our S-76B will set us back well over $4 million; for the same money we could buy a dozen same-capacity fixed-wingers or a 300mph 30-seat twin-turboprop! So we can fairly sum up the present state of helicopter technology as highly imperfect, very expensive and indispensable.

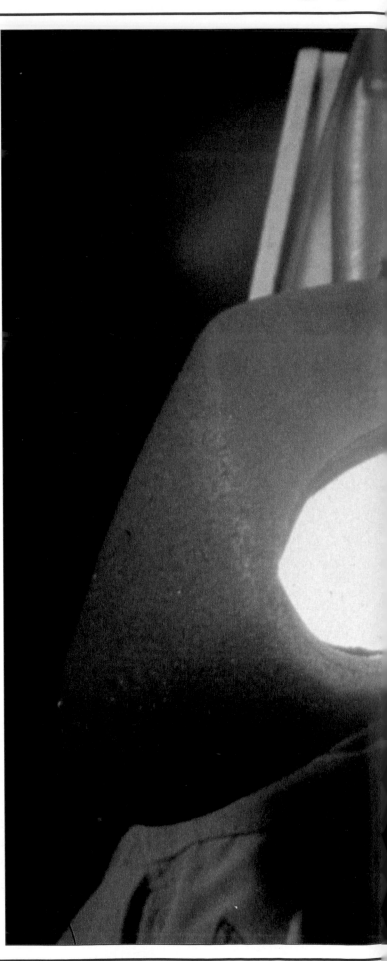

Below: This futuristic helmet is VCASS undergoing test at Wright-Patterson AFB. The "eyes" are screens which show the pilot what is happening outside the cockpit with flight data superimposed over the scene. Airborne versions of VCASS are being studied for the US Army's next-generation LHX family.

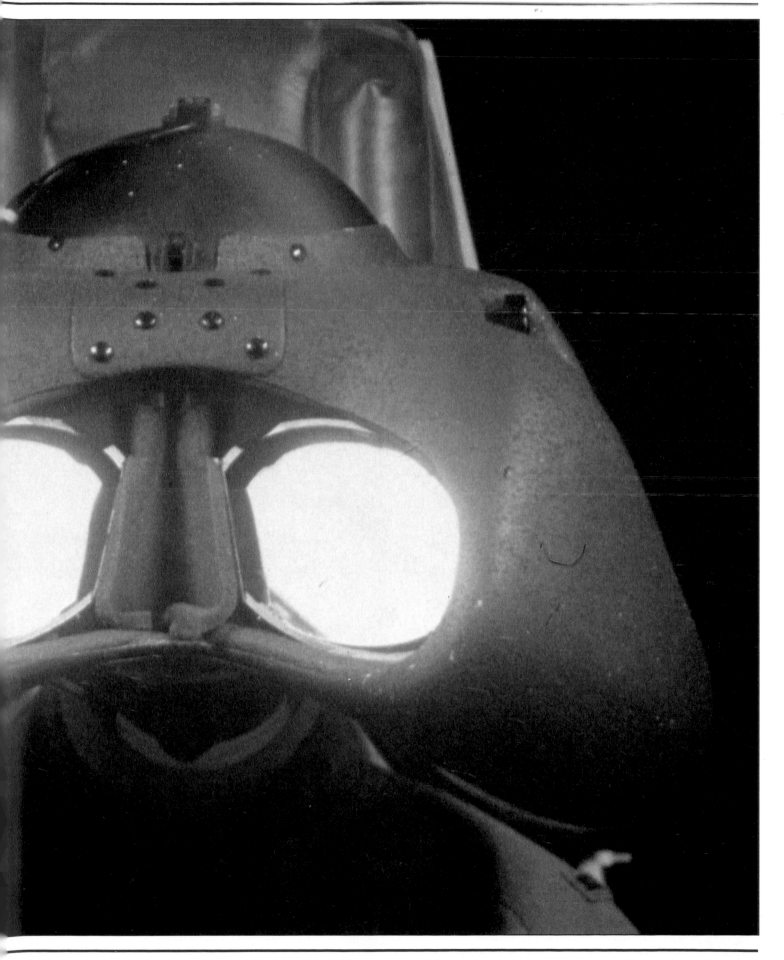

Anatomy of a Helicopter

Key to A 129 components:

1 PNVS (pilot's night vision sensor), comprising a FLIR (forward-looking infra-red) sensor which displays clear pictures in the pilot's cockpit on the darkest night.

2 CPG's instrument panel.

3 Viewing scope for the CPG.

4 The main rotor provides both lift and propulsion. The blades are in effect long, narrow, thin wings. The rotors are driven by the engine(s) via gearboxes and shafting.

5 Special seats are fitted, in this case Martin-Baker armoured "crashworthy" seats which absorb severe impacts without damaging the occupant's vertebrae. Ejection seats cannot be used, because of the main rotor.

6 Pilot's instrument panel.

7 The pilot sits behind and above the CPG. Both cockpits have bullet-resisting flat glass canopies to minimise "glint". In the side panels are sliding windows for direct vision and ventilation. The right panels hinge upward for cockpit access, and in emergency the armoured sidewall can

be blown out by small explosive cords.

8 A cable cutter is needed, because in high-speed flight at low level cables are the greatest single danger to the helicopter.

9 Hinges. Each main-rotor blade has to be controllable in pitch (angle of incidence) and also free to pivot up and down and to front and rear. In most helicopters this articulation is provided by hinges at the root of the blade.

10 The engine air inlets have to be aerodynamically efficient at all speeds and with the helicopter flying

even sideways or backwards. Combat helicopters have inlets shaped to reduce radar reflectivity, and it is essential to filter out dust, sand and salt spray.

11 Hub. The main-rotor hub is the strongest single part of the helicopter. In the A 129 the swashplates that control the pitch of the blades are inside the tubular rotor mast to give added protection against hostile fire.

12 The rotor mast transmits the drive and supports the entire weight of the helicopter. In this helicopter it has a diameter large enough for the installation of an MMS (mast-mounted sight), which would house the PNVS/TADS here mounted on the nose. An MMS enables a helicopter to hide

behind cover and see the enemy without more than a tiny fraction of it being seen.

13 The engine cowling panels are often made strong enough to be used as servicing platforms. The fuel tanks, deep inside the fuselage, are invariably "crashworthy" (do not rupture in severe crashes) and protected against fire by reticulated foam inside and between the tanks.

14 IR jammer. Infra-red homing missiles can be put off the scent by radiating very strong pulses of IR (heat). The missile keeps seeing the hot engine exhausts followed by the even more attractive IRCM (IR countermeasures) and cannot remain locked on the target.

15 The engine exhausts provide a source of IR (heat) on which missiles

can home. Everything possible must be done to cool the plume(s) of hot gas and shroud the hot metal parts within a cool box.

16 The main-rotor blade leading edges are protected against erosion by hard metal skin, usually stainless steel, nickel or titanium. Sometimes an electric heating element is incorporated to discourage the formation of ice.

17 The rear fuselage is sometimes a slender boom joining the tail to a tadpole-like fuselage pod. In this helicopter there is a normal streamlined fuselage from

Below: This three-view drawing of the Agusta A 129 Mangusta attack helicopter is included here to show the main components of a modern battlefield helicopter, and the systems that are fitted to it. Naval helicopters are equipped with systems appropriate to their operating environment, but the basic technology remains the same.

nose to tail. The structure may be metal or of advanced composites reinforced with fibres of glass or carbon. The tail-rotor drive shaft runs inside the spine along the top.
18 The blade tips may be specially shaped to reduce noise and increase aerodynamic efficiency. The actual shape varies from one helicopter type to another.
19 The tail-rotor pylon is today usually shaped like a fin, often swept back to increase the moment arm of the tail rotor (its distance from the aircraft centre of gravity).
20 The tail rotor blades can be metal or composite, and revolve at high speed. The sideways thrust counteracts the torque needed to drive the main rotor. The thrust can be

varied by adjusting the blade pitch with the cockpit pedals to swing the helicopter's nose in the required direction.
21 The tail-rotor gearbox turns the drive through a right-angle and also adjusts the rotational speed (rpm) to the required level.
22 This helicopter has a tailwheel with a long-stroke shock strut, attached to a deep ventral tailfin. Other helicopters have tricycle landing gear, or floats (usually inflatable pontoons).
23 The tailplane (horizontal stabilizer) may be fixed or have its incidence adjusted, either by the pilot or automatically by the main-rotor controls. It normally operates in a diagonal downwash from the main rotor.

24 If a wire aerial (antenna) is fitted it usually denotes the installation of a long-wave HF communications radio, giving long-distance voice contact (for example with army or naval forces).
25 Blade aerials (antennas) are used by VHF (very high frequency) radios. Smaller blades probably mean that UHF (ultra high frequency) radios are installed.
26 Combat helicopters protect themselves with a chaff/flare dispenser. This resembles an outward-facing egg-box. Each of its tubes is loaded with a large cartridge the contents

of which are either millions of strips of radar-reflective chaff or a hot-burning flare composition to attract IR-homing missiles away from the helicopter.
27 Weapon "wings" project from the fuselage to provide attachments for a wide range of attack missiles, gun pods and other loads including auxiliary fuel tanks.
28 Missiles can be carried to attack tanks, ships or other types of target. Here two quad launchers for the TOW anti-tank missile are installed. TOWs are fired individually and guided to the target using a magnifying optical sight.
29 Here rocket launchers are carried on the inboard weapon stations. An armed attack helicopter usually has a mix of weapons.

30 The main landing gears are designed with long-stroke shock struts to absorb the energy in high-rate emergency descents. In really severe crashes nothing must be able to punch up through the floor of either cockpit.
31 Steps to assist entry and egress.
32 Pilot's rear-view mirror, useful to see close formating helicopters and, especially, any hostile aircraft coming up astern.
33 Pitot heads sense the ram pressure of air entering an open forward-facing tube; comparing this with local static pressure gives a measure of airspeed.
34 The RWR (radar warning receiver) has small passive receiver aerials (antennas) which detect signals from enemy radars "illuminating" the

helicopter, and warn the crew. The display shows the identity, direction and lethal range of the threat.
35 TADS (target acquisition and designation sight), comprising a turret which can rotate 120° to left or right, with sensors which pivot vertically. In the left half of the turret is the daylight sensor, consisting of a TV camera and a laser rangefinder/designator. On the right is a FLIR. The TADS feeds displays for the CPG (copilot gunner) but can also provide backup night (FLIR) vision to the pilot.

Helicopter Design

Above: Simulated rescue by the US Navy's first helicopter, an HNS-1 (Sikorsky R-4B), in 1944. This type played a major role in establishing the configuration of today's helicopters.

Right: Vietnam "specials", an HC-130P tanker and Pave Low 3 HH-53H Super Jolly, afford a comparison between fixed and rotating wings. One can see the rise and fall of the rotating blades.

Prior to World War 2 a great Spaniard, Juan de la Cierva, devoted his life to perfecting the autogyro, or as he registered the name the Autogiro. He did not so much set out to invent a new flying machine as make an aeroplane that could not stall and crash. He thus started with an aeroplane fuselage, with a propeller at the front and tail at the back, and tried to replace the wings by a freely spinning rotor. In cruising flight an autogyro is pulled or pushed along by its propeller, and the freely spinning rotor is kept turning by the flow of air past it. The plane of the rotor is inclined backwards, the tips of the blades being high at the front and low at the rear, so the airflow is diagonally upwards through the rotor disc.

There have been autogyros that incorporated a drive from the engine to the rotor, but this was only to give what was called "jump start" capability, today called VTO for vertical takeoff. Autogyros cannot hover, except in a strong wind, and this limits their usefulness. The helicopter, whose rotors are continuously driven under power to thrust air downwards, is the true dragonfly or hummingbird among man's creations. Its ability to operate from small platforms or backyards, and to hover, more than makes up for its high price, high insurance premiums, high fuel bills and generally poor flight performance in comparison with aeroplanes of similar installed power.

An accompanying tabulation compares a modern utility aeroplane, the Cessna Caravan I, with a modern utility helicopter made in the same country with a similar level of technology, the Bell 206L-3 LongRanger III. Both aircraft have been most

Autogyro and Helicopter

Above: Similarity between the autogyro and helicopter is only superficial. The autogyro is essentially an aeroplane, thrust along by its propeller, but whose wings happen to rotate. They are kept turning by the fact that the

competently designed and engineered, and are fairly representative of the current "state of the art". The figures emphasize that the unique capabilities of the helicopter are not gained for nothing. As in most things, aircraft design is a matter of swings and roundabouts, and gains in one area balance losses in another.

Equally significant is the fact that, whereas fixed-wing aircraft can go as fast as the customer wants (the Shuttle Orbiter reaches a typical orbital speed of 15,285kt or 17,600mph, 28,325km/h), the helicopter is still subject to a severe restriction on forward speed. Though not everyone would agree,

resultant aerodynamic force on the blades is always just ahead of the axis of rotation, so there is always a small force in the tip-path plane pulling the blade forwards. The helicopter is totally different. Here the rotor has to

the author believes that this limitation is not absolute. In the pre-Whittle era it was universally believed that there could never be a 500mph (805km/h) aeroplane, but jet propulsion swept this "limit" away for ever. However, the really fast helicopter is difficult to build. Most of the installed power is used in overcoming gravity. The rotor system is not an efficient way of propelling the machine forwards. Perhaps most difficult of all is the fact that the airspeed of the advancing blade (see diagrams of rotor in plan view) is equal to that due to its own rotation added to the speed of the helicopter. Conversely, the speed of the

provide propulsion as well as lift, and its axis is angled sharply forwards. The resultant aerodynamic force is inclined steeply back from the axis of rotation, and a great deal of power is needed to keep the rotor turning.

retreating blade is equal to that due to its rotation minus the speed of the helicopter. A little thought will show that, as the helicopter's forward speed increases, things begin to happen on opposite sides of the disc. Long before the helicopter has reached the speed at which Concorde leaves the runway the tips of the advancing blades run into shock-stall problems as the airspeed over them reaches the speed of sound. On the other side the retreating blades are in even bigger trouble. Some way out from the hub the tangential speed due to rotation is exactly equal to the speed of the helicopter, but in the opposite direction, so at this point the effective airspeed is zero. Between here and the hub the relative wind is backwards, passing over the blade from trailing edge to leading edge, which does not do much for aerofoil efficiency! Towards the tip the angle of attack (the angle at which the blade meets the air) soon reaches that at which the blade stalls. This eliminates lift from a large section of the disc.

COMPARISON OF 1986 HELICOPTER AND AEROPLANE

	Engine	Gross weight	Max seating	Max cruising speed	Service ceiling	Range (see footnote)
Helicopter Bell LongRanger III	485kW (650shp)	4,150lb (1882kg)	2+5	126mph (203km/h)	20,000ft (6096m)	368 miles (592km)
Aeroplane Cessna Caravan I	447kW (600shp)	7,300lb (3311kg)	1+13	213mph (342km/h)	30,000ft (9144m)	1,139 miles (1833km)

Note: helicopter range is with no reserves; aeroplane range full allowances plus 45min reserve.

Above: A Royal Navy Westland Sea King on icing trials (Wessex in foreground) vividly illustrates the airflow through the rotor of a hovering helicopter. In forward flight the flow is inclined at a shallower angle.

Almost everything about the helicopter is asymmetric and complex. Taking out lift from the stalled part of the disc makes the helicopter roll to the left, pitch nose-up and also sink straight down, all at the same time. Manoeuvres that are simple with an aeroplane require the helicopter pilot to make quite different yet time-synchronized movements of both hands and feet. On top of other problems the helicopter inevitably involves sustained high torque transmitted through gears and shafts that cannot be duplicated, complex aerodynamic interactions between the rotors (and with shaft drive there must always be a minimum of two rotors), and ceaseless threshing oscillations and stress reversals that are most undesirable from the viewpoints of noise, vibration and the fatigue life of primary structure. Before 1990 the presence of rotors may also be recognised as simplifying an enemy's task of detecting the helicopter and even identifying its type.

ROTORS

Engines and drive systems are discussed in the next section, so it is logical to begin with the rotors. Together with the drive gearboxes and shafts they make up what are called the dynamic parts. These are the ones subjected to constant motion, high and often rapidly reversing stresses (even in still air), oand when they are made of metal they inevitably have limited fatigue lives. Such parts in aeroplanes are often duplicated or made in a "fail safe" way so that, should one part crack with fatigue, there is no catastrophic breakage. With helicopters this is impractical, and everything has to be designed so that fatigue cracks do not even start.

A helicopter can be arranged in various ways. By far the most common is the MTR (main and tail rotor) or "penny-farthing" configuration. The main rotor provides lift and propulsion, and a small rotor on a horizontal axis at the tail keeps pulling the tail sideways to counteract the main-rotor drive torque (otherwise the main rotor would turn one way and the helicopter the other). Many designers have eliminated the tail rotor by using some form of tip drive, for example by blasting compressed air from the main-

Blade Tip Speed

Right: As soon as a helicopter begins to move forwards the airspeed starts to vary in different parts of the main-rotor disc. It is speeded up on the side of the "advancing blades" and slowed down on the opposite side where the blades are "retreating". Here a helicopter is flying at 130mph, while its main-rotor tips have an airspeed due to rotation of 420mph, but their actual speed oscillates between 290 and 550mph (467 and 885km/h).

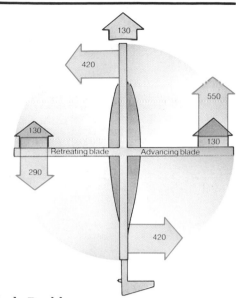

The Retreating Blade Problem

Right: This diagram attempts to illustrate the complex behaviour of every ordinary helicopter main rotor in cruising flight. Density of shading indicates blade pitch angle: darker shading means greater pitch. Round most of the disc the blades give useful lift, as shown by the blue areas. The inner part of the retreating blade is actually pulled backwards through the air, so this is a region of reversed flow (red disc). The outer part reaches such a high pitch angle that the blade stalls (red area near periphery of disc). The small diagram plots blade airspeed across the line AB. The symmetric thin blue lines show the corresponding airspeed when the helicopter is hovering, reaching just 420mph at both tips.

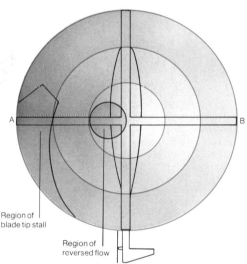

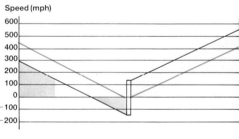

The Torque Problem

Right: Driving the main rotor in the common way, by applying power at the rotor shaft, automatically tries to drive the helicopter's fuselage in the opposite direction. If the rotor moves in the direction of the curved blue arrows, the fuselage tends to rotate in the direction of the red arrow. To prevent this, a tail rotor is added, which throughout flight keeps thrusting the tail sideways in the direction of the straight blue arrow.

rotor blade tips, but these have never enjoyed significant sales.

The "penny-farthing" remains the dominant configuration because of its inherent stability and simplicity. Other arrangements include twin tandem rotors, twin side-by-side rotors, twin intermeshing rotors and twin coaxial rotors. The twin tandem, used in the Chinook, suits a transport helicopter because it opens up the permissible range of CG (centre of gravity) position. Twin lateral rotors were used in the Soviet V-12, the biggest helicopter ever, but have never proved successful. Intermeshing, or "eggbeater" rotors have been used in several successful helicopters, but are unlikely to be seen again. The coaxial arrangement is seen in all the current Kamov types, partly because it makes possible a very compact helicopter for shipboard operations.

Each main-rotor blade is in effect a wing. For efficiency it is very slender, much narrower than aeroplane wings, and centrifugal force prevents it from bending upwards. A diagram shows how the airflow creates intense reduction in pressure (in effect suction) above the front of the blade, and increased pressure along the underside of the leading edge. The result is sufficient lift to overcome the helicopter's weight, and this broadly upward force, like all other rotor forces, is transmitted through the root of each blade into the hub and down through the main drive shaft to a large bearing from which the rest of the helicopter hangs.

Like most things about the helicopter this is just the start of a complex story. In hovering flight all blades are set to the same angle of incidence at all times. Their angle of attack is equal to the angle of incidence reduced by an angle proportional to the vertical downwards velocity of the air through the rotor disc. The pilot

A Slender Wing

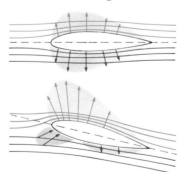

Above: Each blade is a slender wing, but in comparison with most wings it is relatively thick (here this is exaggerated) and often of symmetric profile. At zero incidence, or neutral pitch (upper drawing), pressure is uniformly below atmospheric all round the blade, and there is no lift. At a positive pitch (lower drawing) increased pressure below augments the top-surface suction.

Helicopter Configurations

Right: There are many possible configurations for a helicopter, but only five have been important and three of these are rare. By far the commonest arrangement is the so-called "penny farthing", here represented by a Westland Lynx, in which the torque of driving a single lifting rotor is reacted by a tail rotor. Its almost universal usage shows that, despite its many complexities, it is probably the best overall layout. Next comes the twin tandem rotor arrangement, as used in the Boeing Vertol Chinook. This uses tandem rotors, usually with the blades intermeshing and thus counter-rotating, and with their axes tilted to cancel out any torque imparted to the fuselage. The twin side-by-side configuration has never been popular, though it was used on the biggest helicopter ever built, the Mil V-12. The Kaman HH-43 Huskie featured the "eggbeater" layout, in which two rotors turn in opposite directions on two closely spaced inclined shafts. Last of the configurations depicted is the coaxial (Ka-25 is shown). Here the two rotors are superimposed, one shaft rotating in the opposite direction inside the other. This is a very compact layout.

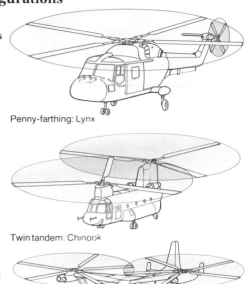

Penny-farthing: Lynx

Twin tandem: Chinook

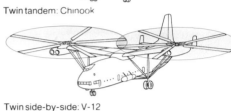

Twin side-by-side: V-12

Twin intermeshing: HH-43

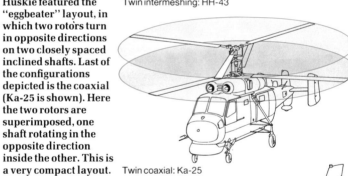

Twin coaxial: Ka-25

Flight Control System

Below: Here an Agusta A 109A is used to illustrate in simplified form how the main elements of a flight control system are arranged. The main rotor hub, with actuators, is shown in greater detail on the facing page.

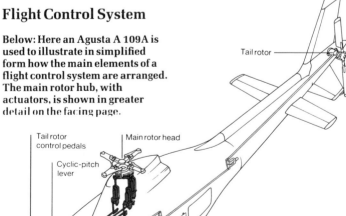
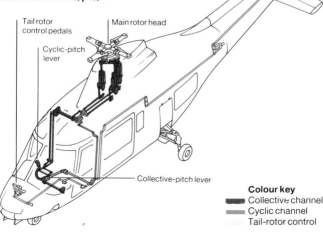

Tail rotor

Tail rotor control pedals

Main rotor head

Cyclic-pitch lever

Collective-pitch lever

Colour key
Collective channel
Cyclic channel
Tail-rotor control

Above: The vital tail rotor has push/pull rods to control the pitch of its blades according to the input demands of the pilot or (as in this AH-64A Apache) the automatic flight controls. Here the blades are set 55° apart, to reduce noise.

has a large lever low down on the left of his seat, pivoted up/down at the rear. This is the collective-pitch lever, or the "collective". Pulling it up increases the angle of incidence of all blades together. The pilot grasps the collective by means of a handgrip which rotates. This handgrip is a twistgrip throttle as on a motorcycle. To take off the pilot smoothly pulls up the collective whilst rotating the throttle to full power. At a certain point the rotor lift will overcome weight, and the helicopter rises.

Increasing power and blade incidence greatly increases the drive torque to the rotor. To keep the helicopter from rotating the opposite way the tail-rotor incidence must be increased at the same time. In almost all helicopters (except for the French and Russians, who are perverse) the main rotor rotates anticlockwise when viewed from above. The tail rotor is controlled by the pedals, and as the power comes on the pilot pushes progressively down on the left pedal.

Once climbing away we want to go somewhere. Further pressure on left or right pedal has the effect of making the helicopter rotate to the left or right, just like the rudder of an aeroplane but without the need for any forward speed. When we are pointing the way we wish to go we can start moving forwards.

This takeoff is, of course, very much non-standard but has the advantage of doing one thing at a time. A real helicopter mission would invariably accelerate straight ahead to get forward speed as soon as possible, and only then turn on course very much like an aeroplane. Before the flight becomes really complex the point must be made that the helicopter lifts off with less power than would be needed if there was no solid surface under the helicopter. This is because of the favourable interaction, called ground effect, of the powerful downflow of air

through the rotor and the ground. This is reduced by strong winds, dense ground cover and other interferences. In performance specifications it is usual to give the helicopter's hovering ceiling IGE (in ground effect) and OGE (out of it). A ceiling of 15,000ft (4572m) IGE means that the helicopter could just hover above an infinite smooth plate held horizontal 15,000ft above the ground. Take the plate away and the helicopter would fall until the air had become dense enough for engine power and rotor lift to support once again the machine without forward speed, perhaps at 8,000ft (2438m).

We were left climbing away facing the way we wished to go. Between our knees is the cyclic-pitch stick, corresponding to the control column of an aeroplane. This does not interfere with the collective setting, but, by means of fixed and rotating swashplates under the rotor hub, it varies the pitch of each blade as it travels round the disc. If we keep the cyclic centred the swashplates remain horizontal, though they can be moved up and down by the collective, varying all blade angles together. In the traditional articulated form of rotor each blade is held in a rotary bearing in the hub, and its pitch is controlled from the upper (rotating) swashplate by a pitch-change arm and a connecting rod (see large drawing of A 109 hub). For the sake of argument we will assume that in hovering flight all blades are at 10°.

Moving the cyclic stick in any direction tilts the swashplates in that direction, the amount of tilt being proportional to cyclic stick movement. Clearly, tilting the swashplates means that, as each blade rotates round the disc, its pitch will be increased over one half of the disc and decreased over the other half. Instead of remaining at 10° our blades now keep oscillating between a minimum of, say, 5° at one point and 15° on the other side of the disc. A small angle

Above: A US Army Black Hawk makes a desert landing, with a little forward speed. Rotor downwash is disturbing the desert surface. This helicopter is 100 per cent IGE (in ground effect), and its rotor gives greatly enhanced lift.

Below: Close-up of a typical modern main rotor, showing hingeless design. This rotor, used on the BO 105 and BK 117, clearly reveals the three inputs to the lower swashplate governing pitch.

IGE and OGE

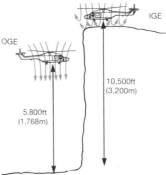

Above: Helicopter hovering ceiling is always much higher when IGE (in ground effect), in which a flat plate is imagined directly beneath the helicopter to deflect the rotor downwash up again. A Lynx has a ceiling IGE of 10,500ft (3200m) compared with a ceiling OGE of only 5,800ft (1768m). IGE measures are idealised, and ignore such disturbing factors as engine hot-gas ingestion.

An Articulated Hub

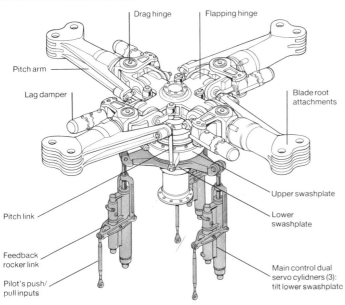

Collective and Cyclic

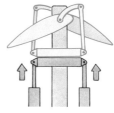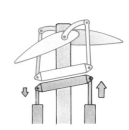

Left: The Italian Agusta A 109A has an articulated hub of conventional design, with four blades attached at the multiple-laminate fixings on the ends of the rotor arms. Pilot control demands come in via the three red hydraulic actuators (shown the same colour in the drawing on the facing page). These tilt, raise or lower the lower (fixed) swashplate, which is also coloured red. This transfers its movements to the adjoining rotating swashplate, from which four arms and push/pull rods adjust the pitch angles of the four blades.

Above: The pilot has two main flight-control levers with which he flies the helicopter. The collective lever, pulled up/down by his left hand, alters the pitch of all main-rotor blades (blue) together. It moves the lower swashplate (red) up or down, twisting all blades equally. Between the pilot's legs is the cyclic stick, and this tilts the swashplates to any desired angle. Tilting the plates makes the blades oscillate in pitch on each rotation, tilting the tip-path plane (rotor disc) and making the helicopter head in the desired direction.

The Rotor Hinges

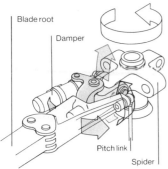

Blade root

Damper

Pitch link

Spider

Above: Traditional articulated rotors have hinges built into the hub. These used to demand repeated lubrication, but today elastomeric (rubber) bearings are used. Blue denotes the flapping or coning hinge, which allows the blade to pivot up and down. Red is the drag hinge. Green is the pitch-change input.

means reduced lift, so the blade tends to fall, rotating downwards about the flapping hinge. A large angle means enhanced lift, which makes the blade rise and pivot upwards about the flapping hinge. The flapping hinges are needed for various reasons, quite apart from cyclic control demands. The reader might ask "What stops the blades from pivoting vertically up, so that the helicopter just falls like a stone?" The answer is that they are kept more or less horizontal by centrifugal force. There is also a physical stop to their upwards movement, called the anti-coning stop, but this is needed only at very low rotor speeds on the ground when the blades could indeed be lifted right up by a gale, causing damage when they fell back.

As the helicopter has no other means of propulsion the main rotor has to be used to move it in the direction in which the pilot wishes to go. Thus, to transition into forward flight the pilot moves the cyclic a little way forward of neutral, at the same time pulling up a little on the collective to prevent the machine settling as it comes out of ground effect. The swashplates tilt and increase the angle of each blade as it moves from the front on to the retreating side, making the blade climb higher as it travels round to the highest point at the rear. From here the angle falls, so the blade also falls as it travels round to the front. This tilts what is called the tip-path plane; the whole rotor disc tilts forwards, though the rotor drive shaft remains vertical (in practice pilots tend to tilt the whole machine nose-down to increase forwards acceleration, but this is not necessary and makes the explanation harder). Tilting the rotor disc naturally tilts the

Right: This Sidewinder-armed AH-1W SuperCobra clearly shows the inclination of the main-rotor tip-path plane in high-speed forwards flight. Note how the forward blade is in high pitch to make it climb up to the rear.

Right: This US Army Apache is seen as it is transitioning from the hover into high-speed forwards flight, and the nose-down attitude is needed for forward acceleration.

resultant lift force on the blades so that it has a horizontal component, and this pulls the helicopter along.

As it accelerates forwards the lift of the rotor increases slightly because of the increased (induced) airflow through the rotor, while the weathervane effect of the tail means that the pedal pressure previously needed to keep straight can be progressively relaxed. Established in forward, or translational, flight the helicopter appears to have settled into a smooth condition in a level attitude, but in reality the situation is complex in the extreme. The blades continuously oscillate between a minimum pitch angle and a maximum, responding by climbing up the retreating side of the disc and descending down the advancing side. This is made possible by the flapping hinges, and the same hinges also enable the blades to even out lift on the left and right sides by the same rising and falling motion quite apart from that induced by cyclic pitch changes. Without these complications the advancing side of the rotor would generate much more lift than the retreating side and roll the helicopter over.

The up/down flapping of the blades causes stresses within the plane of the rotor tending to bend the blades horizontally, alternately increasing and reducing the angular gap between each blade and the next. Such bending would eventually cause fatigue, so a further set of hinges is usually provided which permit the blades to pivot through a small "drag angle" to front and rear; these are called drag hinges. Naval helicopters often have special drag hinges which enable the rotor to be folded, either by hand or by hydraulic power, so that the

helicopter can enter a small shipboard hangar.

Not all helicopters have fully articulated rotors with pitch-change bearings, flapping hinges and drag hinges. Back in World War 2 Bell and Hiller developed semi-articulated rotors with two blades with neither flapping nor drag hinges. Always directly opposite each other, the two rigidly connected blades were pivoted see-saw fashion on top of the drive shaft. At right angles to this "teetering rotor" were added

short rods. On the Bell these carried streamlined weights on the ends and formed a stabilizer bar, while the Hiller rods carried control surfaces resembling short lengths of rotor which were driven to coarse angles by the cyclic stick to tilt the entire head and thus produce the required tilting of the rotor without actually having any cyclic pitch control on the blades.

By 1962 Lockheed-California was flying the first helicopter to have a so-called rigid rotor. By carefully designing a forged hub

Chinook Hub

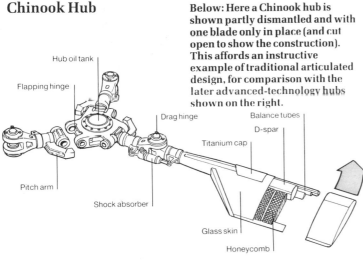

Below: Here a Chinook hub is shown partly dismantled and with one blade only in place (and cut open to show the construction). This affords an instructive example of traditional articulated design, for comparison with the later advanced-technology hubs shown on the right.

Hub oil tank
Flapping hinge
Pitch arm
Shock absorber
Glass skin
Honeycomb
Drag hinge
Titanium cap
D-spar
Balance tubes

New-technology Rotors

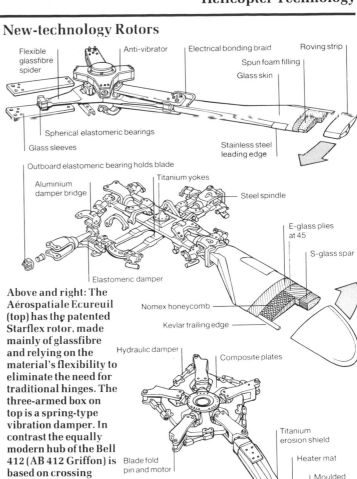

Flexible glassfibre spider
Anti-vibrator
Electrical bonding braid
Roving strip
Spun foam filling
Glass skin
Spherical elastomeric bearings
Glass sleeves
Stainless steel leading edge
Outboard elastomeric bearing holds blade
Aluminium damper bridge
Titanium yokes
Steel spindle
Elastomeric damper
E-glass plies at 45
S-glass spar
Nomex honeycomb
Kevlar trailing edge
Hydraulic damper
Composite plates
Blade fold pin and motor
Titanium erosion shield
Heater mat
Moulded glass/carbon nose
Glass skin
Honeycomb
Carbon wall spars
BERP tip (filament wound)

Above and right: The Aérospatiale Ecureuil (top) has the patented Starflex rotor, made mainly of glassfibre and relying on the material's flexibility to eliminate the need for traditional hinges. The three-armed box on top is a spring-type vibration damper. In contrast the equally modern hub of the Bell 412 (AB 412 Griffon) is based on crossing yokes of forged titanium in which steel blade roots are held in elastomeric bearings. Last comes the very advanced rotor of the EH 101, with five composite blades retained by elastomeric bearings and metal roots in a pentagon plate of composites on a metal core.

offering the right degree of flexibility it was found possible to dispense with flapping and drag hinges, which not only reduced cost and improved reliability but also opened the way to higher speed and dramatically better manoeuvrability. For the first time the Lockheed helicopters showed that a helicopter could manoeuvre like a fighter. Since then different manufacturers have adopted quite different approaches to rotor design – a remarkable thing in an industry so strongly influenced by

Below: Probably to be used by MBB Helicopter Canada on the BO 105 LS (two P&W 205B engines), this completely new titanium five-blade hub started tests in 1986.

Above: A formation of Agusta-Bell AB 205s clearly shows the stabilizer bars on their "teetering" rotors. Proven in some 30,000 examples, the teetering rotor rocks like a see-saw on its hub, the tip-path plane ruled by pilot input and by the masses on the stabilizer bar.

fashion. Rather than indulging in long descriptions some contrasting rotors are depicted in comparative drawings which also explain the different blade constructions.

Early blades were of fairly simple aerofoil profile, often almost symmetrical and with the high thickness/chord ratio of 15 to 20 per cent. Today more efficient profiles, often of reflex Wortmann sections as used in championship

sailplanes, are often used with thickness/chord ratio of only 5 to 8 per cent. Nobody has discovered a practical way of using high-lift devices such as droops, Krügers, slats or flaps on a helicopter rotor, though for various reasons there have been prolonged efforts to blow compressed air from spanwise slits.

Using such a blowing system (see diagram) it is possible to make

a helicopter rotor blade symmetrical in a totally new sense in that the front half is a mirror-image of the rear half. Thus, looking at one edge of the blade, there is no way of knowing whether it is the leading edge or trailing edge. This opens the way to a dramatic breakthrough in helicopter speed. We have already seen that, because of supersonic tips on the advancing side of the

The Circulation-Control Rotor

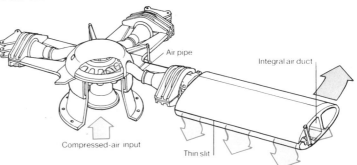

Air pipe
Integral air duct
Compressed-air input
Thin slit

Above: A typical brilliant British invention never funded to completion, the circulation-control rotor has now been picked up by the US Navy and is flying on an HH-2D. Blowing a thin sheet of

air downwards along the trailing edge not only increases lift but could eliminate vibration and, in the longer term, lead to the high-speed "stopped rotor" machine.

Above: The BERP rotor appears to represent the best that can at present be achieved with a conventional helicopter rotor blade. Here the new rotor is installed on a Lynx.

disc and stalled tips on the retreating side, helicopters cannot normally fly faster than about 200mph (322km/h). If only we could slow the rotor down and stop it, with the helicopter still travelling at full speed! Then there would be no such limitation on speed.

Britain's National Gas Turbine Establishment was the first to research the "circulation controlled rotor" with compressed air blown from slits to control the airflow round a blade of elliptical section, with leading and trailing edges identical. The problem with trying to stop a conventional rotor is that on one side the air flows in the reverse direction, from trailing edge to leading edge, and this is unacceptable. With a blade of elliptical profile it makes no difference which side the air comes from, and the circulation round the blade can be controlled by blowing from different slits along the front or back of the blade. The NGTE unfortunately had no budget to continue their work, which has now been picked up by Sikorsky in the USA. The S-72 RSRA (rotor systems research aircraft) was in 1985 beginning an exciting flight-test period which it is hoped will eventually lead in late 1986 to stopped-rotor flight with auxiliary jet propulsion up to speeds around 518mph (834km/h). Severe problems remain to be solved in both the blowing system and the aeroelastic deflection of the two front blades, which become slender forward-swept wings.

The stopped rotor offers enormous potential to whoever can make it work. Meanwhile research continues to improve traditional rotors. Probably the most efficient so far is the Westland composite-bladed rotor with BERP (British experimental rotor programme) tips. These new blades represent the pinnacle of

Above: The Sikorsky S-72 RSRA has been funded by NASA and the US Army and has already, with turbofan auxiliary propulsion as seen here, broken much new ground. With the rotor stopped speed should reach 361mph.

the art of conventional rotor design and were made possible by a combination of computer design, computer-controlled composite manufacture and the development of a new form of blade aeroelastically tailored from root to tip. Inboard the blade has a reflex (upward-curved) trailing edge, while outboard it becomes progressively thinner but with a drooped leading edge of large radius. The tip has increased chord, progressive (curved) LE sweep, and is bodily moved forward to keep c.g. in line. Mass distribution from root to tip is close to the ideal, and an idea of the

careful tailoring of the design is seen in the combination of different kinds of carbon and glass fibres with internal foams, superplastically formed titanium and using nickel coatings to resist erosion and lightning strike. The resulting blade has been made aeroelastically correct both for four-blade Lynx rotors and five-blade Westland 30 rotors. Among other things it extends the forward speed potential of conventional helicopters to "well in excess of 200kt" (230mph, 371km/h).

DYNAMIC PARTS

Under this heading come the engines (described in the next major chapter), gearboxes, drive shafts and control system. Obviously there has to be a speed-reducing gearbox connecting an engine with an output shaft turning at (in the case of the Super

Right: Royal Navy ground crew service a Sea King at RNAS Yeovilton. More than two-thirds of the maintenance needed by traditional helicopters is required by the engines and the associated dynamic parts.

Puma) 23,840rpm with a main rotor (again citing the Super Puma) turning at 265rpm. The gearbox is crucial to the helicopter's continued flight, and indeed it not only transmits the drive but also, in most helicopters, carries the machine's weight as well. The power and torque transmitted through the gearbox are very large, so inevitably this tends to be a massive piece of machinery. In the first really powerful helicopter, the Soviet Mi-6, the gearbox is roughly 6.6ft (2m) square and 9.9ft (3m) high (in other words it would not fit between floor and ceiling in an average room) and without its oil

Dynamic Parts

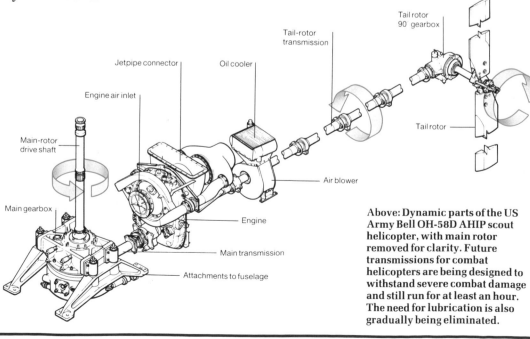

Above: Dynamic parts of the US Army Bell OH-58D AHIP scout helicopter, with main rotor removed for clarity. Future transmissions for combat helicopters are being designed to withstand severe combat damage and still run for at least an hour. The need for lubrication is also gradually being eliminated.

weighs 3.2 tonnes (7,055lb). This is greater than the combined weight of the two monster Soloviev D-25V engines!

In the design of the Lynx in 1968-9 Westland achieved a remarkably compact gearbox using conformal-tooth gears. Since 1980 the same company has perfected a next-generation gearbox which offers a weight saving of 40 per cent and numerous other advantages. Enclosed in a lightweight semi-skeletal titanium case, it has three stages of gearing giving a speed ratio of over 90:1, yet reduces gear tooth stresses, reduces the number of parts, reduces noise, separates

the gear loads completely from the stresses brought into the box from the blades, facilitates the fitting of an MMS (mast-mounted sight) and has many minor advantages. All manufacturers are striving to produce better gearboxes, which in battlefield machines have to permit continued rotor rotation even if the gears should happen to be severely damaged by hostile fire.

In commercial helicopters the uncomfortably rough ride of early helicopters is no longer acceptable, and in military and naval machines the need for smooth flight is obvious to anyone who has

New-technology Gearbox

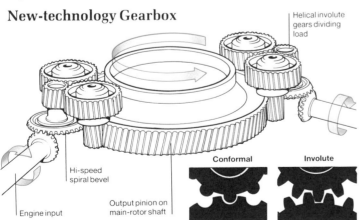

Above: In the 1960s Westland perfected the use of Wildhaber-Novikov "conformal" gears, shown in the left detail sketch. Unlike ordinary involute gears (right), which have line contact, conformal gears mesh with area contact. Such gears are used on the Lynx, the gearbox being very

compact in consequence. Today Westland is testing an AEG (advanced engineering gearbox) in which such gears are arranged in a new way that increases tolerance to battle damage and offers many other advantages as detailed on this page. Inadequate funding is hampering development.

Above: This rotor mast carries the new MBB all-composite bearingless main rotor. In operation only the upper swashplate and rotor shaft above it can be seen to revolve.

tried to use optical sights on distant targets. One of the market leaders in the fight against vibration is Bell Helicopter, which first marketed its Noda-Matic system in the early 1970s. A sketch shows how this hangs the helicopter from four arms which are themselves interlinked by flexible glassfibre straps and pivoted tuning weights. The latter, together with pendulum damper bobweights in the roots of the rotor blades, oscillate just enough at the main rotor blade frequency to cancel out the heavy thumping vibration at this frequency which is normally transmitted to the fuselage.

Noda-Matic works quite well, and has been widely copied, but in 1979 Bell's Dennis Halwes hit on what may prove to be a better method. Called LIVE (liquid inertia vibration eliminator), this hangs the helicopter from two boxes containing inner and outer metal sleeves. The latter are joined by elastomeric (bonded rubber) seals which bear the weight of the helicopter and absorb small movements without any metal-to-metal connection. The key to LIVE is that inside the inner sleeve is a high-density liquid, such as mercury, which is pumped up and down by the vertical movement between the inner and outer sleeves. The energy of pumping the heavy liquid comes out of the vibration input, which is damped out by 80 per cent or more. This kind of development appears to be of the most crucial importance for effective fighting helicopters able to "look" accurately and fire accurately.

Perhaps desirable rather than crucial, engineers in most major helicopter companies are busy developing better flight control systems. Except for the smallest types modern helicopters have hydraulic power units to position the swashplates and control the

Noda-Matic

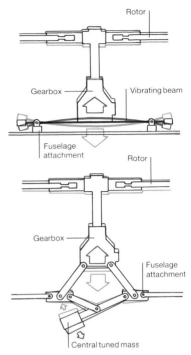

Above: Bell Helicopter Textron has been a leader in the battle to isolate the helicopter fuselage from the vibration inevitably generated by the main rotor. The patented Noda-Matic system has been applied in various ways, two of which are shown here in schematic form. In the upper arrangement the fuselage is hung from the nodes (points of minimum motion) of springy beams with masses on their ends. In the second scheme a central tuned mass is connected to the fuselage suspension by pivoted links.

LIVE

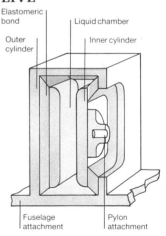

Above: The latest Bell anti-vibration system is slickly but perhaps inappropriately known as LIVE, from liquid inertia vibration eliminator. The fuselage is hung from the outer case of two very simple LIVE units, in each of which is an inner cylinder connected to the rotor pylon. Vibration of the latter is permitted by the elastomeric (rubber) bond between the cylinder and the case. This vibration is damped by the fact that it pumps a heavy liquid from end-to-end inside the case, absorbing the vibration energy.

Right: A generalised plot of cruising speed for helicopters, compound helicopters (with wings and separate propulsion systems) and tilt-wing aircraft. The Rotodyne was typically British in being before its time, unappreciated, and cancelled.

Below: Use of ADOCS (advanced digital/optical control system) technology is expected to make the future US Army LHX helicopter much simpler, more reliable and more survivable on the battlefield (if it can survive funding pressures). This simplified diagram shows how hundreds of today's mechanical control links would be replaced by five optical fibres and a handful of LRUs (line replaceable units) of digital avionics.

Rotary-wing Cruising Speeds

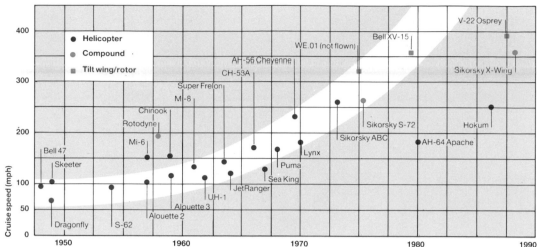

ADOCS

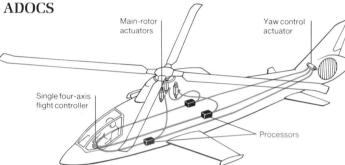

Above: Boeing Vertol's ARTI (advanced rotorcraft technology integration) testbed is an Agusta A 109A. This is the single-seat cockpit, with synthetic displays.

Below: The ARTI hovering. On the nose are the multiple sensors, which feed the displays in the remote cockpit. The ordinary cockpit houses a safety pilot.

machine's flight. A forest of "spaghetti" (hydraulic power piping) surrounds at least part of the main rotor hub(s). In turn the hydraulic power units are controlled by mechanical inputs connected to the cockpit cyclic and collective levers by a seemingly endless succession of push/pull rods, torque tubes and bell-cranks. This seemed natural in the early days of helicopters, but today it looks archaic.

The next generation should have been electrical signalling, the so-called FBW (fly-by-wire) technology in which multi-core flat conductive ribbons wend their way round the helicopter sending not muscular forces but proportional electrical signals. In fact so many builders are now well into the next generation of FBL (fly-by-light) that FBW looks like being largely bypassed.

Again Westland are well up with the leaders, with an MoD contract, in collaboration with RAE Farnborough, for developing and flight testing a complete FBL helicopter, which by early 1986 was almost ready to fly. The accompanying diagram, however, comes from a briefing by the US Army on its proposed LHX, which while being restricted to what might be called conventional helicopter technology will push that technology to the limit. Under the acronym Adocs (advanced

digital optical control system) work is well advanced on FBL systems which appear an absolute certainty for the future LHX. It should be explained that FBL links the cockpit and rotors only by optical fibres, similar to a small coaxial cable but capable of carrying data at seemingly fantastic rates. The small sidestick controller in the cockpit generates output voltages proportional to the pilot demand and these, probably after some "shaping" in a microprocessor, control the hydraulic power units. One of the early tasks with FBL was to demonstrate systems resistant to such interference as EMP (electromagnetic pulse) from nuclear explosions and lightning strikes. When such systems are in use they will offer superb reliability, reduced weight, survivability after battle damage, and enhanced handling and agility.

It goes without saying that all future fighting helicopters must possess the same kind of ACT (active controls technology) "carefree manoeuvring" as tomorrow's fixed-wing fighters. ACT inserts at least one computer into the control loop, so that the helicopter not only responds precisely to pilot demand but also never gets into a dangerous or out-of-control situation. It must also avoid hitting the ground or even a single electricity supply cable or similar hard-to-see obstruction, and this calls for hi-fi sensors much better than radar or the naked eye. (Sensors are discussed later.) To conclude this section, the observation can be made that, though it will mean a major relearning process, the traditional form of helicopter control input has to be discarded. It was logical 45 years ago to accept the collective and cyclic sticks with the aid of which hundreds of thousands of harassed pilots have struggled to become helicopter-qualified. If future generations are going to survive in air combat they must rethink the trajectory-control input, and this is discussed in greater detail in the section on Cockpits which is to be found between pages 30-35.

Right: Assembly line of Apaches in the new McDonnell Douglas Helicopter plant at Mesa, Arizona. Airframes are delivered there from Teledyne Ryan in San Diego.

AIRFRAMES

A brief word needs to be said on this topic, though whereas with aeroplanes the airframe is the basis of the whole machine the helicopter airframe is merely a secondary shell wrapped round the vital dynamic parts. All conventional helicopter airframes are broadly similar, but they do fall into one of several distinct classes. Small machines have a tadpole shape, with a transparent cabin at the front and slim rear boom to carry the tail rotor. Most helicopters in the next size up have a cabin under the rotor for passengers, casualties on stretchers, sensor operators working at consoles or some kind of cargo. The biggest transport helicopters have a cargo hold into which vehicles or freight pallets can be loaded through a rear ramp door. The "gunship" for fighting armour or other aircraft has a fighter-type fuselage just wide enough for tandem cockpits, with sensors and weapons visible externally. The specialized crane helicopter has no fuselage at all, its airframe comprising a mere structural beam linking the cockpit, rotors and landing gear and providing hoists for the slung load.

Efforts to improve the airframes of fighting helicopters are evolutionary rather than revolutionary. Thousands of smaller helicopters still use a structure based on welded steel tube, the front part being faired by light panels of aluminium or even plywood. Most helicopters have light-alloy stressed-skin structures which increasingly include skin panels made of foam-filled or honeycomb-filled sandwich giving great rigidity for light weight. But as with aeroplanes the proportion of airframe made of advanced composites, reinforced with carbon, Kevlar or glass fibres, has grown dramatically in the past five years, and the Bell D292 and Sikorsky S-75 are current research helicopters with essentially all-composite airframes.

Not a lot can be done to make light and agile helicopters truly resistant to SAMs and heavy-calibre gunfire. A great deal can still be done to increase their survivability and also their crashworthiness; in other words to let them make an autorotative or even uncontrolled descent, hitting the ground with a vertical velocity of up to 45ft (13.7m)/s, without bursting into flame or significantly injuring the crew members.

Right: Sikorsky's S-75 ACAP (advanced composite airframe program) is one of two research helicopters now flying with all-composite airframes. Funded by the US Army, the composite structures save weight and cost.

Propulsion

Around 1955 piston engines began to be replaced in all except the lightest helicopters by gas turbine "turboshaft" engines, and this was certainly the biggest single advance in the history of rotary wings. Today modern turboshafts can provide whatever power is needed, within very compact dimensions and for a competitive weight (which is often similar to the weight of the gearbox). Usually the engine installation needs no clutch or cooling system, though fan-assisted cooling is needed by the gearbox and engine oil radiator(s). In Western machines the oil cooler is less obvious than on Mil designs (which appear to have a third engine above the others) but it is there nonetheless, and it absorbs power.

Modern turboshaft engines offer many additional advantages. They are several orders of magnitude more reliable than the piston engine; they can run for prolonged periods at close to their maximum power; they burn less-volatile fuel and are tolerant of a very wide range of fuels; they can be made more tolerant of incoming air contaminated by sand, water, salt, smoke and even birds; they can be designed on a modular basis so that a faulty piece of an engine can be replaced *in situ* without disturbing the rest; and they can be controlled by advanced digital systems which do for the engine what advanced flight controls do for carefree manoeuvring.

The FADEC (full-authority digital engine control) is one aspect of today's concentration not so much on wringing out more power as on getting reliable power for 40 years at the lowest possible cost. This is not to imply that power growth is not also

demanded but, as in the world's airlines, the dominant customer demand is greater reliablility for less of what is called "total cost of ownership". This tends to mean emulating the Soviet designers in making things more brutishly simple, and the challenge is to do

this whilst gaining in efficiency and light weight rather than going backwards.

In bygone days engine designers set their sights squarely on improving component efficiency, increasing compressor pressure ratio, increasing turbine entry

A Modern Turboshaft Engine

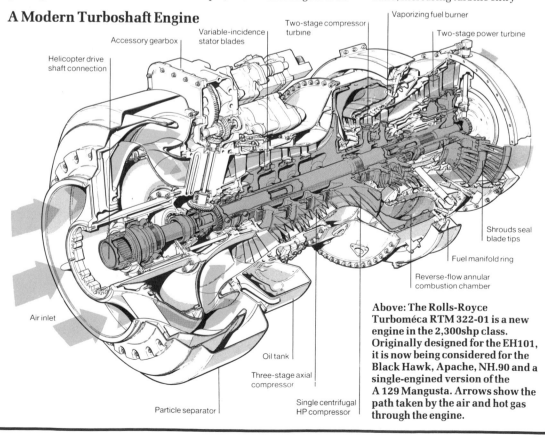

Helicopter drive shaft connection
Accessory gearbox
Variable-incidence stator blades
Two-stage compressor turbine
Vaporizing fuel burner
Two-stage power turbine
Shrouds seal blade tips
Fuel manifold ring
Reverse-flow annular combustion chamber
Air inlet
Oil tank
Three-stage axial compressor
Single centrifugal HP compressor
Particle separator

Above: The Rolls-Royce Turboméca RTM 322-01 is a new engine in the 2,300shp class. Originally designed for the EH101, it is now being considered for the Black Hawk, Apache, NH.90 and a single-engined version of the A 129 Mangusta. Arrows show the path taken by the air and hot gas through the engine.

Left: US Army line crews performing maintenance on the port General Electric T700 engine of an AH-64A Apache. This view shows the all-round access, and also the Black Hole IR-suppressed exhaust systems.

temperature and reducing engine mass and bulk. These endeavours all increase power and together result in higher fuel efficiency, but at considerable penalties in higher price, greater complexity and, probably, increased maintenance requirements. Greater internal pressure make it doubly important to tighten up clearances between fixed and moving parts, and this is especially difficult with the small parts used in helicopter engines, whose HP (high-pressure) turbine blades may be little bigger than thumbnails. Today designers are having to balance these objectives against the need to reduce the numbers of parts, reduce component prices, increase engine life, and if possible fit an engine that can be virtually ignored during the next several years of intensive operation in the harshest environment.

TOMORROW'S ENGINES

At first glance designers may appear to be taking retrograde decisions. The very first small helicopter turboshafts all had single-stage centrifugal compressors, adopted because

they were much less demanding from the viewpoints of design and manufacture than very small multi-stage axials. In 1958 Allison achieved a technological *tour de force* with the Model 250, developed as the T63 with US Army funds to power the LOH (light observation helicopter). This small engine, initially of 250shp, had a miniature axial compressor with six stages of delicate blades upstream of the final centrifugal stage. It handled an airflow of 3.1lb/s at a pressure ratio of 6.3. The engine was developed to give first 317 and then 420shp, and then in 1977, 20 years from the original design, a new version appeared with the axial compressor eliminated! The single centrifugal compressor not only handled an airflow increased to 4.45lb/s but it

achieved a pressure ratio of 8.4 all by itself. These later Model 250 engines give up to 735hp, yet are simpler than ever before.

It is not often that so many objectives can be achieved all at once. One of the keys to today's centrifugal compressors is high-strength flawless titanium alloy, with which a centrifugal impeller can be made with thinner vanes, curved instead of straight (and thus more efficient) yet running at very much higher speed, to achieve the dramatically raised pressure ratio. High pressure ratio can be equated with reduced fuel consumption, and in the past designers had a choice between simple inefficient engines or complicated efficient ones. Before designing a new engine the aircraft mission would be studied and the total weight of

engines and fuel calculated. Obviously it paid to put a simple engine in a short-range helicopter and a complicated one in a long-range aircraft.

Today quite simple engines can achieve excellent fuel economy. It is interesting that the four newest helicopter engines from the French company Turboméca are: the TM319, 443hp, centrifugal compressor; Arriel, 698hp, centrifugal plus one axial; TM333, 912hp, centrifugal plus two axial; and Makila, 1,875hp, centrifugal plus three axial. It does not automatically follow that greater power means more compressor stages, but the more powerful engines tend to be installed in helicopters with great flight endurance where reduced fuel consumption is more desirable.

Left: Fitters at Rolls-Royce's facility at Hatfield working on the dressing of RTM 322 engines for use in the intensive development programme. The engine in the background has a blue-painted test inlet bellmouth, and both are festooned with test instrumentation. This engine well exemplifies modern helicopter power, combining the horsepower and fuel economy of a giant diesel locomotive into a compact 20in (51cm) diameter package.

Top and above: The Société Turboméca has more types of helicopter engine in production than any other company. Largest of the range is the Makila (top), rated at up to 1,875shp and used in the twin-engine Super Puma. In the 912shp class, the new TM333 (above, in the Dauphin testbed) entered production in 1986. A "growth version" to be rated at 980shp, has been selected for the ALH (Advanced Light Helicopter) being developed in India by HAL.

Propulsion

Of course today's demand for more power from a simpler and lighter engine almost inevitably does mean greater maximum temperature, at the inlet to the HP turbine which drives the compressor. To run hotter without losing in reliability or engine life demands turbine blades either made of better material or provided with better internal air cooling. The first aircooled blades were incredibly expensive, and in the first large turbofan engines for widebody jets each set of HP blades often cost almost £1 million. At this time, in the late 1960s, the prospect of replacing metal blades in small gas turbines by Sinide (silicon nitride, a ceramic not very different from common sand) appeared tantalizingly imminent. Today, almost 20 years later it still looks tantalizingly imminent, and in fact experimental helicopter engines are running not only with ceramic turbine blades but also with ceramic bearings in the hot parts of the engine. Whereas traditional ball or roller bearings have to be continuously lubricated and cooled by oil and high-pressure airflows, a ceramic air bearing needs no cooling and uses dynamic airflow to prevent fixed and moving parts from ever coming into contact.

At present the hoped-for all-ceramic hot end is still not quite with us. Instead turbine rotors continue to have discs made by sintering (bonding under heat and pressure) a special heat-resistant metallic powder which, when completed, is so hard and tough it could be neither forged nor machined. Around its edge are fastened on by diffusion bonding a ring of blades each made of special alloy with directional solidification, in which the microscopic crystals of metal are all lined up radially to resist the tremendous tensile stress. Alternatively, and only a few people can do this, the blades may be of so-called single-crystal form in which, like the perfect crystals of silicon or germanium used to make integrated circuits, there are no flaws or joints in the crystalline lattice, resulting in vastly greater strength. As everywhere in the engine, shapes are designed to minimise any local concentrations of stress, even where this mildly interferes with aerodynamic efficiency.

Already HP turbine blades are being run in experimental engine cores at temperatures around 2,516°F (1,380°C) without air cooling, and the trend is still upwards. At such high temperatures it is more important than ever to design the combustion chamber so that, despite the fantastic rate of heat release from a very small space, the gas leaving the chamber and entering the HP turbine has the same temperature everywhere, with no inefficient cooler regions and no dangerous hot spots. Virtually all the latest helicopter engines have combustors of the folded reverse-

Left: Main rotor gearbox of an Agusta A 129. The large black/white object is the bevel gearbox transmitting the drive from the right Gem engine, which is just out of the picture at the left.

Right: The large box above the cockpit of this Egyptian Mi-8 is the filter assembly which keeps out desert sand and other solid matter. Fine filtration of engine air is today seen as extremely important.

flow annualar type. Such a chamber accepts the air flung radially out from the centrifugal compressor (which is now virtually taken for granted, irrespective of whether there are any axial stages upstream) and passes it around the outside, then in at the rear where the fuel is injected and thence forward again on the inside, finally reversing yet again to expand out to atmosphere via the turbines. The need for a 90° bend followed by two 180° bends today results in no significant performance penalty and the folded arrangement makes the chamber and engine much shorter. In particular it enables the turbine to be brought up close behind the compressor so that there is no need for a third bearing chamber (or sump, as the Americans call it) in the middle of the engine.

PROTECTION SYSTEMS

A later chapter looks at the protection of the helicopter, but the engine needs protection also. Though it was claimed earlier that modern engines can swallow all kinds of foreign material, doing so inevitably shortens engine life and can cause immediate damage. Indeed the trend towards higher rotational speeds and the replacement of steel by titanium both increase the likelihood of damage from ingested material. It is therefore desirable to feed the expensive engine with clean air, and because battlefield and naval use tends to mean highly contaminated air some form of filter is needed.

Older helicopters are often seen with large filter boxes or foreign-object deflectors in front of the inlets, examples being the Westland Sea King and Commando and the Soviet Mi-24. Modern engines use more efficient dynamic particle separators which swirl the incoming air round a sharp bend. The centrifugal force acting on each particle of solid material carries it outwards and, while clean air continues round the bend into the engine, the contaminated air (now at a high concentration) is sucked out through a separate channel and discharged overboard as far from the air intake as possible. In the

Left: Maintenance work on the RR Gnome engines of a Westland Sea King, with main rotor folded. This mark of Sea King has a large deflector in front of the inlets to keep out salt and snow.

Dynamic Particle Separation

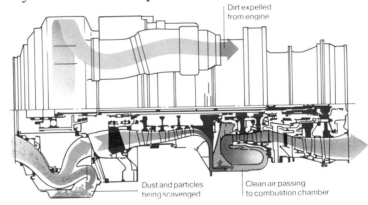

Dirt expelled from engine

Dust and particles being scavenged

Clean air passing to combustion chamber

Left: A simplified cross-section of an RTM 322 turboshaft engine showing how a modern particle separator operates. By introducing a sharp bend in the inlet, the dust and other solid material is forced to swing outwards through its own momentum. While the clean air carries on into the engine, the extracted dust is blown overboard.

Below: Typical of hundreds of types of modern avionic "black boxes", this line-replaceable unit is a Smiths Industries HUM (health and usage monitor) for future helicopters.

same way modern engines filter their lubrication and cooling oil to a much higher standard than previously. Helicopters of the 1960s filtered out particles larger than about 40 microns size (a micron is one-millionth of a metre), 1970s machines filter out everything bigger than about 15 microns, and 1990s helicopters will take out everything above some 3 microns. It has been shown that this can play a major part in extending the life of bearings and other components to an almost unlimited level, certainly much longer than the competitive life of the helicopter.

Backing up unprecedented cleanliness in oil and air is the protection of the entire engine, and probably all the dynamic parts, by a full-time system called a HUM (health and usage monitor). Back in the 1950s designers and operators began the first steps in this direction by recording overloads and mistreatment in handwritten logs, fitting magnetic detectors to attract particles of

metal in the oil (showing something was very wrong, and that complete failure might be imminent) and fitting vibration indicators which sound a warning in the cockpit if engine vibration exceeds a known safe level. Today's HUM goes a thousand times further, and dramatically improves both safety and cost.

A modern HUM installation comprises sensors, a computer, storage, displays, self-checking facilities and a link to ground storage if required. The sensors measure everything significant; numbers of flights, flight hours, engine operating hours, low-cycle fatigue (number of cycles from low to high power and vice versa), all usage at excessive powers or temperatures, stresses in the rotor head and gearbox, torque in the transmission shafting, thermal creep in the turbines and other "hot end" components, and the acceleration and amplitude of all significant vibrations. The HUM also indicates loss of any channel in any system, such as FBW or FBL flight controls, where for safety there is parallel redundancy. The capabilities of a HUM are vast, and the advantages enormous. Should anything go wrong, or be *about to go wrong*, the HUM will give a warning in the cockpit in real time. It can almost eliminate safety problems arising from operating failures in any dynamic component. Not least it can replace today's painfully expensive philosophy, in which the most crucial (and costly) parts have to be

The Useful Load Fraction

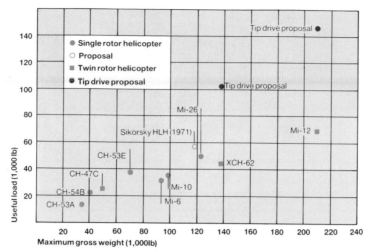

removed (and thrown away) and replaced after expiry of the most pessimistic assumed "safe life", by the far better philosophy of "on condition" maintenance in which, in effect, the operator says "no news is good news" and leaves everything alone until the HUM begins to give warnings.

While inlet systems remove foreign matter, the exhaust systems today have to try to remove heat, to avoid offering juicy targets to IR-homing missiles. This topic is covered in a later section on "Protection".

Some helicopters have unwittingly eliminated that problem by piping the engine exhaust to jets on the tips of the

Above: This graph plots various large helicopters (actual and proposed) on the basis of gross weight and useful load. Clearly, a point on this plot as high as possible but not far to the right is most desirable.

Above right and right: These graphs plot trends in sfc (specific fuel consumption) and weight per horsepower for current and future engines. One graph (top right) displays the evaluation of research carried out by the US Army and NASA to lower sfc over the next 20 years; the other two (middle and lower right) are based on Rolls-Royce data plotted to compare 11 actual engines with those of the next generation (blue ovals).

Performance Trends

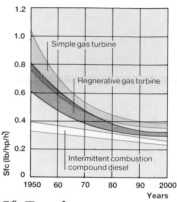

Sfc Trends

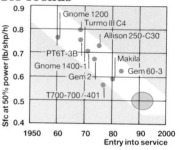

Specific Weight Trends

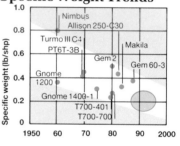

The LHTEC T800 Engine

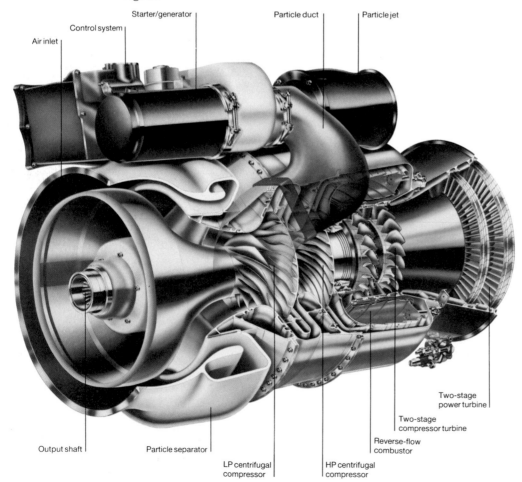

rotor. By the time the gas is discharged it is too cool to attract missiles, but the idea was not to increase protection but to find a better way of driving the rotor. Tip-drive helicopters need no tail rotor, because the only torque transmitted to the fuselage is that due to friction in the rotor bearing. Tip-drive helicopters have been quite successful, but higher fuel consumption is among the reasons why no more are being developed.

A number of schemes have been put forward to try to replace the traditional tail rotor, and most actually flown have involved expelling either engine exhaust or compressed air from a side-facing tail jet. This was first done in the British Cierva W.9 helicopter of 1946. A more sophisticated scheme is the Hughes Notar (no tail rotor) in which compressed air ejected from a slit along the lower side of the tail boom induces a lateral air circulation which results in a side force. A controllable compressed-air jet at the tail governed by the pedals provides yaw control. Hughes (now McDonnell Douglas Helicopter Co) claimed advantages in reduced

Left: It is possible that 5,000 or more may be made of this new engine which is a candidate for the LHX. The LHTEC (Light Helicopter Turbine Engine Co) T800 is a 1,200shp unit embodying the latest high-efficiency design.

noise and vibration, better personnel safety, elimination of the rotor hazard on the ground and the fact that in NOE (nap of the earth) flight there is no rotor to hit the ground.

Of course, the security of any aircraft is enhanced if it can survive the failure of one of its engines. In the early piston-engine days of helicopters it was virtually impossible to provide engine-out safety, because this means in effect carrying around a spare engine. With modern turboshaft engines there is much less of a problem, though many small helicopters are still single-engined, largely on the grounds of cost. Purely for the helicopter market some engine manufacturers have produced twinned powerplants consisting of a single package with two power sections driving into a common high-speed gearbox. Examples are the Pratt & Whitney Canada PT6T and T400 and the Rolls-Royce Coupled Gnome. Such engines could in theory put out combined power well beyond the transmission limit of the helicopter, but each power section is deliberately restricted to a lower power (normally just over half the transmission limit). Should either power section fail, the other is automatically brought up to full power so that flight can be continued almost as if nothing had happened.

Most multi-engined helicopters have two or more quite separate powerplants. Thanks to development of the D-136 engine by the Lotarev bureau the world's biggest and most capable helicopter, the Mi-26, has only two engines. One might have thought so large a helicopter a candidate for a third engine, and in fact three is beginning to be considered a good number for large Western machines. In the case of the CH-53D Super Stallion there was no other way of providing enough power, unless a switch had been made to quite different Allison 701 engines. In the case of the Boeing XCH-62 heavy-lift helicopter, to fly in 1988 after a ten-year delay, the original design was based on use of three engines (Allison 701s) which

Above: A mock-up of the Pratt & Whitney T800, being developed in partnership with Avco Lycoming, and in competition with LHTEC, for the LHX programme. The outlet at upper left is the particle ejector.

Above right: The new high-efficiency fan which blows the air out of the tail boom of the McDonnell Douglas NOTAR helicopter shown at right.

Right: The special test section (between the circular rings) on the tail boom of the NOTAR (no tail rotor) helicopter contains the blowing slit through which air is pumped to counteract main rotor torque.

were designed for the job. The same is true of the extremely important all-new EH101, where three was the deliberately chosen number of engines.

NASA's Lewis Research Center and the US Army are excited at the prospects for compound diesel/turbine engines. Such engines could even replace today's turboshafts by 1995. At first glance

a compound diesel sounds very heavy and complex, but current objectives in the 500-2,000hp class include a specific weight of only 0.58-0.63lb/hp, besides a specific fuel consumption of 0.3lb/h/hp. Garrett is the main industrial researcher, and in 1985 picked up where a previous USAF cruise-missile engine programme had left off.

Above: Dwarfing its stable-mate, the Chinook, the Boeing Vertol HLH (Heavy Lift Helicopter) may fly (ten years late) in 1988. As the most capable helicopter in the West, it needs high-power engines. These are three Allison T701s, each with maximum rating of 8,079shp. The greatest development effort so far has been on the very challenging gearboxes and transmission.

Cockpits

In the case of aeroplanes cockpits got ever more complicated for 60 years from 1914 onwards, and then began to get outwardly simpler. This is because electromechanical dial instruments are progressively being replaced by multifunction displays. It is natural that helicopter cockpits should have followed the same trend, but in this case there are powerful modifying factors. One is that, except for a few very large machines, helicopter cockpits have lacked panel space in which to become really complicated, and more than half current helicopters have no "panel" in the accepted sense but mount instruments and controls on a relatively small binnacle or console inside a largely glazed compartment. Another is that the helicopter has a total manoeuvring capability in three dimensions, which in theory could exceed that of a dragonfly or hummingbird (because with all-round sensors the pilot can see in all directions) but which has never been exploited. A third factor concerns the basic form of the flight control interface.

It would be simple in this chapter merely to pick round the edges and describe how today's "instruments" are rapidly being replaced by multicolour, multifunction, reprogrammable displays. In fact it is necessary to stand further back and recognize that major revolutions are taking place. In the ultimate form tomorrow's helicopter cockpit (probably like tomorrow's combat fixed-wing cockpit) will have no outside vision but will be wholly synthetic. This will not be easy for pilots to accept.

A further problem in structuring this chapter is that from now onwards helicopter cockpits, especially those for air warfare, will increasingly be dominated by displays fed by sensors, and these are the subject of the next section. As far as possible the sensors are not discussed here, and the present chapter concentrates on crew philosophy, human/machine interfaces and basic cockpit design. Crashproof seats and armour are discussed in a subsequent section on "Protection".

COCKPIT DESIGN

No other vehicle makes such severe demands on its operator interface as the modern combat helicopter. Submarines have the same capability of 3-D manoeuvre and the ability to travel in almost any direction without change in attitude, but are extremely limited in motion capability; moreover they are surrounded by a compliant medium likely to be free from other solid objects. (They do, however, present the requirement, not yet met, for synthetic vision.) The jet STOVL aeroplane combines most of the helicopter's problems with flight at substantially greater speeds, but it

is unlikely to slow down over the battlefield, nor usually fly in directions other than dead ahead.

Only the helicopter combines the all-directions motion capability with an intimacy with the Earth that could swiftly prove fatal. The naval helicopter at least has the advantage of operating above a sea/sky interface that can generally be regarded as flat and locally horizontal, and the only obstructions are likely to be ships which are among the easiest of objects to see by eye or by various sensors. The land-battle helicopter is another matter. All-weather, day/night NOE (nap of the earth) flight in hostile airspace, with a mission calling for insertion of troops in a particular corner of a particular field, is probably the biggest single guidance and control

problem in manned aviation.

In the past helicopters have been able to operate only because their pilots have been able to stay constantly in close visual contact with the ground. Night flying posed very severe problems, and all-weather missions were impossible. Today combat aeroplanes can be flown at high speed through hostile airspace by providing the pilot with a HUD (head-up display) through which he can see whatever is visible ahead whilst simultaneously watching numerous accurate flight guidance cues giving aircraft trajectory and also weapon-aiming information. Early HUDs had an FOV (field of view) of about 7.5°, while the very latest (GEC Avionics HUD on F-16C) expands this to 16°. But a 16° FOV would be

Top: With pilot door hinged forward and the main rear door slid back, this MBB BO 105 reveals its interior. The pilot sits in front on the right, and the copilot/ gunner on the left has his seat slid aft so that he can use the roof-mounted sight to guide TOW missiles. In line with the door hinge can be seen the pistol grips of the two cyclic-pitch sticks with which the machine is flown.

Above: Cockpit of another older-technology helicopter, the Kaman SH-2F LAMPS 1 of the US Navy. Though dominated by the radar display, the front panel is littered with traditional electromechanical dial type instruments. Though fully adequate for the mission, this cockpit naturally contrasts sharply with those of the Apache.

The Apache Cockpits

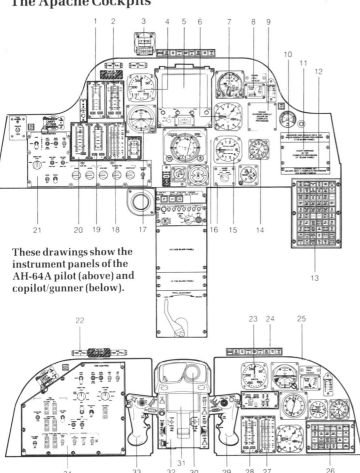

These drawings show the instrument panels of the AH-64A pilot (above) and copilot/gunner (below).

Key to Apache Cockpit Displays
1 Turbine gas temperature display.
2 Torque indicator.
3 Standby compass.
4 Airspeed indicator.
5 VDU displaying height, speed, attitude and other flight information.
6 Sensitive altimeter for NOE flight.
7 Altimeter.
8 Stabilizer angle.
9 APR-39 RWR panel.
10 ALQ-136/ALQ-144 radar/IR jammer power panel.
11 M130 chaff/flare dispenser panel.
12 APR-39(V) panel.
13 Central warning keyboard/lights.
14 Clock.
15 Climb/descent rate indicator.
16 HSI horizontal situation displays for navigation.
17 Attitude director indicator.
18 Engine and rotor speeds display.
19 Oil pressure and temperature indicator.
20 Fuel gauge.
21 Integrated weapons fire control panel.
22 Engine fire extinguisher pulls.
23 Airspeed indicator.
24 Warning captions display.
25 Repeater flight instruments to allow co-pilot/gunner to control helicopter.
26 Central warning keyboard/lights.
27 Engine/rotor speeds
28 Torque display.
29 RH grip: sensor and weapon control.
30 Eyepieces.
31 Video screen.
32 Multipurpose sight system, TADS/PNVS.
33 LH grip: FLIR and other controls plus gun.
34 Integrated weapons fire control panel.

Right: The pilot's cockpit in a production Apache, switched on and ready for flight. All displays on the left and centre of the panel are electronic, though there are still a few traditional dial type instruments. The long console along the right side is devoted to radio and navigation controls.

Left and right: The TADS/PNVS display, seen being tested at left, dominates the CPG (copilot/gunner's) cockpit in the nose of the AH-64A Apache. The cockpit is that of a regular production Apache photographed upon completion at the Mesa assembly plant. Note the battery of switches on the end of the collective lever (left of seat).

useless to a helicopter pilot, and probably lethal. In flying a helicopter the lateral vision seen out of each "corner of the eye" is not merely valuable but vital. Even the forwards vision has to encompass the entire forwards hemisphere, into any part of which the helicopter could be required to dart at a moment's notice. Vision restricted to a 16° tunnel would take away almost all the machine's essential agility.

Any army helicopter pilot will confirm that in battle conditions it is necessary to keep both eyes looking outside roughly 100 per cent of the time. Transport and possibly naval helicopters can fly useful missions with a single pilot. After some agonizing the RAF is applying Wessex and Puma experience, of using a single pilot

aided by a second crewman responsible for navigation and systems management, to its big Chinooks, which had previously had two pilots (and still do in other air forces with no pilot shortage). But a battlefield combat helicopter poses very much greater problems, and despite the US Army's hope that the SCAT (scout/attack) version of its next-generation LHX can be made a fighter-like single-seater the author is prepared to bet that most LHXs will in the event have a second seat.

The problem has some features in common with fixed-wing fighters. In 1957 the British government announced that manned fighters were obsolete; the air war would in future be fought with missiles. Just as this was announced a company in St Louis was building the prototype of an aircraft which was destined to become the world's No 1 fighter of the next 20 years, with well over 5,000 sold. It was the McDonnell Douglas F-4 Phantom, and it had not one seat but two. Ever since there has much argument about whether the right number of seats for a fighter (which also means a ground attack aircraft) is one or two; nobody, even in Britain, any longer believes the correct number is zero.

At times there have been passionate arguments over how a crew of two can best be arranged in a battlefield helicopter. Early machines all had either a single pilot or two side-by-side, but from 1962 Bell and Lockheed pioneered the concept of the modern armed helicopter with a slim fuselage made possible by tandem seating. As in fixed-wing jet trainers the seats have to be staggered to give the backseater a good view ahead. Most authorities in the USA, UK, Soviet Union and Italy appear to consider two to be the best number of humans to have aboard major armed battlefield helicopters for the foreseeable future. This is despite the deeply considered Westland advanced cockpit with "2.5 seats", and the proposal that the LHX/SCAT should be a single-seater.

The "2.5-seat" cockpit, studied by Westland in 1982-3, is shown in an illustration. One pilot is seated in front on the right. Another, or a gunner, sits behind on the left. Both can call up full flight instrumentation on their displays, and both can fly the helicopter via a small sidestick controller. Behind on the right is a third seat which would be valuable in many special missions and to carry local or theatre commanders. All seats are armoured, and the sides and arms are folded up around the occupant. Such a cockpit demands a high level of electronic sophistication, and it could be argued that this ought to enable the pilot to be eliminated entirely.

Left: Europe's advanced anti-tank helicopter is the A 129, being developed by Italy, the UK, Spain and others. Here the stepped tandem seating is seen to advantage.

Below: The cockpits of the A 129 are an excellent compromise between the available and the radical. That for the gunner (left) is dominated by the TOW sight unit and the small missile control joystick below it. The high rear cockpit for the pilot (right) has one electronic multi-function display (partly hidden behind the cyclic stick).

Left: This advanced 2/3-seat combat cockpit was schemed by Westland in 1984. The two pilots (front right and rear left) fly the helicopter via the right-hand sidestick controllers. The third seat is for an observer or passenger. All seats are fully armoured, the sides being pulled up round the occupant.

Ideally we should have just two tandem seats, the rear seat being for the supernumerary.

Some of the fiercest arguments have raged over who sits in front. The consensus today is that in NOE flight the backseater has the better appreciation and awareness of the situation, and better "feel" in controlling the helicopter, so he is invariably the pilot flying the helicopter. Almost without exception he is the aircraft commander. The frontseater, even if he is a rated pilot and provided with a set of flight controls, is normally classed as a copilot/ gunner or weapon system operator. A British Army view is "Even if he has to take over as pilot he is not the captain of aircraft but a 'Driver, Airframe'".

Certainly it is the frontseater in a tandem machine who has the weapon-aiming sensors and sights, while the backseater has all primary flight and navigational information. Sights are covered in the next section, but navigation is a quite different problem which is only now being fully solved. In the pre-1980 era practically no battlefield helicopter had anything approaching the night and all-weather capability needed. In most conflicts friendly surface navaids cannot be relied upon, and to avoid broadcasting one's presence it is desirable to keep one's own emissions to a minimum. The one on-board emitting navaid that is almost universally accepted is doppler radar. This projects narrow beams diagonally downwards ahead and to the rear, and by measuring the frequency shift of the return beams reflected from the ground the cockpit display can read out instantaneous ground speed and drift, and with simple add-ons can give an accurate present position.

Decca Doppler 80 is an example of a popular equipment nothing like as costly as some dopplers and able to feed a versatile display/ control unit called Tans (tactical air navigation system). There are many ways in which doppler can be combined with a magnetic compass and attitude gyros to give comprehensive attitude and position information. The main pilot interface used to be electromechanical instruments such as an ADI (attitude director indicator) and an HSI (horizontal situation indicator) both fed by an AHRS (attitude/heading reference system). Now such instruments are being replaced by large electronic displays, as described later. The doppler/compass system is being continually upgraded in accuracy, whilst trying to find ways to reduce

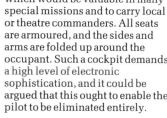

Left: The neat central console of a Lynx contains, at top centre, the sub-panel for the Tans, described on the facing page. This forms part of the Decca Doppler 71 or 80 navigation system. The forward panel of existing Lynx helicopters uses traditional instruments, but a later-technology panel has been designed for the more powerful Lynx 3. The pilot is probably transmitting a "squawk" (identification signal) on the SSR/IFF.

absence of moving parts, such as gyros, torquers, resolvers, slip rings and gimbal mounts, and almost complete lack of sensitivity to g loading and shock. Accuracy in the first helicopter application – the BAe LINS in the EH 101 – will be better than 1 knot.

Today there is one system that is ideal in all respects except one: it is a US system, and users from other countries must be at various kinds of disadvantage. The system is GPS (global positioning system) Navstar and is being developed for all US services under a Joint Program Office at USAF Systems Command. It works by measuring the precise times taken to receive signals from groups of satellites, and it provides extremely accurate and reliable position information for any friendly platform anywhere

on Earth. It will certainly revolutionize the capability of helicopters (and very many other kinds of vehicle), but though companies in many countries (such as GEC Avionics in the UK) have minor roles as subcontractors the basic system remains American. Should the interrogation codes be thought compromised the US command authorities could change it without warning, and this could leave Allied vehicles suddenly lost. Such political problems are already the subject of urgent discussion.

Almost the only aspect of future cockpit development which is obvious is the replacement of traditional instruments and switches by electronic displays. As in aeroplanes, helicopters are already at the stage where the primary flight instruments are becoming electronic displays, and before long we may expect to see the "all glass cockpit" moving into the field of rotary wings. The drawbacks, which are not insignificant, are that such displays are expensive and quite heavy. While large jetliners, and even the Beech Starship, can pack the cockpit with advanced displays, the helicopter tends to be limited by weight and cost considerations.

the strength of the radar emissions to avoid detection.

At best, however, it is merely a marginally adequate system for day or night operations in reasonable visibility. It is flawed by the fact that it broadcasts its presence and lacks the accuracy demanded in poor visibility. An inertial system would give the helicopter the silent autonomy it needs to survive over the battlefield, but for any affordable price the INS (inertial navigation system) again fails on the score of precision. After an hour of hovering the helicopter's position is uncertain within anything up to a mile, and inertial drift is progressive with time. Another alternative is Tercom (terrain comparison, or terrain contour matching), but this is unsuitable for a vehicle that spends the whole day moving short distances in different directions with its wheels almost touching the ground.

Possibly the best of all the self-contained passive systems will prove to be the LINS (laser INS) in which the gyro wheels are replaced by laser light. Heart of the system is a ring laser, a very precise block of low-expansion glass ceramic in the form of an equilateral triangle with almost perfect mirrors at the corners. Laser beams rotate ceaselessly round the triangular circuit in both directions. The slightest rotation of the block makes one beam take longer to cover the round trip and the reverse-flow beam take less. A LINS usually has three ring lasers and three accelerometers, all "strapped down" in a standard avionic box. Advantages include

Left and left below: The first LINS (laser inertial navigation system) to go into production will be that developed by British Aerospace Dynamics for the EH101. The stylized artwork at left shows the RLG (ring laser gyroscope) used in this system. Below left is seen an actual RLG on test, the brilliant white lines being the laser beams. The principle of the RLG is outlined in the text on this page.

Below: A typical modern synthetic panel instrument, created entirely electronically on a form of colour TV display. This Westland presentation, which may be used in the EH101, gives the pilot almost all primary information in one display.

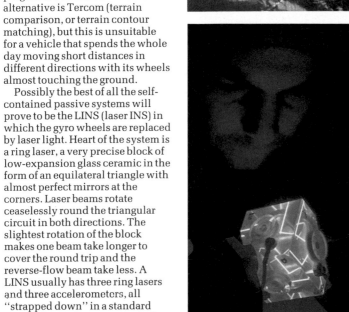

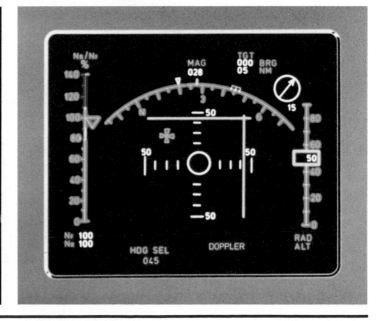

For a start we can take it for granted future helicopters will use digital databuses, either MIL-STD-1553B or an optical equivalent of it passed along fibre-optic links. Miniature digital computers will handle every possible control and management task that can be removed from the crew workload. For example the pilot will have to press a button to start the engine(s), but after that the starting sequence will be computer controlled. The engines will automatically come under digital control which will maintain the required speeds and temperatures as well as constant rotor speed. Even in the engine failure case everything ought to happen without pilot intervention, though he would be kept fully informed on the situation.

Though a few traditional instruments may be retained as a backup, as is the case with the ADAS (Army digital avionics system) UH-60A testbed, the aim is to present all information to the pilot via various displays. These will no longer merely replace traditional instruments but will be extremely versatile and reprogrammable, with instant switching from one mode to another. The chief displays will be large CRTs (cathode-ray tubes) giving computer-generated colour pictures or diagrams. Backing these up will be smaller flat-panel displays, either of the LED (light-emitting diode) type giving bright red or blue-green alphanumerics, or EL (electro-luminescent) or liquid-crystal displays. They will have touch-sensitive screens so that the pilot can change the menu or format, or call up additional information, merely by a fingertip touch.

Changes in the cockpit are arriving in different "generations". A present-generation update applicable even as a retrofit to existing machines is seen in Ferranti's BMMS (battlefield mission management system), which uses a single shadow-mask CRT to display a synthetic real-time plan view of the battlefield,

showing ground forces, danger areas of AAA and SAM systems, friendly platform locations and many other factors, all labelled and keyed by colour. Rather more sophisticated hardware is exemplified by the DCAS (digital core avionics system) developed by Westland, with the RAMS (Racal Avionics management system) providing the pilot interface. RAMS in various forms can manage navigation, communications, mission equipment and HUM monitoring of engine and airframe. Another example of current hardware is the GEC Avionics DCMU (digital colour map unit) which stores maps, and height information, on magnetic tape. Any required part of tape can be quickly accessed to present either a large detailed colour map or a 3-D perspective of the terrain on which video pictures or guidance symbology can be superimposed.

Going on to the future generations, two major lines of development are being pursued which could bring significant changes. One is the wholly synthetic cockpit and the other DVI (direct voice input). Of the two, DVI is easier to comprehend, and is a natural development applicable to existing cockpits. The ability of the helicopter crew to interface with essentially everything in the cockpit except the primary flight controls by means of speech appears likely to bring about a dramatic reduction in workload. At present the workload in the attack helicopter cockpit is on the margin of what skilled and experienced humans can handle. NOE flight, especially at night or in bad weather, leaves no spare brain capacity and no spare hands free to handle navigation, communication, weapon aiming and other extra tasks. Voice control makes things a lot better. Ironically

Digital Avionic System

MIL-STD-1553B data bus

Mission computers
Bus controllers
Remote terminals

Aircraft interfaces

Weapons systems management

Video

Visionics/sensors

Dual channel symbol generators
Remote terminals

Keyboards
Pilot   Gunner/copilot

Radios/AJ data links

Triplex flight control

Cassette/bulk loader mission-planning interface

4-axis digital flight control

Helmet-mounted displays

Digital map   MFD   MFD

Below: Simplified schematic representation of the Harris digital data-bus control system which manages all of a helicopter's subsystems. As in fixed-wing machines, such systems are becoming universal.

Left: A recent picture of a Westland advanced-technology cockpit simulator, being used to help develop the EH101. Six multi-function displays replace virtually all "instruments".

the situation has been made even more acute by the introduction of electronic displays. These are covered in touch screens or peripheral buttons. Controlling them in conditions of extreme workload may seem even more difficult than in the old days of massive individual switches and knobs, but increased automation and modern displays are fast becoming essential. Concentration in the laboratory is one thing, but spending several seconds with the eyes in the cockpit whilst dashing at 150kts (173mph, 278km/h) through a forest is quite another.

USAF Systems Command's Aerospace Medical Research Lab has got as far as experimenting with use of clearly spoken words picked from a concise vocabulary, but Westland in Britain has taken the concept much further. The Westland objective is natural speech, and this presents much greater problems. The speech recogniser has to accept not only isolated words but connected words, and there appear to be advantages in security in tailoring it to the pilot's own voice, inserted by cassette before the mission. Westland expect a DVI cockpit to be cost/effective by about 1988, an obvious adjunct being DVO (direct voice output) so that the cockpit will repeat and confirm the input commands and give warning of any problems.

The synthetic cockpit, or "virtual cockpit" is the brainchild

Below: The actual cockpit of the MBB BK 117A-3M, showing the careful blend of traditional dial instruments and the multifunction electronic displays and keyboards of the British RAMS 3000 (Racal avionics management system). RAMS systems are tailored to the management of every kind of on-board equipment. Earlier RAMS installations are in service in the Navy Lynx and 530MG Defender.

Above: Boeing Vertol is one of the few companies actually to be flying a four-axis sidearm controller. This seems to be the only way to replace the old cyclic/collective.

Below: The rather frightening appearance of a pilot wearing the VCASS, the only existing system on test which presents the pilot with a totally synthetic view.

of the aforementioned Aerospace Medical Research Lab. Though hard to accept, it replaces the pilot's normal view, both of the cockpit and externally, by a synthetic image perceived as being at infinity. It comprises a mix of computer-generated external scenes, which match with the real one, and superimposed cues, symbology, stylized pictures of threats (in some cases with effective radius illustrated) and many other features. The concept is still in a primitive formative stage, but with stealth demands threatening to eliminate cockpit transparent windows it may be forced on us.

The concept is being researched as part of an Aerospace Medical Research Laboratory programme called the VCASS (visually coupled airborne systems simulator). It attempts to present to the pilot a totally adequate synthetic picture, covering 60° to left and right, and assembled from information fed in by on-board sensors, CNI (com/nav/IFF) and weapon systems, and giving a three dimensional image. Pilots see their projected flight path superimposed on a landscape on which threats appear as red mushrooms (size indicating effective range), with yellow symbols indicating threats that are only potentially hostile. Friendly aircraft are white and hostile ones red, while way markers and possible ground targets are black. Vital helicopter information, such as speed/height indications and available weapons, are also superimposed, and the pilot can interact with his aircraft and weapon systems by direct voice command.

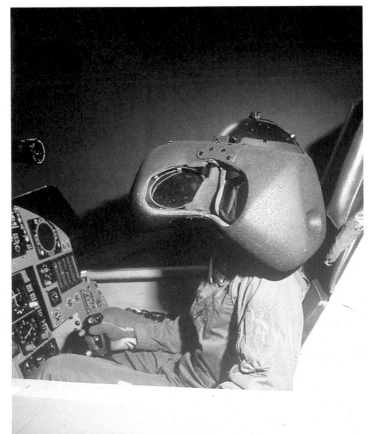

Visionics and Sensors

Helicopters, like fixed-wing aircraft, have to be equipped to do a useful job. In the case of the helicopter the perpetual pressure on the designers and engineers to make things lighter and more compact is accentuated by the fact that, compared with aeroplanes of similar installed power, helicopters can lift less, fly slower and have shorter range for a given fuel capacity. To compound the problem further, while the demand for visionics – a hideous but useful word derived from "vision electronics" – has multiplied and multiplied again, the modern combat helicopter has to spend a far higher proportion of its life in close proximity to the enemy than does any other kind of aircraft. It also probably operates from austere front-line bases or small ships where manpower and facilities to cosset its complex systems are very limited.

It can be taken for granted that every combat helicopter has to be able to fly at night. This is a manageable problem; it merely requires night vision systems, the correct cockpit lighting and, for use in peacetime if not in war, external navigation lights. It also has to have communications radio, and the requirement here is likely to be more severe than for, say, the fighter aircraft because of the need to communicate with at least two branches of the armed forces and possibly with three. The US Marine Corps, for example, would be embarrassed if they could not talk to the US Air Force, Army and Navy. In time of battle this requirement is not only intensified but overlain by the need for absolute communications security, the ability to continue communications at a time of radio silence or severe hostile communications jamming and, in

parallel with the "C" demand, the extra ones that make up what the Americans call C-cubed I, or "command, control, communications and IFF", the I also standing for intelligence. IFF, discussed later, means we do not fire on friendly platforms, and for a helicopter those platforms could be tanks, ships, infantry, submarines, other helicopters or almost anything else, not excepting supersonic fighters.

We have only scratched the surface so far. We have a helicopter that can fly at night and talk to its friends. But to survive it has to fly in NOE (nap of the Earth) situations, where the highest point

of its rotors is far below the tops of the trees and where it is as far as possible concealed from the enemy by terrain and fixed obstructions. Fixed-wing aircraft try to do the same, but they fly higher and in general are better equipped to brush the tops of trees or even electric utility cables and get away with it. For the helicopter, contact with *terra firma* is a reason for terror; it tends to be fatal.

Safe NOE flight demands very advanced and reliable visionics, quite apart from the fact that we want to get to the enemy, perhaps spend a long time in battlefield smoke whilst performing major gyrations about all three axes and

Above: British Aerospace has delivered more than 130 roof-mounted TOW sights for British Army Lynx AH.1s. The fact that such helicopters must operate in inhospitable surroundings places special demands on their sensors.

finally go home to a base that is unlikely to boast an illuminated five-mile runway. Base is likely to be a small unlit forest clearing, or a small boat in a big sea.

Yet all these requirements added together do not equal the one demand that every combat helicopter must fulfil: it must find its targets, and, if required to do so, hit them with its weapons. A few

The EM (electromagnetic) Spectrum

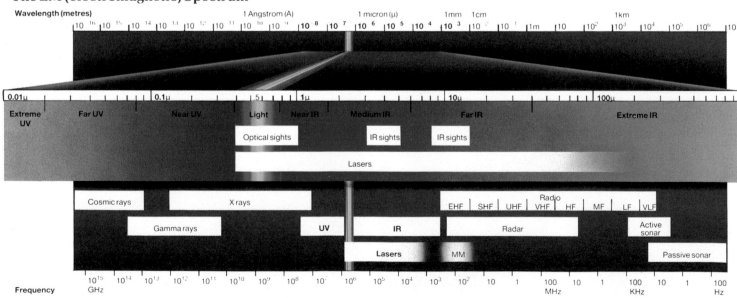

Above: Virtually the entire EM spectrum is shown here in simplified form. Along the top is the wavelength in metres (m), with the wavelengths of 1 kilometre, 1 centimetre, 1 millimetre, 1 micron and 1 Ångström unit

specially marked. Along the bottom is the radiation's frequency, starting with Hertz (cycles per second) on the right and progressing through kilohertz and megahertz to gigahertz. Because it is so important the

portion of the spectrum from 10^{-3}m to 10^{-8}m has been opened out in the centre on an enlarged scale. Near the centre of this region lies visible light, the individual spectral colours of which are illustrated. To the left of

the visible region (ie, shorter wavelengths) lies the ultraviolet, while to the right are the subdivisions of infra-red. At the bottom are mentioned some of the broader species of sensor which operate in these regions.

Above: A Hughes Aircraft engineer adjusts the optics of a roof-mounted TOW sight for a Lynx AH.1.

Right: A British AAC (Army Air Corps) crewman demonstrates TOW missile guidance using the roof-mounted sight of a Lynx AH.1. These sights are now to be upgraded with night and bad-weather capability.

helicopters are lucky enough to be sent on anti-ship attack missions. Apart from the fact that some ships can hit back, this is relatively easy. Ships are big, warmer than the sea and often pump out EM (electromagnetic) radiation right across the spectrum from visible light through IR (infra-red, heat, see EM spectrum diagram) to all the radio and radar wavelengths. Other helicopters search for submarines deep in the ocean. These probably have no means of hitting back (but anti-aircraft defences for a deeply submerged submarine could readily be provided if anyone bothered to ask), but are about a million times

harder than the big surface combatant to find. ASW (anti-submarine warfare) helicopters are a specialized race, though some also double as anti-ship or SAR (search and rescue) machines. A third totally different species is the helicopter for the land battle, and this is the type considered through most of this section.

LAND BATTLE VISIONICS

The broad requirements for the land-battle helicopter are strongly biased towards the killing of hostile armour. Apart from this they have much in common with those of the fixed-wing tactical

attack aircraft. The crews of both may number one or two men, they set out with a knowledge of the enemy's approximate location and movement, and they know the kind of targets they are looking for. Both have to find and hit targets that are on the move. The pre-flight briefing cannot give exact locations, and most of the targets are likely to be small, extremely well camouflaged, protected by vast amounts of anti-air defences (triple-A and SAMs) and moving with the maximum speed and furtiveness the terrain allows. The task of finding targets will before long be left to the automatically self-guided weapons, but these are

mainly still in the development stage. We have to find (the jargon word is "acquire") our targets ourselves. Then, as like as not, we have to steer missiles to each target one by one, guiding each one all the way and keeping the target – if not a whole enemy army – in sight the whole time. And certainly, if we can see them, they can see us.

Few things come anywhere near the human eye for finding targets. At night it needs assistance, because the rate of receipt of photons is inadequate (the common, non-jargon way of expressing this condition is to say it is dark). Night-vision sensors form an important part of this chapter. But how do we use our eyes and the NV sensors? As in the case of fixed-wing aircraft, the ideal would be to integrate the NV sensor closely with our own eyes so that, as we searched in human fashion over the battlefield, the rate of reception of photons was multiplied at least a billionfold. In other words we could see. We can do this today. It is called dropping flares or switching on searchlights No better way of getting shot down could be devised.

There is no great difficulty in rigging the helicopter with a marvellous NV system, but we cannot plug the output signal into ourselves; we have to look at a screen inside the helicopter. Or we can fit NV goggles to our helmet and, looking through them, get a greatly enhanced picture. But suppose we spot a target; how do we either say where it is or aim weapons at it? The accepted

Left: This Aérospatiale Dauphin demonstrator is flying with the Boule Vénus (Venus ball), giving FLIR vision for guiding HOT missiles by night or in adverse weather. Total weight of the ball, with ancillaries, is 198lb (90kg).

Left: A Wessex HU.5 Commando assault transport of Royal Navy No 845 Squadron during Exercise Cold Winter '83. Quite apart from the effect on hardware, blizzard conditions severely attenuate the transmission of many important wavelengths of EM radiation.

method today is to fit the cockpit with sensors which continuously measure the attitude of our helmet, in pitch, roll and yaw. It is not difficult to slave the helicopter's sensors, or a gun turret, so that these faithfully and continuously follow the movements of our helmet. But, however disciplined we may be, we cannot keep our eyes looking straight ahead. Our eyes do most of the searching, the head and helmet following a generally unrelated series of motions which lag in time and in magnitude. What we really want is not a helmet-based system but an eye-based one, and at the time of writing nobody has been clever enough to make one that works (and a few laboratories have tried). Perhaps in a few years we shall be able to tap the human optical system so that we can use our external man-made photomultiplier tubes and image-enhancement devices to multiply the actual photons received by the sensitive receptors of our own retinas. At the moment this is "pie in the sky".

Below: A Land-Rover seen on a pitch-black night through a Barr & Stroud IR18 infra-red imager. Surface temperature and other factors build up a clear picture against the cold background.

Atmospheric Transmittance

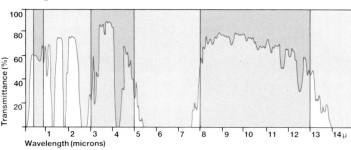

Above: The atmosphere is highly transparent to many EM waves and completely opaque to others. This diagram shows how, at some wavelengths (such as 8-13 microns) there are "windows" giving transmittance of around 80 per cent; ie, clear air is almost

CHOICE OF WAVELENGTH

Any system of visionics or sensors can be arranged in various ways, and to function within a selected bandwidth. Our own bodies use two receptors, typically mounted about 5ft (1.5m) above the ground, facing in the same direction and giving binocular vision, which enables a valuable qualitative perception of target distance to be obtained. Operating wavelength is

completely transparent. The block of red colour shows the limits of FLIRs used in this region. There is another window at 3-5 microns, where different FLIRs (red) are used. At 0.5-0.9 microns LLTVs and NVGs are the sensors used, as shown by a narrow red band.

0.38 to 0.75µ (one µ is one micron, or one millionth of a metre), though we cannot see well beyond the narrow range 0.5 to 0.65µ. In this range different wavelengths give rise to a sensation of colour.

No man-made visionics can quite rival this system, but we do have the ability to extend the bandwidth tremendously, always towards longer wavelengths, and to do a few other things beyond our eyes' capability. Moving to longer wavelengths means that we lose picture definition but gain in

ability to pierce fog and smoke. At IR (infra-red) wavelengths, which are a little longer than light at from 1 to 5,000µ, we get a perhaps unexpected ability to "see" things on a basis of temperature, which puts a whole new slant on any battlefield scene. Though IR sensors have so far always been connected to monochrome displays, which can usually be switched so that hot parts of the scene appear white and cold parts black or vice versa, there is no reason why IR pictures or thermographs should not be coloured. Such pictures immediately betray the presence of anything containing a running engine. Flying over an airfield an IR sensor would show any aircraft with a running engine, an aircraft which had recently parked (with hot engine bays and freezingly cold residual fuel after soaking at high altitude) and a warm blank space where an aircraft had recently been parked. Changing wavelengths thus provides additional information, and also greatly increases the enemy's problems in trying to camouflage his operation.

At longer wavelengths still we enter the vast field of microwaves and radio, at first with millimetric radar, then centimetric radar and finally with the largest radars and communications radios. Some form of search or surveillance radar is almost always fitted to naval helicopters, and of course in summer 1982 in a very successful "crash programme" Thorn EMI fitted a large AEW (airborne early warning) radar to existing Royal Navy Sea Kings. Tactical helicopters for overland use have

Below: A successful "crash programme" in 1982 resulted in the conversion of Royal Navy Sea King Mk 2s from ASW to AEW missions. Here one of 849 Sqn's eight AEWs is on station.

almost never carried radar, their sensors being designed to use much shorter wavelengths.

The greatest shortcoming of the shorter wavelengths is that the signal energy is rapidly attenuated by travel through even relatively clean atmosphere, and the attenuation becomes very rapid in heavy rain or snow. Atmospheric attenuation varies quite sharply with frequency, and there are "windows" at particular frequencies where attenuation is much less. For example millimetric radar at a frequency of 94GHz (one gigahertz is 1,000,000,000 cycles per second) penetrates several times further than radar waves operating at, say, 60 or 180GHz. Rather frustratingly, however, if it is raining 94GHz is just at the peak of the attenuation scale. The reason why the shorter wavelengths of millimetric radar, IR and laser light are acceptable for battlefield helicopters is that the ranges involved are invariably short. A target is seldom as far away as 6 miles (10km).

In theory at least, any available wavelength can be used to detect targets, indicate their direction and measure their range. In practice the apparent wealth of choices is limited by such factors as the need to see small objects, the need to use only what is affordable, and the

wish to minimize one's own signature and, if possible, use only passive sensors. Some of the most useful sensors are passive (ie, they emit no signal themselves), but by using LPI (low probability of intercept) techniques it is likely that emitting sensors will remain viable, though decreasingly so, for perhaps ten more years.

Radar, other than doppler for purely navigational purposes or special large installations for surveillance (eg the US Army SOTAS), has seldom been considered for land-battle helicopters. The chief exceptions are very recent, because MBB in West Germany and Thomson-CSF in France are trying to develop small millimetric radars to warn of obstacles, and particularly of electric cables which are the bane of every tactical pilot's life. MBB

has since 1980 been using the first production BO 105 as a flying laboratory for the evaluation and refinement of a wide range of sensors, and one of the 1985-86 programmes concerns obstacle warning. The first installation was an AEG/Telefunken radar operating at 60GHz, with 125,000 pulses per second emitted from a parabolic aerial and a mirror rotating at 400rpm. Results showed no major problem and fine wires could be detected. In 1986 a more powerful radar was to be flown, with a better presentation and refined algorithms (software procedures) to enable the crew to detect wires at greater distances. MBB have not said how far away they saw cables in 1985, but the figure of 1,312ft (400m) for detecting pylons is not exactly encouraging.

The last thing a battle helicopter pilot wants to do is soar high into the sky, but unless the ground speed is very low the usual procedure on detecting cables is to rise well above them. Detection systems should ideally give both enough warning and a clear picture of the clearance underneath for the helicopter to fly under the wires. Thomson-CSF's system is called Romeo (radar ondes millimetriques d'evitement d'obstacles), and it operates in the atmospheric "window" at 94GHz, which naturally gives finer resolution than 60GHz. Of course, there are special "synthetic aperture" techniques which can combine fantastic angular resolution, better than any human eye, with the good penetration through rain and fog of longer wavelengths. These radars emit their signals in rapid sequences which electronically duplicate the emissions from giant radars with aerials 100ft (30m) or more across. The actual SAR (synthetic-aperture radar) is of manageable size, but nobody can afford to use them in attack helicopters, highly desirable though they may be. In any case, nobody knows how to reconcile SAR with a helicopter that is hovering! Romeo has several novel features which make it especially attractive; for example

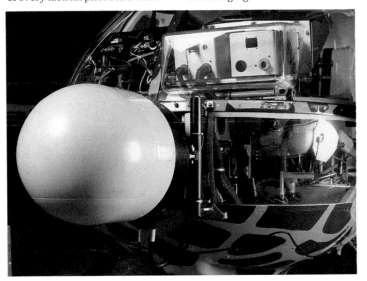

Below: In terrain almost devoid of cover these British Army Lynx AH.1 (TOW) anti-tank helicopters are having to fly at NOE height. Power cables pass far overhead, posing no threat, but it would be a different matter with lower cables, and at night.

Left: As described above, MBB is flying a millimetric radar on its giraffe-spotted BO 105 in a major programme aimed at beating the menace of collision with surface obstacles. This shows the second, larger, radar installation which was being flown in 1986.

Millimetric Attenuation

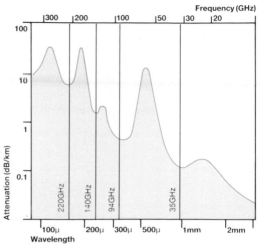

Frequency (GHz)

Attenuation (dB/km)

220GHz 140GHz 94GHz 35GHz

Wavelength

Left: This diagram shows attenuation, the opposite of transmittance, of EM (radar) waves of J-band (X-band) or higher frequency, in the millimetric range. As wavelength gets shorter, attenuation becomes worse, but there are still "windows" at specific frequencies where it is acceptable (red lines).

Right: A plot over a wide range of frequencies, encompassing radars, FLIRs and LLTVs, showing the way atmospheric attenuation increases in the presence of rain or fog. The effects of two rates of precipitation are shown, and it is seen that the effect falls slightly at higher frequencies. Fog is worse.

Effect of Rain and Fog

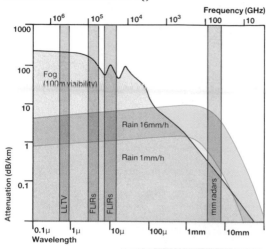

Frequency (GHz)

Fog (100m visibility)

Rain 16mm/h

Rain 1mm/h

Attenuation (dB/km)

LLTV FLIRs FLIRs mm radars

Wavelength

by using CW (continuous-wave) emission its radiated power is less than 1W (one watt), making it hard for the enemy to detect, yet rapid TV scanning gives a totally refreshed picture every 2-3s. From mid-1985 flight test from Bretigny has generally confirmed cable detection at 1,640ft (500m) in clear weather. An accompanying diagram shows how at 94GHz fog and rain attenuation is much less crippling than at IR and optical frequencies.

ENHANCED OPTICS

Thus, despite promising results with a few radars, for all practical purposes all helicopter visionics use shorter wavelengths. As the diagram shows, these have very limited range, especially in rain or fog, but they are affordable, relatively compact, and can be made entirely passive. Broadly they can be divided into two groups, image intensifiers and thermal imagers.

Image intensifiers (II) do not operate at thermal wavelengths but at the much shorter wavelengths of optics, using visible light. A soldier with the best II in the world could see nothing inside a totally

Sensor Sensitivity

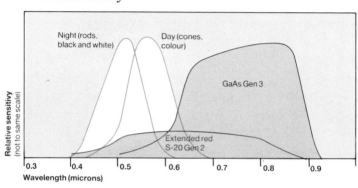

Night (rods, black and white) Day (cones, colour)

GaAs Gen 3

Extended red S-20 Gen 2

Relative sensitivity (not to same scale)

Wavelength (microns)

Above: These curves show the sensitivities of the human eye and two types of image intensifier photocathode over the range of visible and infra-red wavelengths. The eye peaks strongly at two

opaque and perfectly sealed room. The II works because in the real world of the battlefield it is never really dark. On the blackest night billions of photons enter our eyes each second, but this is still inadequate for our brains to construct a clear picture, and we say the scene is black. The II simply multiplies the incoming faint light to construct a visible picture.

clearly defined wavelengths, one by day (the eye's cones, sensitive to colours) and the other by night (the rods, seeing in black/white). Note the improvement in Generation 3 man-made receptors.

All IIs operate by means of a photocathode, a "lens" of material which, when even a sparse beam of photons falls on it, emits electrons. These are then multiplied in a multichannel plate to give a greatly enhanced electron beam which falls on a phosphor screen. The latter, very like a TV screen, is usually coated with a phosphor which emits bluish-green light at

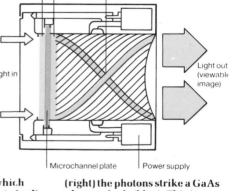

Above: These CN$_2$-H NVGs are made by the French company SOPELEM. The type of helmet mounting can be clearly seen. Power is supplied by a battery fitted on the rear of the helmet.

around 500-520 nanometres (nm) (0.5-0.52µ), which is the wavelength at which the night-adapted eye has peak sensitivity. Early IIs had all kinds of problems. Any significant source of light appeared as a streaked or smeared image unless the device was held absolutely still. Compared with the eye, which has about 7 million "cones" and over 100 million "rods", the man-made device is crude and coarse, and inevitably introduces "noise" and graininess in the image. A sudden bright light made early IIs "bloom out", rather like a radar subjected to hostile jamming. Some even emitted a whistling sound which could be detected by dogs!

Today all IIs are either Gen (generation) 2 or Gen 3. Neither has major shortcomings, and while sensitivity has increased dramatically, bulk and weight have fallen until a single II could easily be held in one hand. Gen 3 devices use wafer-type tubes incorporating GaAs (gallium arsenide) photocathodes which not only have extremely high sensitivity but also detect far into the IR region. This is important because clear starlight has far greater intensity in the IR part of the spectrum than in the visible portion.

Early IIs were often monocular, but today the obvious way to use them in a helicopter is in what

Image Intensifiers

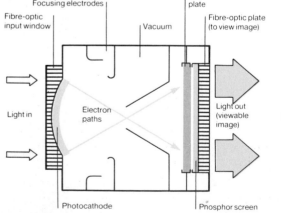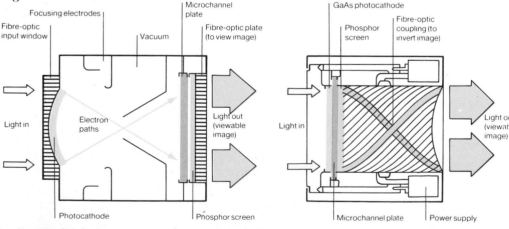

Focusing electrodes Microchannel plate GaAs photocathode

Fibre-optic input window Vacuum Fibre-optic plate (to view image) Phosphor screen Fibre-optic coupling (to invert image)

Light in Electron paths Light out (viewable image) Light in Light out (viewable image)

Photocathode Phosphor screen Microchannel plate Power supply

Above: Longitudinal cross-sections showing the operation of two species of image intensifier. A Gen 2 device (left) receives the sparse photons (yellow arrows) at a fibre-optic input window. This is backed by a photocathode (blue) which emits corresponding

electrons (blue arrows) which strike a microchannel plate (red). The image is formed on a phosphor screen (green) viewed through a second fibre-optic plate. Large green arrows represent photons. In the double proximity focussing type of Gen 3 device

(right) the photons strike a GaAs photocathode (blue). This is separated from the microchannel plate (red) and luminescent screen (green) by the minimum distances permitted by the electrostatic fields between them. New photons (green) are focussed in the output.

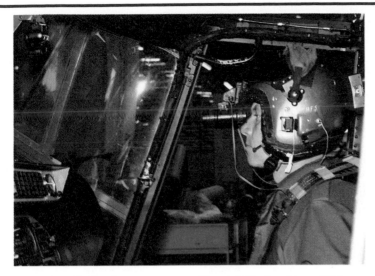

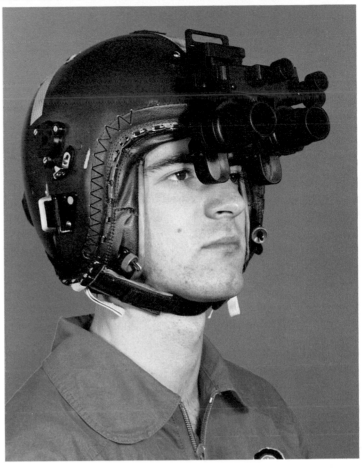

used to be called PNGs (passive night goggles) and today are called NVGs (night vision goggles). Looking like a small pair of binoculars, they can be worn on the helmet during all helicopter manoeuvres, and unlike monocular devices provide the 3-D depth perception essential for safe flight. Powered by small dry batteries, NVGs are almost totally reliable, always in the pilot's LOS (line of sight) and give adequate vision down to illumination of 2mlx (2 thousandths of a lux, the standard unit of illumination) with Gen 2 tubes and only 0.5mlx with Gen 3. The latter would be considered virtually pitch dark by an unaided observer.

There are, however, some obvious difficulties. One is that so far nobody has been clever enough to design a combined NVG/HUD system so that the pilot can have his essential flight data, guidance and weapon-aiming cues whilst looking through NVGs. This means that the pilot must be able to look at the existing head-up and head-down displays in the cockpit, and in turn this demands the use of illumination and filters to see the cockpit by night. Whatever wavelength is chosen to illuminate

Natural Lighting

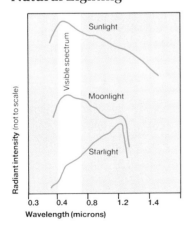

Above: Spectral distribution from 0.4-1.4 microns of sunlight, full moonlight and clear starlight. The vertical scale of radiant intensity (night sky radiance and sunlight irradiance) is broken to save space; the value for sunlight is thousands of times higher than for the others.

Above: A Westland Lynx AH.1 pilot wearing Anvis (Aviator's Night Vision Imaging System) NVGs. These have little effect on comfort or head mobility, but there remain severe problems in achieving a true night-vision cockpit.

Right: An A-10A pilot modelling the advanced Cat's Eyes type NVG. Unlike Anvis and all other current NVGs, Cat's Eyes resembles a pair of small inverted HUDs, the goggle optics themselves being well above the wearer's line of sight.

the cockpit, the enemy may be sure to be able to detect it. Moreover, the problems of making a truly NGC (night goggle compatible) cockpit are still considerable, and it is the author's opinion that this is the wrong way to go in any case.

GEC Avionics in Britain has begun to follow a better path with a progressively improving series of "Cat's Eyes" goggles which instead of being worn close in front of the eyes are mounted further away and higher. The incoming sightlines reach the eyes via reflection in plastic combiners resembling inverted miniature HUDs. This has several results. The large eye relief (distance from the eyes to anything in front) of some 1in (25mm) gives good peripheral vision, which NVGs usually eliminate. HMDs (helmet-mounted displays) can easily be cranked into the system, and the most important of all is that it is possible to combine the NVGs with any other sensor imagery. There are still problems but the prospects are exciting. By day or night all necessary flight data, guidance and weapon-aiming information can be projected on to the pilot's eyeline. (By day the NVGs would be switched off or filtered.) The combiner must incorporate a slide for NVG viewing and a slide for each sensor's image or HUD symbology.

Right: Honeywell's IHADSS (Integrated Helmet And Display Sighting System). What can be achieved depends on funding, and IHADSS has gone further than any rival system. On the other hand in ten years' time such arrangements may seem clumsy.

Alternatively, instead of having a display surface for each input the layers can all be combined downstream and fed to the eyeline combiner or lens as a single video signal.

This is so far little more than thinking aloud. The next stage beyond the combined helmet-borne viewing system, with sensor and cockpit imagery displayed on the eyeline with NVG inputs, would be to miniaturize the II tube so that it could be worn in the form of contact lenses. The ideal would be thin wafers causing no eye discomfort yet microprocessor controlled to enhance incoming

starlight and IR, up to at least 10,000nm (1μ) wavelength, and combining in the same wafer all the required sensor inputs. This may sound ludicrously unattainable, but the level of technology required is no more severe than that used today in astronomic quantities making LSI (large-scale integration) chips. It does, however, call for several problems to be solved which have not yet been even attempted.

Before leaving optical and near-optical wavelengths, LLTV (low-light TV) or LLLTV (low light level) should be mentioned. These devices range from simple

intensified vidicon tubes, which are just an II upstream of a TV camera tube (usually coupled by fibre optics) to complicated "intensified ebsicons" (NATO prefers EBSICON) in which a single vacuum-sealed package contains the II, the vidicon, a special SIT (silicon intensified target) responsive to electrons, and the coupling optics and fibres. LLTV has to be mounted in a power-aimed external turret feeding either "Cat's eyes" type goggles or a big display in the cockpit, and with current progress in NVGs there seems no point in fitting such a heavy and costly installation to display an artificial scene when NVGs can show the real scene. The TADS carried by the AH-64A Apache does include a TV, but for day only.

IR

Though at first glance it may be thought there is no difference in principle between optical devices which enhance EM (electromagnetic) radiation extending into the IR regime, and sensors which detect IR alone, there is one crucial difference. The NVGs and other devices described under "optics" all need the target scene to be illuminated, even though it may look black to the naked eye. The point was made that no II would give any results inside a totally sealed room, where photons were literally absent. IR devices do not need photons. They rely upon the fact that, in the world in which we live, everything is, by comparison with absolute zero temperature – 0° Kelvin (minus 273°C) – intensely hot. Icebergs are a little cooler than human bodies, and boiling water is a little hotter, but even the coldest iceberg is pumping out EM radiation at a very useful rate. After 20 years of research we have more or less solved the problem of making devices which "see" everything on a basis of temperature, just as humans see at shorter wavelengths.

Thus, unlike our light intensifier, our IR sensor would not be at all bothered at being shut up in a lightproof room. The only problem might arise if every part of the room were to be at precisely the same temperature, because then nothing would stand out against anything else. We can get a visual representation of this by removing ourselves from the normal world in which everything responds to daylight falling on it and imagining a world in which there was no light whatsoever except that emitted by each object. To emit light an object must be much hotter than normal room temperatures. Suppose we were able to enter a furnace at 1,292°F (700°C), a temperature high enough to give ample illumination. With no light entering from outside, everything visible would be at the same temperature, and the total absence of contrast would be frustrating. Everything would look the same bright golden-yellow, and we

Spectral Emittance

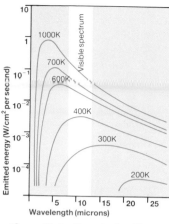

Above: Plots of spectral radiant emittance according to Planck's law for perfect radiation in the visible and IR range. The lowest curve is in the IR, corresponding to an emitter temperature of 200K. A middle curve corresponds to what might be called red heat, whilst the uppermost curve corresponds to an emitter temperature of 1000K, a yellowish-white heat.

should grope about just as if there were no illumination at all.

IR can be used in the real world because hardly any two objects, not even leaves on the same tree, are at precisely the same temperature. If we have a thermal imager it therefore sees contrasts very much like our normal vision (though we have not yet translated the temperature differences into colours). The coldest thing we are likely to find on a battlefield is unlikely to be as cold as minus 40°F (−40°C), and if we rewrite that temperature as 233K (ie, 233

IR Detector Response

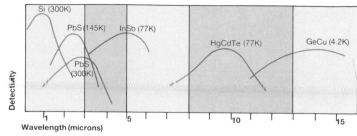

Above: All FLIRs and thermal imagers rely upon the spectral response of some kind of thermal imager, cooled to a very low temperature to minimise background "noise". Here

degrees above zero absolute) we shall appreciate that even at this temperature plenty of radiant energy is being emitted. A diagram shows how, as objects get hotter, not only do they emit much more radiation but the mean (or peak) wavelength gets shorter and shorter. When they are hot enough their emission begins to be visible, first red, then orange and finally yellow and white; but this is quite by the way. The IR sensor merely responds to the intensity of emission over its own spread of wavelengths.

Unfortunately, as with all sensors, there are problems. There is no "perfect" IR detector. Another diagram shows how the detector materials commonly used respond to IR of different wavelengths. Most have to be refrigerated to very low temperatures, so that the possibly feeble incoming radiation is not swamped by the "noise" generated within the detector by its own heat. Germanium/copper responds best

detectivity for different wavelengths is plotted for silicon, lead sulphide at 145K and 300K, indium/antimony, mercury cadmium telluride and germanium copper cooled to 4.2K.

to extremely cold radiation at wavelengths around 15µ. Silicon, on the other hand peaks at about 1µ wavelength, so it would hardly "see" anything except flames and explosions! In between come lead sulphide, indium/antimony and mercury cadmium telluride, and despite its name the last-mentioned is by far the most popular detector. It is refrigerated by liquid nitrogen or by violent expansion of highly compressed gas as in normal refrigerators.

Another of the problems is that IR is attenuated by the atmosphere (see diagram on previous spread). Radiation at 3 to 5µ gets through clean air fairly well, but is soon scattered by smoke or fog. From 5 to 8µ nothing gets through, but transmission from 8 to 13µ is quite good so this is the waveband invariably chosen, and this in turn explains the obvious choice of HgCdTe as the detector. But we next have to build a practical system. Such systems are commonly called FLIRs (forward-

Above: Elements of the HNVS (Hughes Night Vision System), or AAQ-16, include a FLIR turret, here seen mounted under a JetRanger, which is automatically slaved to follow the helmet movements of the wearer of the vizor on which the FLIR image is displayed (see right).

Right: A Hughes Aircraft Company test pilot is here modelling the HNVS helmet with head-up binocular display. On the latter are presented the black/white TV-type picture sent from the FLIR sensor.

looking infra-reds), though this is a misnomer because the helicopter has to look in all directions. TI (thermal imager) is a better acronym, and many kinds of TI – including what are called "common modules" planned to be built into systems for helicopters, aeroplanes, armoured vehicles, warships and many other kinds of platform – are being developed in all advanced countries.

Radiation from the target scene passes through the atmosphere, the shorter wavelengths falling by the wayside but radiation at about 10μ penetrating fog and smoke much better than visible light. Arrived at the helicopter, the greatest possible amount is collected by a telescope system. Any windows or lenses have to be of material offering the greatest transparency to radiation of around 10μ. Glass is extremely bad, and the best choice is germanium, as thin as possible and with an anti-reflection coating. Just as an astronomer's huge optical telescope focusses starlight on a film, so does the TI telescope focus the radiation on the detector elements, which are probably refrigerated HgCdTe wafers mounted in the form of an array. This array is scanned, either in one or two dimensions depending on the detector array pattern. The system employs two spinning mirrors to give simultaneous horizontal and vertical scanning. The HgCdTe semiconductor chips are photosensitive, and they emit an electrical signal exactly proportional to the radiation falling on them. This may be fed direct to LEDs (light-emitting diodes) to create a visible picture, but most FLIRs use an indirect-view arrangement in which the

signal output drives a conventional TV-type raster (line by line) scan which continuously creates a monochrome picture. As noted previously, hot areas are usually white but the pilot can reverse the polarity to make hot items black. Ships usually show up better with a hot-black output.

There is roughly a 10:1 cost difference between a FLIR and cheap NVGs but by 1990 it is very doubtful that any battle helicopter will be without an advanced FLIR installation. In fact FLIR and NVGs complement each other well, and the best that can be envisaged for the near future is a FLIR display combined optically with the NVG

Superimposed Symbology

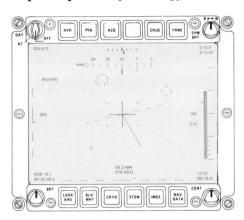

Left: The HNVS (see photos at foot of facing page) can also include a multifunction display mounted on the panel. On this appears the TV-type FLIR picture, on which are superimposed data. This information gives guidance in the horizontal and vertical planes, steering directions, distance to waypoints and other information. Other pages present BIT (built-in test) data.

Above: Newest of the French roof-mounted sights, the SFIM Viviane is representative of the latest technology. It incorporates direct-view optics, a large FLIR imager and a laser ranger and marked-target seeker. Note the screen wiper.

Below: Northrop Corporation's Seahawk FLIR turret undergoing test on a US Coast Guard HH-52A search and rescue helicopter. This system is ultimately destined for the new HH-65A Dolphins, and is qualified for USAF use under the designation AN/AAS-40.

Above: This photograph was taken direct from the TV-type display of a GEC Avionics TICM II (Thermal Imaging Common Module). Developed in collaboration with Rank Taylor Hobson, the TICMs operate in the 8-13μ waveband.

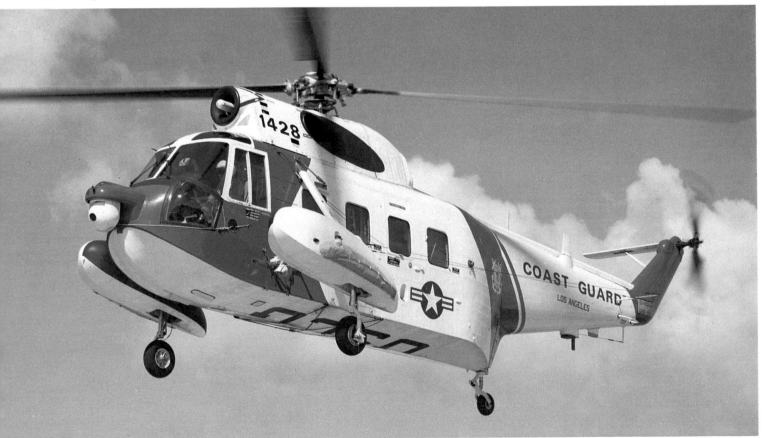

Visionics and Sensors

PNVS

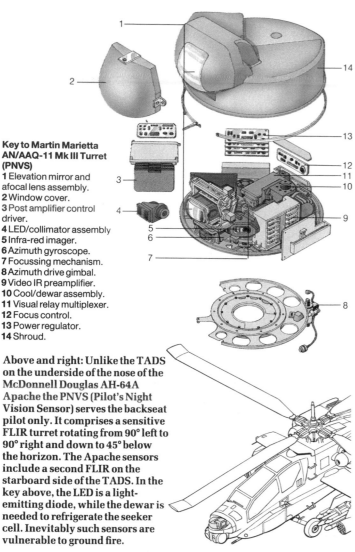

Key to Martin Marietta AN/AAQ-11 Mk III Turret (PNVS)
1 Elevation mirror and afocal lens assembly.
2 Window cover.
3 Post amplifier control driver.
4 LED/collimator assembly
5 Infra-red imager.
6 Azimuth gyroscope.
7 Focussing mechanism.
8 Azimuth drive gimbal.
9 Video IR preamplifier.
10 Cool/dewar assembly.
11 Visual relay multiplexer.
12 Focus control.
13 Power regulator.
14 Shroud.

Above and right: Unlike the TADS on the underside of the nose of the McDonnell Douglas AH-64A Apache the PNVS (Pilot's Night Vision Sensor) serves the backseat pilot only. It comprises a sensitive FLIR turret rotating from 90° left to 90° right and down to 45° below the horizon. The Apache sensors include a second FLIR on the starboard side of the TADS. In the key above, the LED is a light-emitting diode, while the dewar is needed to refrigerate the seeker cell. Inevitably such sensors are vulnerable to ground fire.

vision. There is still no easy way to add flight data and keep down helmet mass and also fly from night into day in a cockpit compatible with NVGs without alteration.

It is interesting that Martin Marietta, whose TADS/PNVS is certainly the most advanced and experienced sensor suite in service outside the Soviet Union (on the US Army Apache), has developed from it a commercially marketed system called Fulvision. This is based entirely upon TI imaging, yet the company claims "thermal imagery 'sees' wires and poles at night better than the eye can see them during the day". This would certainly be the case if the wires were carrying electric power, because they are then significantly warmer than the surrounding background, but cables do not have to be carrying current to be dangerous to helicopters. As previously noted, many researchers have reluctantly come to the conclusion that the only sure way to see cables is with an active RF (radio frequency) emitter.

LASERS

In view of the last comment, it is again interesting to note the widespread belief that neither millimetric radar nor IR is the best way to avoid hitting obstacles in

Below: This front view of an AH-64A Apache is very revealing. In the nose are the TADS below and PNVS above. The yellow TADS sensor is the FLIR (night) and the bluish one the day TV/optical channel.

NOE flight. Several teams, including the US Army Avionics Lab at Fort Monmouth and United Technologies Research Center (working for Sikorsky), have concentrated on so-called lidar (laser radar), the Army contracting with Honeywell for the hardware. Several other companies, almost all in the USA, have also researched this field.

The general problem of wire strikes is covered in a later section, headed "Protective Systems". Two of the main research programmes funded to meet it have been Cotaws (collision and obstacle/terrain avoidance warning system) and Lotaws ("laser" replaces "collision and"). In all published cases the most difficult problem has been the ability to sense very narrow obstacles (small angle) with reliability. The obvious "narrow obstacle" is the wire, either the approximately horizontal one carrying electricity or telephone traffic or the sloping one guying a tall mast. To detect such a target without fail at a distance great enough for a high-speed helicopter to have no difficulty in taking avoiding action calls for a sensor with an extremely fine beam. The beam has to have a "spot size" at a range of, say, 1,500ft (457m) not much bigger than the palm of the hand, and even then this poses severe problems if the spots are always to fill the scanned target plane. The original Fort Monmouth study reckoned the PRF (pulse repetition frequency) had to be 500kHz (500,000 per second), which was considered unrealistic. Such a rate demands excessive average power, complicates the decision logic and, in the present state of the art, would probably affect reliability.

This Army programme began with a YAG (yttrium aluminium garnet) laser, with a PRF of only 360Hz, but it later switched to a much more promising CO_2 (carbon dioxide) laser flown in a CH-53, with PRFs around 50 to 60kHz. UTC Research Center also used a CO_2 laser, and cunningly added an oblique mirror to give a second beam projecting downwards in a narrow conical scan for use in doppler navigation and hover control. Part of the trouble with smaller helicopters is their limited space and payload capability, and it obviously helps if sensors can be made to fulfil several functions. With fixed-wing attack aircraft lasers have been used for navigation, target ranging and weapon-homing purposes, but not for obstacle avoidance. It would appear ridiculous to develop costly helicopter lasers used only for obstacle avoidance and not usable for the other functions, but the difficulty lies in the aforementioned challenge of detecting wires, which demands features that differ from the other requirements. The UTC laser was pulsed at 40kHz, and by 1981 was detecting power lines at a mile (1600m) and a typical field telephone line at 1,640ft (500m).

A Roof-Mounted Sight

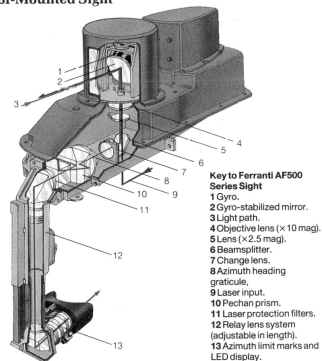

Key to Ferranti AF500 Series Sight
1 Gyro.
2 Gyro-stabilized mirror.
3 Light path.
4 Objective lens (×10 mag).
5 Lens (×2.5 mag).
6 Beamsplitter.
7 Change lens.
8 Azimuth heading graticule,
9 Laser input.
10 Pechan prism.
11 Laser protection filters.
12 Relay lens system (adjustable in length).
13 Azimuth limit marks and LED display.

What is particularly noteworthy is that both UTC and the Army insisted that "Microwave and millimeter radars have been demonstrated to be effective for use as obstacle avoidance systems".

Using CH-53 and UH-60 helicopters the Army programme is now trying to expand the use of CO_2 lasers to encompass target ranging and, notably, ground mapping. Laser terrain mapping is a relatively little explored technique which on paper has much to offer, trading slightly

Below: Though not a normal fit, this Lynx AH.1 of the British Army is on trial with a GEC Avionics Heli-Tele TV system. This has a 20:1 zoom lens and a daylight colour camera. A TICM II thermal imager can be installed.

Above: A Ferranti AF532 roof-mounted sight in a British Army Gazelle. This sight is half the weight of the AF120 and has improved optical performance. The AF580 variant is being evaluated in a US Army OH-58C.

reduced atmospheric penetration for considerably enhanced picture resolution. These activities back-up and complement more familiar night-vision systems, filling in several corners (most importantly obstacle detection) which the NV systems cannot perform.

At the risk of being simplistic the problems of naval helicopters appear to be much simpler. The only real problem is recovering to the ship at night or in bad weather in conditions of radio silence and general signature control.

Above: A cutaway drawing of a sight in the Ferranti AF500 series. It is a typical roof-mounted design of the monocular type, with a gyro-stabilized head and a cockpit down-tube which is adjustable for height and folds away when not in

Comprehensive sensor coverage or resolution is not needed, and most authorities claim either a TI or NVGs alone is sufficient.

TARGETING

Included under this heading are anti-ship attack, anti-armour, delivery of troops to precise locations and various SAR (search and rescue) missions. ASW is discussed in the next subsection. Absent from this listing is air-to-air combat, and here the Western

use. The head can be steered through a total azimuth angle of no less than 240°, and magnification can be either ×2.5 for search or ×10 for identification and for use with the laser designator/rangefinder.

nations appear to have dragged their feet. Almost all the information on the published record emanates from the Soviet Union! Since the early 1970s large-scale exercises by Warsaw Pact (especially Soviet) forces have brought their battlefield deployment of helicopters to a fine art, and their roles have increasingly involved air-to-air combat. This is discussed at greater length in the section on Weapons, but most evidence so far suggests that such fighting would be conducted visually at close range, irrespective of whether the helicopter is operating in the air/air hunter (ie, fighter) role or encounters hostile aircraft unexpectedly.

Today virtually all experience with helicopter targeting in Western nations has been visual. Even the naked eye is still much used, though it would be a poor helicopter that did not even have a pair of gyrostabilized binoculars on board. Magnification not only increases apparent image size but also, by concentrating the incoming light, gives improved visibility in bad weather or in near-dark conditions. To do better it is necessary to increase the wavelength, and most authorities would agree that the best wavelength for battlefield targeting is probably IR at around 10μ. This gives generally very good results by day or night, and almost all targets presented by a mobile army tend to radiate strongly at these wavelengths (not only tank exhausts), and they usually stand out from the background even in

desert summer or arctic winter. Performance is downgraded progressively by rainfall, and a prolonged downpour evens out a great deal of the thermal contrast as well as attenuating the transmission.

While the 10μ region is a good compromise, some advantages in penetration of rain and smoke can be gained by going to much longer wavelengths, in common radar wavebands. The US Army SOTAS (stand-off target acquisition system) was to have used a centimetric radar, with the aerial (antenna) rotating beneath the fuselage of the EH-60B Black Hawk. The aerial was about two-thirds the length of the helicopter; there is no way such a machine could creep unseen through the trees whilst observing the enemy, and so the intention was the EH-60B would fully expose itself in pop-up manoeuvres. Partly for this reason SOTAS was cancelled in September 1981.

NAVAL MISSIONS

As already noted maritime helicopter missions are in general totally different from those over land. Apart from specialized roles such as shipboard AEW (airborne early warning), the chief tasks are anti-ship attack and ASW (anti-submarine warfare).

AEW is crucial to the protection of friendly surface forces, including ships, from air attack. Today only a primitive airpower would send any kind of aircraft to fly over hostile sea or land forces and drop bombs or other freefall stores: more sophisticated weapons would be used, launched from the greatest possible standoff distance. This means that the enemy aircraft must be detected at an even greater distance, if possible so that they can be

destroyed before they release their weapons. Simple geometry shows that for the greatest detection range the surveillance radar should be lifted to the greatest possible altitude, and this in turn means that the best carriers are fixed-wing machines able to cruise at 30,000ft (9144m) or above. Helicopters are used in the AEW role only if no fixed-wing platforms are available. The obvious example is the Royal Navy Sea King AEW (no mark number has been allocated, but they are converted HAS.2s). This has a Thorn EMI Searchwater radar, as used in the Nimrod MR.2. This radar was specially designed for long-range use over heavy seas, and uses pulse compression and frequency agility (random variation of frequency to detect hostile countermeasures), with processors to enhance detection of small targets and also to incorporate and pinpoint IFF (identification friend or foe) responses. The aerial, which rotates in a pressurized radome swung up beside the fuselage when not in use, has a carbon-fibre reflector which is stabilized in pitch and roll.

Today almost all naval helicopters are equipped with radar for use in the ocean

surveillance and anti-ship role. Typical examples are the Ferranti Seaspray and Thomson-CSF Agrion. Both are I-band (previously called X-band) radars of modest size and weight, with pulse compression and frequency agility to reduce sea clutter and target glint and help to defeat hostile countermeasures. A vital part of both sets is their ability to illuminate ship targets to provide an echo source on which missiles (respectively Sea Skua and AS.15TT) can home. Of course any alert ship would at once detect such illumination.

In the longer term a great deal has been done to develop

Conformal Radar

conformal radar, with the aerials forming major parts of the airframe. Ferranti is one of several companies which have permitted tantalizing glimpses of this challenging technology, in this case with the radiating and receiving elements built into the leading edges of the main rotor.

By far the most important armed helicopter role in maritime operations, ASW is made more difficult by the fact that the ocean is almost opaque to most EM radiation. Modern submarines can dive dozens of times deeper than the limit of penetration of visible light, IR or any kind of radar. Recourse must therefore be had to

Left: Ferranti Seaspray (ARI.5979) is the standard surveillance radar in most naval versions of the Westland Lynx. The Mk 3 Seaspray provides 360° scanning, as well as track-while-scan of multiple threats and guidance for the Sea Skua missile.

Below: This Sea King, on the strength of the Royal Aircraft Establishment at Bedford, is carrying out flight development of the Ferranti Blue Kestrel radar, the extremely advanced surveillance radar for the EH101.

Above: Conformal radar is a long-established concept, but it is still in its infancy as far as hardware is concerned. The basic idea is to make the radiating and receiving elements (the aerials or antennas) conform to the shape of the aircraft. Here an EH101 is used as the purely hypothetical example (no plans for conformal radar on this helicopter have been announced). Dielectric antenna radomes are shown on the main-rotor leading edges and on several portions of the fixed airframe structure.

alternative methods of detection and position-fixing, of which the most important rely on high-intensity sound waves and magnetic effects. Of these the sonic (sound waves) method is the more versatile.

Major nations, especially the USA, have many kinds of sonics ASW systems, some on the ocean floor, some moored, some ship-mounted, some towed behind ships, some carried in submarines, some dropped by aeroplanes and some carried by helicopter. Of all the available ASW platforms the helicopter is perhaps the most useful, because it alone can outrun the submarine, turn immediately in any direction and, if necessary, hover. The hovering capability means it can pause above a likely target location and "dunk" a sonobuoy into the sea. It can listen, and then move the buoy to another place and dip it in the sea again. Clearly a buoy that is repeatedly used but never thrown away can be many times more powerful and capable than buoys which have to be used up in hundreds.

Sonobuoys are equipped with sensitive hydrophones which can hear sounds within the sea. Like the electronic devices used within the atmosphere they come in two forms, active and passive. Active buoys are virtually "underwater radar"; they emit intense "pings" of sound, with frequency anything from 10Hz to about 40kHz, and usually in the range 5-20kHz. These travel through the water at about 3,355mph (1.5km/s), much faster than sound in air, and if the expanding waves strike a submerged object a proportion of the signal energy is reflected. Transmission under water is very complex, the waves being distorted by several factors of which the most important is water temperature. Either special

thermometer (bathythermal) buoys are dropped before using any sonobuoys, or the latter themselves contain sensitive thermometers. Armed with an exact knowledge of ocean temperature at each depth the ASW commander can decide on the best depths for his buoys. Today depths approaching 1,640ft (500m) are becoming possible, which demands buoys of tremendous strength to resist colossal water pressures.

Active buoys send out sound waves and listen for the reflections, while passive buoys

Above: Operator station of the GEC Avionics Tattix. This advanced and flexible system largely automates the processing of ASW acoustic sensors and solves navigation, intercept and attack problems.

merely listen. The latest buoys are either miniaturized or hundreds of times more capable than older buoys of the same size. Their hydrophones are not only fantastically sensitive but they can also measure the exact direction of the sound's source. Sounds can be

received from many underwater sources. Old submarines were unmistakable, but modern submarines are designed to be very quiet, and the crew try never even to drop an indiarubber on the floor! This tends to make the active buoys more important, and these can give range as well as direction. Dropped buoys separate on entering the water, a float and VHF radio aerial remaining on the surface and the active/passive operating section sinking rapidly to the preset depth chosen by the operator. Most passive buoys listen over a wide frequency band from 10Hz to 2.4kHz, while active buoys usually work at around 10kHz.

Two of the most important new sonars for the 1990s are the British (Plessey, with GEC Avionics) HISOS (helicopter integrated sonics system) and the American (Bendix) Helras (helicopter long-range active sonar). Performance is classified, but it can be said they multiply by about ten the detection ranges possible on average submarines. They work at lower than normal frequencies and use advanced mosaic integration and microprocessor control. Both buoys have capabilities which in 1980 could not have been achieved with a shipload of transducers and

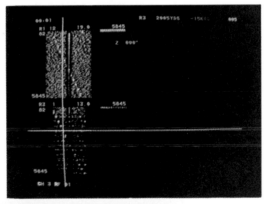

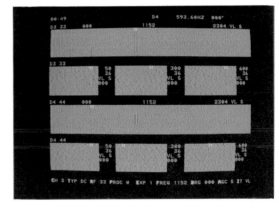

Above: Tattix (top picture) was derived from the GEC Avionics AQS-902, a modular processor of sonobuoy and dipping sonar data. In the active display (above left) two Ranger buoys present range/doppler and range/history displays, each format being annotated. In the passive display (above right) a broadband analysis and three vernier (narrow-band) windows are shown for two DIFAR buoys. Annotation is extremely comprehensive.

Left: Fitting the explosive charge which will launch this SSQ-41A sonobuoy from an SH-2F of US Navy squadron HSL-32.

Right: The SSQ-53 passive DIFAR sonobuoy is made in different versions by Magnavox (left) and Sparton (right). On entry to the sea the parachute is jettisoned and, while the hydrophone unit sinks, the float inflates and holds the antenna upright at the surface. The battery is activated by sea-water, and the transmission of data normally begins 1-3min after entry to the water.

Sonobuoy Deployment

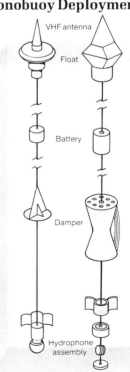

VHF antenna

Float

Battery

Damper

Hydrophone assembly

generating capacity. At the same time the point must be made that the submarine is not exactly deaf either, and it will hear the helicopter (at least its rotor downwash), the sound of the dipped sonar entering the water and the sound waves emanating from it. Fastened to a large object very deep in the ocean the helicopter is severely constrained, and it is conceivable that, like U-boats in 1942-44, future submarines will hit back. They could suddenly spout underwater-launched self-homing SAMs. Should this happen, the tethered helicopter would hear it coming but be unable to avoid it.

Magnetic effects depend on the fact that several thousand tons of metal, even deep in the ocean, exert a measurable distorting effect on the Earth's magnetic field which can be detected by an aircraft flying at low level. In general the terrestrial "lines of force" tend to be concentrated, passing through the submarine hull rather than through the water. Thus the previously very uniform angle of dip is rather suddenly altered, first one way and then the other. The distortion caused by a submarine is fairly specific and identifiable, and can be distinguished from that due to, say, a wreck. The problems are that the Earth's field is by no means uniform and contains its own non-constant variations which can exceed the "anomalies" caused by submarines. Second, the anomalies involved are only of the order of a few gammas (a gamma is an extremely small unit of magnetic flux density) while the Earth's field might be 50,000 to 70,000 gammas. Third, the aircraft itself distorts the field, so the MAD (magnetic anomaly detector) has to be as far from most of the aircraft as possible. Not least, modern submarines are constructed as far as possible from non-magnetic materials to minimize the anomaly they create.

Modern MAD sensors usually work on the principle of NMR

Above: One of the latest and most advanced dipping sonars is HISOS 1, or Cormorant. The sensor array, here shown deployed, is by Plessey Marine, and the acoustic processor and display is by GEC Avionics.

Left: Looking up at a Bendix AQS-13B dipping sonar being deployed from a US Navy SH-3H Sea King. This widely used buoy is probably the final model in a long series started by the AQS-10 in 1955. It operates on frequencies of 9.25, 10.0 and 10.75kHz.

(nuclear magnetic resonance), though all earlier MADs, such as the widely used Texas Instruments ASQ-81(V), use optically pumped helium atoms. NMR involves the absorption of RF (radio frequency) energy by certain atomic nuclei, which "spin" in a magnetic field. Under particular conditions the nuclei resonate, at exact frequencies. Thus, any disturbance

in the magnetic field results in sudden change or loss of resonance, and the effect is so sensitive that – provided the Earth's field has been accurately mapped in advance – unbelievably small but characteristic distortions caused by deeply submerged submarines can be detected. The detector is usually packaged in a glassfibre "bird" which is towed as

far from the helicopter as possible, at the lowest safe height above the waves. It is shaped so that brushing the waves will not endanger the helicopter but will be noticed by the pilot. Any excessive tension on the winch cable and instrumentation channels normally fires an explosive device to jettison the MAD "bird" before the helicopter is put at risk.

Above: The US Navy's AQS-14 is an MCM (mine countermeasures) sonar, used for minehunting. One is seen in front of an RH-53D Sea Stallion aboard USS *Shreveport* in the Suez area in 1984.

Right: The most used helicopter MAD sensor in the Western world is the Texas Instruments ASQ-81(V), here seen mounted on a Lynx Mk 81 of the Royal Netherlands Navy.

In recent months Crouzet in France and CAE Electronics in Canada have both begun marketing more advanced MAD systems in which the sensitive head is mounted directly on the helicopter. Crouzet's Mk 3 was flight tested on an Aéronavale Lynx, initially on a long boom projecting ahead of the nose and more recently on a compact lateral arm projecting on the right side of the fuselage. Dowty Electronics is a UK partner on this installation. The CAE ASQ-504(V) has been fully developed and has impressive brochure performance, eliminating delays (inevitable with a towed bird) and giving true "on top" position information.

SENSOR LOCATION

This final subsection concerns mainly overland helicopters, because in naval operations the only sensor fixed to the helicopter is usually radar. Dealing briefly with the latter, there has been surprising diversity of opinion. Most of the early helicopter radars were mounted with a dorsal aerial, either above the cabin ahead of the rotor (Agusta-Bell) or on the fuselage aft of the rotor (Westland). In the early naval Lynx and several other types the aerial is in the nose, where it has a perfect view but only over the forward sector. The Soviet naval Kamov helicopters (Ka-25 Hormone and Ka-27 Helix) have all-round vision from a chin radar, and almost certainly so does the Mil Mi-14 Haze. The SH-60B and Lynx 3 have almost flush chin-mounted aerials giving all-round vision, and so will the EH 101.

For land-battle use most of the earliest sensors were mounted on the cabin roof, with periscope optics at a convenient height for the gunner (or whatever the second man was called). Introduction of more complicated, non-optical sensors led to nose installations, partly because of the sheer size and complexity of the sight installation. As early as 1962 papers had been published suggesting the MMS (mast-mounted sight), but for 20 years this was rejected by most of the major customers, most notably by the US Army.

One of the problems is the sheer difficulty of achieving sufficient pointing accuracy with a massive installation such as TADS/PNVS – which, operating today on the AH-64A Apache, sets the standard for at least the next several years. With narrow-FOV imagers such as form the central part of TADS the lens has to be huge and heavy by any standard, and its mass dominates the mechanical design of the whole system. All the sensors have to be stabilized to cancel out motion of the helicopter, and equally they have to be driven precisely to point in the desired direction – possibly slaved to an HMS (helmet-mounted sight). When the AAH (advanced attack helicopter) was being planned in the early 1970s the MMS was considered to pose

too great a technical risk, and the nose mounting was adopted even though this means exposing the whole helicopter to enemy fire whenever it is engaging the enemy.

In the author's view there is now such a wealth of evidence (admittedly, almost all gained with exercises and simulations) of the improved survivability of MMS helicopters that the Apache ought to be modified without delay. This would drastically shift the centre of gravity backwards, and in any case Martin Marietta has stopped developing a mast-mounted TADS. At the same time the general consensus is that helicopters with nose-mounted sights are about ten times as likely to be shot down as those with an MMS. In the long term this must surely make the nose-mounted sight obsolete, and the adoption of such an arrangement for the proposed Eurocopter PAH-2 is certain to be rethought long before this helicopter is delivered in 1993. Apart from PAH-2 every new tactical helicopter known to be under development will have a stationary "drainpipe" up the centre of the rotor to take one of the MMS groups to be marketed by such companies as Martin Marietta, Ferranti, McDonnell Douglas and SFIM.

Below: A prototype of the SFIM Ophelia mast-mounted sight on MBB's distinctive research BO 105. The 265lb (120kg) stabilized platform contains a FLIR sensor, TV camera and laser rangefinder. Tests showed that the MMS did not degrade the helicopter's handling.

Mast-mounted Sight

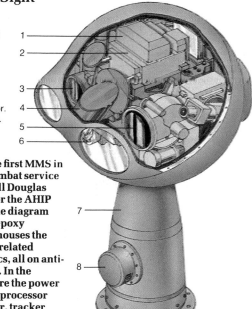

Key to McDonnell Douglas mast mounted sight
1 Laser rangefinder/designator.
2 Stabilized platform.
3 TV camera.
4 Boresight assembly.
5 Thermal imaging sensor.
6 Multiplexer electronics.
7 Composite post.
8 Heat exchanger.

Right and below: The first MMS in the world to enter combat service will be the McDonnell Douglas type in production for the AHIP OH-58D (shown in the diagram below). The carbon/epoxy spherical container houses the array of sensors and related processing electronics, all on anti-vibration mountings. In the helicopter fuselage are the power supply and the main processor with digital computer, tracker unit and digital scan converter.

Armament

Historically the first weapons mounted on helicopters were hand-aimed machine guns (MG15 on Fa 223s in 1944), followed by spin-stabilized rockets fired from fixed forward-facing tubes (US Army H-19, 1954). In 1955 there came a great leap forward when light helicopters were equipped with the Nord 5203 (later SS.10) wire-guided anti-tank missile. The missile, though difficult to guide accurately, represented a major breakthrough in man-portable lethality against the heaviest armour. Fitting it to helicopters added an element of high mobility over long distances, and from that time onwards the missile-armed helicopter has been one of the chief foes of armoured forces.

Today the armed helicopter is one of the principal weapons of the land battle, with a philosophy and understanding that has, in the author's opinion, been pioneered by the Soviet Union. For 25 years Soviet writings have taken it for granted that the helicopter is a foil and counterpart to motor/rifle divisions and armoured forces, with the ability shared by no other aircraft of taking, occupying and holding ground. Western nations have been so inclined to emphasize the helicopter's other battlefield roles of troop transport, resupply, reconnaissance/scout, casevac and armed escort (for support helicopters) that the helicopter's central role as a weapon in its own right has been largely ignored. When the Lynx was designed as the WG.13 there was to have been an armed "gunship" version, but this was of interest only to the French which in the end cancelled its order. The British Army has never had a true fighting helicopter, and only today – more than 20 years after the first Cobras – the notion of how to use armed helicopters is at last beginning to permeate Western defence staffs.

This book is no place for pontificating on how to win (or lose) land battles, but the capabilities of properly designed armed helicopters are going to be increasingly evident between now and year 2000. It is also evident that, so far, helicopters have been lumbered with bolted-on weapons originally designed for other applications. A few "centres of excellence", such as General Electric and McDonnell Douglas Helicopter Co (previously Hughes Helicopters), have developed important helicopter guns, but in the main the effort has been directed towards creating interfaces between helicopters and guns, missiles, rockets, torpedoes and other stores originally designed for fixed-wing aircraft. The point should also be made here that, since helicopter armament varies so greatly, depending on the mission, the rest of this section is divided not into "missions" but into categories of weapon.

Below: The Gecal 50 is a modern replacment for the "fifty-calibre" Browning. Here the three-barrel version is shown on a doorway pintle mount on the side of a US Army UH-60A Black Hawk. Firepower is vastly increased, but far more ammunition is needed.

Above: A product of Emerson Electric, the MiniTAT turret (now known as the FTS, flexible turret system) is seen here on the underside of a Bell UH-1H. The weapon carried is the 7.62mm General Electric M134 Minigun, which has all-round coverage at angles down to 70° below the horizontal.

Below: The DGP is a rotating 0.5in machine gun mount which is so designed that the gun's sight remains at the gunner's eye level in all firing positions (right), unlike conventional mounts (left) which cannot always be aimed from a comfortable seated position.

AEREA Door Gun Post Firing Positions

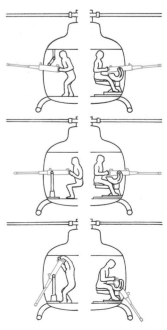

indeterminate area target. Problems included unwieldiness of the basic vehicle, including near-impossibility of holding the desired pitch attitude, severe large-amplitude vibration and the absence of any proper sight system (often there was just a Chinagraph cross or ring on the windscreen).

Today fixed guns have gained in importance. This is partly because so many manufacturers have identified the gun pod as a potentially large market, and most pods can be bolted on a helicopter as easily as on an aeroplane. A second factor is the emergence of more controllable and agile helicopters, with dramatically reduced vibration, and a third is the development of accurate sight systems. Another factor is the realization that the helicopter will play an increasingly important role in air-to-air combat, against both aeroplanes and other helicopters. This has long been understood in the Soviet Union, and in 1985 at least two sets of research programmes in the USA, involving both simulations and actual flying, threw up many unexpected results including the likelihood that properly equipped helicopters could score as high as 8:1 or even 12:1 against modern fixed-wing fighters! (One is reminded of the very first helicopter air-combat test, in Germany in 1942, when expertly flown Bf 109Gs and Fw 190As failed to get an Fl 282 on a single frame of camera-gun film.)

Fixed guns vary from 5.56mm to 30mm. As the accompanying table shows, characteristics of helicopter guns vary very widely.

Above: Most add-on installations for heavy-calibre guns (cannon) are for fixed weapons firing axially, ie directly ahead. This is a 20mm Oerlikon KAD cannon mounted on a Westland Army Lynx. The belt feed can be seen between the fuselage and gun cradle, carrying ammunition from containers in the fuselage.

GUNS

The first guns mounted on helicopters were rifle-calibre machine guns on gimbal or pintle mounts and aimed by hand (MG15 on Fa 223, late 1943). In Korea machine guns were set up in doorways, and this is still a common practice despite obvious shortcomings in vulnerability, limited arc of fire (to one side only) and blockage of the doorway. Almost all current LMGs have been mounted in this way, with ammunition fed from boxes inside or outside the cabin. Cannon of up to 20mm calibre are also occasionally so mounted, the chief type being the French GIAT M621, which is claimed to be suitable for helicopter use on account of its "low recoil forces", though in fact these are four to seven times higher (depending on whether a muzzle brake is fitted) than for the much faster-firing American M197. In general, all guns aimed by hand from helicopter doorways have extremely poor accuracy, even with tracer ammunition. More than 25 years ago a saying grew up "Whatever you hit, call it the target". Such weapons are still used to improve morale and to "keep the enemy's heads down" during approach to a DZ or troop landing zone, but they are becoming increasingly rare.

Fixed guns invariably are arranged to fire straight ahead. Such guns are almost universal on fixed-wing fighters, but until recently they have been rare on helicopters. This is largely because of their limited effectiveness. Accuracy has been even poorer than for pintle-mounted guns, and experience showed that fixed guns were of value only for suppressive fire, and for the occasional

HELICOPTER GUNS

Country	Gun	Calibre (mm)	Mounting types (helicopters)	Rate of fire (rds/min)	Gun wt (lb/kg)	Muzzle vel. (ft(m)/s)	Remarks
Belgium	FN MAG 58	7.62	ETNA CMP, TMP	900	24(10.9)	2,800(853)	
France	GIAT M621	20	Type 19A001	340 or 740	104(47)	3,380(1,030)	
	GIAT AM30/781	30	not announced	750	143(65)	2,600(792)	intended for HAP; gun weight includes 22lb (10kg) of electronics
FRG	Rheinmetall Rh 202	20	HBS 202	1,000	165(75)	3,415(1,050)	APDS ammunition 3,773ft (1,150m)/s
South Africa	GA1	20	chin turret	600	86(39)	2,362(720)	tested in prototype Armscor Alpha-XH1
Soviet Union	UBK, UBT	12.7	various	1,200	47(21.5)	2,820(860)	also four-barrel rotary in this calibre (Mi-24)
	GSh	23	not known	2,800	159(72)	2,920(890)	
Switzerland	Oerlikon KAD-B	20	KAD-B/HS 820	850	150(68)	3,445(1,050)	
	Oerlikon KBA	25	fixed at side	570	247(112)	4,462(1,360) max	m.v. with 128g/150g APDS; 3,600ft (1,100m)/s with 180g
USA	GE XM214	5.56	internal and pod	10,000	33(15)	3,248(990)	weight includes electric or hydraulic drive; five barrels, rotary
	M60	7.62	M16,M23,M24, M41,XM59	600	23(10.4)	2,800(853)	
	GE M134 (GAU-2B)	7.62	SUU-11,FTS, XM27E1,M21	2,000/ 4,000	67(30.4)	2,850(869)	six barrels, rotary
	Hughes EX34	7.62	HGS-55	570	28(12.7)	2,808(856)	scaled-down Chain Gun
	Hughes Heligun	7.62	fixed or pivoted	6,000	30(13.6)	2,850(869)	two superimposed barrels, self-powered
	Browning M2,M3	12.7	XM13,ETNA HMP, Lucas and others	500/900	84(38)	2,930(894)	weight is heavy barrel (HB) version
	GECAL 50 (3)	12.7	fixed or pivoted	4,000	68(30.8)	2,900(884)	linked or linkless feed, choice of barrel lengths, three barrels
	GECAL 50 (6)	12.7	fixed or pivoted	8,000	98(44.5)	2,900(884)	six instead of three barrels
	Hughes Mk 11 Mod 5	20	Mk 4 pod	700 or 4,200	195(88.4)	3,400(1,036)	two barrels
	GE M197	20	GPU-2/A pod, Flex WS, Universal turret	400/3,000	145.5(66)	3,400(1,036)	three barrels, rotary
	GE XM195	20	M35	750	265(120)	3,400(1,036)	modified M61 six-barrel rotary (6,600 rd/min)
	GE GAU-12/U	25	studies	3,600	276(125)	3,600(1,097)	AP ammunition 3,495ft (1,065m)/s; five barrels, rotary
	GE 225	25	chin turret in AH-1S	0 to 2,000	180(81.6)	4,400(1,341)	m.v. with APDS, HEI m.v. is 3,600ft (1,097m)/s
	GE GAU-13/A	30	GPU-5/A pod	2,400	339(154)	3,400(1,036)	AP ammunition 3,238ft (987m)/s; four barrels, rotary
	GE XM188	30	—	0 to 2,000	110(50)	2,600(792)	three barrels, rotary
	Hughes XM230	30	—	625-750	123(55.8)	2,600(792)	single barrel Chain Gun; weight is entire AH-64A unit
	Hughes M129	40	XM8, M28 etc	420	45(20.4)	787(240)	grenade launcher; XM8 installation 238lb (108kg) with 150 rounds

Armament

The development by General Electric at Burlington, Vermont, of the six-barrel rotary cannon in 1951-53 has exerted a major influence and led to a large family of such guns covering the entire range of available calibres and with from three to seven barrels (seven-barrel guns so far fixed-wing only). These have considerably increased the maximum rate of fire attainable, though high rates of fire tend to demand heavy weights of ammunition and usually high-power gun drives (though some of the rotaries are self-powered). Among the non-rotaries are the Soviet GSh-23 and American Mk 11, both with a pair of barrels which fire simultaneously (in the rotaries all barrels fire consecutively).

Until recently helicopter guns were almost ignored as air-combat weapons, but were regarded as desirable for use against personnel and soft-skinned vehicles. Since 1980 various trials have been flown to evaluate use of the larger and more powerful guns against the thin top armour of AFVs, including main battle tanks. Using various forms of armour-piercing ammunition, with muzzle velocities up to 3,773ft (1,150m)/s with discarding sabot 20mm calibre, helicopters have demonstrated the ability to destroy almost all armour when firing from above, but the capability appears unlikely to be realizable in view of the anti-aircraft firepower of all sensible armies. It is particularly worth noting that the Soviet Union has not attempted to fit helicopters with high-power trainable guns for use against armour, preferring rapid-fire 12.7mm four-barrel guns which appear a good compromise between penetration, lethality, ammunition weight and range. In Afghanistan Mi-24s have fired quite accurately from ranges of about 3,280ft (1km), showing both a stable vibration-free helicopter and excellent sight systems. The Mi-24, incidentally, is one of the few helicopters to have a super-accurate air-data system giving a readout of airflow angles and speeds in hovering, and near-hovering, flight. This was installed to assist accurate aiming of rockets but also increases gunfire accuracy.

There is no inherent problem in mounting small guns at the sides of a helicopter, either bare with fuselage ammunition or complete in a streamlined pod. High-power guns are another matter, and they pose problems of installed weight, recoil force and severe muzzle blast effects, as well as muzzle flame at night which destroys the crew's night adaptation. In the past shock-absorbing mountings have reduced recoil forces transmitted to the fuselage, but today such mountings introduce inaccuracies in aiming which are multiplied by whip of long cannon barrels. This was no problem when helicopter guns were little better than scatter guns, but with today's all-weather precision aiming systems much more has to be done to point the barrel(s) in the desired direction.

Above: Weapons available for the UH-60A Black Hawk include these General Electric guns, both aimed by hand on door mounts. The large one is the Gecal 50 and the smaller the 7.62mm M134.

Below: This McDonnell Douglas 530MG Defender is carrying an ETNA TMP-5 twin machine-gun pod on its left stores pylon. Both it and the rocket pod are boresighted to the helicopter's longitudinal axis.

Though it is naturally costlier and heavier, almost all guns in US and Soviet attack helicopters are fitted in powered turrets. One obvious exception, the powerful GSh-23 in the Hind-E, was first seen in Exercise Druzhba '82. Just how the gun was used was not evident, and Western observers have been curiously reluctant to offer explanations. In the author's view this high-power gun was fitted in a large-scale evaluation of its value against surface targets and aircraft. The Mi-24 has an important anti-aircraft role, and the rapid-fire 23mm weapon could kill NATO aircraft at quite long ranges if aimed accurately. It will be instructive to see if it is mounted on either the Havoc or the Hokum, about which little is so far publicly known. The former is shown, in the only (Washington artist) illustration publicly revealed, to have a large single-barrel gun firing ahead from under the nose. The gun is depicted in use against surface targets, firing directly ahead, though it may be mounted in a turret. It is certainly much

52

A Modern Helicopter Turret

Key to Lucas Aerospace Helicopter Gun Turret
1 Ammunition feed.
2 Geared ring (mounted on floor of helicopter).
3 Hydraulic connectors which allow turret to traverse.
4 400 rounds capacity magazine.
5 Valve block.
6 Gearbox.
7 Hydraulic motor for azimuth movement.
8 Re-cocking/charging actuator (to discharge round in the event of a misfire).
9 Recoil damper.

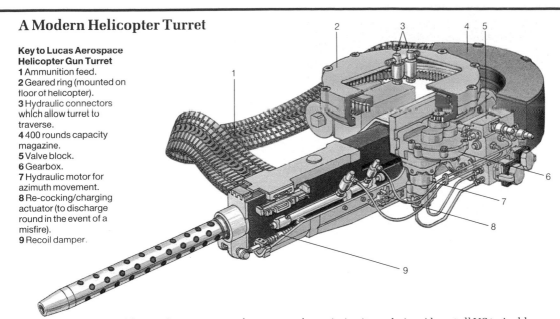

Position of remote magazine in helicopter

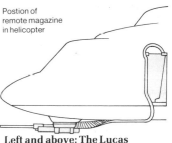

Left and above: The Lucas Aerospace HGT (Helicopter Gun Turret) has been designed to fit a precision-aimed 0.5in (12.7mm) gun into existing helicopters with maximum flexibility and minimum projection. The turret has a close-fitting streamlined casing and can draw ammunition from either an integral or a remote magazine (above diagram). Slewing rate and elevation/ depression can reach 80°/sec.

larger than 12.7mm calibre, and may possibly use standard 23mm ammunition, though most of the Soviet single-barrel guns of this calibre are obsolescent.

Mounting a helicopter gun in a powered turret, or at least aiming it with precision under remote power control, appears to be the preferred form of installation to countries with experience and finance enabling them to make a choice. Almost all US trainable guns are driven electrically, invariably from the helicopter's basic 28-volt DC system, though some external pods incorporate their own nickel/cadmium battery. Electric power is often used to drive rotary cannon, and many types of ammunition, including the standard US M50 series of 20mm, have electrical priming instead of percussion. One exception to electric-powered rotaries is the GAU-12/U, which in the Harrier II uses bleed air, but this high-power 25mm gun is so important that helicopter applications are being studied and

it is included in the data table. In parentheses, Britain's poor showing in aircraft guns has been partly rectified by a new 25mm version of the Aden, but this single-barrel gun is not known to have any helicopter application.

A few helicopters have had guns with limited pivoting in one plane only, to overcome the difficulty of tilting the whole helicopter in pitch. An example is the M621 carried on the right side of the Gazelle with elevation limits of +6°/−4°. Sometimes there are problems in reconciling the heavy recoil forces with aiming accuracy of a small helicopter. Possibly the biggest recoil force of any helicopter gun is the 1,212/1,653lb (550/750kg) of the Rheinmetall Rh 202, which has to be withstood beneath the fuselage of the BO105 used to test the HBS 202 armament system. So far as is known, no helicopter has an automatic bias in

Above: The four-barrel gun of the Soviet Mi-24/Mi-25 Hind D is mounted in an extremely neat chin turret which is aimed by the gunner in the front cockpit directly above it. Few details of the gun are known with any certainty.

Below: An SA.342M Gazelle, fitted with a rocket pod on one side and the massive 20mm GIAT M621 cannon on the other. This gun can be elevated and depressed through a small range of angles in order to bring it to bear on ground targets.

The FFV Uni-Pod

Below: One of the most popular gun pods for helicopters and light fixed-wing aircraft is the Swedish FFV Uni-Pod 0127, accommodating an M3 0.5in (12.7mm) gun. The complete loaded pod weighs 260lb (118kg), or 199lb (90kg) with only spent cases and links.

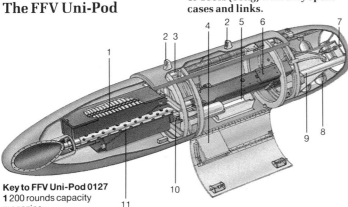

Key to FFV Uni-Pod 0127
1 200 rounds capacity magazine.
2 14in suspension lugs.
3 Recoil damper.
4 Ejection chute for spent links.
5 Ejection chute for spent cases.
6 Charger unit.
7 Air ventilation outlet.
8 Compressed air bottles (part of gun charger system).
9 Access pipe for cocking tool.
10 Feed chute.
11 Cal 0.50in M3 Browning machine gun.

its flight-control system to cancel out recoil forces, though such subsystems are a feature of some modern fighters (such as the F-15, whose gun is offset well outboard on the right side).

Most helicopter turrets of which details are known have been developed by Emerson Electric or General Electric of the USA. The titles of these companies might be thought to explain the use of electric power for traverse and elevation, but in fact they are such large corporations that they have "across the board" capabilities in hydraulic and bleed-air motors and all other available drive systems. A few guns have an external power source for recocking in the event of a misfire or other stoppage in action. There is no reason why this should not be a repeatable actuation powered by one of the on-board power systems, but usually it is a one-shot device energized by a pyrotechnic cartridge. Hopefully, in-flight stoppages will become very rare: the Hughes XM230 Chain Gun, so called because its simple rotating-bolt action has a chain drive, has established a level of reliability not far short of perfection.

In the AH-64 Apache this gun is mounted with powered elevation (+11°/−60°) and traverse (110° to left and right), but it can hardly be described as turret-mounted as the whole gun is exposed, carried in a simple cradle. Some chin turrets have unrestricted all-round traverse, though usually this is limited by the twist of the ammunition feed. In practice, with the present state of the sighting and sensor art, there seems little point

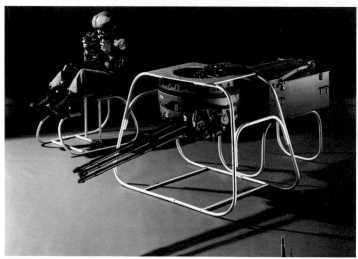

Above: The business end of an original AH-1G HueyCobra, showing the M28 chin turret. In this case, rather unusually, the turret is fitted with two M134 7.62mm Miniguns. Normal combined rate of fire of the two guns is either 4,000 or 8,000spm (shots per minute). This armament would be used against soft-skinned targets and personnel.

Left: A later General Electric scheme is the UTS (Universal Turret System), which fits under the nose and is controlled by the remote gunner as shown. The UTS can be fitted with a range of guns, that shown being the M197 three-barrel 20mm cannon, firing 400 to 3,000spm.

Left: The nose of a US Army AH-64A Apache, showing the PNVS/TADS systems, and, below the fuselage, the M230 Chain Gun. When not in use this gun is spring-loaded to rest in a nose-up attitude.

in being able to aim where the crew cannot see, and the Apache traverse is close to the limit of TADS movement in azimuth, and greater than the traverse of the PNVS. In normal flight the gun, like those in other helicopters, is inert and locked fore/aft. In action it can be aimed manually by the copilot/gunner, or it can be slaved to the TADS/PNVS, which in turn can if necessary be slaved to the special IHADSS (integrated helmet and display sight system) worn by both crewmembers. Thus, in emergency, the gun can be aimed merely by one of the crew looking at the target, though for best accuracy the target should be acquired in the copilot/gunner's HDD (head-down display).

The chin position is almost the only one possible on small tactical helicopters. It helps if the heavy gun can be well back from the nose, and especially if the magazine (which may be even heavier) can be near the centre of gravity, because otherwise the helicopter will suffer marked change in trim on firing off its ammunition. On the

Apache, for example, the 1,200 rounds of ammunition (XM789/799, Aden or DEFA type) weigh some 2,100lb (952kg), but it is located very near the c.g. under the rotor gearbox, the feed passing to the left of the rear cockpit. Curiously, the French HAP version of the proposed Franco/German Eurocopter at present is planned to have a large and very heavy GIAT 30mm cannon mounted right in the nose. Unless the ammunition feed is inordinately long the magazine will also be far ahead of the c.g. Because of the weight of the gun so far forward the weapon wings of this Eurocopter version are expected to be moved several feet to the rear compared with the other versions.

One possible advantage of mounting the turret right in the nose is that it eliminates danger of the crew being injured by the turret in a crash landing. At high rates of descent the complete turret may be pushed up into the fuselage. In the Mi-24 Hind-D there are so many chin sensors and weapons that they probably serve to cushion the impact, but in the Apache the big gun is the only item other than the landing gear to project below the fuselage. The turret has been specially designed to thrust up between the front and rear crewmembers, injuring neither.

ROCKETS

Unguided but spin-stabilized rockets were among the very first weapons to be mounted on helicopters. They come in a great variety of shapes and sizes, and are made by at least 56 companies in the non-Communist world. Some of the largest have fixed stabilising fins and are fired either from individual racks or from groups of rockets hung one under the other, each supported by the one above. Most have folding fins and are fired from pod or box launchers.

Every known type today appears to have a solid-propellant motor, which occasionally is of the two-stage type, a high-thrust boost charge being followed by a low-thrust sustainer. Rockets can be fitted with various warheads – for example Forges de Zeebrugge of Belgium offers a choice of 14 on the 2.75in (69.85mm) calibre alone – for use against soft-skinned surface targets, armour, fortifications, ships, ordinary buildings and aircraft, and with incendiary, smoke, anti-personnel and many other uses.

Range used to be limited in practice to a few hundred feet because of dispersion and the impossibility of accurate aiming. Continued refinement has reduced dispersion to the point where, with a good sight system, an aircraft or even a truck is likely to be hit by a single round on a close-range dive attack, and many manufacturers claim useful ranges against large targets (in dive attacks) of up to 6.2 miles (10km).

To give an example of effectiveness, rockets designed for attacks on HASs (hardened aircraft shelters) are typically designed to penetrate 1.6in (40mm) of steel, or 47in (1.2m) of concrete, or a composite of 142in (3.6m) of earth and 12in (300mm) of concrete before exploding and radiating about 600 fragments each capable of penetrating 0.315in (8mm) of aluminium plate.

On a typical trajectory from an attacking helicopter the projectile accelerates to around 3,280ft (1,000m)/s at motor burnout about 2,625ft (800m) ahead of the launcher. Speed then decays to half this value at a range of 9,022ft (2,750m). Even speeds of this order still give considerable penetrating power, and TBA (Thomson Brandt Armements) in France is marketing a series of "flechette" type warheads each packed with high-density darts of 10:1 length/diameter ratio. On a typical helicopter pass the F2/AMV 68mm size (22 rounds fired, each with 36 darts) would in 4.5s result in

Hydra 70 Warheads

M261
The Hydra 70 is a proven system of 70mm (2.75in) folding-fin rockets. The M261 warhead contains ten high-explosive sub-munitions for use against armour, materials, personnel and many other targets. The M267 is a smoke-generating training version.

M247
The M247 is a shaped-charge warhead for use against armoured targets. The charge is detonated on impact at the correct stand-off distance by an M438 base-mounted fuze. The only problem is that the rocket must strike the target.

M255
The M255 is a flechette warhead which contains approximately 2,500 28-grain flechettes plus three tracers for many missions including air-to-air as well as air-to-ground. The usual fuze for helicopter operations is the M439 airburst-type set to 500-6,000m height.

M264
Another warhead for the Hydra 70 family of rockets is the M264 smoke screen type. It provides up to five minutes of effective smoke screen for target marking or obscuration. In helicopter missions it would be triggered by an M439RC fuze, with airburst remotely set, giving variable range of engagement.

M262
The M262 is a specialized illumination warhead used against ground targets at night. It provides approximately one million candlepower illumination for a total time of roughly two minutes. This head is another usually fitted with the M439RC remote-set airburst fuze.

M?
The Department of Defense had not allocated a designation number to this warhead as this book went to press. It is a special long head packed with discs of radar chaff for jamming, decoy and effective countermeasure avoidance. It is another of the heads triggered by the M439RC fuze, though seven other fuzes are available, some of them nose-mounted.

Above: One of the latest US Army Bell AH-1S Modernised HueyCobra attack helicopters (with flat-plate canopy and new low-airspeed sensor boom) engaged in a rocket-firing run. The rockets are of 2.75in (70mm) calibre, and have flick-out fins of a type different from those on the Hydra 70 series. Note how the rocket smoke has been blown downwards by the rotor downwash.

Left: There are various ways in which helicopter-launched rockets may be carried. The very largest, such as the awesome Soviet 240mm (9.45in), are carried individually. Most small-calibre rockets are loaded into tubes in a streamlined pod or box launcher. Intermediate calibres are carried in external groups. This MBB BO 105CB is armed with the RWK 051 system for a total of 30 SURA D-81 rockets. These 81mm (4.94in) weapons each weigh from 12.7-14.2kg (28.0-31.3lb) depending on warhead.

Above: Probably the most important anti-armour guided missile in the West today is the Hughes TOW, seen here being fired from a McDonnell Douglas 530MG Defender with an MMS (mast-mounted sight). Note how the fins and control surfaces are already almost fully deployed, a split second after leaving the tube launcher. The turret under the nose is the HNVS (Hughes night vision system) with helmet FLIR.

Above left: One of the earliest of all helicopter-launched guided missiles was the Aérospatiale AS.11, with optical (human eye) sighting and wire guidance, the operator having to keep a flare on the missile aligned with the target. Here sparks fly as drops of incandescent carbon blast from an AS.11 leaving a Westland Wasp of the Royal Navy.

Left: TOW is an important weapon on Lynx AH.1 helicopters of the British Army of the Rhine, which are also being updated with new roof-mounted all-weather sights. Here Army Air Corps personnel load the four right-hand tubes of a TOW-equipped Lynx. This helicopter can fire eight TOW missiles and then reload the tubes from missiles in the cabin.

Below: TOW (Tube-launched Optically tracked Wire-guided) is very widely used, with deliveries well on the way to the half-million mark. This cutaway shows all salient features of the original BGM-71A TOW 1. The later Improved TOW and TOW 2 are identical except for more powerful warheads and new fuze systems, giving greater armour penetration.

blanket coverage of an area 2,280ft ×230ft (1,000m×70m) with 792 darts each penetrating 0.315in (8mm) of steel plate.

MISSILES

The first combat experience with guided missiles fired by helicopters was gained by France in Algeria. In the prolonged and bloody war that ended in 1962 the French used hundreds of the most powerful helicopters available, armed with guns, rockets and the new SS.10 and SS.11 missiles. Though the FLN (Algerian nationalists) had no armour, the missiles were used as in today's Afghan war to blast hideouts in rocky terrain. Occasionally they were used against urban buildings. Though more difficult to guide than today's missiles, they were often surgical in precision and devastating in effect.

The same rather challenging manual command to LOS (line of sight) guidance was used on the Soviet AT-3 Sagger, which proved deadly to many Israeli armoured vehicles in October 1973 (though then usually fired from the ground). Today, however, this method of guidance is fast on the way out. Perhaps its best-ever performance was with AS.11 missiles fired by British Army Scouts in the Falklands, but this was due mainly to the exceptional skill of the operators and the good optics of the Avimo-Ferranti 120 roof-mounted sights.

By 1960 Nord-Aviation (today Aérospatiale) was developing a second-generation guidance method known as Saclos (semi-active command to LOS) which greatly reduced the operator's problems. All he has to do is keep his magnifying optical sight on the target. A sensitive IR goniometer (angular detector) in the sight measures the difference in angle between the LOS to the target and

bright flares in the tail of the missile and automatically generates an error signal to reduce the difference to zero. This "TCA" (télécommande automatique) guidance has since been used on many later helicopter-launched missiles, including the Franco-German Euromissile HOT and, in an Americanized form, on the Hughes BGM-71 TOW family. These are the most widely used anti-armour missiles in the Western world.

Almost all current helicopter-launched anti-armour missiles follow the same general principles. Since they invariably use a hollow, or shaped, charge warhead, penetration of armour depends on

TOW Cutaway

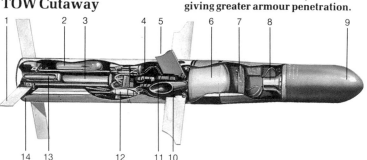

Key to TOW missile
1 Flick-out control fins.
2 Gas bottle.
3 Launch motor (booster).
4 Batteries.
5 Flick-out wings.
6 Flight motor (sustainer).
7 Electronics.
8 Safety/arm unit.
9 Warhead.
10 Motor nozzle.
11 Gyro.
12 Control actuators.
13 Wire dispenser.
14 IR source (for missile tracking).

warhead diameter, which has to be as large as possible. Already an excellent weapon, TOW has been upgraded twice. I-TOW (Improved TOW) has a more powerful warhead within the original 5in (127mm) diameter, and can be loaded into existing launch tubes. TOW 2 has an even more powerful head, with the same 6in (152mm) diameter as the missile body, and as it incorporates many other changes requires upgrading of the entire system. Lasers and thermal imagers are being incorporated into TOW night sights, and the Venus (viseur ecartométrique de nuit stabilisé) has been added to the HOT system to give night firing capability. Sight magnification is selected at the highest available level during missile guidance, which in one way eases the problem of LOS accuracy yet magnifies the errors and in rough air or a vibrating helicopter emphasizes the difficulty of holding the sight on target. The best a good operator can normally hope for is to keep the missile

within a circle of 79in (2m) diameter at maximum range, which is barely adequate to guarantee a good hit.

Almost all current missiles are fired from a storage container, launch tube or some other attachment under the thrust of a boost motor, which gives a powerful kick to bring the missile up to speed. Thereafter a long-burning cruise motor maintains the speed, but at quite a short distance downrange the cruise motor burns out. Thereafter the missile coasts, the speed falling away until as the weapon nears maximum range it is travelling at about half the motor burnout speed. This is inevitably reflected in worsening manoeuvrability, and the greater the manoeuvre demands the more rapid is the decay in speed. When firing near extreme range it is obvious to the operator how sluggish the missile is becoming. Much coarser and more prolonged control demands are needed, and the task of holding the missile on the LOS becomes

HOT Installation

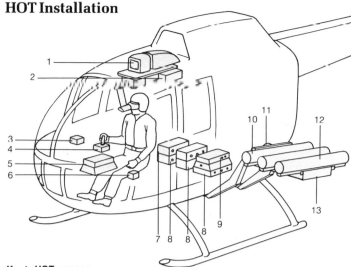

Key to HOT weapon system installed on MBB BO 105
1 Gyrostabilized sight.
2 Localizer (part of guidance equipment, detects IR tracer).
3 Steering indicator (artificial horizon).
4 Sight control unit.
5 Control selection unit.
6 Firing system.
7 Sight electronics box.
8 Electronics boxes for localizer, guidance, and launch ramp control.
9 Slaving electronics box.
10 Ramp selector switch units and cables.
11 Actuator.
12 Six launch ramps.
13 Two launch ramp supports.

HOT 2 Cutaway

Key to HOT 2 missile
1 Missile container plug.
2 Glass fibre tubular container.
3 Hollow charge warhead, ignition triggered by distortion of nose cone upon impact.
4 Fuze.
5 Sustainer motor.
6 Booster motor.
7 Guidance module containing decoder, gyroscope, battery, control wire, sustainer jet deflector, and IR tracer.
8 Thermal battery, pyrotechnically primed on firing.
9 Safety locking mechanism.
10 Electrical connector system.
11 Arming wire.

Left: For comparison with TOW opposite, this illustration shows internal arrangement of the European HOT 2. In the first second of flight the boost motor accelerates the missile to 263mph (240m/sec), and this speed is then maintained by the sustainer motor to the target.

Below left: Standard anti-armour helicopter of the Heer (West German army), the MBB BO 105P is officially known as the PAH-1. Here in NOE flight among spruce, a PAH-1 searches for targets using its roof-mounted sight.

Above: This diagram shows the disposition of major elements in the installation of HOT missiles into an MBB BO 105. Customers have various options, but the arrangement depicted is that of the West German army's PAH-1, with six launch tubes and a roof-mounted sight.

Below: A dramatic picture of a PAH-1 (MBB BO 105P) firing a HOT missile while trying to maintain a "hull-down" position behind trees. Many of the old rules of armoured warfare apply to the anti-armour helicopters.

ever more difficult. In any case the long time of flight is always a great drawback. It prolongs the exposure of the helicopter's sight system (and, if the sight is foolishly mounted in the nose, of the entire helicopter); it warns the enemy of the attack, and it may give the target vehicles time to get hull-down or in some other way counter the oncoming missile(s).

For the future everything possible must be done to increase missile speed all the way to the target. TOW's burnout velocity is not far short of Mach 1, and if this could be held to extreme range the results would be much better. In

the author's view there is little practical advantage in going for missile ranges significantly greater than the 2.5 miles (4km) of today's weapons, and over such short ranges there is probably no very great difference in missile bulk and weight between a ram-rocket (which is launched as a rocket and quickly changes into an air-breathing ramjet) and a two-stage rocket as used in current weapons. A future missile cruising at Mach 1.2 would reach 2.5 miles (4km) in about 9s, compared with 17s for today's HOT, and would retain immediate crisp agility all the way to the target.

Above: Already a useful and well-equipped battlefield helicopter, the UH-60A Black Hawk has been made vastly more effective by the add-on ESSS (external stores support system). These strong braced "wings" can carry extremely heavy loads, in this case 16 of the heavy (99lb, 45kg) Hellfire missiles.

Left: Primary carrier of Hellfire, and fully equipped to guide it, the McDonnell Douglas AH-64A Apache is the US Army's future front-line attack helicopter, entering full combat service in 1986. This Apache was photographed firing a brightly painted test Hellfire.

Latest and probably most formidable of current weapons are the Soviet AT-6 Spiral and the US Army's Rockwell AGM-114A Hellfire. Both are hefty weapons, significantly bigger and heavier than their predecessors and able to fly at about the speed of sound out to ranges "far in excess of present anti-armor systems" (a Hellfire claim); AT-6 range has even been put as high as 6.2 miles (10km). Both home on laser light diffused from the target, the designating laser being either in the launch helicopter or aimed by friendly ground forces. The missile has an optical telescope in the nose feeding error signals through microelectronic guidance cards to work the control surfaces. Further aft is the hollow-charge warhead, of some 7in (178mm) diameter in both missiles, firing its armour-piercing jet straight through the guidance section. Amazingly, the motor in the first batches of Hellfires left a smoky trail, but doubtless this remarkable oversight has been corrected with the main production.

With missiles in this class it is possible not merely to dispense with guidance wires but also to adopt LOAL (lock-on after launch) as a standard procedure. Having established beyond doubt the presence and rough location of the enemy armour, a succession of missiles can be fired by a helicopter which does not expose itself at all. Each is guidance-coded to a particular friendly laser designator, the lasers all being aimed at different targets. The missiles come into sight over a wood, hill or whatever is hiding the helicopter and each detects and locks-on to its own particular target. Homing is thereafter automatic. AT-6 firings have probably not been observed by the

Hellfire Cutaway

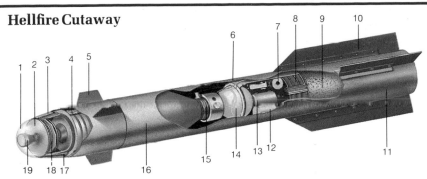

Key to Hellfire missile
1 Glass nose.
2 Cassegrain telescope.
3 Laser seeker.
4 Guidance avionics.
5 Control canards.
6 Guidance section.
7 Pitch gyro.
8 Autopilot circuit boards.
9 Motor.
10 Fixed fins.
11 Control section.
12 Yaw/roll gyro.
13 Battery.
14 Air bottle.
15 Fuze.
16 Hollow charge warhead.
17 Impact switch.
18 Gyro.
19 Detector pre-amp.

Above: Hellfire is the first of a new generation of anti-tank missiles in the West with self-contained homing guidance. The laser receiver in the nose is coupled to the fin control system to steer the missile automatically towards laser light scattered back from the designated target. Each missile responds only to light from a particular laser.

Above: Another potential carrier of Hellfire is the greatly upgraded Westland Lynx 3, the prototype of which is seen here with a varied assortment of eight Hellfire plus two self-defence Stingers and an Oerlikon 20mm KAD cannon.

Right: Many weapon manufacturers are studying the problems of self-defence missiles which might also be used by helicopters against surface targets. The main future French weapon in this class is the Matra Mistral, carried in twin tubes with nose eyelid doors. Here seen mounted on a Gazelle, Mistral looks set to achieve widespread sales.

West, but there is no reason to doubt that this missile also has LOAL capability. Hellfire originally followed a rather lofty trajectory which, while it offered better effectiveness in plunging on its targets from above, ran the risk of entering low cloud and losing the vital guidance lock. As the terrain on each firing cannot be pre-ordained there may even be a case for equipping missiles with some form of ground-proximity or terrain-avoidance system, or alternatively with a programmed memory so that, should the laser signal be lost, the missile quickly noses down to lose height below cloud level.

Increasingly, tactical helicopters will have to be well-armed in the air-to-air role. For many years desultory experiments have taken place using such familiar weapons as Sidewinders and even the big radar-guided Sparrow, the latter being carried by a Kaman NUH-2C Seasprite. The remarkable fact remains that – almost certainly excepting the Soviet Union – no country appears to have carried out any comprehensive research into the air-combat helicopter. A trivial amount of thought has been applied to helicopters used in an air-defence role, especially with the fleet, but the fact that helicopters are important multirole assets which can even hunt and shoot down other aircraft seems hardly to have been recognised. Only since 1981 has the US Army begun to consider the possibility of offensive air-combat operations, and the OH-58D near-term Scout Helicopter is expected to be equipped with AAMs (air to air missiles) when a suitable type is available.

Several promising weapons are likely to become available in the fairly near term. One species, used purely in the anti-aircraft role, is MLMS (multi-purpose lightweight missile system), closely related to ADSM (air-defense suppression missile) and in both cases derived from FIM-92A Stinger, the US Army standard infantry SAM (surface-to-air missile). Compared with Stinger the MLMS has a longer-burning flight motor, and it would certainly replace plain IR homing guidance by "two-colour" POST (passive optical seeker technique) guidance using UV (ultraviolet) as one of the two "colours". A "fire and forget" weapon, MLMS is expected to be carried in two-tube boxes which are reloadable and house the refrigeration system for the missile seekers and the modular guidance electronics. The loaded twin launcher weighs about 99lb (45kg) and several can be stacked to give a multiple launch capability.

A particularly attractive missile now in advanced development is the French Matra Mistral. A close-range IR-homer, this weighs only 37.5lb (17kg) and has range limits of 1,000-20,000ft (300m-6km) at Mach 2.6. It can be carried in paired tubes, which with sensor refrigeration weigh 154lb (70kg). Instantly reacting, and fitted with a modern laser proximity fuze, Mistral is likely to be seen in very large numbers on tomorrow's battlefield helicopters.

Among several novel alternatives are a new class of dual-role missile with capability against both air and surface targets. There is an obvious problem with the warhead, in that the best warhead for bringing down aircraft would not penetrate the hide of a battle tank, while a hollow-charge warhead might have little effect on an aircraft. Despite this two important Western missile programmes are intended to yield dual-role missiles.

One sidesteps the warhead problem entirely by not having a warhead, at least not one of conventional form. Under development since 1981, initially for USAF fixed-wing aircraft, Vought's HVM (hypervelocity missile) is fired from 20-tube launchers in the same way as ordinary rockets. This missile differs in having precision guidance by a CO_2 laser, which provides target range/doppler data and subsequent coarse and fine beams for missile capture and terminal guidance out to a range of about 3.73 miles (6km). The second unusual feature of HVM is that its motor accelerates it to "more than 3,355mph

Left: Developed with money from Saudi Arabia, the French Aérospatiale AS.15TT is a radar-guided development of the long-established family of wire-guided weapons. It homes on target reflections from the helicopter radar, which in the case of the SA.365F Dauphin is the Agrion housed in the dish under the nose.

(5,400km/h)'', sufficient for the heavy slug of metal in the nose to punch straight through the target. The metal is expected to be depleted uranium, but another super-high-density material might be chosen.

The other dual-role missile is Adats (air-defence anti-tank system), an extremely promising system being developed as a private venture by Oerlikon-Bührle of Switzerland and Martin Marietta of the USA. In this case the missile does not rely on kinetic energy but on a warhead, and to try to get the best of both worlds this consists of a shaped charge to pierce tank armour surrounded by steel fragments for use against aircraft. This is the only significant compromise in what is otherwise a very attractive system which by 1986 had captivated the attention of almost every armed force in the world! The system does require a surveillance radar, but with obvious LPI features to reduce the chances of hostile detection, and the guidance method is the unusual one of laser beam riding. The Adats missile is 81in (2.05m) long and weighs about 112lb (51kg), which is to be expected in view of its dual warhead. One of the most attractive features of Adats is its extremely high speed, which is Mach 3; thus, it takes only 6s to go all the way to its maximum effective range of 3.73 miles (6km). The motor is smokeless, and the enemy's chances of interfering with the missile close to zero.

Future missiles in this class may be carried, a dozen or more at a time, with quick-change warheads. There would always be an anti-tank and an anti-aircraft round ready to fire. Either might have staring focal-plane array seekers using completely passive guidance, and so in all probability will future anti-ship missiles. At present helicopter-to-ship missiles

Right: The Royal Navy Lynx, originally an anti-submarine helicopter, has gained a tremendous anti-ship capability from the fitting of four BAe Dynamics Sea Skua missiles. These home on target-reflected signals from the specially coded Ferranti Seaspray radar.

come in various forms, a very few (such as the French AM.10 Lasso) even having wire guidance. Most of the current large crop make use of the fact that ships offer almost perfect radar targets, despite the shortcomings of illuminating such well-equipped targets with uninvited radar waves. Again, almost all contemporary anti-ship missiles are sea skimmers, cruising as low as possible above the waves in order to minimize the chance of detection or interception.

Sea Skua Cutaway

Key to Sea Skua missile
1 Fixed fins.
2 Sustainer nozzle.
3 Gyros and gyro-drive gas bottle.
4 Electronic pack.
5 Warhead with DA fuze.
6 Radome.
7 Semi-active radar receiver aerial.
8 Homing electronics.
9 Moving wings.
10 Thermal battery bay.
11 Radar altimeter.
12 Sustainer motor.
13 Boost motor.

Aérospatiale's small AS.15TT, purchased by Saudi Arabia for use from that country's Dauphin 2 helicopters, has an unusual form of radar command guidance which continuously tries to reduce to zero the difference between the LOS from the helicopter to the target and from the helicopter to the departing missile, though without trying to make the missile climb above its cruise altitude of 40in (1m). The British Aerospace Sea Skua is rare in having semi-active

radar homing guidance, a passive receiver inside the nose radome always steering the missile towards the source of reflections from the target of the helicopter's Seaspray radar. The much bigger AM.39 Exocet uses active terminal radar guidance, its Adac head containing its own small radar which sweeps through a wide arc and is reported to pick up a typical major surface vessel at a range of about 7.5 miles (12km).

Probably the most powerful anti-ship missile at present carried by helicopter is the British Aerospace Sea Eagle, which arms Indian Navy

Below: the British Aerospace Sea Skua is the only advanced-technology anti-ship missile available for all the world's helicopters. It achieved a perfect score in the Falklands in May 1982 when still not cleared for combat.

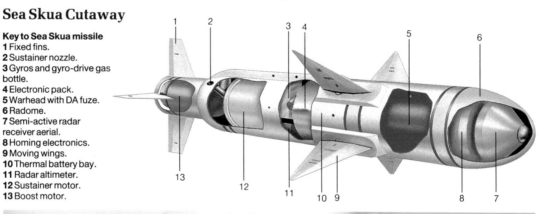

Right: Biggest of the Western helicopter missiles, the Aérospatiale AM.39 Exocet has so far found only limited sales (so far as published information goes). It is a sea-skimming missile with a range of 25-43 miles (40-70km) depending on missile type and firing conditions. In this case the carrier is an AS 332F Super Puma.

Sea Kings. Air-breathing propulsion gives this a range of at least 62 miles (100km), twice the limit for the helicopter-launched Exocet, and it also has more advanced microprocessor guidance control with special ECCM provisions. Like Exocet it has an inertial strapdown system to keep it pointing in the known general direction of the target during the main cruise portion of flight, lithium batteries then being energized to switch on the MSDS active radar seeker which has the advantage of a body diameter of 15.75in (400mm). In the next decade the ANS (anti-navire supersonique) should come into use, in which advanced ramjet propulsion will enable a cruising speed of Mach 2 to be matched with a range of about 115 miles (185km). ANS will only have the same body diameter as Exocet (13.78in, 350mm) but will be longer and heavier and the warhead will be enlarged from 353lb (160kg) to 397lb (180kg). Air for the ramjet engine will enter via four ram inlets, one ahead of each wing root. Surprisingly, active radar homing is expected to be used, in preference to passive IR homing which would eliminate the possibility of alerting the defenders.

One of the most promising ASM families is Penguin, by Norway's Kongsberg company. Unlike so many rivals it does not broadcast its onset but instead uses passive IR homing, which also has the advantages of separating real targets from decoys and being a fire-and-forget system. Penguin Mk 2, launched from ships, has been developed into the Mk 3 missile for use from fixed-wing aircraft, with

Penguin Mk 2 Mod 7 Cutaway

Key to Penguin Mk 2 Mod 7 missile
1 Passive infra-red (IR) target seeker.
2 Canard.
3 Altimeter.
4 Control unit.
5 Inertial navigation unit.
6 265lb (120kg) warhead, DA fuze.
7 Fuze.
8 Solid propellant sustainer motor.
9 Folding wings.
10 Booster motor.

Above: It was a great feather in the cap of the Norwegian Kongsberg firm when its IR-homing Penguin Mk 2 anti-ship missile was adopted by the US Navy for the SH-60B and other helicopters.

Below: Italy developed the Marte Mk 2 (Sea Killer) system, using radar guidance to steer a long but slim two-stage rocket towards the target ship. It is carried by the Italian Agusta-Sikorsky SH-3.

smaller wings and extended range. For helicopters, however, Grumman of the USA is assisting development of a folding-wing "Mod 7" version of the big-wing Mk 2, retaining the surface-launched missile's boost motor, for future deployment from US Navy SH-60Bs. Mk 3 cannot be used from platforms flying slowly, or even hovering. US designation is AGM-119.

In the past few helicopters, in the West at least, have been able to use anti-radar missiles. The position has now been rectified by development by British Aerospace of the advanced-technology Alarm. Only a fraction of the size and weight of its predecessors, Alarm is small enough to be clipped to a helicopter as an extra, not unduly affecting the existing weapon load (complete with launcher and on-board equipment it weighs 617lb, 280kg). Its great versatility and passive nature give a wholly new capability to both overland and naval helicopters, but the author has yet to meet a senior helicopter officer who is even aware of the possibilities.

Left: The most important anti-submarine weapon is the torpedo, and the US Mk 44 is still an important torpedo in the West. Here one of these familiar acoustic-homing weapons is seen hung under a Sea King HAS.5 helicopter of Royal Navy No 824 Squadron. Just visible is the inflatable buoyancy flotation bag on the outer side of the float.

Right: Most helicopter-launched anti-submarine torpedoes are quite complicated weapon systems, with automatically deployed parachutes to limit the rate of descent and prevent damage on entry to the sea. Here a Mk 46, a product of both Honeywell and Gould, streams its drag-chute canopy on departure from a Kaman SH-2F Seasprite. Prolonged trials are needed to ensure clean separation from the helicopter, and correct entry to the water.

Below: The Westland Sea King HAS.5 is one of the world's best anti-submarine helicopters. This splendid photograph shows one with the full kit of sensors and weapons, the latter including two Mk 44 A/S torpedoes on the left side. On the far side are the MAD towed body, and two Mk 11 depth charges. Also visible are the front and rear MIR-2 ESM receiver boxes, on each side of the nose and on each side of the rear fuselage.

TORPEDOES

Virtually all helicopter-launched torpedoes are members of the AS (anti-submarine) family, smaller and lighter than the heavyweight torpedoes deployed against large surface vessels. Taking the US-developed Mk 44 and Mk 46 as examples – and they are by far the most widely used weapons in this category – a typical diameter is 12.75in (324mm) and launch weight about 510lb (231kg). AS torpedoes tend to be visibly much shorter than the heavyweights, the Mk 44 and 46 having lengths of some 100in (2.54m) compared with 177-275in (4.5-7m) for the non-helicopter weapons. Some helicopters could carry heavy anti-ship torpedoes, but, so far as the published record shows, have never done so in practice.

There are many major variables in AS torpedo design. Two of the basic choices concern propulsion and guidance. Early torpedoes were usually driven by piston engines running on stored compressed air, but today the invariable choices are either an electric motor or an engine running on a stored chemical fuel. Most helicopter torpedoes use electric propulsion (almost the only exception being the American Mk 46), the energy being stored in an Ag/Zn (silver/zinc) battery. The main drawback to such a system is the limited energy density (stored energy per unit volume or unit mass), which imposes rather

severe limits on torpedo range and endurance. For much greater ranges and the ability to make repeated "try again" attacks there is no alternative to some form of chemical energy conversion system, such as Otto fuel (monomethyl hydrazine, as used for example in the on-board emergency power system of the F-15 fighter). Probably the most advanced torpedo at present nearing service is the US Mk 50, which has an electronically controlled turbogenerator driving the pump-jet propulsor via a high-speed rare-earth (probably samarium/cobalt) permanent-magnet motor. The supersonic impulse-type turbine is driven by a recirculating working fluid passed alternately through a lithium-fuelled reactor and a condenser.

Control systems are equally interesting. For short-duration missiles the answer is invariably dry gas stored at very high pressure and used to pressurize a total-loss hydraulic system driving the controls. Torpedoes have longer mission times – a Mk 46 would take nine minutes to run to its limit of 6.8 miles (11km) even if it could average 40kt (46mph, 74km/h) – and here the answer is a hydraulic pump with a return oil system. Fairey Systems uses pairs of ring mains, one HP and the other LP, with stored pressure handling vital control activity immediately the weapon enters the water and before the propulsion engine has run up to speed.

Guidance still occasionally

involves some form of command sent along trailing wires, but the overwhelmingly more important methods are acoustic. Almost all today's helicopter torpedoes use active acoustic (sonar) homing, in which a "pinger" in the nose of the weapon sends out waves of intense sound in the hope these will be reflected from a target. A common mode is to set out on a preplanned heading towards the expected target position, but an equally attractive alternative is to travel in circles of predetermined diameter and depth in the hope that at some point the target will be detected.

Compared with radar the relatively low speed of sound, even in the ocean, introduces a significant delay into reception of the reflected waves.

Warheads are typically 50-220lb (22.7-100kg) in full "warshot" torpedoes (much bigger for anti-ship heavyweights). Future submarine targets need new technology, and all current effort appears to be applied to the development of directed-energy warheads. These are far more lethal than plain blast-type heads, but put increased demands on the terminal guidance system. To be

effective against a thick and smooth deep-diving submarine hull a D/E head has to detonate not only at the right place against the target hull but also at the right angle. Of course, the torpedo also has to be designed to dive as deep as the enemy submarine, typically 2,500-3,000ft (760-915m) for the latest AS torpedoes. The British Sting Ray has been described as the only lightweight torpedo capable of penetrating all modern submarine hulls.

MINES

Helicopters can "sow" sea mines and also emplace many varieties on land. The USA and other major countries deploy a wealth of sea mines, for both moored and bottom deployment, and only a selection are illustrated in the main section of this book. Among land mines one of the specialist companies is Italy's Tecnovar, whose DAT system has been specially developed for rapid deployment from helicopters. It involves the MATS/2 anti-armour mine, weighing 8.8lb (4kg) including a 5.7lb (2.6kg) explosive charge, and the TS/50 anti-personnel mine which weighs 0.42lb (0.19kg) including a 0.11lb (0.05kg) filling of RDX. Both are completely undetectable, and unaffected by any of the established mine-clearing methods, and hundreds can be laid in seconds from automatic dispensers conveyed as a slung load, with electronic programming of the drop.

Left: An Aéronavale Super Frelon carrying a portly L4 torpedo on the right-hand pylon. The main task of these helicopters is protecting the French nuclear deterrent submarines.

Below: Special trials with the Lynx 3 prototype carrying the Italian Tecnovar DAT mine dispenser system. This carries either 1,536 AP anti-personnel mines or 128 AT anti-tank, or a combination of both.

Protective Systems

Helicopters are generally thought of as tricky and fragile beasts, liable perhaps to suffer catastrophic consequences from a single bullet strike. Though their relatively slow speed makes them – once clearly seen – much easier targets than fast jets, they can be made at least as tough as the latter, and a few attack helicopters have been designed to withstand strikes by cannon shells of up to 20mm or even 23mm calibre. This means an across-the-board design philosophy that duplicates wherever possible, with the parallel channels or structural members as physically far apart as can be arranged, and with unduplicated items made of multiple steel laminates, solid forged titanium or advanced fibre-reinforced composites. Certain areas, such as transmission bearings, may be protected by ESR (electro-slag remelt) steel.

A few special places can be armoured, but helicopters tend to be limited in available useful load capacity, and extensive armour protection cuts severely into the fuel and weapons that can be carried. Some fixed wing machines have portions of the airframe deliberately made to have an armour effect; for example the entire cockpit area of the A-10 is made from a titanium "bath" thick enough to stop AP cannon shells. The author does not know any helicopter in which armour on a major scale forms part of the structure, though there are plenty of examples of structural design deliberately made resistant to battle damage. Armour as such appears to have been confined to lightweight boron carbide panels around the crew seats, high-strength Kevlar-based sandwich panels, ceramic tiles and occasional flexible curtains. Fuel tanks seldom receive any protection beyond being made self-sealing and filled with reticulated foam to prevent collection of explosive vapour. Most tanks are called crashproof or crash-resistant, but this is hardly meant to be taken literally. One of the more obvious weak links in the chain of protective devices concerns the cockpit transparencies. No helicopter known to the author has glazed panels that could truthfully be called bulletproof, though several companies (notably Sierracin) are hopeful of continuing progress in transparencies that stop AP projectiles, have acceptable weight and offer undistorted vision.

Personal protection for helicopter crews encompasses armour, crash-resistant seats and special provisions to prevent burns and flash from high-power lasers. Future seats will invariably incorporate lightweight armour, such as boron carbide and other ceramics, in the back and seat. The arms will fold back, for easy entry, thereafter being pivoted back to envelop the occupant and provide protection from the sides (as described on page 32). NBC (nuclear, biological and chemical) detection systems are being devised which not only encompass

Apache Survivability Features

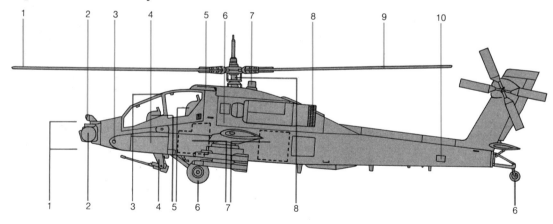

Reducing Helicopter Detectability
1 Low flicker rotor.
2 Radar jammer transmitting antenna.
3 AN/APR-39(V)1 radar warning receiver.
4 AN/ALQ-136(V)1 radar jammer.
5 Radar jammer receiving antenna.
6 Space/weight/power for AN/AVR-2 laser warning receiver.
7 AN/ALQ-144 IR Jammer.
8 Simple IR suppression system (no moving parts).
9 Low aural signature.
10 M-130 chaff dispenser.

Crashworthiness Features
1 Load-absorbing structure.
2 Recessed protected sensors.
3 Roll bar effect protects crew.
4 Collapsible turret mount avoids crew.
5 Energy-absorbing seats.
6 Load-absorbing collapsible landing gear.
7 Crash resistant fuel system.
8 Static mast retains rotor.

Above and right: From the start of design, the AH-64A Apache was planned to set a new high standard in ability to survive over a modern battlefield. The side elevation above shows special features designed to reduce the Apache's detectability and improve its crashworthiness. Diagrams at right show features intended to protect the crew against hostile fire.

Apache Crew Protection

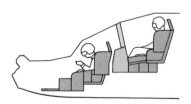

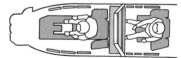

Crew Compartment Armour

Blast/Fragment Shield

Transparent Blast Shield

Right: An Apache main-rotor blade root after demonstrating its ability to operate for 5.2 hours after a "worst case" (main spar) strike by a high-explosive incendiary cannon shell. This endurance was ten times the US Army's stated requirement. Note the separation of the thin stainless-steel skins and the mass of glassfibre.

Left: Seen here in true NOE flight, the A 129 is Europe's only example so far of a truly durable, crashworthy battlefield helicopter. This view, however, reveals the plain jetpipes, which in future will be protected.

Right: The lightest advanced-technology aircrew helmets are the Alpha family developed by the British firm Helmets Ltd. This particular aircrew helmet has a semi-rigid visor cover for use by helicopter pilots.

the area around the helicopter but also detect contaminated ground terrain. Advanced helmet systems are nearing production which not only incorporate NVGs and magnetic HPS (helmet pointing systems), for slaving weapon-aiming systems to the wearer's head position, but also nuclear flash-blindness protection and tailored laser protection. At present the helmet faceplate for US Army crews can counter three wavelengths (530, 694 and 1,060nm), but by year 2000 a successor helmet will incorporate a variable-wavelength protection system.

STEALTH

Transparencies already play a major role in trying to create a less-observable helicopter. The classic case concerns the AH-1 Cobra, whose shapely curved canopies have in US Army versions been replaced by severe flat plates which are much less likely to reflect sunlight. At first it might be thought such an attempt at improving the ''stealth'' design of a helicopter was almost laughable. They are such intrusively noisy

machines, with rotor ''slap'' often heard for minutes before the machine comes into view, that the whole notion of stealth might seem irrelevant. In fact helicopters can be made quieter, their radar cross-section can be significantly reduced, and elimination of glint from the canopy removes a previous pinpoint indication of location and may leave an enemy aware of the presence of helicopters but highly uncertain (within 90° azimuth or more) of their location.

Mil, Westland and other manufacturers have revised the detail design of rotors, changed over the position of the tail rotor to reverse its direction of rotation, and made many other changes to such important machines as the Mi-24 Hind and Lynx. Reversal of the tail rotor has had a remarkable effect in reducing rotor slap, though the truly quiet helicopter is exceedingly hard to design. Hughes has added a further contribution with the Notar (described earlier), though again the result is still a long way from achieving aural stealth.

There has been a considerable amount of interesting research on

Right: The Martin-Baker HACS (Helicopter Armoured Crashworthy Seat) has been developed in several forms, with different kinds of seat pan, fixed wraparound armour or with foldback and removable side panels. All use the same impact attenuation system in which soft stainless-steel tubes are deformed by being forced through dies as the seat slides down.

Below: This pattern of Martin-Baker HACS was designed for the Eurocopter PAH-2 version. Furry cushions nestle inside the surrounding panels of carbon-fibre ceramic armour.

HACS

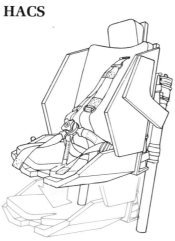

Above: A close-up of the business end of an AH-1T SeaCobra of the US Marine Corps. Even though this is an advanced Cobra with twin engines and the powerful M197 three-barrel cannon it still retains the original curved cockpit canopy, which glints in sunshine, betraying the helicopter's presence from great distances.

Left: A late-model US Army Cobra, known as a Modernised AH-1S, on exercise with an A-7D Corsair II. Noteworthy for its projecting low-airspeed sensor attached to the top of the canopy, this has the standard Army flat-plate canopy which greatly reduces dangerous glint. Crew vision is slightly improved, and flight performance is not affected to any significant degree.

techniques for reducing radar cross-section, though most of it is classified. In all efforts of this nature it is important to remember that the opposition never stays in the same place. There is little point in developing a helicopter for the 1990s that is hard to detect on radars of the 1960s. Today air-defence radars can not only "see" small helicopters through smoke, rain and a surprising amount of trees and other vegetation, but they have considerable ability to identify the actual helicopter type. Airborne radars looking down from above have a more difficult basic task, but usually have fewer obstructions in the way. Either way, protecting the helicopter from radar detection is likely to need more than a typical 1986 kit of chaff and jammers. Virtually all fighting helicopters are equipped with a passive RWR (radar warning receiver), in the later models with the ability to identify particular hostile emitters and indicate their location. As described in the section on cockpits, future panel displays will give the pilot a graphic picture of the best future track to avoid detection. Active countermeasures seem at best an admission of failure.

Above right and right: MEL Katie (killer alert, threat identification and evasion) is a lightweight low-cost RWR applicable to all light combat helicopters. Above are seen all elements of the system, the four black discs being the spiral helix receiver aerials (antennas). The display (right) shows types of threat.

IR Suppressed Jetpipe

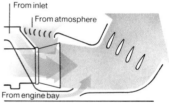

From inlet
From atmosphere
From engine bay

Left: A Rolls-Royce helicopter exhaust system with IR suppression to reduce externally visible gas and hot metal parts. The engine gas (red) is mixed with three streams of cold air (blue). The cool mixture is then expanded through shielded upward-facing nozzle fishtails.

So far little has been done to shape helicopters for minimum RCS, but in time the urgent need for a closer approach to true stealth design must make this essential. Basically, helicopters are a better prospect than aeroplanes, because they have fewer and smaller "wings" and "tail surfaces". Their rotors, however, pose severe problems. Not only are they often relatively highly reflective but they have a fundamental blade-passing frequency which the latest radars can detect. Composite blades offer the prospect, in time, of reduced rotor reflectivity, despite the probably continuing need for leading-edge capping of nickel or some similar erosion-resistant material. There is also the possibility that before long front-line helicopters will have an exterior clad in RAM (radar-absorbent material), though whether this can be merely painted on is hard yet to say. RAM coatings are already in service on the B-1B, and probably have more effect on cost than on weight. The subject is still highly classified, but the trend

Left: The Advanced Sea King, here seen with Sea Eagle cruise missiles, is well equipped with RWR and ESM systems. The boxes projecting on each side of the nose are the forward receivers of the Racal MIR-2 ESM system.

towards reduced radar, visual and aural observability is inevitable.

One wavelength missing from that list is IR, heat. The chief heat source is clearly the engine exhaust stack(s). Most current helicopters still have plain pipes projecting to the sides or upwards, and though these do not get very hot they are perfectly adequate as an IR source for the latest heat-seeking AAMs. IR signature can be greatly reduced by extending the pipes upwards and encasing them as far as possible in a cool surrounding tube, but for full protection one has to go to the remarkable bulk (and, one suspects, weight) of a comprehensive mixer of exhaust gas and cold fresh air in a mighty box. The size of the mixer box for a 1,500hp engine can be seen on the AH-64 Apache. Originally this helicopter had cooling fans to promote mixing, but the production "Black Hole" suppressor is passive, and also incorporates the suction exit pipe from the inlet particle suppressor of each engine, and also the exhaust pipe from the gas-turbine APU (auxiliary power unit). Details of the mean and maximum visible temperatures anywhere behind the engines of the Apache are classified, but the operators claim it is low enough not to attract the attention of current missiles.

Left: This tail-on view of an Apache firing 70mm rockets at a ground target shows the Black Hole IR-suppressed engine exhausts. Each T700 engine discharges its hot gas into a large box with baffle plates which mix it with cooling air, the mixture leaving via vertical slits.

IR Suppression

Unsuppressed IR signature | Suppressed IR signature

COUNTERMEASURES

Any EM (electromagnetic) wavelength used for war purposes will immediately trigger the development of corresponding countermeasures to render use of that wavelength difficult or impossible. For 44 years the classic countermeasure, usable at most radar wavelengths, has been chaff. A cheap passive method, it comprises billions of small strips of aluminized Mylar film, or similar lightweight material, each strip having a length chosen to match a particular hostile radar wavelength. Originally tightly packed in bricks, dispenser magazines or ejectable cartridges, most chaff is arranged to burst quickly upon release into a huge cloud much larger even than the vehicle that wishes to protect itself. Such RBC (rapid-bloom chaff) can within 1.5s of system initiation generate a cloud with a radar signature much more attractive to hostile defences than that of the helicopter which was originally targeted.

It cannot, however, duplicate the helicopter's signature. The role of most chaff is to blanket the scene so that hostile radars cannot penetrate the chaff cloud and see what is happening beyond it. Dispensed chaff trails behind the aircraft and offers limited protection, but chaff fired laterally in cartridges can cover a larger angular area, or blot out regions above or below. When fired at the correct time chaff can either cause a radar-guided missile to break lock and become unguided (though most modern missiles in these circumstances continue to home on the target's last known or predicted future position). Clever

Above: The large red area shows the approximate lethal envelope of an unsuppressed Bell UH-1H in which IR-homing missiles will lock-on. The small roughly circular region shows the lethal radius with a suppressed jetpipe, IR paint and an ALQ-144 active IRCM jammer, whose pulsed heat radiation makes missiles break their IR lock.

Left: This Marine Corps AH-1T SeaCobra, seen operating near Grenada, is fully protected by a Sanders ALQ-144 IRCM pulsed active jammer (behind the rotor mast) and a Lundy ALE-29A chaff/flare dispenser.

Below: Based on diagrams by Chemring Ltd, these stylized representations depict various ways in which the tiny reflective dipoles known as chaff behave as they fall through the sky. The different motions are self-explanatory, though they have a major effect on cloud bloom rate, cloud density, rate of fall and polarization response to hostile radars. Chemring have identified 14 different kinds of chaff motion.

How Chaff Works

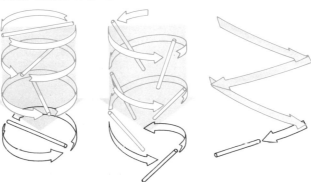

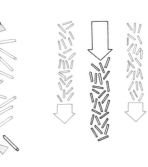

Above: Flares being rippled away from the cartridge dispensers on each side of a CH-53A Sea Stallion of the US Marine Corps.

Left: An SH-60B Seahawk hovering over USS *Crommelin*, showing (angular boxes each side of the nose) the ALQ-142 ESM system. Note also the APS-124 main surveillance radar and the towed MAD bird.

Below: The badge of the US Army's ARJS, seen on an EH-1H during Border Star '85, shows how the external jammer pods interfere with SAM guidance, making missiles miss.

anti-aircraft missiles can be taught either to recognise the "noisy" reflection from a chaff cloud for what it is, or at least to label it as "uncertain", and increasingly we shall see missiles that fly straight through chaff clouds all ready to lock-on again to the real target.

Active jammers are more difficult for enemy defence systems to counter. They can not only jam the enemy's radars and communications, but they can process his radar signals and re-broadcast the same signals, or exact copies, in such a way as to create the apparent existence of false helicopters at different places in the sky. What is more difficult to

do is to get the enemy intent on destroying the false helicopters and then disappear one's self! Extra helicopters merely dilutes the enemy's effort so that fewer weapons are brought to bear on the real helicopters. In any case jammers are costly, need large amounts of electrical power and are far from insignificant in bulk and weight. In an air force such as that of Britain, which cannot afford jammers for its front-line fast jets, there is not much chance of anything in this line for the helicopters, except years hence for the cast-offs from the fixed-wing squadrons. Thus, the larger British helicopters might later get some

ALQ-101(V) pods, but these hefty packages are too much of a burden for helicopters of Lynx size and hardly seem worth the problems.

On the other hand, though one cannot do anything about the need for radiated power – in other words, if you want 500kW pulses, you have to have the capacity to pump out 500kW pulses with no cheating – modern microprocessors can significantly improve ECM performance and reduce the bulk and weight. LHX countermeasures requirements appear not to have leaked into the technical press, but they are likely to demand internal installation of a sophisticated high-power jammer

not far short in capability of the ALQ-165 ASPJ (airborne self-protection jammer) being produced for the latest US fighters. So far the author knows of no helicopter with any kind of comprehensive jammer installation operating at RF wavelengths, other than single research machines testing the jamming of enemy communications, such as the Sikorsky EH-60A.

It is a matter of historical fact that more than 90 per cent of the world's close-range AAMs home on the IR radiation emitted by hot parts of the target. As long ago as 1949 Sidewinder was in

IR Flare Performance

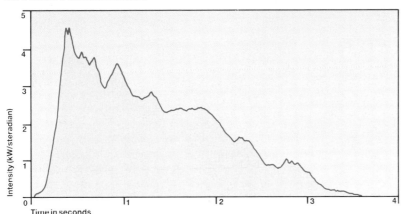

An IR Flare

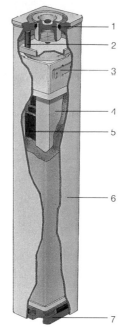

Key to Schermuly Infra Red Decoy Flare
1 Impulse cartridge.
2 Piston.
3 Safety and initiation mechanism.
4 Flare pellet.
5 Priming composition.
6 Outer case.
7 End cap.

Above and left: The Schermuly 1×1 (1in by 1in size) is a typical IR flare. At left is a plot showing how IR power (in kilowatts per steradian of solid angle) falls away over a period of seconds.

companies as Sanders, Loral, Itek, Northrop, Eaton, ITT, Dalmo Victor, Westinghouse, Lundy, Tracor, Cincinnati Electronics, Raytheon and Xerox, for example – have a commercial interest in producing what the customer wants, or even what he is likely eventually to want. Several of these famous names have addressed the problem of defence against IR-homing missiles.

The simplest answers are flares and IRCM sets. Flares are merely hot pyrotechnics fired in cartridges identical in shape and ballistics to chaff cartridges and loaded into cells of the same dispenser. Millions of TV viewers have seen flares being ejected from Israeli fighters attacking targets in the Lebanon in 1983. Gradually the users of front-line helicopters are getting round to protecting them with cartridge dispensers, which are relatively light and cheap and are simple bolt-on packages needing merely instrument connections to a panel display telling the crew what kinds of cartridges are in which cells. Sometimes particular cartridges are fired automatically on a signal from an RWR or an IR warning receiver, but usually the crew is given the information and left to take decisions on when "carts" are justified.

The trouble with cartridges is that they are soon all gone. Many helicopters in the USA and Soviet Union have now been equipped with a permanent IRCM installation that forms part of the aircraft. These are called IRCM sets or IR jammers, and they pump out intense IR radiation at a pulsed frequency carefully chosen to cause such confusion to an

Quick Fix II Black Hawk

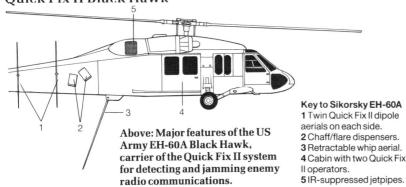

Above: Major features of the US Army EH-60A Black Hawk, carrier of the Quick Fix II system for detecting and jamming enemy radio communications.

Key to Sikorsky EH-60A
1 Twin Quick Fix II dipole aerials on each side.
2 Chaff/flare dispensers.
3 Retractable whip aerial.
4 Cabin with two Quick Fix II operators.
5 IR-suppressed jetpipes.

BAe Pulsed IRCM Jammer

Key to BAe Active Infra Red Jammer
1 Optical assembly.
2 Electrically powered IR lamp (graphite element in sapphire envelope).
3 Cover with 16 IR-transparent windows.
4 Fuselage attachment point.
5 Motor to rotate optical assembly at high speed.
6 Cooling fins.

This pulsed IRCM jammer for helicopters was developed by British Aerospace Dynamics. A novel optical enhancement system maximizes depth of modulation.

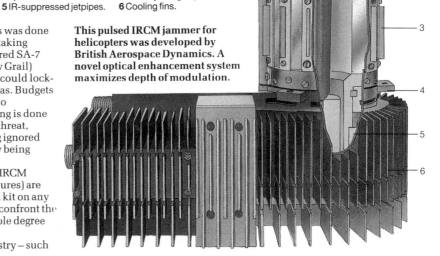

development, and when this missile became operational in its initial form in early 1956 the world's users of military aircraft must already have considered how best to counter it. This clearly should have extended to helicopters as well as to aeroplanes, yet the author cannot find evidence of much being done until late 1972, almost 30 years after the heat-homing AAM became public knowledge! By early 1973 the US Army had modified an OH-6A Cayuse and an AH-1G Cobra with simple exhaust deflectors made of asbestos/metal sandwich whose outer layer remained cool enough never to

emit detectable IR. This was done because the Army was taking losses from shoulder-fired SA-7 (then called Strela, now Grail) missiles, whose seeker could lock-on to the plume of hot gas. Budgets worldwide seem to be so overstrained that nothing is done to counter a perceived threat, countermeasures being ignored until losses are actually being suffered.

Nevertheless, active IRCM (infra-red countermeasures) are fast becoming standard kit on any helicopter intended to confront the enemy. To a considerable degree this is because the US countermeasures industry – such oncoming missile that its seeker head gives up and it breaks lock. Virtually all such IRCM jammers known to the author work in the same way, known originally as the "hot brick" method. The heat source is a block of ceramic, possibly aluminium oxide, which is heated to incandescence. This would take a daunting electric current, so the usual heat source is a propane burner. It has always seemed odd to the author that designers fly a helicopter with white-hot engine combustion chambers and then rig up a totally separate system, even using a different fuel, to heat a ceramic block which might be only inches away. Be that as it may, the bright block is then encased in a kind of lighthouse whose windows can be modulated alternately IR-transparent and IR-opaque. Note: we are dealing here with IR at much shorter wavelengths and millions of times greater intensity than the IR that enters an FLIR or other sensor looking at the world around the helicopter. The window material for IR jammers is likely to be something highly transparent at the shorter IR wavelengths, such as calcium fluoride.

When pulsed, mechanically or by some other method, the IRCM jammer acts like an overwhelmingly powerful beacon whose intermittent emissions swamp those from the helicopter's jetpipes. A microprocessor controls the pulsing according to preset codes which are picked according to the expected type of missile to be encountered. Seeing the flickering source, the missile (according to 1986 rules) instantly decides that it is slightly off-target. In its search to find the true target

the missile is likely to depart increasingly from the true one. The most widely used of these protective devices are the Sanders ALQ-144, which gives all-round coverage, and the Xerox ALQ-157 whose emitters look out on each side, each covering a 180° sector. The most common Soviet jammer looks similar to the ALQ-144.

OPTICAL COUNTERMEASURES

Helicopters have in the past been so visually and (especially) aurally obtrusive that it may seem pointless to attempt any form of countermeasure. Much can be done by tactics and proper use of terrain, as explained in the final major section of this book, but

Self-screening Smoke

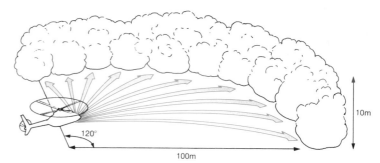

Above: Sweden's FFV company has pioneered the HSSS (helicopter self-screening system). It is a modular system based on a five tube launcher which fires volleys of smoke rockets. A normal salvo covers a 120° arc about 330ft (100m) ahead of the helicopter, and can screen the aircraft with smoke impervious over the spectral range 0.4-14 microns. This blots out human vision, lasers and IR seekers. Smoke persistence is 2-30 sec.

Above: IRCM jammers are intense sources of IR (infra-red, or heat), which is radiated according to programmed modulation in a way designed to cause a heat-seeking missile to break lock. This is the Sanders AN/ALQ-144 transmitter and microprocessor control unit.

Right: Most IRCM transmitters use electrically-heated ceramic blocks as sources of IR radiation. Seen here is an emitter in the Loral AN/ALQ-157 installation on a US Marine Corps CH-46E. The grey disc higher up is a radar warning receiver (RWR) aerial.

Left and below: Two frames from a sequence showing the effect of firing an FFV HSSS launcher. The picture (left) was taken at the moment of firing while (below) we see smoke still dense enough to protect after 20 seconds have elapsed. Wind speed for this test was 10 mph (4.7m/sec).

Right: Loading smoke ammunition into an FFV self-screening smoke launcher. The helicopter is a Swedish Boeing Vertol HKP4 (Model 107). The 90mm smoke cartridges are packed in sealed tubes. A complete loaded installation weighs 95lb (43kg).

there still remains the crucial problem of how to defend helicopters after they have been forced to unmask over contested or hostile territory. With modern quick-reacting SAM systems there is a need for a rapid-deploying screen impervious to both visual and IR wavelengths. The generally accepted answer is a smokescreen, but one using modular generators or launchers and emitting precisely tailored smoke.

Best-known of the current OCM (optical countermeasures) suppliers is FFV of Sweden. This company offers a range of generators, including pods for flank screening for ASW helicopters working with friendly surface vessels and generators that inject IR smoke material into the engine exhaust. A special kit for attack helicopters is the self-screening launcher which comprises two five-tube rocket launchers which in 2 seconds can fire ten 84mm projectiles to a distance of 330ft (100m) ahead of the helicopter over an azimuth arc of 120°, giving an immediate screen 33ft (10m) deep which in typical wind conditions lasts at least 30 seconds. The smoke is impervious over the entire spread of wavelength from 0.4-14µ. Inside 4 minutes the tubes can be reloaded by the helicopter crew and a second volley fired. The system is light (launcher 15.4lb, 7kg, and each rocket 6.2lb, 2.8kg) and ASW or transport helicopters are recommended to have six launchers for all-round protection.

COLLISIONS

Probably the greatest single hazard to battlefield helicopters, transcending even hostile defence systems, is collision with obstructions, and especially with power cables and other wires. The problem of early detection of wires was emphasized in the Visionics section. If the helicopter does collide with a wire the effect can usually be minimized by fitting a strong deflector to divert the wire either under or above the nose.

In the author's view the obvious extra requirement is a simple cartridge-powered wire cutter, nearly half a million of which flew on RAF bombers in World War 2. Amazingly not one such cutter appears to be installed on any modern battlefield helicopter, and the presence of a nose-mounted sight unit makes wire deflection more difficult. A further complication is that, at least in heavily industrialized areas such as Western Europe, many of the most obtrusive cables carry very high-voltage electric power and come in groups of up to a dozen spaced two or three metres apart.

Below: One of the worst problems in low NOE (nap of the Earth) flight is the danger of wire strikes. Some helicopters are being fitted with prominent cable cutters; this US Army OH-58D AHIP has a cutter above the nose and another below. There has been some debate about whether the MMS should break off in a wire strike.

The Future

Above: The extreme simplicity of future rotors is evident from this bearingless four-blade main rotor for helicopters in the 2-3 tonne class. It has been flying since January 1986 on a BO 105.

Left: The Sikorsky S-69 (XH-59A) is so far the only ABC helicopter to have flown. It uses two closely superimposed rotors with very rigid blades, the advancing blades giving equal lift.

Below left: Sikorsky artwork showing a stopped-rotor helicopter as it might appear in USAF service around the year 2000. The circulation-controlled rotor is stopped with blades all at 45° and the machine then becomes an aeroplane capable of Mach 0.8.

Helicopters in their present form will always be limited in terms of speed, agility and fuel economy in cruising flight, in comparison with aeroplanes. The best that can be done is improve aerodynamic and structural efficiency with advanced composite structures in rotor blades and fuselage, modern computerized FBW or FBL flight controls and, in the longer term, develop the rigid coaxial ABC (advancing-blade concept) rotor, in which only the advancing blades give lift, or the stopped-rotor concept to the point at which one can become the preferred solution.

Clearly the helicopter is a very different beast from the transonic V/STOL. To a first-order approximation, the bigger and slower the downwards-accelerated jet which supports the machine in hovering flight, the lower the noise and fuel consumption and the greater the efficiency. The other side of the coin is that the helicopter, which rates tops in hovering flight, is a very poor animal in translational, or cruising, flight. Here the V/STOl jet shows up far better, quite apart from having much higher speed and agility. What many engineers have sought is a vehicle that comes midway between the two, better at hovering than the jet, yet better in going from A to B than any helicopter.

There have been many contrasting answers, not one of which has gone into production. But now at last one of the answers is on the brink of usage which, on present announced requirements for the US forces alone, will take

care of almost 1,000 aircraft, and worldwide civil and military sales could multiply this several times. This vehicle is the Bell/Boeing V-22 Osprey.

We had much discussion before including it in this book, because it is not really a helicopter at all, even in hovering flight (though it does have cyclic and collective pitch controls). It is more properly an aeroplane fitted with very large propellers which can be tilted upwards to lift the machine without forward speed. Compared with a helicopter the downward jets from the propellers in hovering flight are relatively small and fast-moving, so in this mode it is rather less efficient than a helicopter. In cruising flight, however, it is lifted by its wing and pulled along by its propellers, so it is one of the quietest and most efficient flying vehicles ever. Thus, if you want a

Osprey Performance

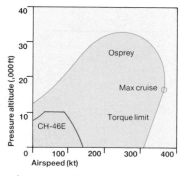

Above: A graphic indication of the quantum jump in flight performance provided by the V-22 Osprey (in comparison with today's helicopters, not V/STOL jets) is afforded by this plot of its flight envelope compared with that of a CH-46E Sea Knight, both in USMC trim.

vehicle which only occasionally, for short periods, has to be able to hover then the V-22 is probably the best possible answer.

Whether one quibbles about the inclusion of this machine in a book about helicopters or not, the fact remains it is likely to take away a very large part of the market for which the helicopter was previously the only answer. One of the strangest features is that this paragon of virtues did not burst on the world suddenly. The first tilt-rotor research aircraft, the Bell XV-3, first flew well over 30 years ago on 23 August 1955. In most essentials the XV-3s had features similar to the Bell XV-15 which reopened the tilt-rotor story on 3 May 1977 and whose brilliant success has led to tomorrow's Osprey. While the author has no wish to sound like a salesman for Bell/Boeing, the ability of the Osprey to cruise at over 300mph (483km/h), much quieter and with far less vibration than any helicopter, and at dramatically lower direct operating cost (per seat-mile or per ton-mile), must to any impartial observer mean that the helicopter's day as a trucking system is over. This may not yet have fully dawned on the world's competing helicopter manufacturers, and it may not fully have dawned on the world's commercial air carriers either. It will be summer 1987 before we hear the first Osprey flying, but the odds are that it will be a quiet and unobtrusive aircraft, in sharp contrast to many of today's helicopters. Though obviously important in permitting operations into city centres, it is also important in the difficult struggle

Helicopter Vibration Levels

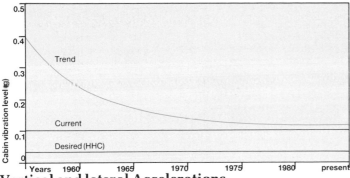

Vertical and lateral Accelerations

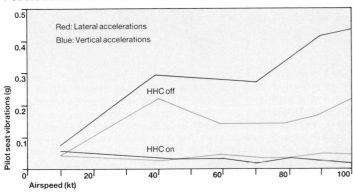

Red: Lateral accelerations
Blue: Vertical accelerations

HHC off

HHC on

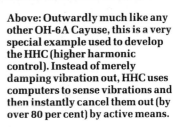

Above: The upper diagram shows how pilot-seat vibration (measured in g) has been brought down over the years. The lower plot shows the dramatic reduction in vibration resulting from switching in the McDonnell Douglas HHC system (see photo at right).

Below: First flown 32 years ago, the tilt-rotor concept has been dramatically resurrected by Bell with the XV-15 (this is the No 2 aircraft). Its great success has now led to the Bell/Boeing V-22 Osprey, due to fly in the second half of 1987 and planned for use by all US forces.

Above: Outwardly much like any other OH-6A Cayuse, this is a very special example used to develop the HHC (higher harmonic control). Instead of merely damping vibration out, HHC uses computers to sense vibrations and then instantly cancel them out (by over 80 per cent) by active means.

to make front-line helicopters have low-observables, or stealth, characteristics.

As emphasized in many current Salamander books, stealth is clearly going to be the single most important design feature not just of helicopters, or even of aircraft in general but of all future military operations. This is hard enough to achieve by the man in the balaclava and blackened face, and it might be thought impossible for a machine putting 10,000hp through thrashing rotors.

Nevertheless the basic rule has now firmly sunk in that future helicopters must be designed so that they are very difficult to detect. If they are detected, their crews must be immediately warned of the fact. If they are fired at, they must try to avoid being hit. If they are hit, they must be ballistically tolerant and able to continue the mission. If they cannot continue, they must try to hit the ground under some degree of control and at minimum relative speed, both horizontally and vertically. If this is not possible and the result is a crash, the crew must be able to walk away and the helicopter be both worth recovering and recoverable. Taken together, these simply stated requirements will exert a profound influence on the design of fighting helicopters for the 1990s and into the next century, even to the extent where flight performance may have to be degraded.

FLYING THE MISSION

Helicopters able to plug into the American GPS Navstar system will have a navigation system as perfect

The Navstar System

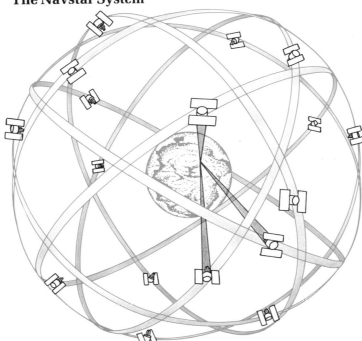

as could be devised. From the South Pole to downtown Manhattan they will always know their position (and speed, if they need to be told that) with as much accuracy as any aircraft commander could ever want. But knowing one's exact position does not prevent a collision with something on the ground or even a ship or another helicopter, and future operations are likely to be required "for real" in the worst weather that the force commander can find. Fixed-wing aircraft can be equipped with a GPWS (ground-proximity warning system), but virtually all combat helicopters operate in proximity to the ground that would keep a GPWS shrieking warnings continuously.

No other aircraft operates so constantly in such close intimacy with our planet as the combat helicopter. Even the dusting and spraying ag-plane flies from one site to another at "sensible" levels, but the NOE (nap of the Earth) profile is today's helicopter's best chance of survival. Clearly there comes a point where, if the helicopter is not designed for the job, the ground becomes a far

Left: The Navstar GPS (global positioning system) promises to revolutionize navigation. It consists of a constellation of satellites, orbiting in six planes around the Earth, which constantly broadcast satellite position co-ordinates and timing information. By pressing a few buttons, linking them to this system of satellites, users anywhere on Earth can obtain their exact position, accurate to within a few feet.

worse foe than the enemy. One is reminded of a poster seen on many fast-jet crew rooms: "Effectiveness of triple-A 25%; effectiveness of SAMs 50%; effectiveness of the ground 100%". One is also reminded of what happened in South Vietnam, where in one four-year period 55 men died in 14 helicopters which collided with *the only electric power line in the country.*

One feels inevitably that to design tomorrow's fighting helicopters the starting point (after agreeing on the missions) is to create a totally competent all-round, all-seeing, computer-controlled system of visionics and protective systems which can give the crew not merely a far better all-weather day/night picture than they could get in broad daylight but also comprehensive

information on hidden defences. In the past the combat-helicopter pilot has had virtually no worthwhile assistance in avoiding enemy fire. Even today a helicopter equipped with an RWR (radar warning system) is often thought to be "one up on the neighbours", but this should have been the situation 30 years ago. Most RWRs merely tell the pilot he is being "painted" by a hostile radar, and some indicate which quadrant contains the emitter. Knowing that an enemy radar is in a particular 90° sector is better than nothing, but again we should have got beyond this stage before 1945 (some companies did). The means exist today to present tomorrow's pilot with a near-perfect synthetic picture showing the exact location of all hostile defences, including those detected by other friendly

aircraft seconds previously, as well as the actual tracks of hostile triple-A fire and the numerically quantified positions of oncoming SAMs (which, with full information, can often be avoided).

It is probably fair to claim that tomorrow's cockpit, which may have purely synthetic vision, will eliminate the hazard of collision with obstacles. After only five years or so of effort, sufficient experience has been gained to claim that anything that could serious disturb the helicopter can be detected at a distance great enough for a controlled avoiding action. Just which wavelength to use depends who you talk to, both millimetric radars and lasers having their passionate adherents and the Fulvision system even championing the cause of infrared. Avoidance of obstacles, and

wires in particular, is as important as seeing the enemy and directing weapons. The wire will probably remain the greatest obstacle threat throughout the foreseeable future, and seeing it in time without an unacceptable system false-alarm rate is still not easy. Some are horizontal, and can be deflected and severed if struck. Others, such as guys for tall TV masts, can be almost vertical and must be avoided at all costs because the first part to encounter them would be the rotor.

AFFORDABILITY

What can be done in this world is almost always a matter of what can be afforded. It is tempting to get carried away and propose a "helicopter 2000" with an unglazed stealth nose, covered in low-observables RAM (radar-absorbent material) and packed internally with fabulous full-colour displays right the way round to show what is happening in every direction. This could be designed today, but the US Army could probably afford to buy about a dozen, and the British Army might be able to afford the instruction manuals. In the past displays have also been heavy, but the prospects here are fairly bright.

When one studies the real world one is also constantly reminded of the increasing emphasis being placed on not only capital cost but also ongoing costs, so that the true objective is minimum total cost of ownership over 20 or 30 years (because tomorrow's systems will probably obsolesce less rapidly and have to last longer). This tends to put a brake on the most exciting "far out" technologies, and favour solutions that are thoroughly familiar and proven. On the other hand, nobody wants to buy today's helicopter for service in the period 1995-2025.

By far the biggest decisions in the history of helicopters will be those taken by the US Army in the next few months concerning its LHX family of combat helicopters. The production run for the original customer alone is expected to be about 4,500, so this is a programme that every company in the US helicopter industry has decided it cannot afford not to win. To make things harder the customer's spread of ROCs (required operational capabilities) are so wide as to make a single winning design impractical; indeed for the two types to have much degree of commonality would be a remarkable achievement, and one that is not expected.

The biggest number (2,408) is needed of LHX/Utility, to replace the Huey in all its transport versions carrying a squad of 6 or 8 men, or internal/external cargo. This clearly must have a capacious cabin. The other version, SCAT (scout/attack), is expected to account for 2,127, split into 1,100 gunship attack models and 1,027 scouts. SCAT is regarded almost as a rotary-wing fighter, with the

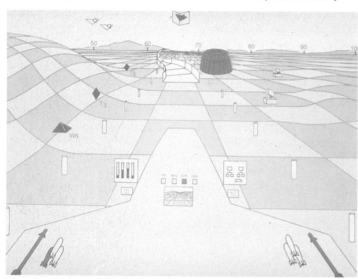

Left: Under development by the USAF Aerospace Medical Research Laboratory, VCASS (visually coupled airborne systems simulator) is a purely synthetic view of the outside world generated in the pilot's helmet. Inputs are drawn from all onboard sensors, weapons and CNI systems. The red dome is the lethal envelope of a defence system; friendly aircraft are white, and hostiles red.

Below: Under development by Hughes Aircraft, this helmet visor display is seen as a possible way of reducing pilot workload in the LHX helicopter. The display is hoped to allow a single pilot to fly NOE (nap of the Earth) at night or in bad weather.

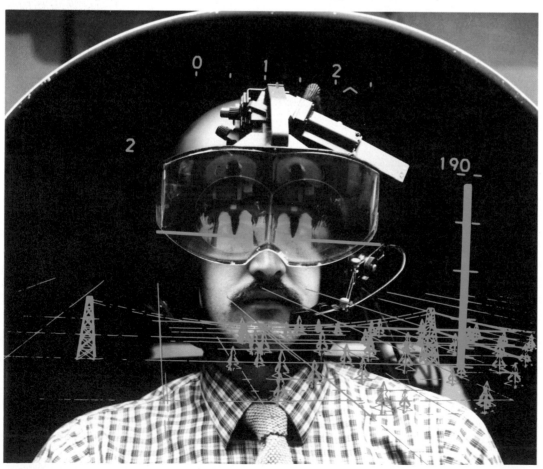

Left: This special AH-64 Apache has been modified by McDonnell Douglas Helicopter Co to have a front cockpit rebuilt to represent that of a single-seat LHX. Called the Advanced Digital Flight Control System demonstrator, it began flying with an active cockpit at the end of 1985.

Centre left: The Sikorsky S-75 is one of two ACAP (Advanced Composite Airframe Program) helicopters with airframes entirely of composite materials. The technology reads across direct to the LHX.

Below left: Bell's Model 249 ARTI (Advanced Rotorcraft Technology Integration) is a modified Cobra with hands-off FBW (fly by wire) flight controls.

Below: The Hughes NOTAR (no tail rotor) helicopter, here on ground test, is a possible research tool for the McDonnell Douglas LHX research programme (see below).

highest speed and all-round combat manoeuvrability possible. Of course, all versions must have the most comprehensive sensors, displays, EW/ECM installation, communications, navigation and (especially for SCAT) weapon-aiming systems, for use in any conditions around the clock.

At first the LHX programme looked like the world's one giant chance to take a great leap forward. Industry was even encouraged to explore radical solutions, and there seemed every prospect that both versions might be 350mph (563km/h) machines of very compact design and unprecedented capabilities. The Utility at least looked like a candidate for the tilt-rotor, already being used on a large size scale in the V-22 Osprey, while the SCAT

could have assumed any of a number of forms. But in March 1985 the US Army issued an edict saying, in effect, "No unconventional designs need apply". Exactly what the Army's thinking was in 1986 was uncertain, and this customer recognizes the magnitude of the opportunity presented by LHX, but it appears to be eager to try to confine the newness to visionics and systems. However, in June 1986 it did announce that tilt-rotor designs might, after all, be acceptable for LHX candidates.

This kind of thinking always has its foundation in politics and finance. One sympathizes with the wish not to buy vast quantities of something that might later prove difficult to build for the agreed price, less reliable than prediction,

NOTAR Technology

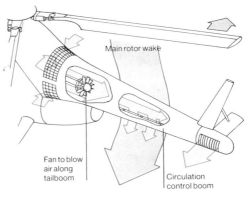

Above: The NOTAR is being considered for the future LHX helicopter. Instead of having a noisy and vulnerable tail rotor, the NOTAR machine blows compressed air from a slit along the tail boom. The airflow round the tail boom (cross-section, right) generates the necessary side thrust, with tail jet control.

Above: The Shadow (Sikorsky Helicopter advanced demonstrator of operator workload) is an S-76 modified to have an LHX type single-seat cockpit grafted on the nose. Sensors feed a helmet-mounted display, HUD and panel displays.

unexpectedly limited in some aspect of performance or longevity, or in any other way unsuitable. Frankly, the collective expertise of the Army and the US helicopter industry ought to be adequate to ensure that nothing like this happens. To disqualify all radical approaches seems to be potentially damaging and shortsighted. One is inevitably reminded of what Lord Hives told his team at Rolls-Royce on the day World War 2 began: "Gentlemen, we must win this war. There won't be much point in coming a good second".

ON COMING SECOND

Discounting unhappy episodes such as "south-east Asia", the West has had almost no experience of losing a major conflict since the dawn of aviation. This perhaps inevitably colours our thinking in procurement, deployment and even our ability to visualize future conflicts. In the realm of fixed-wing airpower, the whole multi-billion dollar NATO front line

would probably never live to see "Day One" of any genuine shooting war with the Soviet Union. Helicopters, however, are different. Because they are not inescapably tied to the most heavily overtargeted points on this planet some might survive to play a role in such a war (though as this is written a pre-emptive strike would probably catch more than 99 per cent at known locations).

What is at least equally important is the fighting ability – in the narrowest sense of the term – of the helicopters Western nations will deploy in the rest of the century. Whilst not wishing to give the very mistaken impression that the Russians are "ten feet tall", and that they build unstoppable hardware, one has only to study the scene around us in 1986 to conclude that perhaps the West no longer has a supposed qualitative superiority to make up for a quantitative inferiority. In fact the quantitative inferiority in front-line helicopters is not great (though widening all the time), and

very much less serious than in almost all other categories of weapon for land and land/air warfare. But if quantitative inferiority is going to be accompanied by qualitative inferiority the future looks bleak.

The maddening thing is that, in almost any single facet of helicopter design, the West is almost certainly technically ahead of the Soviet Union. The problem is a long-term failure to think ahead and build fighting helicopters calculated to beat the competition. With the Mi-8 the Mil bureau created a machine heavier, more capacious and more powerful than a Sea King and built it in numbers unheard-of for so large a machine (over 11,000 to

date). With the Mi-6 and Mi-26 the same bureau built an airlifter which dwarfs in capability not only everything in the West but anything planned in the West. With the Mi-24 the same bureau, led by Marat Tischchyenko, has created what is easily the most useful all-round battle helicopter in the world, a machine which perfectly fits the Soviet concept of the helicopter as a battlefield weapon which fights alongside the tank and APC but which happens to fly. A distant derivative is the Havoc, reported by NATO as the Mi-28, which addresses itself more particularly to the use of the helicopter as an aerial weapon, without being compromised by having any troop transport capability.

With difficulty we included this helicopter in the main section of this book. But we were unable to include another helicopter, called Hokum by NATO, which (reasonably enough from its coaxial-rotor configuration) is ascribed to the design team of the bureau named for the late Nikolai Kamov, which is led by S.V. Mikheyev. So little is known about it that most of the present "knowledge" may later prove to have been wrong, and we would have been unjustified in trying to include it as a major entry in this book. But – in the words of a senior US Army officer with a Southern drawl – "This is just about the fight'nest helo there is". To have omitted it from a book with the title of this volume would have been inexcusible, but we would have been unjustified in giving it a main entry because too much would have been speculation. In early 1986 not much had appeared in public beyond a crude side elevation published by the US Department of Defense and a much better Dutch drawing which is probably based on the crude one, coupled with the statement that "Hokum will give the Soviets a significant rotary-wing air superiority capability".

Like Kamov predecessors it has twin turbine engines driving coaxial rotors, and a tail probably without moving surfaces. There the resemblance stops. The fuselage is slim, because there is thought to be no internal cabin. At the front is the cockpit, said to have side-by-side seats. The engine/rotor group might have been

Above: Bell's D292 is one of the two ACAP (Advanced Composite Airframe Program) helicopters. An all-composite LHX would have reduced radar signature.

Right: In a conventional helicopter (top diagram) the advancing blade has high lift and climbs, while the retreating blade (with much lower airspeed) has poor lift and falls, despite very high blade angles. When two such rotors are superimposed, as in the conventional coaxial machine (centre) the two rotors must be widely separated, and rotor lift falls away rapidly once a modest speed (below 200mph, 322km/h) is exceeded. In contrast the ABC (advancing-blade concept) helicopter has rigid rotors capable of being mounted close together. Lift is equal on both sides of the helicopter, and total lift actually increases until the speed has reached a value far in excess of 300mph (482km/h), provided there is adequate engine power.

The ABC Helicopter

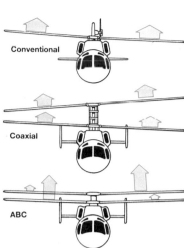

expected to be based on that of the Ka-27 Helix family, but this is not the case. Diameter of the supposed four-blade rotors is estimated at 59ft 8in (18.2m), implying engines of over 4,000hp. Fuselage length is put at 52ft 6in (16.0m), almost half as long again as Helix; and, most significantly, level speed is said by the DoD to reach 217mph (350km/h). This is an exceptional speed for a conventional helicopter. Were ABC type rigid rotors to be used the speed could be even higher, but according to *Jane's*, "wide vertical separation of the contra-rotating rotors implies a conventional drive system, as opposed to anything as advanced as Sikorsky's ABC system". What makes this statement odd is that in the only available drawing the rotors are much closer together than in previous Kamov helicopters!

With a gross weight estimated in the 12,000lb (5443kg) class, very much less than half that of the Helix family, one begins to feel a certain confusion among Western analysts. Nobody is going to build a helicopter in this weight category with coaxial rotors of 60ft (18.3m) size. This is especially the case with four-blade rotors as implied by the Washington artwork. Clearly, either Hokum has rotors of some 45ft (13.7m) diameter or its gross weight is some 30,000lb (13600kg). All the indications are that it is packed with guns, various kinds of missiles (carried on "wings"), armour and self-protection systems.

According to DoD "The system has no current Western counterpart". Apart from asking "Why not?", this throws renewed emphasis on LHX/SCAT, but as this is written even this potentially huge programme is under threat. It could have given the US Army, and later other Western nations, the world's best fighting helicopter. As it is, the insistence on its being a "conventional helicopter" has robbed it of any hope of flying faster than Hokum. Indeed the feeling in the DoD and even the US Army as this was written was "What's the point in LHX if it's going to be slower than Hokum?" We have already had too many errors in Western procurement, one of the more publicised ones in 1985 being the cancellation of the $1.8 billion Sergeant York mobile AA gun system "Because its range is less than the firing range of Soviet helicopters". If we cancel LHX because (on the customer's orders) it has been made slower than Hokum we shall be well on the way to guaranteeing "a good second" in any future war.

Hokum

Above: The supposed Kamov Hokum is estimated to have a speed of 217mph (350km/h), and – though said to have a conventional rotor system – has always been drawn with closely spaced rotors.

Below: This Boeing/Sikorsky LHX, a suggestion by the two companies in partnership, could not be in service before 1992, by which time the Warsaw Pact will have helicopters newer than Mi-24s.

Below: Artwork by Bell Helicopter, showing two of that company's ideas for the LHX. Both are similar single-seat SCAT machines, one having external weapon carriers.

Left: A McDonnell Douglas Helicopter Co suggestion for the single-seat SCAT (scout/attack) version of LHX, showing substantial lifting wings used to unload the conventional rigid rotor and carry weapons. It uses the company's NOTAR technology (p.75), with extra louvred jets at the tail to provide yaw control.

The Aircraft and their

The next – and largest – section of this book includes colour drawings of each of the principal types of helicopter (and tilt-rotor) currently in service or planned to come into service with the world's military and naval operators. Some explanations are necessary in order to interpret the following pages correctly. The reader is also again referred to the glossary at the back of the book wherein should be found all the acronyms and technical terms which might otherwise prove puzzling.

The most basic question concerns what is included and what is omitted. Perhaps the most encouraging aspect of today's helicopter industry is that there was clearly not going to be room for absolutely everything. There were quite detailed discussions about the wisdom of including – for example – the Westland Sea King as well as the Sikorsky S-61, while omitting the Hiller 1100 Hornet, the Westland 30 and nearly a dozen other proposed new helicopters which are not actually in production. We believe that the overall content is the best that can be done at present, including, as it does, all helicopters currently in military service, on order, or those that seem likely to obtain firm military orders in the near future.

Arranged around the large drawing of each helicopter are all the weapons known to have been carried by that machine, together with other externally visible loads such as auxiliary fuel tanks and minesweeping gear, and in many cases features of technical interest such as sensors, countermeasures, engine inlet filters and avionics aerials (antennas). In each case we have illustrated the widest possible range of ordnance items and mission equipment. Many of the items are peculiar to one country or one customer only, while others may not be in regular operational service even though the helicopter has been cleared to carry it, or is planned to at some time in the future.

In the particular case of the Soviet helicopters, obvious lack of detailed knowledge has necessitated a little guesswork in the appearance of some external stores, and in the case of the Mil Mi-28 Havoc this certainly extends to the helicopter itself. It was only after careful study that the decision went in favour of including this important helicopter rather than leaving it out, because it is very imperfectly known in the West.

In the accompanying text the Specification is invariably either that published by the manufacturer or, in the case of Soviet types, that disseminated by the US Department of Defense (though occasionally with comments by the author). Often the manufacturer does not publish a "maximum speed", but only a "never-exceed speed" and a "maximum cruising speed". In such cases we have sometimes corresponded with the manufacturer to establish what is meant. Usually a "never-exceed speed" can be reached only in a dive, and the "maximum cruising speed" is the accepted "maximum speed". The maximum rate of climb invariably means in forward flight; vertical ROC is always lower.

When it comes to weights, mission radii and range/endurance one is up against so many variables it is impossible to be precise and readily comprehensible. Figures published by some manufacturers are for harsh conditions with heavy weapon loads at sea level, while others (though they are reluctant to admit it) are clearly for the most favourable condition at high altitude. There is an international association of aerospace constructors (AICMA), and one day this august body may care to formulate a series of rigid guidelines so that it will be possible to compare all the world's aircraft on an identical and fair numerical basis.

In the section on Avionics the treatment depends on the style of helicopter. For the simplest machines details are given of all the communications radio, intercom and such things as blind-flying instruments and navigation lights. For the more sophisticated helicopters such things may be omitted, because they can be taken for granted. Instead the text for these machines concentrates on the more advanced and specialized equipments carried, and lists alternative equipment fits where these have been announced. In all cases the specifications and equipment fits refer to military and naval versions of each helicopter, rather than to any civil counterparts.

Weapons

Below: A US Army AH-64A Apache firing 2.75in folding fin aerial rockets (FFARs); two pairs of Hellfire and anti-tank missiles are carried on the inboard pylons, while a 30mm M230 A1 gun is mounted in the chin position. The AH-64 is the ultimate expression of the US Army's need for an "all-can-do" fighting helicopter.

Aérospatiale SA 316B Alouette III

Origin: France (licence-built in India, Romania and Switzerland), first flight 28 February 1959.
Type: Light utility helicopter.
Engines: One Turboméca turboshaft engine, (316B) 870shp (649kW) Artouste IIIB flat-rated at 570shp (425kW), (319B) 870shp (649kW) Astazou XIV flat-rated at 600shp (447kW).
Dimensions: Diameter of three-blade main rotor 36ft 1.9in (11.02m); length (rotors turning) 42ft 1.5in (12.84m), (blades folded) 32ft 10.9in (10.03m); height (to top of rotor head) 9ft 10in (3.0m).
Weights: Empty (316) 2,474lb (1122kg); maximum loaded 4,850lb (2200kg).
Performance: (316): Maximum speed at SL 130mph (210km/h); maximum cruising speed 115mph (185km/h); maximum rate of climb 850ft (260m)/min; hovering ceiling OGE 5,000ft (1524m); range (six passengers) 300 miles (482km). (319): Maximum speed at SL 136mph (220km/h); maximum cruising speed 122mph (197km/h); maximum rate of climb 885ft (270m)/min; hovering ceiling OGE 5,575ft (1700m); range (six passengers) 375 miles (605km).
Background: The first flight of the original Alouette II, then designated SE 313B, on 12 March 1955 was one of the significant dates in the history of the helicopter. This was the dawn of the age of the turbine-engined helicopter, and Aérospatiale's predecessors sold 1,300 Alouette IIs in 46 countries by 1975. Seating a pilot and passenger in front and three passengers on a bench behind, the SA 318C Alouette II could lift a total load of 1,323 lb (600kg) on an early Astazou engine flat-rated at 360shp (269kW). In 1968, to meet Indian needs, development began of the SA 315B Lama, combining a strengthened Alouette II airframe with SA 316B engine and dynamic parts. By May 1985 the parent firm had sold 387, with low-rate production continuing. Others are assembled in Brazil as the Hélibras Gaviao, and production continues in India by HAL as the Cheetah with over 140 delivered. The Alouette III introduced a bigger seven-seat cabin and greater power. Aérospatiale delivered 1,455 to 74 countries. Switzerland built 60, Romania still builds the IAR-316B, with over 185 delivered, and HAL in India had delivered 257 by early 1983 with the name Chetak, with many added since.
Design: All engines fitted to production Alouettes have been of the single-shaft type, so the drive incorporates a freewheel for engine starting and autorotation. The main planetary gearbox has 16:1 ratio. The main rotor is fully articulated and has all-metal blades. The airframe is simple, the cabin having large glazed panels in a light-alloy frame; the tail boom on the Alouette II is a welded steel-tube spaceframe, while that of the III is a semi-monocoque. Landing gear comprises skids on the II, with removable ground-manoeuvring

wheels; the III has fixed tricycle wheels, and all versions have the option of inflatable pontoons.
Avionics: Few versions have much beyond communications radio, though naval Alouette IIIs can have SFENA autostabilization and ORB 31 surveillance radar and a lightweight MAD installation. Additional equipment has been fitted in Indian and Romanian machines.
Armament: Though the tip-drive Djinn was the first helicopter to carry guided missiles (SFECMAS 5200, later called SS.10) the Alouette II and III were the first to deploy them in service. Alouette IIs were armed mainly for research and evaluation purposes, but the Alouette III as made in France, India and Romania has appeared with a very wide variety of weapons. The first production weapon fits were both of pintle or tripod-mounted guns fired from the side doorways. One standard installation mounts a 7.62mm AA52 with 1,000 rounds on a tripod firing through the right doorway (the door being locked open or removed) or through an aperture cut in the door. The quadruple folding rear seat is removed. A more powerful installation fits a 20mm MG 151/20 or, more recently, GIAT cannon in a turret-like mount in the left doorway, the door being removed together with all seats except that of the pilot. The ammunition box can hold 480 rounds. Alternatively for ground attack up to four rocket launchers can be carried on external jettisonable arms, the most common types being French pods with 68mm tubes. The first wire-guided anti-tank missile ever to go into production for helicopter use was the SS.10, but this was soon replaced by the larger and heavier AS.11 of which four can be fired using the APX-Bézu 260 gyrostabilized sight mounted on the cockpit roof above the gunner sitting beside the pilot. In the anti-ship role, which was pioneered by the SA 316B, two AS.12s can be carried. Trials with the HOT missile were successful, but this is carried by the Gazelle, BO 105P and other newer helicopters in operational service. The Mistral was also tested from Alouettes. The French Aéronavale version, not yet withdrawn, carries up to two Mk 44 AS torpedoes, or one torpedo and the MAD installation, or two AS.12 missiles. The Romanian IAR-316B is offered with all previously developed weapon fits, but the ICA has devoted all its development effort to the locally designed IAR-317 (described separately on later pages). In India HAL announces that it is developing an armed version of the Chetak for the IAF and Navy, carrying four ASMs of an unspecified type.
Future: With virtually no new machines being built in France, future development is confined to licensees, and to modification of existing Alouettes. Both India and Romania have plans for revised avionics and equipment.

Above: France's Aéronavale is one of the operators of a naval version of the Alouette. Note the orange flotation bag (uninflated).

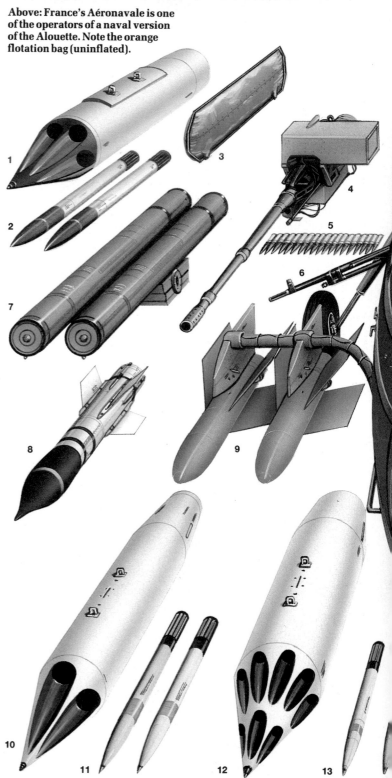

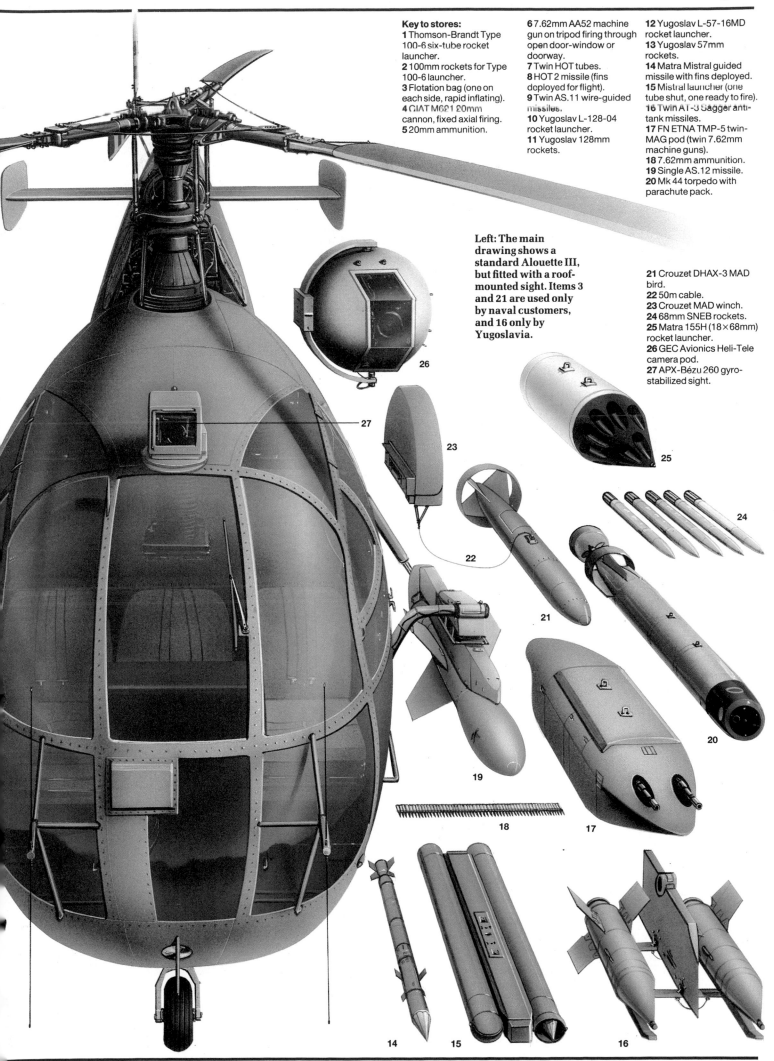

Key to stores:
1 Thomson-Brandt Type 100-6 six-tube rocket launcher.
2 100mm rockets for Type 100-6 launcher.
3 Flotation bag (one on each side, rapid inflating).
4 GIAT M621 20mm cannon, fixed axial firing.
5 20mm ammunition.
6 7.62mm AA52 machine gun on tripod firing through open door-window or doorway.
7 Twin HOT tubes.
8 HOT 2 missile (fins deployed for flight).
9 Twin AS.11 wire-guided missiles.
10 Yugoslav L-128-04 rocket launcher.
11 Yugoslav 128mm rockets.
12 Yugoslav L-57-16MD rocket launcher.
13 Yugoslav 57mm rockets.
14 Matra Mistral guided missile with fins deployed.
15 Mistral launcher (one tube shut, one ready to fire).
16 Twin AT-3 Sagger anti-tank missiles.
17 FN ETNA TMP-5 twin-MAG pod (twin 7.62mm machine guns).
18 7.62mm ammunition.
19 Single AS.12 missile.
20 Mk 44 torpedo with parachute pack.

Left: The main drawing shows a standard Alouette III, but fitted with a roof-mounted sight. Items 3 and 21 are used only by naval customers, and 16 only by Yugoslavia.

21 Crouzet DHAX-3 MAD bird.
22 50m cable.
23 Crouzet MAD winch.
24 68mm SNEB rockets.
25 Matra 155H (18×68mm) rocket launcher.
26 GEC Avionics Heli-Tele camera pod.
27 APX-Bézu 260 gyro-stabilized sight.

81

Aérospatiale SA 321 Super Frelon

Origin: France, first flight 7 December 1962.

Type: Heavy helicopter for assault transport or (G) ASW.

Engines: Three free-turbine turboshaft engines, (except K) 1,550shp (1156kW) Turboméca Turmo IIIC6 (G) or IIIE6 (H and L), (K) 1,870shp (1395kW) General Electric T58-16.

Dimensions: Diameter of six-blade main rotor 62ft 0in (18.9m); length (rotors turning) 75ft 6.7in (23.03m), (ignoring rotors) 63ft 7.8in (19.4m); height (over tail rotor) 21ft 10.2in (6.66m).

Weights: Empty (G) 15,130lb (6863kg), (H, L) 14,775lb (6702kg), (K) 14,420lb (6451kg); maximum loaded 28,660lb (13000kg).

Performance: Maximum speed at SL 171mph (275km/h); maximum cruising speed at SL 155mph (250km/h); maximum rate of climb 1,312ft (400m)/min; hovering ceiling (published IGE only) 7,120ft (2170m); range (SL with 7,716lb/3500kg useful load) 633 miles (1020km).

Background: When France embarked on a submarine-based nuclear deterrent it recognised the need for a heavy helicopter able to follow each SNLE (missile submarine) far out from its base as it left on patrol to make certain it was not being followed by a hostile submarine. The result is the SA 321G. The original SA 3200 Frelon (Hornet) prototype, flown on 10 June 1959, was appreciably smaller than the production machine. It was designed in collaboration with Sikorsky and used virtually the same rotors and dynamic parts as the S-61, though Fiat was assigned complete responsibility for the gearboxes (a role repeated by Fiat on many other Aérospatiale helicopters). Sikorsky also contributed amphibious expertise in the sealed hull and stabilizing floats to give a capability of alighting on water, though routine operations from water were not envisaged. The production helicopter was bigger and more powerful, with a sixth main-rotor blade and many other changes. The first production 321G flew on 30 November 1965. Subsequently 24 of this version entered service, together with foreign sales (almost entirely military) bringing the total to 99.

Design: The SA 321 series are essentially the same size as the S-61 Sea King but, on the basis of installed power, 50 per cent more capable. They also have a considerably larger fuselage. The original 321G has a capacious combat compartment amidships which, despite the large amount of ASW and other equipment, provides room for numerous rescuees who can be hoisted aboard by the 606lb (275kg) hoist normally fitted above the main sliding door forward on the right side of military versions. All versions have the same full-section rear ramp door which can be lowered in flight. All models also have a folding tail, with a small horizontal stabilizer on the right side of the five-blade tail rotor, and the same fixed tricycle landing gear with twin wheels throughout. The amphibious versions (the G and, on customer option, others) have the stabilizing floats added; the G additionally has collapsible oleo struts to reduce overall height for stowage aboard ship, such as the helicopter carrier *Jeanne d'Arc*. In the transport role the H, K and L (the three export military variants) can seat from 27 to 37 troops, or carry up to 11,023lb (5000kg) of cargo either internally or as an external slung load. For casevac missions the interior can be equipped for 15 stretchers and two medical attendants. Addition of stabilizing floats has no effect on payload. The Israeli Chel Ha'Avir has re-engined its SA 321K helicopters for reasons of politics (regarding France as a less-reliable source of spares than the USA) and flight performance, the GE engines giving a better margin at maximum weight in hot environments.

Avionics: Probably the most comprehensively equipped variant is the original 321G, which normally operates in groups of three or four helicopters each equipped with the full range of sensors and weapons. This version can have a nose-mounted radar and other radars above both stabilizing floats, the latter having all-round coverage. The two types used are the Omera-Segid ORB 31D, a member of the Héraclès I family, and the same supplier's later ORB 32WAS, one of the Héraclès II series. The former is specifically used for detecting, tracking and designating surface targets for AM.39 Exocet missiles. The elliptical dish aerial is pitch/roll stabilized and gives a typical ship range of 50 miles (80km) in rain. The later radar has all-round coverage and is used for station holding in ASW, navigation, weather mapping, tac-sit updating, and guidance in attacks on designated targets. It has a large display console which shows sonar contacts in decimal form, and primary echoes and secondary data simultaneously, transponders eliminating sea clutter even at low levels. Crouzet Nadir Mk 1 doppler is fitted, together with a cable-connected MAD (almost certainly the DHAX-3). Other Super Frelons normally carry only navigation and communications avionics, including the doppler, and an all-round surveillance radar above either or both floats (if these are fitted). Among exports the most comprehensive avionics fit is carried by the Israeli 321K, which has eight or nine aerials not seen on other variants. Details are classified, but the radars fitted use a different aerial installation, recessed inside the float(s) and with an almost flat top instead of a hemispherical one.

Armament: Most variants are unarmed (even, it appears, the 321Ks which have been used for several assaults into hostile territory). The only model normally equipped with weapons

is the 321G which has provision for four anti-submarine homing torpedoes, usually of DTCN L4 type, carried in pairs on each side. For use in the anti-ship role two AM.39 Exocet missiles can be carried. Exocets can also be carried by the export versions provided a compatible target-designation radar is fitted.

Future: Customer interest in a major update, including re-engining with the Makila, is low. Modifications will probably be restricted to upgrading equipment for individual customers.

Below: The main illustration shows an SA 321G of the Aéronavale, but with many non-standard features such as the Israeli radar on the starboard float.

Above: A production SA 321G retained by Aérospatiale for special test programmes, seen during the initial carry and firing trials of the AM.39 Exocet. This big anti-ship cruise missile is not normally carried by the SA 321G.

Key to stores:

1 Crouzet DHAX-3 MAD towed body.
2 External long-range (ferry) fuel tank, 500 litres (110gal).
3 Radar installation (Israeli 321K variant).
4 Rescue hoist (standard on most versions).
5 DTCN Murène 324mm lightweight torpedo with parachute pack.
6 Mk 46 anti-submarine torpedo.
7 DTCN L4 airborne 533mm (21in) torpedo.
8 Main radar, Héraclès I or II series.
9 AM.39 Exocet anti-ship missile (not normally carried).
10 Exocet launch pylon (not standard fit).
11 Fixed twin-wheel landing gears (in this version, plus floats).
12 Engine air inlets ice and debris shield.
13 HS.12 dipping sonar sensor.
14 Surveillance radar (321G, both floats).

Aérospatiale SA 330 Puma

Origin: France (licence-built in Indonesia and Romania), first flight 15 April 1965.

Type: Medium transport helicopter.

Engines: Two Turboméca Turmo free-turbine turboshaft engines, (B, E) 1,328hp (991kW) Turmo IIIC4, (C, H, L) 1,575hp (1175kW) IVC.

Dimensions: Diameter of four-blade main rotor 49ft 2.6in (15.0m); length (rotors turning) 59ft 6.6in (18.15m), (ignoring rotors) 46ft 1.5in (14.06m); height over tail rotor 16ft 10.4in (5.14m).

Weights: Empty (H) 7,795lb (3536kg), (L) 7,970lb (3615kg); maximum loaded (B, E) 14,110lb (6400kg), (C, H) 15,432lb (7000kg), (L) 16,535lb (7500kg).

Performance: Maximum speed, varies with subtype from 174mph (280km/h) for early B/E to 163mph (263km/h) for late models at maximum weight; maximum cruising speed (typical) 160mph (258km/h); maximum rate of climb (L, max wt) 1,200ft (366m)/min; hovering ceiling OGE (L, max wt) 7,545ft (2300m); maximum range (standard fuel, SL, no reserves, typical of all) 342 miles (550km).

Background: The SA 330 was designed to meet a 1961 requirement of the ALAT (Aviation Légère de l'Armée de Terre) for a medium assault helicopter for day or night operation in all weather and all climates. In February 1967, when several prototypes were flying, the Puma was selected for use by the RAF so that the helicopter could be included in a major British/French government collaborative programme which also resulted in production being shared by Westland, initially with portions of cabin structure being made at the former Fairey works at Hayes. Production deliveries began in spring 1969, the military versions being: 330B for the ALAT and Armée de l'Air, 330E for the RAF (with comprehensive British avionics, fuel flowmeters and jettison system and other additional equipment), 330C initial export version (with 1,400shp/1044kW IVB engines), 330H upgraded export version with more powerful IVC engines and the final 330L with completely new composite rotor blades. Licences were sold to Nurtanio of Indonesia, which assembled 11 Pumas from CKD kits, and also to ICA of Romania where by spring 1985 no fewer than 112 ICA-330Ls had been delivered, with manufacture continuing. ICA is the only current source, other producers having switched to the Super Puma. Total Aérospatiale sales amounted to 692.

Design: Basically the 330 is conventional, with a capacious cabin (length 19ft 10in, 6.05m) under the main rotor hub in a fuselage of metal stressed-skin construction. The engines are arranged parallel ahead of the main gearbox, each with its exhaust pipe angled away to the side. Directly behind the rotor shaft is a drive to the oil-cooler fan, with the exhaust above the spine carrying the tail rotor shaft above the tail boom. An unusual feature is that, though there is no rear ramp door, there is a large removable hatch (with circular rear-view window) in this location which can be used as an emergency exit and to permit carriage of long projecting items. A large jettisonable sliding door on each side gives excellent access to the cabin, while the cockpit has its own door on each side and a door to the cabin. The cockpit can have from one to three seats. The main rotor hub is fully articulated and is controlled by a lower swashplate with three twin-cylinder power units in the duplicated 2,500lb/sq in (175kg/cm²) hydraulic systems. In all early Pumas (prior to 1976) the main rotor blades are all-metal, with a row of light trailing-edge pockets hot-bonded to the rear of a spar which is extruded and machined in light alloy. The later Pumas have blades with a spar wound from glassfibre roving (continuous "rope") bonded with adhesive inside a composite skin of glassfibre and carbon fibre, with the space filled with lightweight honeycomb and with a thin sheath of stainless steel on the leading edge to resist erosion. The tricycle landing gear has twin wheels and is retractable, the main units being housed in glassfibre fairings on each side of the fuselage. A customer option, not adopted by many military buyers, is four pop-out inflatable emergency flotation bags, two on each side. Normal internal seating is for 16 equipped troops, but 20 can be carried in a high-density configuration. In the casevac role six stretcher casualties and six seated patients can be carried. The hoist, usually fitted, has a capacity of 606lb (275kg). Maximum cargo load is 6,614lb (3000kg), though the later 330L can carry 7,055lb (3200kg) as a slung load. Great attention has been paid to all-weather operation and the engine inlets can be deiced by hot bleed air and protected by add-on external snow/ice shields or, in desert regions, by large filter boxes. If necessary the main and tail rotor blades can have electrothermal deicing, and the Puma was the first non-Soviet helicopter to be certificated for all-weather operations.

Avionics: No regular service Pumas have more than routine communications, navigation and domestic avionics, though SAR models do have nose radar (usually Bendix or RCA). Many have tactical HF and HF/SSB radio, IFF/SSR and a UHF homer as well as the usual UHF/VHF sets. Many customers have specified full blind-flying instrumentation, radar altimeter, Decca Navigator with Flight Log (used by RAF Pumas), VOR/ILS and a doppler navigator. Many Pumas are equipped with the Thomson-CSF TMV 026 ESM system, with DF receiver aerials on each side in the nose and on each side of the front and rear fuselage, and an omnidirectional aerial projecting under the fuselage.

Armament: Most Pumas normally operate unarmed. The range of weapons illustrated is believed to complete all those cleared for use by customers, but as the chief roles are transport and SAR the main requirement has been payload rather than firepower. Romanian IAR-330Ls are offered with the full range of available weapons, including the door-mounted GIAT cannon, axial fixed machine guns and wire-guided missiles.

Future: Aérospatiale has a major, and increasing, programme of modification and upgrading for existing operators. Avionics, inlet and blade deicing and special mission equipment are all involved. No customer Puma has yet been re-engined with the Makila.

Below: The Puma is a good-looking machine even with landing gear extended and special air-inlet filters added. This is an RAF Puma HC.1, which serves with 33Sqn in the UK (with NATO commitments) and 230Sqn in Germany. Today the RAF is studying the prospects for a replacement for the 1990s.

Key to stores:
1 GIAT 20mm gun on Type 19 A001 doorway mount.
2 20mm ammunition.
3 Rescue winch.
4 Twin AS.12 missiles.
5 Quad HOT launch container.
6 HOT 2 missile.
7 Cardoen PJ-1 bomb (manually dropped) with packing tube.
8 TOW 2 (fins deployed).
9 Twin TOW missile launcher.
10 Matra Mistral missile (fins deployed).
11 Twin Matra Mistral launcher.
12 FN 7.62mm GPMG on doorway pintle mount.
13 7.62mm ammunition.
14 GEC Avionics Heli-Tele TV camera.

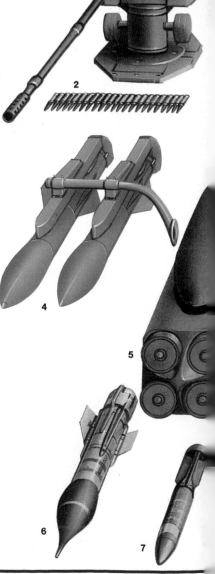

Below: As noted in the text, these weapons are carried by a minority of Pumas. The version illustrated is an SA 330H of the French Air Force fitted out for search and rescue operations.

3

14

12

13

9

11

8

10

Aérospatiale AS 332 Super Puma

Origin: France, first flight 13 September 1978; licence-built in Indonesia.

Type: Multirole transport helicopter.

Engines: Two Turboméca Makila free-turbine turboshaft engines, (most) 1,780shp (1327kW) Makila IA, (suffix 1 versions) 1,877shp (1400kW) Makila IA1.

Dimensions: Diameter of four-blade main rotor 51ft 2.2in (15.6m); length (rotors turning) 61ft 4.2in (18.7m), (ignoring rotors) (B, F) 48ft 5in (14.76m), (M) 50ft 11in (15.52m); height overall 16ft 1.7in (4.92m).

Weights: Empty (B) 9,259lb (4200kg), (F) 9,744lb (4420kg), (M) 9,535lb (4325kg); maximum loaded (B, F, M) 19,841lb (9000kg), (slung load) 20,613lb (9350kg).

Performance: Maximum cruising speed at SL 174mph (280km/h); hovering ceiling OGE 6,890ft (2100m), (Suffix 1 versions) 5,250ft (1600m); range (SL, standard fuel, no reserve) 394 miles (635km), (F_1) 460 miles (740km).

Background: Aérospatiale began design of this improved Puma in 1974. As the subsequent sales record showed, there was little wrong with the existing SA 330 Puma, but the company could see the advantages of various major updates to make the helicopter more competitive in civil as well as the existing military markets, both as a result of service experience and the development of new technologies. New engines formed the main plank for the upgraded machine, together with many smaller changes to increase payload, reduce noise and maintenance requirements, and increase survivability in the face of hostile fire or in a crash.

Design: The Super Puma, which is proving as massive a sales success as its predecessor, is remarkable for looking so much like the original. The new engines do not show externally, and the intake grilles are fitted to some Pumas. Likewise the rotor hub was little changed, temptation to use a glassfibre Starflex type being resisted, and the new composite blades are available on the later Pumas also. Again, the traditional tail rotor was retained, flight tests with a Fenestron showing no significant improvement. Even the new engine failed to offer the expected 30 per cent reduction in specific fuel consumption, but it does achieve 18 per cent and also offers a welcome power reserve which enabled a stretched 332M to be offered with cabin 30in (0.76m) longer. Thus, while the original 332B can seat 17 troops in anti-crash seats or 21 in normal seats, the longer M_1 can carry 25. The maximum slung load is increased to 9.921lb (4500kg) in all Super variants. Other changes include widely separated duplicated hydraulics and electrics, energy-absorbing structures, self-sealing fire- and crash-resistant tankage, wide-track single-wheel main legs whose levered suspension can "kneel", a longer nose and a large ventral fin with tailskid. Main and tail rotor blades have a new more efficient aerofoil section, and all have the option of electrothermal deicing. All versions have a dual cockpit, though the 332 can be flown solo in VFR conditions. Customer options include a range of long-range or auxiliary ferry tanks, in the cabin and in the main-gear fairings.

Avionics: All versions carry VHF/UHF com, and army (and most other military or naval) models have tactical HF and HF/SSB radio. Standard navaids include a radio compass, doppler, Decca navigator and Flight Log, VOR/ILS with glidepath, VLF Omega, radio altimeter and SFIM 155 autopilot which can be approach-coupled to the ILS or to an MLS. SAR versions can have neatly installed nose radar, usually Bendix RDR 1400 or RCA Primus 40 to 50, as well as Crouzet Nadir or Decca doppler nav computer, a roller-map display, polar indicator, route mileage indicator, hover indicator and ground speed and drift indicator. Naval 332F versions normally carry the OMERA Type ORB 32 Héraclès II search radar, with the display on a tactical table in the centre of the cabin, as well as an Alcatel HS 12 sonar station at the rear. Helicopters whose missile fit includes the semi-active AS.15TT have to have the OMERA radar replaced by Thomson-CSF Agrion.

Armament: All published weapon and equipment fits are illustrated. Many military Super Pumas are unarmed, but provision is made in all B and M versions for a 20mm cannon, or two machine guns or two rocket launchers (the most common being 36×68mm or 19×2.75in). For the ASW mission the AS 332F series can carry two AS torpedoes as well as sonar, MAD and sonobuoys. In the ASV role the obvious main weapon is AM.39 Exocet, though alternatives include six AS.15TT radar-guided missiles, or one AM.39 and three AS.15TT.

Future: Its worldwide sale (well over 350 sold by 1986), boosted by licence-production by Nurtanio in Indonesia which assembles (and increasingly makes parts for) a version designated NAS-332 ensures a continuing future for this helicopter. The wide usage of military and naval Super Pumas ensures that there will be an ongoing programme of improvements, some of them available as modifications to existing machines, and upgrades of equipment and weapons. Photographs show that several export customers have military and naval versions equipped with the TMV 026 ESM system, or a development of it, and the aggressive development and sales policy of French industry and government will ensure that everything possible will be done to maintain the AS 332 family in the most competitive posture, despite the great difficulties of competing against US products.

Above: Seen with landing gear extended, this particularly colourful AS 332B is one of twenty-two operated by the Singapore Air Force.

Below: The subject of the main illustration is an AS 332F Super Puma in Kuwaiti grey naval livery armed with two AM.39 Exocets. Some items shown (for example 1) are carried only by army versions.

Key to stores:
1 LCT Orchidée J-band doppler radar for battlefield surveillance.
2 HS.12 dipping sonar.
3 GIAT 20mm gun and ammunition, with 19A001 mounting.
4 Crouzet DHAX-3 MAD sensor.

5 Thomson-CSF Class A sonobuoy (eg, DSTV 4M/TSM).
6 Thomson-CSF Class F sonobuoy (eg, DSTV 7).

7 Alkan Type 8020 sonobuoy dispenser (eight A or 16 F).
8 AS.15TT missile.
9 AM.39 Exocet anti-ship missile.
10 Cardoen PJ-1 bomb and container.

11 Weather radar.
12 Surveillance radar (Héraclès II or Agrion).
13 Mistral missile and twin launcher.
14 Sting Ray advanced torpedo.

15 BAe Sea Skua anti-ship missile.
16 DTCN Murène anti-submarine torpedo.
17 DTCN L4 acoustic torpedo (all torpedoes shown with parachute packs).

18 Brandt 68-22 rocket launcher with three SNEB 68mm rockets shown.
19 Cabin air inlet.
20 Ice and debris inlet filters.
21 GEC Avionics Heli-Tele camera pod.
22 Composite blades.
23 Fixed inverted slat.

Aérospatiale SA 341/342 Gazelle

Origin: France, initially with collaboration by Westland, first flight 7 April 1967.

Type: Light multirole (including reconnaissance, training, close-support, casevac and anti-armour).

Engine: One Turboméca Astazou turboshaft, (341) typically 590shp Astazou IIIA or IIIB, (342) 858shp Astazou XIVH or M.

Dimensions: Main-rotor diameter 34ft 5.38in (10.5m); length of fuselage 31ft 3.19in (9.53m); height overall 10ft 5.2in (3.18m).

Weights: (342L) Empty 2,150lb (975kg); maximum 4,188lb (1900kg).

Performance: Maximum speed (clean, sea level) 164mph (264km/h); cruising speed 148mph (238km/h); hovering ceiling OGE (342) 9,430ft (2875m); range with 1,102lb (500kg) useful load (341) 223 miles (360km).

Background: The Gazelle was originally designed in 1965 to meet a French army requirement for a light observation helicopter faster than the Alouette family, but it would probably have been developed in any case to meet an obvious eventual need for an Alouette successor. The prototype even used the same Astazou II engine and transmission system as the Alouette Astazou, but introduced a new streamlined fuselage in place of a bubble-type cabin and open lattice tail. It also introduced two major advances, the German Bölkow rigid rotor with glassfibre/plastic blades and the Aérospatiale "fenestron" shrouded multiblade tail rotor housed in a duct inside the fin. During prototype construction the British government opened talks on joint helicopter developments and eventually the SA 341 was adopted as a standard type by all British services with co-production by Westland Helicopters. The Gazelle is no longer produced in the UK but remains in licence production in Egypt and Yugoslavia.

Design: The Gazelle airframe is entirely light-alloy stressed skin, with almost the complete cabin glazed with transparent mouldings held in a welded frame. Most of the floor area and centre fuselage is skinned with honeycomb sandwich panels, only the tail boom being sheet. The tail fin and horizontal stabilizer (with two small fins) are fixed. The main rotor hub is not fully rigid because flapping hinges are retained, and the blades can be folded manually. The engine is installed directly aft of the main gearbox in a simple cowl open at the front, and in the SA 342M anti-tank version used by the French ALAT (army light aviation) has an upward exhaust deflector giving some protection against IR missiles. Standard accommodation comprises two pilot seats at the front, with dual control, and a three-seat bench at the rear which can be folded down to leave a flat rear floor for carrying cargo. Alternatively up to 1,540lb (700kg) can be slung externally from a central hook. For rescue

Left: An SA 342M on Aérospatiale development flying, with lateral pods of Thomson-Brandt rockets and the 20mm gun. The Astazou engine has an interim jetpipe, not fully protected against IR-homing missiles.

Below: The main illustration shows an SA 341 as produced by SOKO in Yugoslavia, carrying the Soviet weapons used by that country. Around it are displayed a selection of weapons used by other nations.

purposes a 300lb (135kg) hoist can be installed. In the casevac role the left pilot seat can be removed and two stretchers (litters) installed one above the other on the left side, leaving seats for the pilot on the right and a medical attendant behind. The SA 341 and 342 differ mainly in engine power, gross weight and in the design of the fenestron. All versions normally have steel-tube landing skids, to which small wheels can be attached for ground handling, but skis or pontoon floats are options.

Avionics: All Gazelles are equipped for night-flying and with normal communications, which for military examples includes HF as well as UHF and VHF, and internal intercom and beacon homing receivers. Most customers have specified full blind-flying instrumentation but not the optional autopilot. Other options include VOR, Tacan, IFF, radio compass and radio altimeter, the latter being almost universal. The British Army and Royal Marines AH.1 is equipped with Decca Doppler 80 navigation radar with an automatic chart display, and an option is a Nightsun searchlight. During the 1982 South Atlantic war a REME (Army) workshop installed on 16 AH.1s weapons, IFF, smoke dispenser, armour and other gear. During that campaign two Marine Commando Gazelles were shot down by small-arms fire and one from 656Sqn was brought down by a SAM. The latest Gazelles of the SA 342M type – 128 of which have been delivered to the ALAT – have a SFIM autopilot, Crouzet Nadir self-contained navigation system and Decca Doppler 80. Armed Gazelles normally have a gyrostabilized sight installed in the roof of the cockpit, in some cases with optics which can be swung across for use from either front seat. When wire-guided missiles are carried the usual sight is (AS.12) APX-Bézu 334, (HOT) APX 397.

Armament: All Gazelles have provision for installing cantilever tubular weapon beams on each side. On these can be hung a variety of weapons as illustrated, including two rocket pods or two 7.62mm gun pods or four AS.11, two AS.12 or four/six HOT missiles. A single 20mm GIAT M.621 cannon can be attached to the right side of the fuselage; GIAT

is developing a self-contained M.621 pod complete with 150 rounds to improve the installation of this gun. Yugoslav Gazelles carry a specially developed weapon fit including a twin launcher for four AT-3 missiles.

Future: With some 1,200 produced, apart from licence

construction, the Gazelle is near the end of its new production life, but updating of helicopters in service will continue and will be especially important to Egypt and Yugoslavia. EW equipment is already being exported by French manufacturers for foreign Gazelle operators.

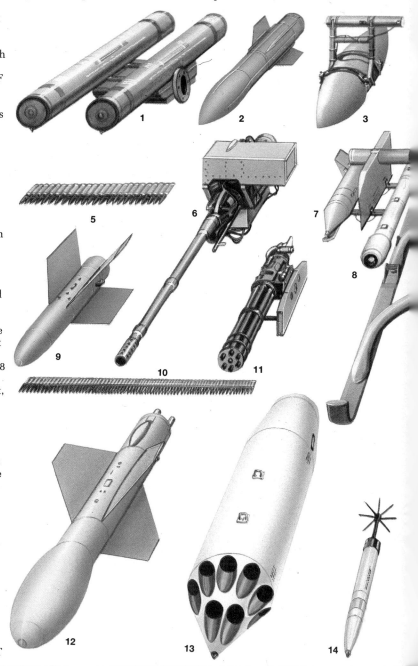

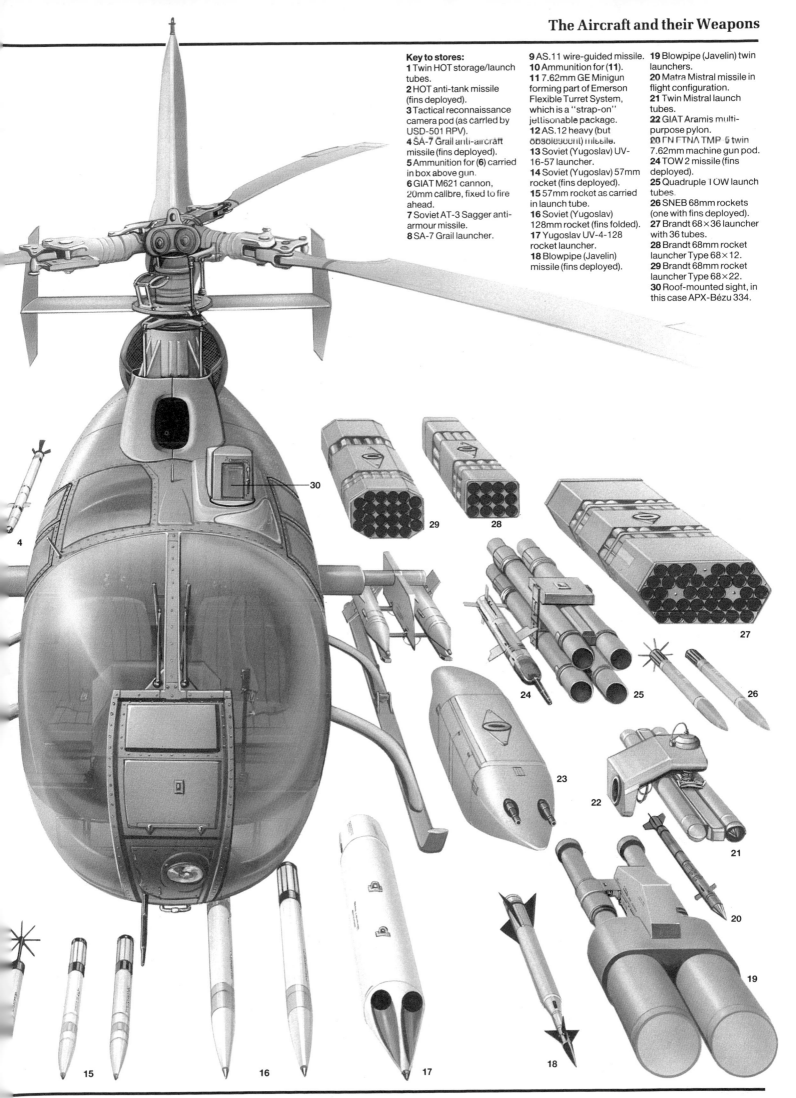

Key to stores:
1 Twin HOT storage/launch tubes.
2 HOT anti-tank missile (fins deployed).
3 Tactical reconnaissance camera pod (as carried by USD-501 RPV).
4 SA-7 Grail anti-aircraft missile (fins deployed).
5 Ammunition for (6) carried in box above gun.
6 GIAT M621 cannon, 20mm calibre, fixed to fire ahead.
7 Soviet AT-3 Sagger anti-armour missile.
8 SA-7 Grail launcher.
9 AS.11 wire-guided missile.
10 Ammunition for (11).
11 7.62mm GE Minigun forming part of Emerson Flexible Turret System, which is a "strap-on" jettisonable package.
12 AS.12 heavy (but obsolescent) missile.
13 Soviet (Yugoslav) UV-16-57 launcher.
14 Soviet (Yugoslav) 57mm rocket (fins deployed).
15 57mm rocket as carried in launch tube.
16 Soviet (Yugoslav) 128mm rocket (fins folded).
17 Yugoslav UV-4-128 rocket launcher.
18 Blowpipe (Javelin) missile (fins deployed).
19 Blowpipe (Javelin) twin launchers.
20 Matra Mistral missile in flight configuration.
21 Twin Mistral launch tubes.
22 GIAT Aramis multi-purpose pylon.
23 FN ETNA TMP 5 twin 7.62mm machine gun pod.
24 TOW 2 missile (fins deployed).
25 Quadruple TOW launch tubes.
26 SNEB 68mm rockets (one with fins deployed).
27 Brandt 68×36 launcher with 36 tubes.
28 Brandt 68mm rocket launcher Type 68×12.
29 Brandt 68mm rocket launcher Type 68×22.
30 Roof-mounted sight, in this case APX-Bézu 334.

Aérospatiale AS 350/AS 355 Ecureuil

Origin: France, first flight 27 June 1974; licence-built in Brazil.

Type: Light utility multirole helicopter.

Engine(s): (350B) one 641shp (478kW) Turboméca Arriel 1 turboshaft engine, (350B₁, L₁) 684shp (510kW) Arriel 1D, (350D Astar) 615shp (459kW) Avco Lycoming LTS101-600A-3, (355) currently two 420shp (313kW) Allison 250-C20F turboshafts, to be replaced (except in N American export version) by two 509shp (380kW) Turboméca TM319.

Dimensions: Diameter of three-blade main rotor 35ft 0.9in (10.69m); length (rotors turning) 42ft 5.4in (12.94m), (ignoring rotors) 35ft 10.3in (10.93m); height overall (B) 10ft 3.6in (3.14m), (L₁) 10ft 11.5in (3.34m).

Weights: Empty (B) 2,348lb (1065kg), (L₁) 2,562lb (1162kg), (355M₂) 2,998lb (1360kg); maximum loaded (B) 4,299lb (1950kg), (B, slung load) 4,630lb (2100kg), (L₁) 4,740lb (2150kg), (L₁, slung load) 5,070lb (2300kg), (M₂) 5,600lb (2540kg), (M₂ slung load) 5,732lb (2600kg).

Performance: Maximum cruising speed at SL (B) 144mph (232km/h), (L₁) 143mph (230km/h), (M₂) 139mph (224km/h); hovering ceiling OGE (B) 7,380ft (2250m), (L₁) 6,300ft (1920m), (M₂) 4,429ft (1350m); range (SL, max fuel, no reserve) (B) 435 miles (700km), (L₁) 407 miles (655km), (M₂) 437 miles (703km).

Background: Following Aérospatiale's long-enduring success with the Alouette family the SA 340 Gazelle was planned as a successor. Later the SA 360 Dauphin was also planned as an "Alouette replacement". It is therefore remarkable that, with both the Gazelle and Dauphin established, room was found for yet a third "Alouette successor". This, the AS 350 Ecureuil (Squirrel) was a totally new design, though very similar to the Gazelle in size. Where it differs from the Gazelle most notably is in having totally new engine(s) and rotors, the main hub being of the advanced-technology Starflex type. The cabin is in all respects slightly bigger than that of the Gazelle, and the airframe differs in generally being skinned in thermoformed plastics instead of light-alloy honeycomb panels. The Ecureuil is also more fuel-efficient than the Gazelle, having both a smaller and newer engine, or, in the important AS 355 Ecureuil 2/Twinstar family, twin engines. Already numerous progressively improved models have appeared, of which military members are the B, upgraded L₁ and twin-engined M₂.

Design: Though a typically clean and efficient Aérospatiale design, the AS 350 was noteworthy in adopting every available modern technology in order to reduce operating costs, maintenance costs and noise. A particular result of this is the use of a wholly new dynamic system. This includes a new and simplified gearbox with nine gearwheels (compared with 22 in the Alouette II) and simpler transmission (with nine bearings instead of 23). The main rotor hub is of the Starflex type, in which the blades are gripped between upper and lower cruciform spiders of glassfibre by single balljoints of rubber/steel sandwich construction. These joints permit the blades to rotate about any axis – flapping, drag, coning or pitch-change – without the need for any conventional bearings, lubrication or maintenance. The blades themselves are produced by a computer-controlled process with filament-wound glassfibre and an anti-erosion stainless-steel sheath along the leading edge. The initial 350B has blades of symmetric profile, but later versions have a lifting (OA 209) profile with a larger chord. It is especially noteworthy that the tail rotor is conventional, rather than the Fenestron type used on the Dauphin family. Each of the two blades has a glassfibre spar and wraparound metal skin. There are swept upper and lower fins, an inverted-profile tailplane (horizontal stabilizer) and, in all current versions, skid landing gear, military models having taller skid struts with steps to ease access. The standard interior has two front bucket seats and two two-place bench seats at the rear. There are various options for armed and casevac roles, and military versions have a large sliding door on each side. Other options are a cargo sling (1,984lb/900kg on the 350, 2,500lb/1134kg on the 355) and a 298lb (135kg) electric rescue hoist.

Avionics: Standard equipment includes VHF, HF/SSB, VOR/Loc/glideslope, intercom, DME, marker beacon receiver and radio compass, with Collins or Sperry autopilot as options to the usual French SFIM. Options include a nav coupler, radar altimeter and full IFR instruments.

Armament: All military versions except the original 350B have fuselages reinforced for axial armament, the most basic elements of which are 20mm or 7.62mm guns, Matra 68mm Brandt rocket launchers and a choice of HOT or TOW anti-tank missiles and sight systems. The Armée de l'Air AS 355M is configured to launch Matra Mistral IR-homing missiles. The Brazilian-built Helibras HB 350B Esquilo is available with various locally produced weapons, the Brazilian Navy UH-12 version carrying the Avibrás LM-70/7 launchers each with seven 70mm SBAT rockets, an FN twin 7.62mm pod and a 7.62mm MAG door pedestal.

Future: By May 1985 a total of 1,018 AS 350s and 504 AS 355s had been sold by Aérospatiale, making this one of the world's fastest-selling helicopters. The combined total by 1986 neared 2,000, exclusive of Helibras production. From 1987 the twin-TM319 version will be available, and this will probably become the preferred military version. New avionic, equipment and weapon fits are certain to become available throughout the long future stretching ahead of this helicopter family.

Above: This Ecureuil is a military AS 350L₁, with a single Arriel 1D engine. A crew member is manning a pintle-mounted FN MAG-58/7.62mm machine gun in the door.

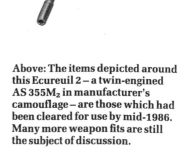

Above: The items depicted around this Ecureuil 2 – a twin-engined AS 355M₂ in manufacturer's camouflage – are those which had been cleared for use by mid-1986. Many more weapon fits are still the subject of discussion.

Right: Another single-engined version, this Ecureuil is one of six AS 350Bs used for survey and utility duties by the Royal Australian Navy. Flotation bags are orange.

Key to stores:
1 Pylon and adapters for axial-firing armament.
2 Twin launcher and support systems for Mistral missile.
3 Mistral (SATCP) homing missile.
4 GIAT M621 20mm gun in fixed installation.
5 TOW anti-tank missile (launcher not shown but usually quadruple; HOT is a possible alternative).
6 FN ETNA TMP-5 twin 7.62mm machine gun pod.
7 Avibras LM 70/19 rocket launcher.
8 SNEB 68mm rocket.
9 Brandt 68-12 launcher for SNEB rockets.
10 SBAT-70 (70mm) rocket for Avibras systems.
11 Avibras LM 70/7 launcher.
12 FN 7.62mm machine gun in Avibras Helicopter Armament System.
13 Starflex rotor hub.

Aérospatiale SA 365 Dauphin/Panther

Origin: France (licence built in China), first flight (360) 2 June 1972.

Type: multirole light helicopter with specialized variants.

Engines: (360) One 1,050shp (783kW) Turboméca Astazou XVIIIA turboshaft, (365F) two 700shp (522kW) Turboméca Arriel 1M turboshafts, (365M) two 912shp (680kW) Turboméca TM333-1M turboshafts, (366) two 680shp (507kW) Avco Lycoming LTS101-750A-1 turboshafts.

Dimensions: Diameter of four-blade main rotor (F, M, 366) 39ft 1.7in (11.93m) (earlier models smaller); length (rotors turning) 44ft 2in (13.46m), (ignoring rotors) (F, M) 39ft 8.8in (12.11m), (366) 37ft 6.5in (11.44m); height (M) 13ft 4.2in (4.07m).

Weights: Empty (F) 4,788lb (2172kg), (M) 5,070lb (2300kg), (366) 5,992lb (2718kg); maximum loaded (F, M) 9,039lb (4100kg), (366) 8,928lb (4050kg).

Performance: Maximum speed (F, M) 184mph (296km/h); maximum cruising speed (F) 177mph (285km/h), (M) 170mph (274km/h), (366) 160mph (257km/h); maximum rate of climb (F) 1,280ft (390m)/min, (M) 1,575ft (480m)/min; hovering ceiling OGE (F) 3,937ft (1200m), (M) 8,200ft (2500m), (366) 5,340ft (1627m); range at SL with max standard fuel (F, M) 547 miles (880km), (366) 472 miles (760km).

Background: Few helicopters have passed through more major changes between prototype and production than the Dauphin. There was no military requirement, and the SA 360 was planned as a rather larger and more powerful general utility machine to succeed the Alouette III. The 360 had an articulated main rotor, single engine and fixed tailwheel landing gear. Though put into production as the 360C, development continued and next led to the twin-Arriel 365C, of which 78 were delivered. Next came a near-total redesign, leading to today's civil 365N and military 365M, naval 365F and US Coast Guard 366. All have twin engines of different types, a completely new fuselage and tail, Starflex hingeless hub and retractable tricycle landing gear. Capability was enormously enhanced, internal fuel capacity being almost doubled and maximum seating increased from ten to 14. A major breakthrough came in 1979 when the SA 366G-1 won a massive order from the US Coast Guard for a short-range recovery helicopter. After severe problems and delays this was delivered (from Aérospatiale Helicopter Corporation in Texas) from November 1984, this HH-65A Dolphin version being burdened by an exceptional load of special mission equipment. Aérospatiale expected to go on from here to an Aéronavale ship-based naval version, but in the event this, the 365F, was entirely funded by the gigantic Saudi Arabian Sawari contract; in early 1986, apart from

an Irish order for fishery protection and SAR, Saudi Arabia remained the only customer, for 20 anti-ship AS.15TT machines plus four with different (ORB 32) radar for SAR duties. Likewise the 365M for land warfare has been funded purely with the hope of export sales, the most immediate prospect being Angola (the Marxist MPLA, not the pro-Western Unita).

Design: From the start the Dauphin featured the patented Fenestron tail rotor, with 13 high-speed blades articulated for pitch-change only, running in a shroud forming part of a large vertical fin. Another new feature was plastics-composite main rotor blades, though in early versions these were attached to a hub very similar to that of the Gazelle, but with four instead of three blades and increased diameter; the blade construction and profile were also similar to the Gazelle. All current advanced Dauphin 2s have a totally different Starflex rotor with upper and lower cruciforms of carbon and glassfibre retaining half-ball sockets of steel and rubber allowing the blades limited freedom of movement without the need for hinges, lubrication or maintenance. Another change is an enlargement of the fin and Fenestron (now with only 11 blades) to increase efficiency and reduce noise, and both the profile and structure of the main-rotor blades has been greatly modified. Each blade now has two Z-section carbon-fibre spars, a carbon-fibre skin, solid glassfibre leading edge with stainless-steel anti-erosion sheath, and Nomex honeycomb filling. The landing gears all retract to the rear, the twin-wheel nose unit being steerable. The 365F has strengthened legs and a deck arrester hook. Considerable development effort has been needed to perfect the four completely different engine installations, and the 365M will probably be further developed to reduce radar and IR signatures. All current models have a fixed tailplane carrying twin fins offset 10° towards the left. Fuel is housed in five belly tanks which in the 365M are crashworthy and self-sealing. Normal seating in a passenger role is a pilot and one passenger in front and two lateral quad seat units behind, with perfect access via three forward-opening doors on each side. If fitted the rescue hoist has a 295ft (90m) cable and is rated at 606lb (275kg). Maximum slung load is 3,527lb (1600kg).

Avionics: Standard options include VHF/HF nav/com, with UHF for military customers, ADF, DME, VOR, ILS and a self-contained navigation system. The Dolphin has dual UHF/VHF and UHF/FM and HF, plus a digital data link for automatic transmission of position, heading/track, fuel state, ground speed and wind. By 1986 Dolphins will begin to receive the Northrop Sea Hawk FLIR to improve capability at night or in bad weather or high seas. The

Above: This Dauphin is the prototype 365M Panther. It is seen here powered by two of the new TM333 engines, and armed with two GIAT 20mm cannon pods (one each side).

365F (SAR) has the Thomson-CSF Héraclès II ORB 32 surveillance radar. The Irish machines have Bendix L500 radar, and such aids as SFIM autopilot, Nadir II nav computer, Crouzet ONS 200A long-distance navaid, five-screen EFIS cockpit displays and ESD Cina B doppler. The 365F (attack) has the distinctive Thomson-CSF Agrion 15 radar in a roll-stabilized dish under the nose giving all-round vision; this radar, with a large-diameter rectangular aerial, has TWS capability enabling it to track ten targets simultaneously. It can guide the AS.15TT missiles and also provide OTH target designation for larger missiles fired from shore or ship launchers. Standard equipment includes a searchlight and auto transition to and from low-level hover in any wind. Aérospatiale offer an ASW version with Alcatel HS 12 sonar, DHAX-3 MAD, and a sonobuoy installation. Development of the new 365M was proceeding in 1986, one major equipment being the Viviane multisensor night and bad-weather sight mounted on the cockpit roof. This replaces various sensor/sight systems mounted in the noses of mockups. The M will also have nose equipment which increases the fuselage length.

Armament: Clearly Aérospatiale is still at a fairly early stage in what looks like being a 25-year development programme with the Dauphin family. The first definitive armed version was the Saudi 365N, prime armament of which in the anti-ship version is four AS.15TT, which uses semi-active guidance to home on a ship illuminated by the Agrion radar. Eight HOTs is envisaged as basic armament of the 365M.

Future: The problem with the Dauphin is the severity of the competition and the small customer base. In 1986 the armed tactical version was named Panther.

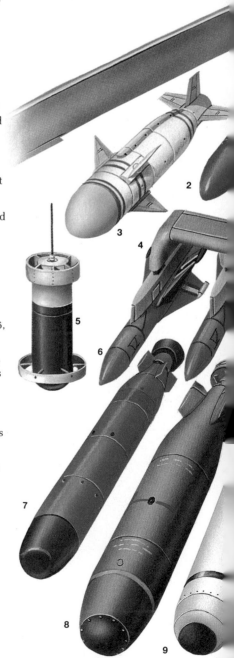

Below: Though not many Dauphins or Panthers have been sold, apart from the major Sawari (Saudi Arabian) contract, this family of helicopters has been offered with an exceptional range of sensors. Here a naval SA 365F (attack) version is shown with Agrion 15 radar, matched to AS.15TT missiles.

Key to stores:
1 APX 397 or similar stabilized sight.
2 Crouzet DHAX-3 MAD sensor.
3 BAe Sea Skua anti-ship missile.
4 Lateral armament pylons.
5 HS.12 dipping sonar.
6 AS.15TT anti-ship missiles.
7 DTCN Murène torpedo.
8 DTCN L4 torpedo.
9 Mk 46 torpedo.
10 Sonobuoys (various, on ASW version).
11 Thomson-CSF Agrion 15 radar (surveillance and AS.15TT guidance).
12 Aérospatiale-Euromissile Vénus FLIR turret, for use with HOT.
13 SNEB 68mm rocket and Brandt 68-12 launcher.
14 Brandt 68-22 rocket launcher.
15 SNEB 68mm rockets and Brandt 68-36 launcher.
16 Quad HOT launcher and HOT-2 missile.
17 Quad TOW launcher and TOW missile.
18 Matra Mistral missile.
19 FZ launcher for 19 rockets of 68mm (two rockets shown).
20 M621 pod for GIAT 20mm gun.
21 FN ETNA HMP pod for 0.5in MG3 gun.
22 Viviane sight (replaces Item **1**).

Agusta A 109A

Origin: Italy, first flight 4 August 1971.

Type: Multirole light helicopter.

Engines: (A) Two 420shp (313kW) Allison 250-C20B turboshaft engines, (K) two 723shp (539kW) Turboméca Arriel IK turboshafts.

Dimensions: Diameter of four-blade main rotor 36ft 1in (11.0m); length (rotors turning) 42ft 9.8in (13.05m), (ignoring rotors) 35ft 1.5in (10.706m); height overall (fin) 10ft 10in (3.3m).

Weights: Empty, equipped (utility) 3,439lb (1560kg), scout/attack/air defence 3,638lb (1650kg), anti-tank 3,946lb (1790kg), (109K) 3,516lb (1595kg); maximum loaded 109A varies with mission from 5,137lb (2330kg) for casevac up to 5,732lb (2600kg) for most military missions, (109K) 6,283lb (2850kg)

Performance: maximum cruising speed (A, max wt) 169mph (272km/h), (K) 162mph (261km/h); max climb at SL (K) 1,740ft (530m)/min; hovering ceiling OGE (A, max wt) 4,900ft (1493m), (K) 10,990ft (3350m); range (max standard fuel, no reserve) (A) 345 miles (556km), (K) 333 miles (537km).

Background: Agusta got into helicopters in 1952 with a licence to build the Bell 47, since when the company has built many helicopters to Bell, Sikorsky and Boeing Vertol design. Its own A 106 light naval helicopter was built in small numbers but the A 109 is in a different class, and has become one of the world's major helicopters in the 2.5-tonne category. From the start the A 109, a totally "clean sheet of paper" design, has been noteworthy for its graceful lines and attractive appearance, with a well faired twin-engine and gearbox group, upper and lower swept fins and fully retracting landing gear (except in the latest 109K version).

Design: In all basic respects the A 109 is a conventional helicopter, with a fully articulated main rotor and an airframe flush-riveted and bonded from light alloy. The main-rotor blades are of bonded light-alloy construction, with the "droop snoot" profile maintained by a bonded honeycomb core. The tips are cropped diagonally at the leading edge, and the tip caps and leading edges are of stainless steel. Each blade is attached by a multi-laminate root strap which offers optimum flexibility in bending and torsion. The landing gear was from the start a tricycle wheeled type but began with twin main wheels folding into streamlined pods, then twin wheels folding into sponsons and then to sponson-mounted single wheels before finally settling in its present neat form in which each single mainwheel is carried by a vertical shock strut which retracts directly upwards and inwards on upper and lower parallel arms, the lower arms carrying the bay doors. The free-castoring nosewheel retracts forward. The 109 sits very low on the ground and shows how far design has come since helicopter landing gears were often grotesque

to overcome problems of ground resonance. Fuel is housed in left/right bladder cells extending vertically immediately ahead of the main gears, there being no room under the floor. The vertical tails are fixed, and carry a long skid, but the small symmetric tailplanes are pivoted and connected to the collective. Normal accommodation is for two in the cockpit, which can have dual controls, and six passengers in two triple benches in the cabin. There are four car-type doors, all opening forward in civil and passenger versions, but the many military and naval versions usually have left/right sliding cabin doors openable in flight and offering unrestricted access. These A 109A Mk II military models normally have dual controls, rotor and transmission brakes, inlet particle separators and optional exhaust IR suppressors, armoured seats, flotation bags, strong cargo floor, rescue hoist, provision for a 2,000lb (907kg) slung load, provision for external weapons, and, in naval models, fixed gear, folding blades (optional on other versions), auxiliary tankage and upgraded avionics. The more powerful 109K for hot/high countries also has fixed gear and a longer nose for more avionics, stainless-steel main and tail rotor blades, an AC electrical system, greater fuel capacity and many other changes.

Avionics: The basic avionics fit for all A 109s is by Collins, with a great diversity of nav/com equipments depending on customer requirement. Standard kit includes VOR/ILS, with VOR/Loc, glideslope and marker beacon receiver. Navaids can include Loran or Omega, and other options include a Sperry AFCS/autopilot, radar altimeter, Sperry Primus 300SL or Bendix/FIAR RDR-1500 weather radar, FLIR, passive ESM, modular ECM jammers, IRCM, special naval search radar or Otomat guidance radar, MAD (but no sonics) and various sights.

Armament: The Aerial Scout kit normally includes a pivoted 7.62mm or 12.7mm gun and two XM157 launchers. Attack roles can include many guns or rockets, or up to eight TOW missiles (Argentine only, Mathogo missiles). The ASW version can carry one or two AS torpedoes plus six marine markers. Otomat guidance is for missiles fired from friendly warships. The Mirach-100 is a large target drone or surveillance RPV with a one-way range of 560 miles (900km).

Future: Agusta delivered about 150 of the original A 109A in 1978-81, since when about the same number have been delivered of the Mk II version incorporating various mostly minor improvements. Hellenic Aerospace Industries is making major fuselage components for an initial 77 Mk IIs in 1985-87. Nothing has been disclosed of sales of the A 109K, aimed at Middle East and African customers.

Key to stores:
1 HOT missile and tubes.
2 BAe Sea Skua anti-ship missile.
3 FN ETNA TMP-5 twin 7.62mm machine gun pod.
4 Whitehead Motofides A244/S torpedo.
5 Mk 46 AS torpedo.
6 TOW (fins deployed for use).
7 AEREA 12.7mm heavy machine-gun pod.
8 Chaff/flare dispenser (one of three species).
9 Mk 44 torpedo.
10 Twin 12.7mm heavy machine-gun pod.
11 AIM-9 Sidewinder (various species).
12 AS.12 heavy missile.
13 Argentine Mathogo anti-tank missile.
14 Smoke canisters (various).
15 Elettronica RWR (ESM) passive receivers.
16 Telescopic Sight Unit (TSU) for TOW firing.
17 Marine markers (various).
18 AEREA HI-7-80 rocket launcher (7×81mm).
19 Brandt 12×68mm rocket launcher.
20 Brandt 22×68mm launcher, with 68mm rocket shown.
21 Twin Stinger launcher (with missile).
22 7.62mm M134 Minigun in FTS or XM27E1 installation.
23 HL-18-50 rocket launcher for 50mm rockets (also 14 or 28-tube versions).
24 ASQ-81 MAD towed bird.
25 7.62mm GPMG on pintle mount.
26 12-tube FZ type rocket launcher.
27 FN ETNA HMP and MRL 70 (combined 12.7mm M3P gun and four-tube 70mm rocket pod).
28 Remotely controlled twin-7.62mm gun installation.
29 MG3 axial machine gun.
30 AEREA Door Gun Post (12.7mm).
31 Meteor Mirach-100 RPV.
32 APX 397 gyrostabilized sight, used with HOT missile.

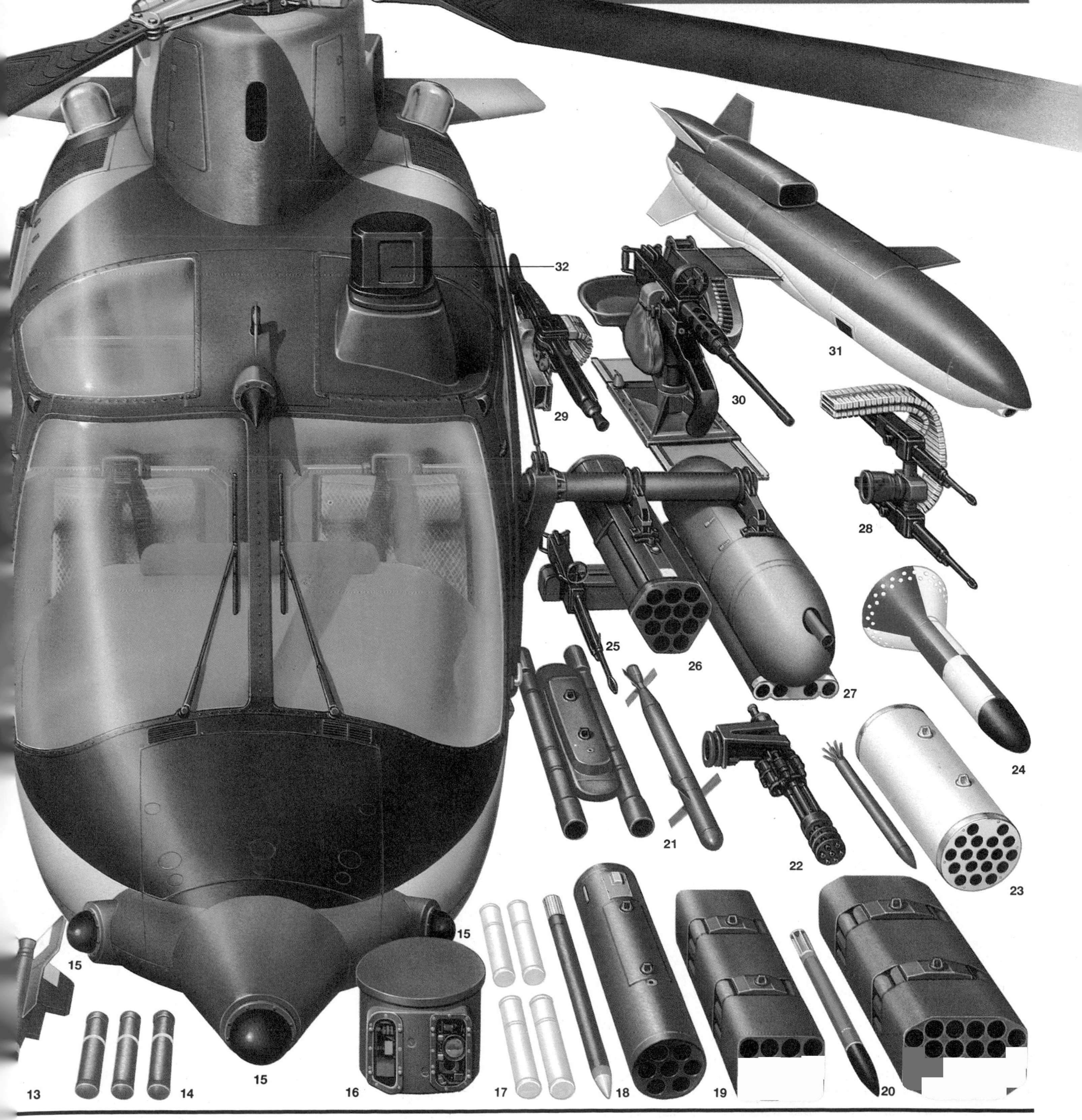

Below: Thanks to Agusta's aggressive development and marketing strategy, the A109A has already been cleared with an exceptional diversity of stores. The basic machine is marketed in many versions for particular roles, each with its own fit.

Right: This A109A has not had its beautiful shape marred by a roof-mounted sight. The more powerful A109K has fixed landing gear and other changes.

13
14
15
15
15
16
17
18
19
20
21
22
23
24
25
26
27
28
29
30
31
32

Agusta A 129 Mangusta

Origin: Italy, first flight 11 September 1983
Type: Attack, anti-armour and scout helicopter.
Engines: Two 952shp (708kW) Rolls-Royce Gem 2 Mk 1004D turboshaft engines (see under Future).
Dimensions: Diameter of four-blade main rotor 39ft 0.5in (11.9m); length (rotors turning) 46ft 10.6in (14.29m), (ignoring rotors) 40ft 3.3in (12.257m); height (over tail rotor) 10ft 10.5in (3.315m).
Weights: Empty equipped 5,575lb (2529kg); maximum loaded 9,039lb (4100kg).
Performance: Maximum speed at SL 161mph (259km/h), (dash limit at 6,560ft/2000m is 196mph/315km/h); max rate of climb 2,090ft (637m)/min; hovering ceiling OGE 7,840ft (2390m); basic mission with full weapon load is fly 62 miles (100km) to battle area, mainly in NOE mode, loiter 90min (inc 45min hover) and return to base with 20min reserve.
Background: Like the A 109A, of which it was originally a derivative, this anti-armour helicopter underwent several changes of configuration, weight and power. Originally it was similar to the A 109 in weight, with C20 engines of 420shp, but continued growth in 1978-80 resulted in a switch to engines of more than double the power. The Mangusta (Mongoose) was designed to meet the requirements of the Italian army (Esercito), and its all-round capability is such that it obviously meets the needs of almost all other modern armies. The current plan is to equip two squadrons each of 30, with another six for training, deliveries starting in early 1987. It would be strange if many other orders did not follow.
Design: Though originally based on the A 109A, the A 129 soon became a totally new helicopter, with dynamic parts of wholly new design marking a great upgrading in power and capability. The main rotor is larger than that of the A 109A and has composite blades with a glassfibre spar, composite skins, Nomex honeycomb cores and stainless-steel leading edge sheath. The tip, which will be frangible, may be of BERP type in the production helicopter (various forms are being tested on the five flying prototypes). All parts of the main and composite tail rotor and transmission are designed to have ballistic tolerance against hits by 12.7mm projectiles, and to have "considerable tolerance" against 23mm. All bearings in the articulated main hub are elastomeric, requiring no maintenance, and all parts of the helicopter are designed for easy access and minimal maintenance requirements. The fuselage makes extensive use of composites and metal honeycomb panels. All parts are designed to withstand 12.7mm fire, and the A 129 meets the stringent crash demands of MIL-STD-1290. External paint is IR absorbing and has a low optical

signature. The nose gunner and backseat pilot both have Martin-Baker HACS 1 (helicopter armoured crashworthy seat) seats, with flat-plate canopies with hinged doors and explosively jettisoned side panels. Typical of the advanced damage-resistant design features is the use of three separate hydraulic systems for flight control, one of them driven off the tail-rotor gearbox, and two further systems for rotor and wheel braking. The tailwheel type landing gears are designed for ground impacts at vertical velocities up to 15ft (4.6m)/sec. Left and right fuel systems, with crossfeed, have particularly advanced protection systems and digital control. The engine installations are designed for minimum noise and exhaust IR signature. Dual Dowty Boulton Paul/Nardi hydraulic power units drive multilaminate glassfibre rotor swashplates, the flight control system being mechanical with dual FBW backup for the main rotor and FBW for the tail rotor with mechanical backup.
Avionics: The A 129 has been designed to fly by day or night in any weather. All operative items are linked by a Harris IMS (integral multiplex system), an advanced digital data bus which controls FBW flight manoeuvres, engines, navigation, communications, flight director, autopilot, full condition monitoring for engines/fuel/transmission/electrics/hydraulics, flight performance/caution/warning systems, and weapons fire control. The IMS computer can store ten complex flight plans or 100 waypoints, and works in conjunction with doppler and radar altimeter for NOE control. In the cockpit are MFDs giving complete displays of all navigation, performance, radio, weapon and warning information, with synthetic maps showing targets and hostile defences. The main nose sensor (likely to move to a mast, already tested) is a PNVS, with FLIR information presented through an IHADSS worn by both crew members. Other devices include a GEC Avionics omni air-data system and comprehensive radar and laser warning receivers and various radar jammers, IR jammers and chaff/flare dispensers.
Armament: Inner stations stressed to 661lb (300kg) and outers to 441lb (200kg) can all be elevated 3° and depressed 12°. Initial basic armament of eight TOW on the outers can be supplemented by various gun or rocket pods on the inners, alternatives to TOW including eight HOT or six Hellfire. Other weapons include self-defence air-to-air missiles. Such as Sidewinder or Stinger.
Future: In April 1985 Agusta signed an agreement with Westland for an A 129 Mk 2, probably powered by a 2,308shp (1721kW) RTM 322 engine, to meet a remarkably tardy requirement for the UK. Another proposal is the Gannet naval version (for

shipboard or shore-based anti-shipping operations, and marine support) with radar, chin turret and Marte 2 or Sea Skua missiles. Later Agusta might build a big-cabin 12-seat battlefield support version with SLAR and chin turret.

Above: To the author it seems typical of West European planning that the Eurocopter should be planned to duplicate the A129 which is already in production. Agusta is studying the possibility of fitting a large-calibre gun.

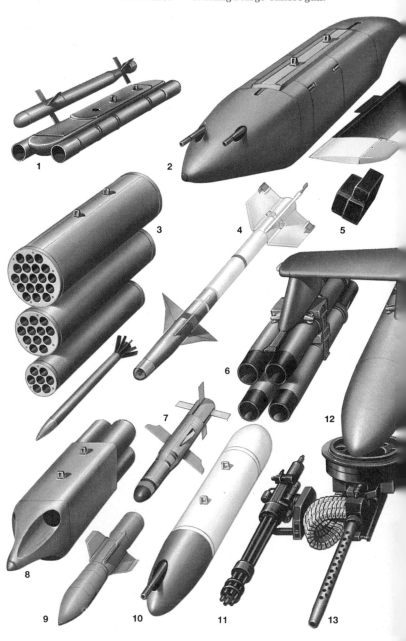

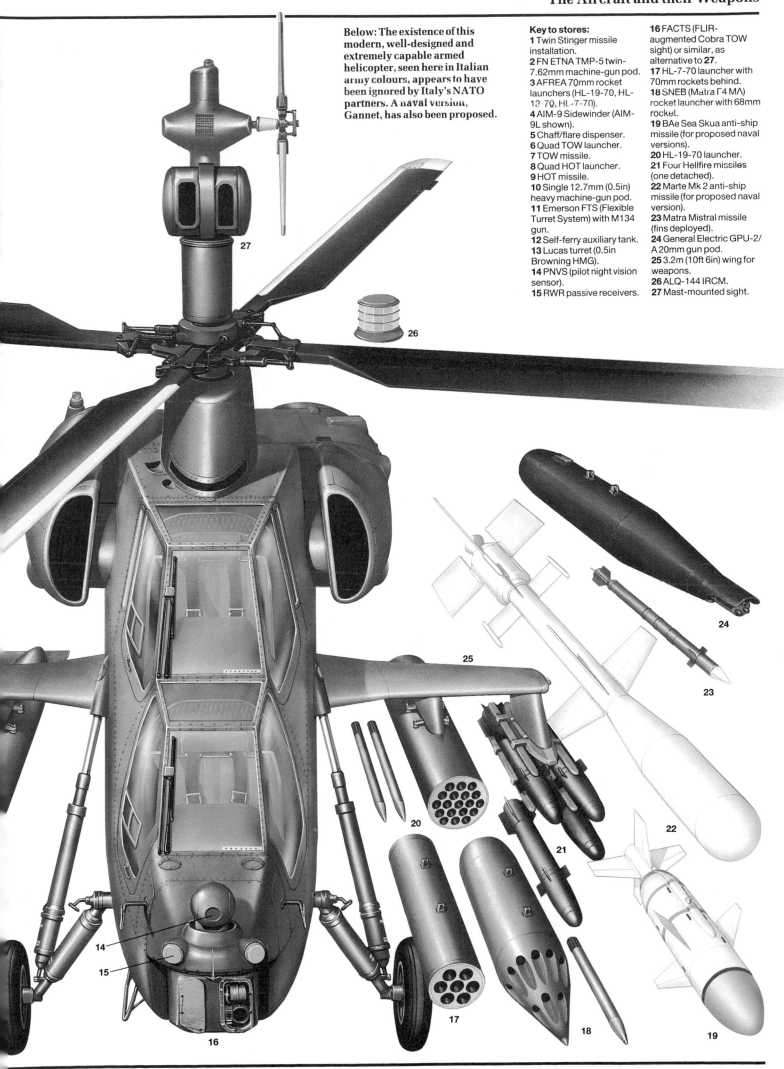

Below: The existence of this modern, well-designed and extremely capable armed helicopter, seen here in Italian army colours, appears to have been ignored by Italy's NATO partners. A naval version, Gannet, has also been proposed.

Key to stores:
1 Twin Stinger missile installation.
2 FN ETNA TMP-5 twin-7.62mm machine-gun pod.
3 AFREA 70mm rocket launchers (HL-19-70, HL-12-70, HL-7-70).
4 AIM-9 Sidewinder (AIM-9L shown).
5 Chaff/flare dispenser.
6 Quad TOW launcher.
7 TOW missile.
8 Quad HOT launcher.
9 HOT missile.
10 Single 12.7mm (0.5in) heavy machine-gun pod.
11 Emerson FTS (Flexible Turret System) with M134 gun.
12 Self-ferry auxiliary tank.
13 Lucas turret (0.5in Browning HMG).
14 PNVS (pilot night vision sensor).
15 RWR passive receivers.
16 FACTS (FLIR-augmented Cobra TOW sight) or similar, as alternative to 27.
17 HL-7-70 launcher with 70mm rockets behind.
18 SNEB (Matra Γ4 MΛ) rocket launcher with 68mm rocket.
19 BAe Sea Skua anti-ship missile (for proposed naval versions).
20 HL-19-70 launcher.
21 Four Hellfire missiles (one detached).
22 Marte Mk 2 anti-ship missile (for proposed naval version).
23 Matra Mistral missile (fins deployed).
24 General Electric GPU-2/A 20mm gun pod.
25 3.2m (10ft 6in) wing for weapons.
26 ALQ-144 IRCM.
27 Mast-mounted sight.

Agusta-Bell 212

Origin: Italy, based on original Bell 212 of USA, first delivery of AB 212 early 1971.

Type: (212) multirole utility, (ASW) ASW and ASV.

Engine: One 1,290shp (962kW) Pratt & Whitney Canada PT6T-3B Turbo Twin Pac coupled turboshaft with two power sections, (212ASW) 1,875shp (1398kW) PT6T-6.

Dimensions: Diameter of two-blade main rotor 48ft 0in (14.63m); length (rotors turning) 57ft 1in (17.4m), (ignoring rotors) 42ft 4.7in (12.92m); height overall 14ft 10.3in (4.53m).

Weights: Empty (212) 5,800lb (2630kg), (ASW) 7,540lb (3420kg); maximum loaded (both) 11,177lb (5070kg).

Performance: Cruising speed (212, SL) 127mph (204km/h), (ASW) 115mph (185km/h); max rate of climb (212) 1,860ft (567m)/min, (ASW) 1,300ft (396m)/min; hovering ceiling OGE (212) 10,000ft (3048m), (ASW, 10,500lb/4763kg) 1,300ft (396m); max range (212, both engines, no reserve) 307 miles (494km), (ASW, in ASV mission, 10 per cent reserve) 382 miles (615km).

Background: Having been a Bell licensee since 1952, Agusta was well placed to move on from building over 1,100 Model 47s (including many ship-based versions) to the Model 204 "Huey" in 1961. After building 250 the company moved on to the 205 and then in 1971 to the effectively twin-engined 212. Extensive experience with the Agusta-developed 204AS, for operation from small decks on ASW missions, enabled the company to develop the more capable 212ASW, initially for the Italian navy. By 1986 over 120 of this naval version had been delivered to numerous customers, for use in ASW, ASV, Elint, SAR and standoff guidance roles.

Design: Based on the Bell 212, the Agusta-Bell 212 is almost identical and differs mainly in avionics and equipment fits. The 212ASW is, however, an extensively modified machine, packed with mission equipment and with many features not found in any other 212 variants. Normally no hauldown gear is fitted, but the structure is locally strengthened and fitted with deck lashing points. Special provisions are made for protecting the airframe and engine against salt-water corrosion. Standard landing gear comprises skids with paired handling wheels. The electrical system is greatly uprated, and a separate hydraulic system serves the 600lb (272kg) rescue hoist, sonar cable and other utilities. The cockpit is equipped for dual pilots, and in most missions two other crew are needed. A sliding door on each side with a jettisonable panel admits to the cabin in which it is possible to fit seven seats or four stretchers and an attendant seat. Options include a 5,000lb (2268kg) cargo sling, emergency inflatable pontoons and internal or external auxiliary fuel tanks.

Avionics: The basic 212ASW has full day/night equipment for all-weather operation. The AFCS has a GE gyro platform and Sperry four-axis autopilot with various auto navigation modes and auto approach to hover. It is possible to fly hands-off from cruise to sonar hover in any wind and sea state. Navaids include ADF, Tacan, doppler, UHF homer, radar altimeter and ASW nav computer. Other basic equipment includes a data link, IFF/SIF transponder and normal HF and UHF transceivers. In the ASW mission the chief sensor is a Bendix AQS-18 adaptive-processor variable-depth sonar, for dunking to depths up to 450ft (137m) (note: Bendix literature gives max depth as 1,000ft, 305m). The auto-nav system enables the sonar to be located without delay over any desired dip point of a complex search pattern, the helicopter thereafter holding precise position irrespective of wind or sea. For the ASV mission the chief sensor is the Ferranti Seaspray surveillance radar, the "very efficient" all-round scanner being mounted above the cockpit in an installation claimed to give high discrimination in rough seas. The radar is integrated with the auto-nav system to give a continuously updated picture of the tactical situation. Provision is also made for installation of "the most advanced ECM systems", installations by Elettronica and Selenia being the most commonly used. For use in the standoff missile guidance role, in which the 212ASW provides mid-course passive guidance for Otomat 2 cruise missiles launched by friendly ships, the main sensor is the SMA/APS series search radar used together with a TG-2 real-time target data transmission system.

Armament: Standard weapons in the ASW role are two Motofides 244AS or similar AS torpedoes, or two depth charges. In the ASV mission the primary weapons are two Sea Skuas or Marte Mk 2 anti-ship missiles, though other weapons have been flown. The main drawing shows a variety of other ordnance for use in the general surface-attack role.

Future: Though for some missions the Agusta-Bell Griffon, based on the Bell 412 with four-blade rotor, offers superior performance and reduced noise and vibration, the 212ASW remains in production because no other helicopter in this class can fly the ASW mission so effectively, claims Agusta. It is doubtful that the basic 212 will be developed further, and the Griffon's new rotor offers a cruising speed of 144mph (232km/h) and other advantages, and so will probably become the preferred choice of many customers.

Right: It is remarkable what a high proportion of the weapons and stores cleared for use on the AB212, seen here in Italian navy colours, have not been fitted to the original Bell product.

Left: This AB212ASW of the Italian Marinavia is using its Bendix AQS-18 dipping sonar, the basic ASW sensor usable to a depth of 450ft (137m).

Key to stores:
1 BAe Sea Skua anti-ship missile.
2 Quad Bofors RBS 70 missile launcher, with RBS 70 self-defence missile.
3 SNORA 81mm rocket installation (with rocket shown).
4 AS.12 attack missile.
5 Hydraulic rescue winch.
6 Mk 44 AS torpedo (Mk 46 can also be carried).
7 FFV TP 42 torpedo.
8 Whitehead Motofides A244/S torpedo.
9 Marte Mk 2 anti-ship missile.
10 Oerlikon KBA 25mm cannon.
11 25mm ammunition.
12 Schermuly day/night flame float.
13 ELT/161 Colibri RWR/ESM receivers.
14 Misar Manta mine.
15 FN ETNA HMP and MRL 70 (combined 12.7mm [0.5in] gun pod with four 70mm rocket tubes).
16 70mm rockets (for item 15).
17 AEREA HL-12-70 rocket launcher.
18 SNIA BPD 50.8mm (2in) launcher (28 tube model).
19 ARF/8M2 2in rocket.
20 81mm SNORA rocket.
21 AEREA HL-7-80 launcher for 81mm rockets.
22 425lit auxiliary fuel tank.
23 FN ETNA TMP-5 twin MG pod, two 7.62mm guns.
24 FN ETNA EMA (external mounting assembly).
25 FN ETNA pintle-mounted 7.62mm MG.
26 Assorted mines for item 27.
27 Valsella Meccanotecnica scatter-drop box (average 1,000 mines).
28 ASQ-81 MAD towed bird.
29 Bendix AQS-18 dunking sonar.
30 Misar MR-80 parachuted mine.
31 GEC Avionics Heli-Tele TV camera pod.
32 SMA/APS search radar.

Bell 205 (UH-1/Huey family)

Origin: USA, first flight (204) 22 October 1956, (205) 16 August 1961; made under licence by Agusta of Italy, AIDC of Taiwan, Dornier of West Germany and Fuji of Japan.

Type: Utility transport.

Engine: One Avco Lycoming T53 turboshaft engine, (D) 1,100shp (821kW) T53-11, (H) 1,400shp (1044kW) T53-13.

Dimensions: Diameter of two-blade main rotor 48ft 0in (14.63m); length (rotors turning) 57ft 9.7in (17.62m), (ignoring rotors) 41ft 10.8in (12.77m); height overall (tail rotor) 14ft 5.6in (4.41m).

Weights: Empty (H) 5,210lb (2363kg); maximum loaded 9,500lb (4309kg).

Performance: maximum level and cruising speed (same) 127mph (204km/h); max rate of climb 1,600ft (488m)/min; hovering ceiling OGE 4,000ft (1219m); range (SL, max fuel, no allowances or reserve) 318 miles (512km).

Background: The original Bell 204 was the prototype XH-40 built for the US Army in 1956. Little did even Bell think it would be the first of a family of helicopters to be made in greater numbers than any other military aircraft of any kind since World War 2, nor that later developments would carry a *payload* greater than the *loaded weight* of the XH-40! This loaded weight was 5,800lb (2631kg), and the original T53 engine was rated at 770shp (574kW). When the power of the free-turbine T53 reached 1,100hp (821kW) the UH-1D was built as the first of the stretched Model 205s, distinguished by a longer cabin enabling far greater internal loads to be carried. Whereas the XH-40 carried 5/6 passengers, and the UH-1B eight (or three stretcher casualties), the UH-1D could carry 12 armed troops or four casualties, and the 1,400shp (1044kW) UH-1H increased the load to a maximum of 14 troops or six stretchers, or 3,880lb (1759kg) of freight. Though the UH-1H remains by far the most numerous current version, with production only completed in early 1986, Bell has taken the same basic design – universally known as the Huey from the 1962 designation of HU-1, though the official US name is Iroquois – much further in the 212, 412 and 214, the latter being a 17,500lb (7938kg) machine with a much bigger cabin and 3,250shp (2424kW)!

Design: All members of this great family have a conventional light-alloy semi-monocoque fuselage, and all production models except the 412 have a traditional two-blade articulated rotor with metal blades. Like the original wartime Bell 47 the rotor is semi-rigid across the hub, rather like a see-saw, and its plane of rotation is largely determined by a "stabilizer bar" with heavy balls on the tips which is rigidly connected to the rotor but at right-angles to the blades. The Huey was the first helicopter in production with a turbine engine mounted close behind the rotor gearbox, above the fuselage, thus enabling the payload cabin to be disposed equally ahead of and behind the main-rotor axis, without the need for a diagonal drive shaft between the pilots from an engine in the nose. All production models have the fuselage low-slung on skid landing gear, customer options including ground-handling wheels and emergency inflatable nylon flotation bags. Fuel (186gal/844lit in the UH-1H) is housed in five flexible cells immediately behind and beneath the floor of the cabin. All versions have a hydraulically powered elevator (horizontal stabilizer) which is automatically positioned by the flight-control system to keep the fuselage more or less level, its inverted aerofoil section always tending to exert a download to counter the high forwards pull of the main rotor. Among customer options are a cargo hook, rescue hoist, auxiliary fuel tanks and a cabin heater.

Avionics: Standard nav/com equipment includes UHF and VHF/FM radio, ADF, VOR and IFF transponder, intercom and gyromagnetic compass. Full night lighting is standard including a controllable searchlight. The US Army plans to update 2,700 UH-1H helicopters with new blades (see Future) and a completely new avionics suite including: HF/FM com for NOE flight, UHF/AM com, radar altimeter, DME, doppler radar, APR-39 RWR, ALQ-144 IRCM jammer, XM130 chaff/flare dispenser, infra-red suppressed engine exhausts and many other updates including a night-vision cockpit.

Armament: Though most Hueys fly unarmed it is doubtful if any helicopter has been cleared to carry such a wide range of weapons (a natural result of its worldwide employment). Many of the ordnance fits illustrated are peculiar to their country of origin, at least at present.

Future: Bell delivered 3,573 of the UH-1H version alone to just one customer, the US Army. Another 1,357 were built for foreign military customers, apart from Italian, Taiwan and Japanese production. The US Army plans to keep at least 2,700 upgraded -1H versions in service beyond year 2000, and Bell and Boeing Vertol are jointly delivering 6,000 composite rotor blades made mainly of glassfibre with Nomex core and leading edges of polyurethane, sheathed in stainless steel over the outer section.

Above: A pintle-mounted M60 is being fired from the doorway of this UH-1E, which belongs to the Navy rather than the US Marine Corps and has forward-firing fixed armament. In its numerous versions the "Huey" was very much the right helicopter at the right time, and only now is it beginning to appear long in the tooth.

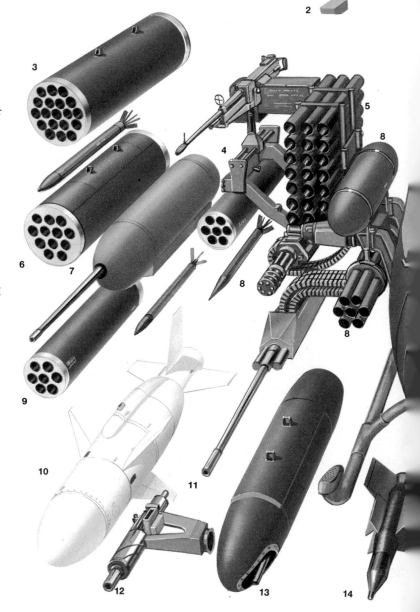

Key to stores:
1 ALQ-144 IRCM beacon.
2 SOTAS Quick Fix aerial.
3 US 19×2.75in rocket launcher, with one rocket shown.
4 Avibras Helicopter Armament System, comprising 7.62mm gun and (below) LM-70-7 rocket launcher (one rocket in front).
5 SNORA 81mm rocket installation, with rocket.
6 SNIA BPD HL-12-70 rocket launcher.
7 XM31 20mm cannon pod.
8 M21 MAMEE armament subsystem: 7.62mm M134 Minigun with 3,000 rounds in tank above, plus M158 launcher for seven 2.75in rockets.
9 SNIA BPD HL-7-80 rocket launcher.
10 BAe Sea Skua anti-ship missile.
11 Oerlikon KBA 25mm cannon.
12 M129 40mm grenade launcher (others similar).
13 FFV Uni-Pod 0127, with 12.7mm (0.5in) gun.
14 Argentine Mathogo anti-tank missile.
15 FFV smokescreen launcher.
16 M5 ball turet, with M75 40mm grenade launcher.
17 Cardoen AS 278 depth charge.
18 Cardoen PJ-1 manually dropped bomb.
19 Emerson FTS (Flexible Turret System) Minigun.
20 Bofors Bantam anti-tank missile.
21 Martin Pescador supersonic missile.
22 AS.12 attack missile.
23 Mk 44 AS torpedo.
24 Browning 0.5in (12.7mm) M3 heavy MG (also quad installation).
25 Twin 7.62mm MG installation.
26 M3 0.5in (XM213) in XM60 armament system
27 Mk 46 torpedo.
28 FN ETNA external mounting assembly with (lower) HMP gun pod.
29 FN ETNA EMA (upper) pintle-mounted 7.62mm MG.
30 Oerlikon RAK 052 launcher, 12 SURA-D 81mm rockets.
31 Pintle-mounted M60 7.62mm GPMG.
32 Brandt 68-22 rocket launcher, with 68mm rocket.
33 Brandt 68-12 rocket launcher.

Below: As the most numerous helicopter in the Western world, the Bell 205 has naturally been cleared to use an exceptional diversity of stores. Obviously, only a small selection, adapted to particular roles, would be carried by any one helicopter.

Bell 206/406 (OH-58 Kiowa)

Origin: USA, first flight 8 December 1962
Type: Observation and utility helicopter.
Engine: One Allison Model 250 turboshaft engine, (OH-58A, CH-136, 206B) 317shp T63 700, (OH-58C) 420shp T63-720, (OH-58D) 650shp Model 250-C30R.
Dimensions: Diameter of main rotor, (most, twin-blade) 35ft 4in (10.77m), (OH-58D, four-blade) 35ft 0in (10.67m), length (rotors turning, most) 40ft 11.7in (12.49m), (OH-58D) 42ft 2in (12.85m), (ignoring rotors, most) 32ft 7in (9.93m), (OH-58D) 33ft 10in (10.31m); height overall (most) 9ft 6.6in (2.91m), (OH-58D, MMS) 12ft 9.5in (3.9m).
Weights: Empty (OH-58A) 1,464lb (664kg), (C) 1,818lb (825kg), (D) 2,825lb (1281kg); maximum loaded (A) 3,000lb (1361kg), (C) 3,200lb (1451kg), (D) 4,500lb (2041kg).
Performance: Maximum cruising speed (all) 138mph (222km/h); maximum rate of climb (A, C) 1,780ft (543m)/min, (D) 1,540ft (469m)/min; hovering ceiling OGE (A) 8,800ft (2682m), (C) 9,700ft (2956m), (D) 11,200ft (3414m); range with max fuel, SL no reserves, (A, C) 305 miles (491km), (D) 345 miles (556km); endurance (A, C) 3h 30min, (D) 2h 30min.
Background: In 1961 the US Army organised an LOH (light observation helicopter) competition which, in the context of the day, was as important as is LHX in 1986. The competition was won by the Hughes OH-6A, but following much acrimony the contest was reopened in 1967 and in March 1968 Bell's OH-58A Kiowa was announced as the revised winner, and 2,200 were ordered. This launched the JetRanger programme, and led to the very similar OH-58B and the OH-58C with uprated engine, flat-glass canopy and improved instruments and avionics. Today, until 1991, Bell is rebuilding a planned 578 OH-58As to OH-58D standard in the AHIP (Army helicopter improvement progam). A total rebuild, they fill the Near-Term Scout requirement until LHX becomes available. Five AHIP prototypes were tested in 1983-85.
Design: In all important respects the OH-58 family are conventional helicopters, though they feature the Bell semi-rigid seesaw "teetering" main rotor. The A, B and C have aluminium-alloy blades, with honeycomb stabilized interior profile, but the D has four composite blades with a hollow glassfibre spar and Nomex cores filling the afterbody skins. Main-rotor blades fold on the OH-58D, and on the earlier models the two blades can be folded after customer modification. A rotor brake is fitted as a customer option to the A and C. The fuselage and slender tail boom are light-alloy monocoques, with some honeycomb sandwich skin panels, and the tail comprises fixed vertical fins and inverted-aerofoil horizontal surfaces. All models have a rupture-resistant

(OH-58D, self-sealing) tank below and behind the cabin with filler on the right. Landing gears are aluminium-alloy skids, the A and C having the option of inflight-inflated pontoons for emergency water landings. All models have a pilot and copilot/observer side-by-side, and the cabin can be devoted to weapons and equipment or house a triple bench seat or two single seats. The TH-57 trainers have dual control, and some models (eg TH-57C) have a 1,500lb (680kg) cargo sling. All models have hydraulic flight controls, and the OH-58D has an hydraulic SCAS (stability control and augmentation system). Bell is also marketing a further upgraded model, the 406CS (Combat Scout), which has most of the OH-58D upgrades plus the 735shp Allison 250-C34 engine. The CS omits the MMS, except at customer request, as well as the integrated digital cockpit and data-management system of the US Army helicopter. Though cleared to the same maximum weight as the OH-58D the CS has the much reduced empty weight of 2,283lb (1035kg), and thus can carry more fuel and weapons. Bell hopes to sell CS versions on the strength of their versatility and quick-change weapon fit.
Avionics: Most military Model 206 helicopters have the expected basic fit of VHF, AM and FM, intercom, ADF, IFF, gyromagnetic compass, radar altimeter, and in many instances such basic navaids as VOR/LOC and Tacan. The OH-58D for the US Army has a dramatically upgraded fit which includes an MMS with a TV and FLIR. The crew have night-vision goggles, and other new upgrades include day/night instrumentation, an AHRS, doppler radar, strapdown INS, laser ranger/designator and an airborne target handoff system. Armed versions include various sight subsystems.
Armament: Most military Model 206 helicopters are unarmed, though as the main illustration shows a wide range of weapons has been cleared for use on customer request. The only standard fit on US Army OH-58C Kiowas is the M26 armament subsystem. This

was devised by Hughes as part of the original LOH competition in 1961-62. It is a compact self-contained installation of an M134 Minigun fed with 2,000 rounds of NATO 7.62mm ammunition. The ammunition box is on the floor of the cabin, and the gun is mounted outboard on the left side of the fuselage with limited angular movement in elevation only. Main armament of the OH-58D is two Stinger AAMs, while the 406CS can carry most of the weapons illustrated.

Future: Deliveries of "at least 578" OH-58D AHIP Kiowas to the US Army began at the end of 1985. Deliveries will continue until 1991. For foreign buyers the 406CS is obviously superior and Bell hope it will find customers for at least the next five years.

1

2

3

4

5

6

7

8

9

10

11

Left: Visibly distinguished from miles away by their mast-mounted sights, the first five OH-58Ds (of which these are two) are undergoing US Army operational testing at Yuma, Arizona. Though all will be rebuilds, the force of 578 D-models will be a giant programme.

Key to stores:
1 Depth bomb (carried by Swedish Agusta-Bell HKP-6 version).
2 CASA 04.080 rocket launcher (80mm Oerlikon rockets).
3 US standard 7×2.75in rocket launcher, with rocket.
4 AEREA HL-12-70 rocket launcher, with rocket.
5 AEREA HL-7-80 with one 81mm rocket.
6 Quad HOT launcher, with missile in front.
7 Nightsun searchlight.
8 Twin Hellfire missiles.
9 FFV Uni-Pod 0127 for 0.5in Browning gun.
10 Twin Stinger launcher with one missile.
11 Twin TOW launcher, with missile in front.
12 AEREA twin flare system (two Mk 5 flares).
13 Philips BOH 300 chaff, flare and smoke dispenser.
14 Cable cutter.
15 FFV self-screening smoke cartridge launcher.
16 Quad Bofors RBS 70 launcher with missile.
17 AEREA twin 7.62mm GPMG pod.
18 AEREA multi-task pod (0.6in M3 machine gun plus six 2.75in rockets).
19 TP 427 (TP 42) torpedo (Sweden).
20 FN ETNA TMP-5 twin 7.62mm machine-gun pod.
21 7.62mm Minigun (fixed or in Emerson FTS installation).
22 MG3 Browning 0.5in gun on pintle mount.
23 McDonnell Douglas mast-mounted sight (OH-58D only).

Left: Though an MMS is shown fitted, the main drawing depicts a basic Model 206 rather than an OH-58D. The most capable member of the family is the Model 406CS Combat Scout, a Bell private venture.

Bell 209 (AH-1 HueyCobra/SeaCobra)

Origin: USA, first flight 7 September 1965

Type: Armed attack and anti-armour helicopter.

Engine(s): (AH-1G) one 1,400shp Avco Lycoming T53-13 turboshaft, (J) one 1,800shp Pratt & Whitney Canada T400-400 turboshaft with twin coupled power sections, (S) one 1,800shp T53-703 turboshaft, (T) 1,970shp T400-402 with coupled power sections, (T/700 and W) two 1,625shp General Electric T700-401 turboshaft engines.

Dimensions: Diameter of two-blade main rotor (G, J, S) 44ft 0in (13.4m), (T) 48ft 0in (14.63m); length (rotors turning) (G) 52ft 11.4in (16.14m), (J) 53ft 4in (16.26m), (S) 53ft 1in (16.18m), (T) 58ft 0in (17.68m); (ignoring rotors) (G, J, S) 44ft 7in (13.59m), (T) 48ft 2in (14.68m); height overall (main blades at rest) (G, S) 13ft 6in (4.11m), (J) 13ft 8in (4.16m), (T) 14ft 2in (4.32m).

Weights: Empty (including crew and fluids other than fuel) (G) 6,073lb (2755kg), (J) 7,261lb (3294kg), (S) 6,479lb (2939kg), (T) 8,030lb (3642kg); maximum loaded (G) 9,500lb (4309kg), (J, S) 10,000lb (4536kg), (T) 14,000lb (6350kg).

Performance: Maximum level speed at SL (G, T) 172mph (277km/h), (J) 207mph (333km/h), (S, with TOWs) 141mph (227km/h); maximum rate of climb (G) 1,230ft (375m)/min, (J) 1,090ft (332m)/min, (S) 1,620 (494m)/min, (T) 1,785ft (544m)/min; hovering ceiling OGE (T) 1,200ft (366m); range (SL, max fuel, 8 per cent reserve) (G) 357 miles (574km), (S) 315 miles (507km), (T) 261 miles (420km).

Background: Bell studied armed helicopter possibilities in the 1950s, and in 1963 flew the company-funded Model 207 Sioux Scout. This was a greatly modified OH-13G Sioux (Model 47) with a streamlined nose housing a pilot and gunner in tandem, and with weapon wings and a chin turret. It was clear that a true armed helicopter needed much more power and using the familiar UH-1B/C Huey as a basis the company-funded Model 209 HueyCobra appeared in late 1965 just as the US Army was recognising an urgent need for armed helicopters in Vietnam. It bought 110 Cobras as early as April 1966, as an interim machine pending development of the bigger and very complex Lockheed AH-56A Cheyenne. In the event the latter was cancelled in 1972 while the Cobra was

bought in ever-greater numbers. The US Army took 1,075 AH-1Gs, others going to Israel and (in the anti-ship role) to Spain. The twin-engined AH-1J SeaCobra was developed for the US Marine Corps (with TOW, Iran) and has been upgraded to the AH-1T Improved SeaCobra. From this the much more powerful 1W (previously 1T+) SuperCobra has been developed, deliveries to the Marines beginning in March 1986. The 1S is the current US Army model, both new production and rebuilds. The current new-build "Modernized AH-1S" is in production also for Israel, Jordan and Pakistan, and is licence-built in Japan.

Design: The original AH-1G retained most dynamic parts of the UH-1B/C but introduced a new narrow fuselage with stub wings to carry weapons and also help unload the rotor in cruising flight. All models seat the pilot above and behind the co-pilot/gunner who manages the nose sight system and fires the chin turret. The pilot normally fires the wing stores and can also fire the turret when it is in its stowed (fore/aft) position, which it assumes whenever the co-pilot/gunner lets go of the slewing switch. In emergency the co-pilot/gunner can fly the helicopter and fire the wing stores. Current 1S versions have a low-glint flat-plate canopy.

Avionics: Most versions have FM and UHF com, and a single-channel secure voice link, HSI/VSI, gyrosyn, DF, radar altimeter, IFF, radar beacon and (1S) doppler. Early G and T models had a simple pantograph optical sight slaved to the turret, but all TOW Cobras (S, T and Iranian J) have a TOW M65 system telescopic sight unit in the nose. The current 1S has the FACTS (FLIR-augmented Cobra TOW sight) or LAAT (laser-augmented airborne TOW) sight, both giving a stabilized magnified target picture with (FACTS) vision through darkness and smoke or (LAAT) precise ranging. Other -1S updates include the APR-39 RWR, IR suppressor and ALQ-144 IR jammer, and a digital fire-control computer and pilot HUD sight.

Armament: Initial 1Gs had the Emerson TAT-102A (Minigun) turret, later replaced by the M28 with one or two Miniguns and/or one or two M129 40mm grenade

Below: All US Army Cobras are various forms of AH-1S, with single T53 engine and, in current models, the flat-plate canopy.

launchers. The 1J introduced the GE turret with M197 gun, but the 1S now has a Universal Turret whose M197 can be replaced by other 20mm or 30mm weapons. Normally the M197 has a 750-round magazine which represents a 60sec supply, but in practice the ammunition lasts much longer because a 16-round burst limiter is included in the firing circuit. The long barrels could obstruct wing store firing when slewed (limit, 110° each side) so the turret is centred before firing wing weapons. The wealth of stores combinations is obvious.

Key to stores:
1 Mk 82 GP bomb (Mk 81, Mk 115 and CBU 55 fuel air explosive other options).
2 M20/19 rocket launcher with 2.75in rocket.
3 M157 launcher with 2.75in rocket.
4 M16 Minigun pod (GE 7.62mm gun).
5 XM260 launcher with 2.75in rocket (LAU-68 similar).
6 Quad Hellfires (one missile shown detached).
7 M28 Minigun 7.62mm.
8 TAT turret, two M28 Miniguns, or two 40mm grenade launchers or one of each.
9 M129 40mm grenade launcher.
10 M197 three-barrel 20mm cannon.
11 FACTS (FLIR-augmented Cobra TOW sight).
12 GE GAU-12/U 25mm gun.
13 M230 30mm Chain Gun.
14 Complete M197 installation.
15 Emerson FTS (Flexible Turret System) with M28 Minigun.
16 M35 system with XM195 (M61 Mod) 20mm gun.
17 Quad TOW launcher, with missile in front.
18 Dispenser, eg M130 or ALE-39 chaff or SU-44 flares.
19 Self-defence Sidewinder (AIM-9L shown; AN/AGM-122A Sidearm antiradiation

Future: Prolonged development of the Army 1S has probably reached its limit, though new customers keep emerging. Though very expensive the tremendously capable 1W SuperCobra is likely to be the baseline for any further version. The Super can carry eight TOWs or Hellfires at speed increased from 141mph (227km/h) to 184mph (296km/h) even on a hot day. It introduces anti-air capability with the M197 backed by AIM-9L Sidewinder AAMs. The USMC is tasking the Super with almost every kind of armed-helicopter mission.

missile is another option).
20 Twin Stinger launcher with one missile.
21 ALQ-144 (or other) IRCM jammer.
22 Laser sight unit.

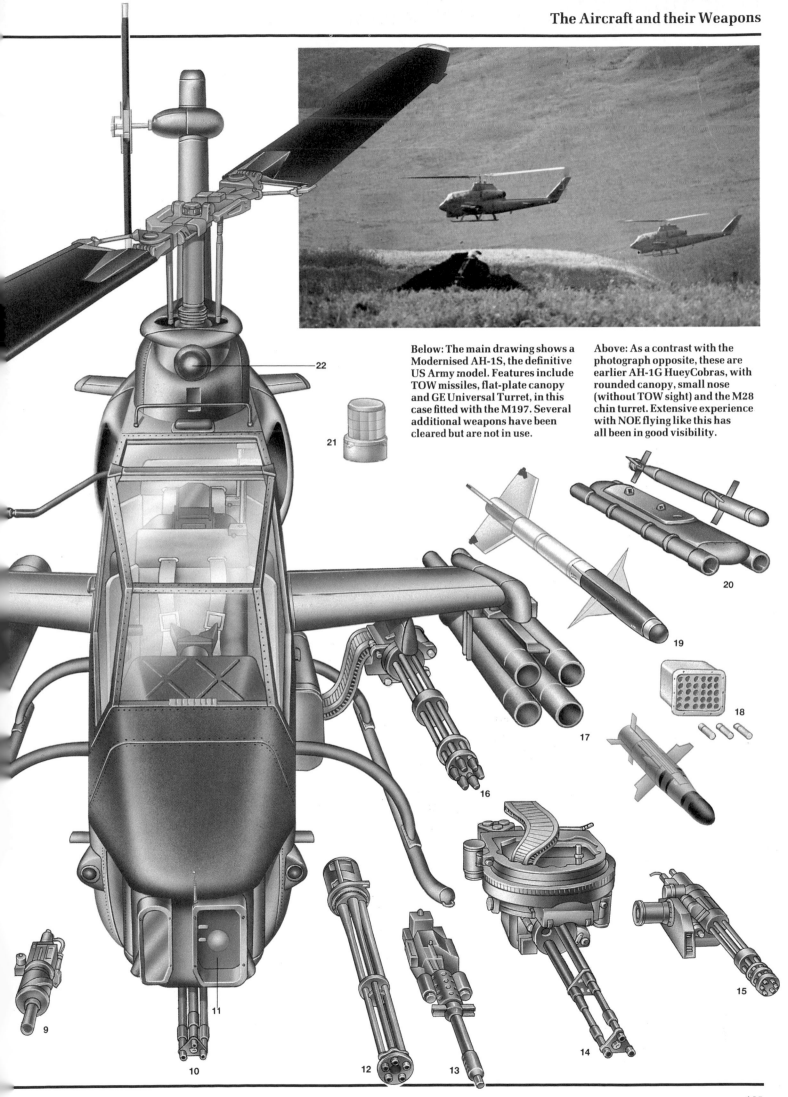

Below: The main drawing shows a Modernised AH-1S, the definitive US Army model. Features include TOW missiles, flat-plate canopy and GE Universal Turret, in this case fitted with the M197. Several additional weapons have been cleared but are not in use.

Above: As a contrast with the photograph opposite, these are earlier AH-1G HueyCobras, with rounded canopy, small nose (without TOW sight) and the M28 chin turret. Extensive experience with NOE flying like this has all been in good visibility.

Bell/Boeing Vertol V-22 Osprey

Left: Artist's impression of an MV-22A Osprey of the USMC departing on an assault transport mission from a carrier offshore. The main payload is expected to be 24 combat-equipped troops.

Below: It is difficult to be precise about the appearance of future Osprey variants because as this book went to press some features, as well as weapons and equipment fits, were undecided.

Origin: USA, joint development by two companies, first flight schedule February 1988.

Type: Multi-mission VTOL aircraft (see Background for variants).

Engines: Two advanced turboshaft engines in the 5,000shp class, to be chosen from the 6,000shp Allison 501-M80C (already selected by US Navy), General Electric GE27 or 6,693shp Pratt & Whitney PW3005.

Dimensions: Diameter of each three-blade rotor 38ft 0in (11.58m); distance between rotor axes 46ft 6.7in (14.19m); length (excluding nose gun) 57ft 4in (17.47m); height (fins) 17ft 4in (5.28m), (spinners vertical) 21ft 9in (6.63m); total width over rotors 84ft 6in (25.77m).

Weights: Empty not yet published; maximum loaded (VTOL) 47,500lb (21546kg), (STOL, 20° forward tilt) 55,000lb (24948kg).

Performance: (estimated) Maximum cruising speed at maximum STOL weight 391mph (629km/h); guaranteed sustained cruising speed in adverse combat missions 288mph (463km/h); hovering performance, see missions in Background; takeoff run at maximum STOL weight less than 500ft (152m); unrefuelled ferry range 2,418 miles (3891km).

Background: The concept of using tilting rotors for a VTOL is quite old, Bell having flown the first XV-3 convertiplane in August 1955. The chief advantage of using tilting rotors is that in cruising flight the machine becomes an aeroplane, freed from the speed limitation of a helicopter. Though it was a complete success the XV-3 project was eventually dropped, not to be resurrected until in 1973 NASA and the US Army awarded Bell a contract for two XV-15s. Unlike the XV-3s these had twin engines on the wingtips, the whole nacelles being pivoted. Flown in May 1977 the XV-15s proved so outstanding that plans were made for an enlarged derivative with a transport fuselage able to fly military missions. A Joint-Service JVX (advanced vertical lift) aircraft programme was launched in April 1983 with a Navy contract awarded jointly to Bell Helicopter and Boeing Vertol for what became the V-22 Osprey. Six prototypes and four static test aircraft are being built, but the plan to use the existing T64-717 engine in these

was cancelled. Now a completely new engine will be used from the start, delaying first flight from August 1987 until early 1988. The US Marine Corps expect to buy 552 MV-22A assault transports to carry 24 combat troops over a radius of 230 miles (370km) and hover at

3,000ft (914m) at full load in air at 91.4°F (33°C). The US Army plans to buy 231 MV-22As for use in the medium cargo (5,760lb; 2613kg) and casevac roles. The US Navy has a need for 50 HV-22A combat SAR machines to fly to a radius of 530 miles (853km), hover OGE at 7,000ft (2134m) and return with four survivors. The USAF requires 80 CV-22A long-range special mission transports to carry 12 special-mission troops or 2,880lb (1306kg) of cargo (such as an F100 fighter engine) over a radius of 806 miles (1297km) and hover mid-mission OGE at 5,000ft (1524m).

Design: Basically the Osprey has to be an aeroplane, with a fixed high-mounted wing (with slight forward sweep) carrying the pivoted engine/rotor groups on its tips. High-speed shafts link the two engine gearboxes to give engine-out safety. Other cross-shafts rotate the nacelles in unison, driven by a gearbox in the fuselage. Boeing Vertol is building the fuselage, which has a side-by-side cockpit and a rear cabin 24ft 0in (7.32m) long and 72in (1.83m) wide and high. At the rear is a full-section ramp door, and in the MV-22A there are 12 folding seats along each side. Grumman build the twin-finned tail, Bell the wings, nacelles, shafts and rotors, Lockheed-Georgia the flaps and ailerons, Menasco the twin-wheel nose gear, Dowty Canada the twin-wheel main gears which fold into large sponson fairings, and General Electric the digital FBW flight-control system. Landing is impossible in the aeroplane (forward flight) mode, because rotor (propeller) diameter is too great. After VTO it takes about 12

seconds to transition into forwards flight. After VL (vertical landing) the blades can be folded inwards, nacelles rotated horizontal and the wings folded back for very compact ship stowage or for camouflage on land. Pneumatic deicers along the leading edges are an option, as are long-range tanks in the sponsons (normal tanks are in the wings), an inflight-refuelling probe, a rescue hoist and armament.

Avionics: No schedule of avionic fit has yet been published, but it will certainly include equipment for self-contained flight and navigation at all altitudes by day or night or in any weather. The FBW flight controls will include provision for auto-hover in winds, at any chosen height AGL. Other equipment will include comprehensive ECM/IRCM installations.

Armament: All versions will have provision for a chin turret (for example with a GAU-12/U or similar gun), and for self-defence AIM-9L Sidewinder AAMs. Many other weapons are awaiting funding.

Future: The initial planned buy of 913 Ospreys is expected to be at least doubled by civilian and foreign customers, making this a major programme. What is even more significant is that, as explained in the introductory sections to this book, the Osprey almost certainly represents a large and permanent shrinkage of the market for traditional helicopters.

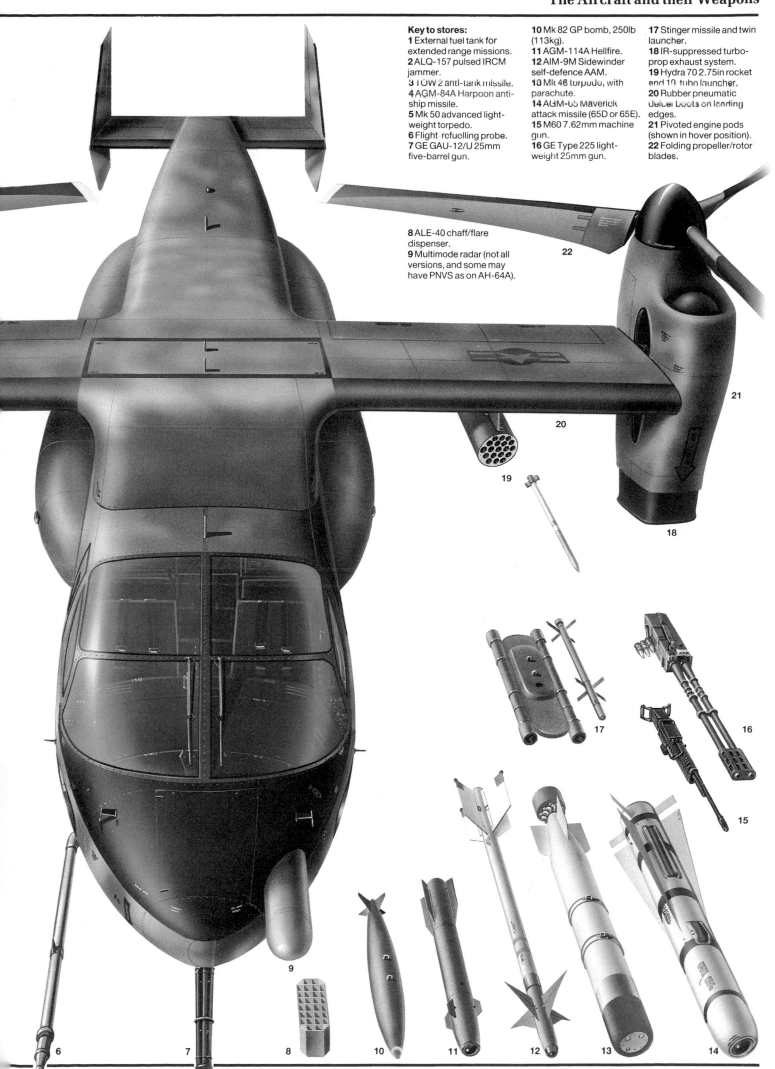

Key to stores:
1 External fuel tank for extended range missions.
2 ALQ-157 pulsed IRCM jammer.
3 TOW 2 anti-tank missile.
4 AGM-84A Harpoon anti-ship missile.
5 Mk 50 advanced light-weight torpedo.
6 Flight-refuelling probe.
7 GE GAU-12/U 25mm five-barrel gun.

8 ALE-40 chaff/flare dispenser.
9 Multimode radar (not all versions, and some may have PNVS as on AH-64A).

10 Mk 82 GP bomb, 250lb (113kg).
11 AGM-114A Hellfire.
12 AIM-9M Sidewinder self-defence AAM.
10 Mk 46 torpedo, with parachute.
14 AGM-65 Maverick attack missile (65D or 65E).
15 M60 7.62mm machine gun.
16 GE Type 225 light-weight 25mm gun.

17 Stinger missile and twin launcher.
18 IR-suppressed turbo-prop exhaust system.
19 Hydra 70 2.75in rocket and 19-tube launcher.
20 Rubber pneumatic deicer boots on leading edges.
21 Pivoted engine pods (shown in hover position).
22 Folding propeller/rotor blades.

Boeing Vertol 107 and KV107

Origin: USA, first flight 22 April 1958.

Type: Multirole transport, SAR, ASW and MCM helicopter.

Engines: (E) Two 1,870shp General Electric T58-16 turboshafts, (D/F) 1,400shp T58-10s, (KV) 1,400shp CT58-140 made by IHI under licence.

Dimensions: Diameter of each three-blade rotor 50ft 0in (15.24m); length (rotors turning) 83ft 4in (25.4m), (ignoring rotors) (KV) 44ft 7in (13.59m), (others) 44ft 10in (13.66m); height overall 16ft 10in (5.13m).

Weights: Empty (E) 11,585lb (5255kg), (KV basic) 11,576lb (5250kg); maximum loaded (E) 21,400lb (9707kg), (KV) as E or 19,000lb (8618kg).

Performance: (KV at 19,000lb, 8618kg) Maximum speed at SL 158mph (254km/h); cruising speed 150mph (241km/h); maximum rate of climb 2,050ft (625m)/min; hovering ceiling OGE 8,800ft (2682m); range with standard fuel 222 miles (357km), (E with 2,400lb/1088kg payload and 30min reserve) 633 miles (1019km).

Background: Vertol designed the Model 107 in 1956, and the prototype flew with 860shp T53 engines. After evaluating prototypes designated YHC-1A the US Army switched interest to the much bigger Chinook, but in February 1961 the Model 107 won a Marine Corps medium assault transport competition and entered production as the CH-46 Sea Knight. This led to the HH-46 for SAR, RH-46 for MCM and Navy UH-46 for vertical replenishment. Canada uses CH-113 Labrador and CH-113A Voyageur SAR transports, Sweden the HKP4 with RR Gnome engines, and since June 1962 all production (until 1965, except for the USA and Canada) has been licensed to Kawasaki of Japan whose KV107 is built in many versions.

Design: The 107 has a simple stressed-skin fuselage with a side-by-side cockpit and a main cabin 24ft 2in (7.37m) long and 72in (1.83m) wide and high. At the rear a powered ramp enables small vehicles to be driven in or pallets winched aboard, and the ramp can be removed or left open in flight. Most versions can seat 25

equipped troops or other passengers, or carry 7,000lb (3175kg) of cargo. The KV107A-4 seats 26 troops, or can be converted to carry 15 casualty stretchers. All shipboard versions have power folding blades and deck hold-down gear, and every 107 has a sealed fuselage to permit limited operations from smooth water. The fixed twin-wheel landing gears can be fitted with skis. The engines are installed above the rear fuselage on each side of the large fin-like rear rotor pylon, with a high-speed shaft linking the front and rear rotor gearboxes. The rotors counter-rotate and both can be driven by either engine. Fuel (normally 291gl, 1324 litres) is housed in the sponsons, and extended-range tanks can be fitted in the cabin or attached externally on each side of the fuselage. Most 107s have metal blades with extruded D-spars of steel and light aluminium/glassfibre trailing boxes bonded on. Boeing Vertol has been reblading almost all surviving 107s with new glassfibre blades, and also upgraded 273 Sea Knights to CH-46E standard with Dash-16 engines, an improved SAR rescue system and crashworthy seats and fuel systems. In 1980-88 Boeing Vertol is also delivering 354 SR&M (safety, reliability and maintainability) kits to reduce operating costs of HH-46A, CH-46D and CH-46E helicopters beyond year 2000. In June 1986 Boeing of Canada completed two major programmes to refurbish and update Voyageurs and Labradors to fit them for long service in an advanced SAR role, with additional fuel, new hoist, weather radar, APU, water dam, upgraded cockpit and improved systems and equipment. Military versions of the KV107IIA currently available are: the A-3 for MCM with minesweeping and retrieval equipment, long-range external tanks, towing hook and cargo sling, the A-4 tactical transport

Below: One of the most recent actions involving US Marine Corps helicopters was the invasion of Grenada, in which this CH-46E took part. If the jetpipes were fitted with IR suppressors the paint would stay on the fuselage.

mentioned previously, A-5 long-range SAR helicopter with no less than 833gal (3785 litres) of fuel and such extra gear as a domed observation window and four searchlights, and four SM versions for the Saudi Ministry of the Interior all with special role equipment.

Avionics: Standard equipment on current versions includes a stability augmentation system and auto-speed trim system, and HF/VHF/UHF radio. Most 107s have a radar altimeter, doppler, VOR/ILS, Tacan and IFF, and options include an AFCS, autostabilization equipment and a wide range of passive RWR and IR receivers, chaff/flare dispensers, ALG-157 IRCM set, and (rarely) an active ECM jammer. There has been no announcement concerning shielding of the engine exhausts to hide the hot metal and plumes.

Armament: Almost all Model 107 helicopters are unarmed. The first to carry weapons routinely were the Swedish HKP4s which today carry the FFV Tp 427 AS torpedo. Other weapon options are shown on the artwork.

Future: Though Kawasaki continues in low-rate production

of the KV107IIA, with about 150 delivered, virtually all effort at present is now directed towards upgrading surviving Model 107s to extend their life and reduce costs and maintenance. Kawasaki has not yet introduced glassfibre blades, and there are several other possible upgrades which the Japanese company has been considering.

Right: The main drawing shows a Kawasaki KV107IIA-4 of the Japan ground self-defence force. These differ considerably in detail and equipment from the Marines' CH-46E, the Swedish HKP4 and the Canadian CH-113. No weapons are routinely carried by Sea Knights in US service.

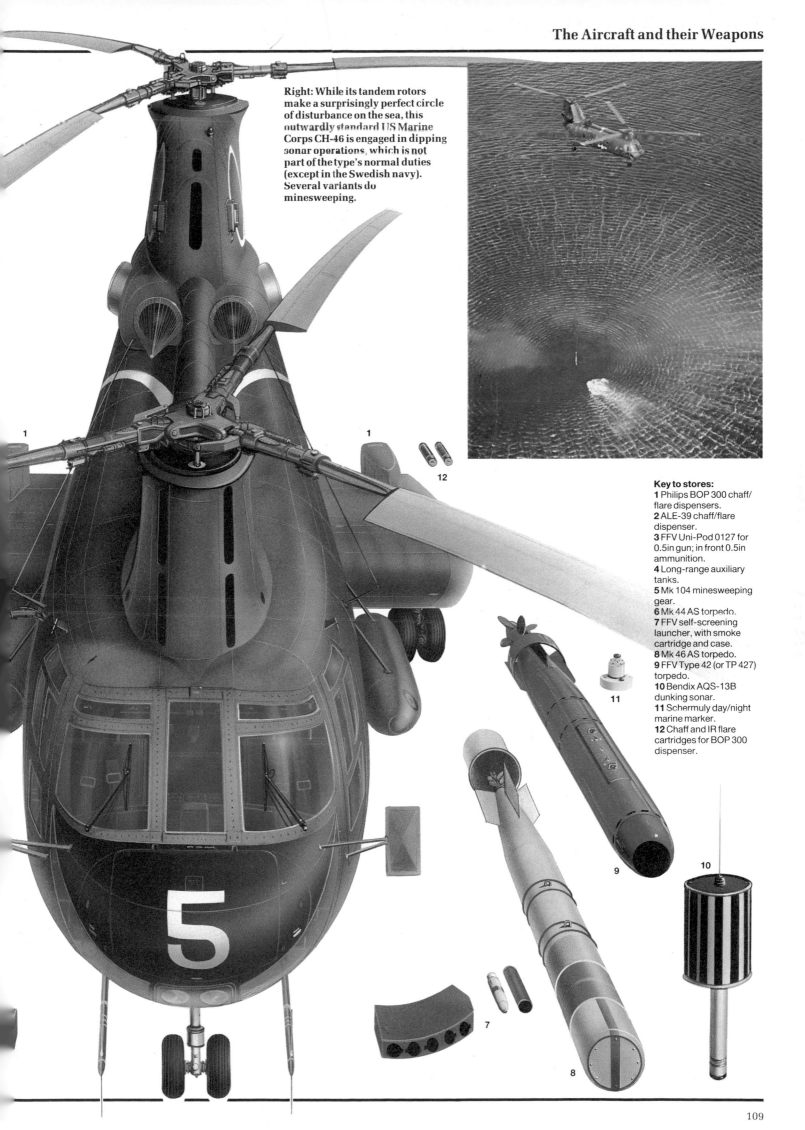

Right: While its tandem rotors make a surprisingly perfect circle of disturbance on the sea, this outwardly standard US Marine Corps CH-46 is engaged in dipping sonar operations, which is not part of the type's normal duties (except in the Swedish navy). Several variants do minesweeping.

Key to stores:
1 Philips BOP 300 chaff/flare dispensers.
2 ALE-39 chaff/flare dispenser.
3 FFV Uni-Pod 0127 for 0.5in gun; in front 0.5in ammunition.
4 Long-range auxiliary tanks.
5 Mk 104 minesweeping gear.
6 Mk 44 AS torpedo.
7 FFV self-screening launcher, with smoke cartridge and case.
8 Mk 46 AS torpedo.
9 FFV Type 42 (or TP 427) torpedo.
10 Bendix AQS-13B dunking sonar.
11 Schermuly day/night marine marker.
12 Chaff and IR flare cartridges for BOP 300 dispenser.

Boeing Vertol 114 (CH-47 Chinook)

Origin: USA, first flight 21 September 1961.

Type: Medium transport helicopter.

Engines: Two Avco Lycoming T55 free-turbine turboshafts, (A) 2,200shp T55-5 or 2,650shp L-7, (B) 2,850shp L-7C, (C) 3,750shp L-11, (D) 4,500shp L-712.

Dimensions: Diameter of each three-bladed rotor 60ft 0in (18.29m); length (rotors turning) 99ft 0in (30.18m), (ignoring rotors) 51ft 0in (15.54m); height overall 18ft 7.8in (5.68m).

Weights: Empty (C) 20,378lb (9243kg), (D) closely similar; maximum loaded (C) 46,000lb (20866kg), (D, US Army) 50,000lb (22680kg), (D, hover OGE at SL) 54,600lb (24766kg).

Performance: Maximum speed at SL (C, at 33,000lb/14969kg) 190mph (306km/h), (D, at 50,000lb/22680kg, 59°F, 15°C) 183mph (295km/h); maximum rate of climb (C, 33,000lb, 14969kg) 2,880ft (878m)/min, (D, 50,000lb, 22680kg) 1,333ft (406m)/min; hovering ceiling OGE (C, 33,000lb, 14969kg) 14,750ft (4496m), (D, 50,000lb, 22680kg) 5,600ft (1707m); mission radius (C, payload 7,262lb, 3294kg) 115 miles (185km), (D, payload 23,030lb, 10446kg) 35 miles (56km); ferry range (D) 1,279 miles (2058km).

Background: After evaluating the Model 107 (YHC-1A) in the late 1950s the US Army ordered a much bigger YHC-1B (Model 114), to meet a battlefield mobility requirement calling for an internal payload of 4,000lb (1814kg) and an external slung load of up to 16,000lb (7258kg). The Chinook, redesignated as the CH-47 in 1962 (a year after first flight) proved a great success, and in 1963 the CH-47A was operational with the 1st Cavalry Division (Air Mobile). Since that time the external appearance of production versions has hardly altered, but capability has dramatically increased by virtue of fitting much more powerful versions of the original engine, glassfibre blades and upgraded systems and equipment. Since 1968 large numbers of CH-47Cs have been made under licence by Elicotteri Meridionali in Italy, and in 1986 Kawasaki is initiating licence manufacture of the CH-47D in Japan.

Design: Essentially the Model 114 is a scaled-up Model 107, the only obvious difference being that there are two forward landing gears, carried on a strong frame inside long sponson fairings along each side. These fairings house the pressure-fuelled crashworthy fuel tanks, normal capacity (D) being 858gal (3899 litres). Much more than half the weight on the ground is carried by the twin nose gears, which are far aft. The rear wheels are single (unlike the Model 107) and are steerable for ground manoeuvring. The fuselage is basically a metal stressed-skin structure, but about 15 per cent of the CH-47D is of composite construction, chiefly glassfibre. Aft of the two-seat cockpit is a cabin 30ft 2in (9.2m) long, 99in (2.51m) wide at the floor and 78in (1.98m) high. The floor is equipped to load and secure high-density cargo, and loading is facilitated by the full-section rear ramp door which can be removed or left open in flight. The fuselage is sealed for operation from water, and provisions are installed for a power-down ramp and water dam to permit ramp operation whilst afloat. Normal equipment of the C and D includes fore and aft cargo hooks (RAF Chinook HC.1s have three hooks rated at 28,000lb, 12700kg on the centre and 20,000lb, 9072kg at front and rear) and a hydraulic winch for rescue and cargo handling. There is a door on each side of the cockpit and a large door with integral steps at the front right of the cabin. Up to 44 equipped troops can be carried, or 24 stretcher casualties plus two attendants. Current blades have a D-spar in glassfibre, with Nomex cored rear section with crossply laminate skins. Blades are designed to withstand 23mm strikes, and all can be folded by hand. Boeing Vertol delivered 732 CH-47A/B/C to the US Army, of which a planned 436 are to be rebuilt to CH-47D standard in 1985-92. In addition 90 have been sold to foreign air forces, the biggest user being the RAF (41), which has developed an electrothermal blade deicing system being made available to all CH-47 users. In Italy EM has supplied at least 152 to various air forces, and Kawasaki in Japan expects to build at least 55 for home use.

Avionics: Standard equipment includes night and all-weather instruments and navaids including gyromagnetic compass, ADF, VOR, ILS, radar altimeter and redundant AFCS. The RAF Chinooks have improved navaids including Decca TacNav with Mk 71 doppler and Mk 19 area nav system, as well as Tacan, ADF and VHF homing. Communications include HF/SSB. Most users have IFF, and a few have fitted ECM and IRCM such as the ALE-40 dispenser and ALQ-157 pulsing IR jammer shown in the main illustration.

Armament: Few Chinooks carry weapons as a matter of course, though all those depicted have been cleared for use.

Future: Boeing Vertol has tested various major derivatives, notably the Model 347 of 1970 which was much longer, had bigger four-blade rotors and retractable landing gears, as well as optional fixed wings. There is no plan to build any major derived version today, the chief new helicopter (initially a commercial transport) being the neat Model 360, to fly in 1986, which almost achieves CH-47D capability and power in Model 107 overall size.

Left: A US Army M198 155mm howitzer forms a15,600lb (7076kg) slung load for a CH-47D Chinook of the same service.

Below: The main drawing (an RAF Chinook HC.1) is generally representative of the CH-47D and Agusta (Meridionali) CH-47C, though it must be emphasized that the weapons depicted are seldom carried in normal operation.

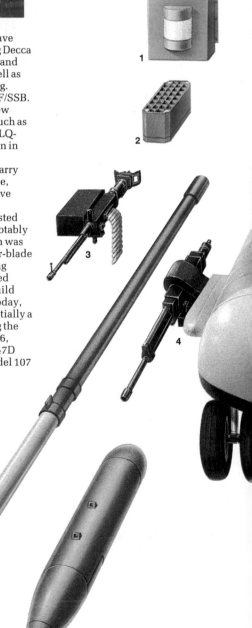

Key to stores:
1 ALQ-157 IRCM jammer.
2 Tracor ALE-40 chaff/flare dispenser.
3 M60D 7.62mm machine gun in M24 system (two guns, left/right).
4 20mm gun, axial firing.
5 Extensible flight-refuelling probe.
6 SUU-11B/A Minigun 7.62mm pod.
7 Radar warning receiver.
8 Spectrolab SX-16 Nightsun searchlight.
9 M129 40mm grenade launcher.
10 19×2.75in rocket launcher, with two rockets shown.
11 Stonefish mines (various).
12 FN 7.62mm GPMG on pintle mount.
13 HF communications aerials.

EH Industries EH101

Origin: Joint project by Italy and the UK, first flight 1986-87.
Type: Multirole helicopter with ASW, ASV/ASST, utility transport and airline versions.
Engines: Three turboshafts, (prototypes) 1,729shp GE T700 401, (production) intended to be 2,308shp Rolls-Royce Turboméca RTM 322.
Dimensions: Diameter of five-blade main rotor 61ft 0in (18.59m); length (rotors turning) 75ft 3in (22.94m), (helicopter folded) 52ft 0in (15.85m); height (folded) 17ft 0in (5.18m).
Weights: Basic EH101 empty 15,500lb (7031kg); disposable load (naval) 13,410lb (6083kg), (utility) 14,436lb (6548kg); maximum loaded (naval) 28,660lb (13000kg), (other versions) 31,500lb (14288kg).
Performance: (T700 engines) Normal maximum speed at SL 184mph (296km/h); cruising speed 173mph (278km/h); time on station for dunking cycle with maximum weapon and mission load 5hr; ferry range 1,150 miles (1850km).
Background: In 1978 the British MoD (RN) selected a Westland study, the WG.34, to meet a requirement for an SKR (Sea King Replacement). Physical size was restricted to that of its predecessor by frigate decks and hangars, but by installing three new-technology engines and using the very newest materials in the airframe a tremendous increase in capability was promised. In 1980 Westland linked with Agusta of Italy to form EH Industries to develop a range of versions of a common design. This is needed in the first instance for ship and shore operation by the Royal and Italian Navies, though the airline and utility transport versions may be certificated first because they are less complex.
Design: Though conventional in all main respects, the EH101 uses outstandingly advanced technology in rotor design, structural materials, powerplant and, especially, avionics. The main rotor has five blades (with diameter actually less than that of the Sea King), and these are naturally of the dramatically superior BERP type. Construction is entirely composite, mainly by computer-controlled filament winding, apart from abrasion-resistant leading edges and electrothermal deicers which are standard on the naval version. The latter also has power folding. Blades are retained by multipath loading in elastomeric bearings held in a new-technology hub with a titanium core surrounded by advanced composites. Most of the fuselage is metal, but the rear section and tail is of composites, the utility model having a rear ramp door and slimmer tailboom. There is a large symmetric tailplane and a swept fin pylon inclined to the left. The steerable twin-wheel nose gear and single-wheel main gears retract hydraulically. All versions have a main cabin 21ft 4in (6.5m) long, 94in (2.39m) wide at the floor (max

width 98.4in/2.5m) and 72in (1.83m) high. The utility version can seat 28 equipped troops or carry a 15,000lb (6084kg) slung load, the internal load being fractionally lower. All versions have provision for flight in all weather including severe icing, triple hydraulic systems, three independent alternators and a gas-turbine APU.
Avionics: No helicopter so far announced can quite equal the avionic systems of even the basic EH101. All functioning equipments and systems are linked through a standard 1553B multiplex digital bus and dual redundant computers. The latter control the bus and also manage flight control, navigation, systems and weapon management, HUM (health and usage monitoring), performance and cockpit displays. Flight control and navigation is handled by an SI/OMI AFCS of dual/duplex digital type with FBL fibre-optic data links, an advanced flight deck with all data displayed on colour MFDs, BAe ring-laser INS (first in production anywhere), GPS Navstar, doppler, Litton Italia strapdown AHRS and a complex communications subsystem. Mission avionics will vary. RN machines will have the GEC AQS-903 acoustic processing and display system, designed for this helicopter, handling complete information from eight buoys with a single operator. The all-round surveillance radar will be Ferranti Blue Kestrel, and a dipping sonar will be carried. In the ASST role equipment will be carried for OTH surveillance and tracking and for midcourse guidance of missiles fired by friendly surface forces. In EEZ patrol equipment will be adequate for absolute coverage of an area 230×460 miles (370×740km) twice in each sortie.
Armament: Items already selected are illustrated. In the EEZ/customs/fisheries mission it will be possible to cover suspects with small arms whilst boarding. The Royal Navy, unlike almost all other potential customers, ses the EH101 as a pure ASW platform and has no plans for anti-ship weapons.
Future: EHI members are building ten pre-production helicopters, the first being due to fly in December 1986. Early examples will prove

the basic machine and systems, the first naval development helicopters being P5 (RN) and P6 (Marinavia). Following civil deliveries in 1990, both navies should receive EH101s from 1991.

Left: By 1986 the appearance of the basic naval EH101 had at last become finalized. This model shows the proposed Royal Navy version in the ASW role armed with up to four torpedoes.

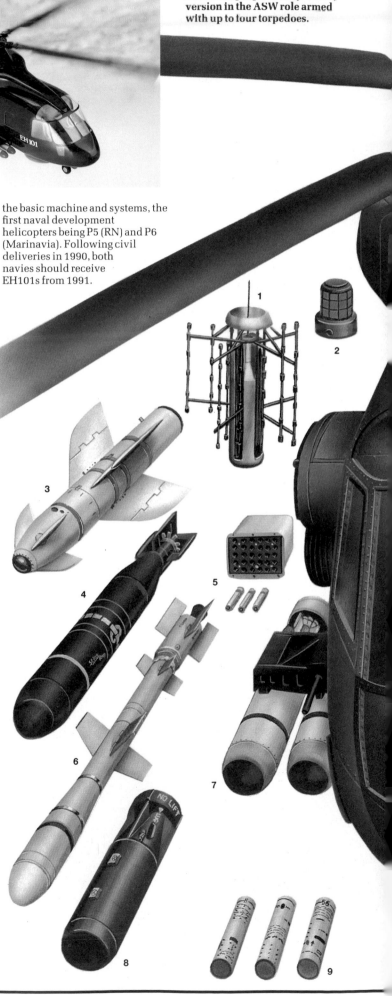

Below: The main drawing (an EH101 in Italian naval service) shows that, five years before the start of operational service, the range of ordnance and equipment planned is already exceptional.

Key to stores:
1 Plessey HISOS dipping sonar array.
2 ALQ-144 IRCM pulsed jammer.
3 Penguin Mk 2 Mod 7 anti-ship missile.
4 Sting Ray advanced torpedo.
5 ALE-40 (or other) chaff/flare dispenser.
6 Marte Mk 2 (Sea Killer anti-ship system).
7 Mk 46 torpedoes (normal load is four of any type of AS torpedo).
8 Mk 11 depth charge.
9 Marine markers.
10 ESM installation (various).
11 Blue Kestrel radar (RN)
12 Sonobuoys (various).
13 BAe Sea Skua anti-ship missiles.
14 AM.39 Exocet.
15 AGM-84 Harpoon cruise missile.
16 BAe Sea Eagle anti-ship cruise missile.
17 BAe Alarm anti-radar missile.
18 AEREA Door Gun Post with 0.5in Browning.

Eurocopter HAC/HAP/PAH-2

Origin: Joint project by France and Germany, first flight 1988.
Type: Escort (HAP) and anti-tank (PAH/HAC) helicopter.
Engines: Two 1,225shp MTU/Turboméca MTM 385-R turboshaft engines.
Dimensions: Diameter of four-blade main rotor 42ft 7.8in (13.0m); diameter of tail rotor 8ft 10.3in (2.7m); other dimensions not settled.
Weights: Empty, not yet fixed; mission takeoff about 10,582lb (4800kg); maximum loaded (design figure) 11,023lb (5000kg).
Performance: (estimates) Maximum cruising speed (HAP) 174mph (280km/h), (PAH) 155mph (250km/h), (HAC) between HAP/PAH; maximum rate of climb 1,970ft (600m)/min; hovering ceiling OGE (HAP, HAC at 25°C) 3,281ft (1000m), (PAH at 10°C) 6,562ft (2000m); mission endurance 2hr 50min.
Background: In 1968-70 France was teamed with Westland in the design of a slim-body anti-tank version of the Lynx. France then pulled out, causing collapse of the project. MBB, which had been in partnership with Agusta on the BO 115, then collaborated with Aérospatiale on the design of the proposed HAC-3G (*Hélicoptère Anti-Char* 3rd generation) for France and PAH-2 (*Panzerabwehr Hubschrauber* 2nd generation) for West Germany, ignoring the existence of the precisely similar Italian A 129. From 1978 the project awaited a decision to go ahead. Six years later (by which time the A 129 was in the air) a go-ahead was agreed on 29 May 1984. Despite the existence of the proven Gem engine a completely new engine is also being designed. MBB has system leadership though work is shared between the two countries on an equal basis. A third version, the French HAP (*Hélicoptère d'Appui et Protection*), is intended for escort and general fire support.
Design: Everything disclosed so far suggests that the Eurocopter group is designing a series of completely conventional helicopters, fractionally bigger and heavier than the A 129, similar to a Lynx and much lighter and less capable than a Lynx 3. MBB, a pioneer of composite blades, has been developing an advanced hub with the blades retained in elastomeric bearings located between upper and lower starplates, each of wholly composite construction, bolted together on each side of a titanium spacer. This configuration "permits almost unrestricted installation of a mast-mounted sight". The hub is claimed to offer such advantages as a compact and robust structure, low aerodynamic drag, a very small number of parts and great ease of maintenance. Aérospatiale, which has been developing the blades, likewise claims "about 10 per cent performance improvement over most present-day systems", though models so far revealed do not show BERP type

tips. Of course this helicopter will need the same extreme agility as other anti-tank helicopters, and it is being developed to survive strikes from 23mm fire and to keep flying for 30min after loss of oil from the main transmission bearings. The fuselage is conventional, with fixed tailwheel landing gears and twin auxiliary tail fins. The stepped cockpits with flat windows will have armoured impact-absorbing seats and probably dual flight controls. Seating, however, will not be common, the German preference being for the accepted layout with the copilot/gunner in front and the French demanding the pilot to be seated in front.
Avionics: All three helicopter types will share a common digital 1553B data bus system, though the actual equipments fitted to the PAH-2 will be mainly German and those fitted to the HAP and HAC-3G will be mainly French. One of the biggest current development tasks is designing the system architecture, which again is being integrated between the partners but without any official contact with either Westland or Agusta who are designing similar digital systems for the EH101 and already have a complete system fully developed in the A 129. All Eurocopter versions will have a decentralized computer, central operating unit, two symbol generators and the usual MFDs in the cockpits. Other common equipment will include a four-axis autopilot, and comprehensive ECM including both radar and laser warning receivers. All versions have totally different sensor fits. The PAH-2 is (remarkably) planned to have its sight in the nose, the installation being almost an Apache TADS/PNVS for both crew. The HAC-3G will have an MMS with three wavelengths (TV, FLIR and laser) for detection, tracking and ranging, for the backseat gunner, and a nose-mounted night-vision sensor for the pilot. The HAP will have a roof-mounted sight with direct optics, TV, FLIR and laser.
Armament: HAC-3G and PAH-2 will have forward-mounted wings carrying the sole armament. HAP-2 will carry eight HOT 2 inboard and four self-defence Stinger 2 outboard. HAC-3G will (it is hoped) from the start carry eight of the third-generation ATGW-3 missiles, which will also be a retrofit on PAH-2. HAP will have a 30mm GIAT 30781 gun in a chin turret, with 450 rounds. The gun's weight will be balanced by moving the weapon wings further back. Normal load will be two twin Mistral AAM pods and two launchers each with 22 SNEB 68mm rockets.
Future: The first version to be delivered is planned to be the HAP, for the French Armée de Terre, for delivery from 1992. Next will come the West German Heer (army) PAH-2, entering service from 1993, and last the French HAC-3G due to enter service from 1996.

Above: A model showing the 1985 configuration of the Eurocopter (MBB/Aérospatiale) HAC-3G. This, the French anti-armour version, is the only one to have an MMS. In mid-1986 the whole programme had become increasingly uncertain.

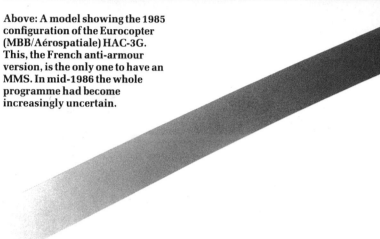

Right: Though the Eurocopter project may for the second time grind to a halt, it is potentially very important. The main illustration shows the PAH-2 in Heer (West German army) camouflage. Many features remain undecided in 1986.

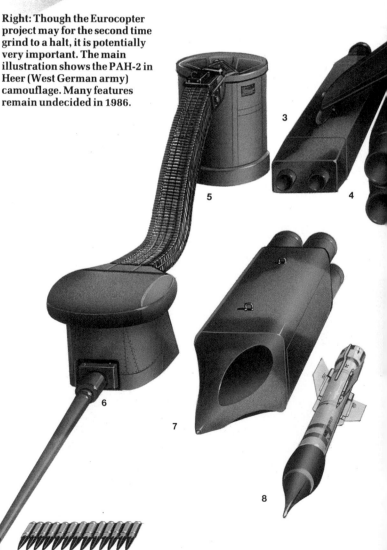

Key to stores:
1 ALQ-144 IRCM pulsing beacon jammer.
2 ALE-39 chaff/flare cartridge dispenser.
3 Matra MICA self-defence missile box.
4 Quadruple launchers for EMDG ATGW3 long-range anti-tank missiles (missile not yet built).
5 Magazine for 450 rounds of 30mm ammunition.
6 GIAT 30781 gun (HAP only).
7 Quadruple launcher for HOT 2 missiles.
8 HOT or HOT 2 missile.
9 PNVS night-vision system.
10 TADS FLIR sight.
11 TADS day TV/laser/direct optical sight.
12 TOW 2 missile (alternative weapon fit).
13 Matra Mistral twin launcher.
14 Mistral air-to-air missile.
15 SNEB 68mm rockets, shown with anti-armour sub-projectiles (part of Multi-Dart 68 system).
16 Stinger self-defence missile.
17 Brandt 12×68 rocket launcher.
18 Brandt Armements 22×68 rocket launcher (Multi-Dart 68 system).
19 Twin Stinger launcher.
20 Weapon wing in forward location.
21 Mast-mounted sight (HAC-3G version only).
22 RWR passive receivers.

ICA IAR-317 Airfox

Origin: Romania (derived from French Alouette III), first flight April 1984.

Type: Light attack and combat training helicopter.

Engine: One 858shp Turboméca Artouste IIIB turboshaft engine.

Dimensions: Diameter of three-blade main rotor 36ft 1.9in (11.02m); length (rotors turning) 42ft 1.5in (12.84m), (blades folded) 35ft 7in (10.845m), (fuselage only) 32ft 1.8in (9.8m); height (rotor head) 9ft 10in (3.0m).

Weights: Empty 2,535lb (1150kg); maximum loaded 4,850lb (2200kg).

Performance: (max wt) Maximum cruising speed at SL 118mph (190km/h); maximum rate of climb 886ft (270m)/min; hovering ceiling OGE 4,920ft (1500m); range at SL (standard fuel) 326 miles (525km), (max fuel) 503 miles (810km).

Background: As a long-time licence builder of the SA 316B Alouette III, ICA, of Brasov, Romania, had since the mid-1970s been studying ways of modifying this helicopter. These studies crystallized into a redesign of the forward fuselage along narrow gunship lines, with just two seats in tandem. By leaving the engine and dynamic parts almost unchanged the development effort was minimised and the prototype got into the air on schedule. After flying about 100hr very successfully this helicopter was modified with military equipment and weapons. This is the first time a completely new helicopter has been developed by a licensee.

Design: Almost all changes are confined to the forward fuselage, though the twin-fin tail is now made of glassfibre instead of light alloy. Almost the entire fuselage is duralumin, the lower bath-like metal structure retaining full (narrow) width right forward to the chisel-like nose. The seats, for front gunner and rear pilot, are armoured and crashworthy with vertical and horizontal adjustment. On each side of each cockpit is a large forward-hinged transparent door, all four being jettisonable in emergency. The lower half of each door pane, like the large forward windscreen, is of shatterproof toughened material, but no attempt has been made to make all parts of the helicopter stand up to cannon fire. Instead of skids, ICA designed a simple tricycle landing gear. The nose gear has been made steerable, and options include skis, floats or emergency flotation bags. Other options include air conditioning (heating is standard), a 386lb (175kg) rescue hoist, rescue sling seat, external cargo sling, deck-lock harpoon, sand filter and flares. Dual flight controls and primary instruments are standard, and the gunner/copilot can also have a repeater gyro horizon and directional gyro.

Avionics: These are naturally fairly basic and comprise a VHF navaid and a marker beacon receiver, radio compass, intercom, radar altimeter and, as an option, an additional communications radio. The pilot's instrument panel, raised above as well as behind the copilot/gunner, normally has an airspeed indicator, altimeter, magnetic compass, VSI (vertical speed [rate of climb and descent] indicator, also called a variometer), artificial horizon, directional gyro, turn and slip indicator, collective-pitch indicator, clock and indicators of fuel contents, oil pressure and temperature, turbine entry temperature and outside air temperature. Other equipment in the cockpit includes night lighting, windscreen heating and demisting, windscreen wiper, landing-light switch, and switches for navigation and anti-collision lights, alternative static source, rotor brake, mission selector and fire extinguisher (and rescue hoist if fitted). Standard equipment in the front cockpit of the combat version will include a Type PKV roof-mounted stabilized missile sight and a forward-looking Type RAD optical gunsight which can also be used when firing fixed armament carried on the outriggers.

Armament: Rather unusually the Airfox carries fixed forward-firing guns, the standard fit being two 7.62mm (FN or similar) machine guns on the lower flanks of the nose. Other weapons can be carried on the twin cantilever beams attached on each side immediately aft of the rear cockpit. Up to three stores attachments can be provided on each side for a total external load of 1,653lb (750kg). Basic loads can comprise four Soviet/Romanian UV-4-130 or UV-12-57 rocket launchers or four machine-gun pods, or four bombs of up to 220lb (100kg). Alternative loads can include six AT-3 Sagger anti-tank missiles or various other tactical or naval weapons. At the 1985 Paris airshow the prototype was exhibited with a wide range of ordnance, all of Romanian origin. Some of the stores comprised dispensers for flares, chaff and other ECM payloads, and ICA have made the point that the extremely low cost of this helicopter, which can be flown solo, makes it particularly suitable for use in the EW/ECM role.

Future: ICA stated they hoped to have two more Airfox prototypes flying by the end of 1985, and to begin series production in early 1986. The initial customers are the Romanian armed forces, but at Paris in 1985 it was stated that "more than one foreign country" had then shown interest in the military version. The extremely low price and modest operating cost of this already well developed light helicopter should enable ICA to sustain a substantial production programme for customers seeking a simple training and liaison machine which, in emergency, could also take its place in the front line.

Below: Surrounded by Soviet and other Romanian aircraft, the Airfox made its public debut at the 1985 Paris airshow. At that time the exact standard of build of the production machine had not been finalized, but many third-world forces showed interest.

Right: When work on this book started, in 1985, the IAR-317 was unknown outside Brasov. It suddenly appeared at the Paris Salon in that year, and even a year later (mid-1986) the helicopter is still in the flight development stage, though a production line is beginning to take shape. Though its outward appearance is ungainly, this helicopter could find a ready market in third-world countries interested in limited-war situations. On cost/effectiveness grounds it could be highly competitive.

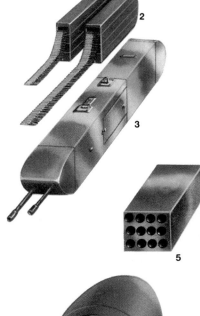

Key to stores:
1 Triple installation of AT-3 Sagger anti-tank missiles.
2 Twin ammunition magazines for GMP 2 pod.
3 GMP 2 twin-7.62mm machine gun pod.
4 UV-12-57 (box type) rocket launchers.
5 Flare/chaff dispensers (in front, flare cartridge left, chaff cartridge right).
6 125lit (33 US gal) long-range external tank.

7 Fixed 7.62mm machine gun in gondola.
8 7.62mm ammunition.
9 Landing gear skids (Alouette type).
10 50kg GP bomb.
11 100kg GP bomb.
12 57mm rockets, with fins deployed.
13 UV-4-130 launcher for 130mm rockets.
14 Emergency flotation gear (Alouette type).
15 PKV missile sight.
16 Engine intake screen box (Alouette type).

Kaman H-2 Seasprite

Origin: USA, first flight 2 July 1959. Data for current production SH-2F.

Type: Multirole shipboard helicopter, with capabilities for ASW, ASST, SAR, observation and utility transport.

Engines: Originally one 1,250shp General Electric T58-8B turboshaft; later two T58-8B; (current 2F) two 1,350shp T58-8F; (future 2G plan) two 1,625shp General Electric T700-401.

Dimensions: Diameter of four-blade main rotor 44ft 0in (13.41m); length (rotors turning) 52ft 7in (16.03m), (blades and nose folded) 38ft 4in (11.68m); height (rotors turning) 15ft 6in (4.72m).

Weights: Empty 7,040lb (3193kg); maximum loaded 13,500lb (6124kg) (pre-1985 SH-2F 12,800lb/5806kg).

Performance: (max weight) Maximum level speed at SL 150mph (241km/h); cruising speed 138mph (222km/h); maximum rate of climb 2,440ft (744m)/min; hovering ceiling OGE 15,400ft (4694m); normal range with max fuel 411 miles (661km).

Background: Charles H. Kaman was one of the pioneers of the helicopter. He invented a new form of flight control system in which blade incidence is controlled not by torque forces applied at a pivoted root but by aerodynamic forces imparted by pilot-controlled servo flaps hinged well outboard on the trailing edge of each blade. Early Kaman helicopters had intermeshing "eggbeater" rotors, but in the H-2 the company applied the servo-flap system to a machine of conventional "penny farthing" configuration. A helicopter of outstandingly clean and neat design, it has since been progressively upgraded, notably by dramatic increases in power.

Design: At a time when most helicopters looked ungainly, the Seasprite showed that helicopters can be streamlined. As it was designed for use from the restricted decks of US Navy warships it was also made extremely compact. It was one of the first helicopters fitted with haul-down and deck locking gear, folding rotor blades and even a nose which can split open and fold to each side to reduce length. The fuselage is a conventional stressed-skin structure, with no suggestion of the pod-and-boom configuration common in the 1950s. In the nose is the side-by-side cockpit with a large aft-sliding door on each side. The pilot and copilot/Tacco (tactical co-ordinator) have almost perfect view to all sides. In the rear cabin is the sensor operator who manages the radar, sonics and MAD. With the sonobuoy package removed the SH-2F can carry a considerable amount of internal or external load, or four passengers or two stretcher casualties. Engines are above the cabin, originally on the centreline ahead of the gearbox and today one on each side of the streamlined pylon structure. Up to 396gal (1802 litres) of fuel is housed in protected tanks in the

centre fuselage, which is watertight and was originally built with inflatable buoyancy bags (since replaced by smoke markers). The twin-wheel main gears have Dowty Liquid Spring shock absorbers and high-pressure tyres, and pivot forwards to retract into the lower fuselage. The single tailwheel, which in the current F version is moved well forward, can be freed to castor except at takeoff and landing but does not retract. All current Seasprites have the Kaman "101" main rotor, with a simplified titanium hub and retention straps holding manually folded blades made of aluminium alloy and glassfibre. From 1987 all-composite blades will be retrofitted.

Avionics: Originally the H-2 was designed for SAR and liaison, and though night and all-weather capability was required a fairly simple avionic suite met the requirement. Today's SH-2F has to meet the vastly more challenging demands of ASW and ASST, in the so-called LAMPS (light airborne multi-purpose system) Mk I programme. Key element was an over-the-horizon targeting capability, provided by the Canadian Marconi LN-66HP surveillance radar. In the ASW role the key items are a battery of 15 Difar and Dicass sonobuoys ejected from tubes in the left side, with comprehensive sonobuoy data links, receivers and recorders, and a Texas Instruments ASQ-81(V)2 MAD trailed in a "bird" on the right side. Navaids include Teledyne ASN-123 doppler/tacnav. Export Seasprites are offered with Bendix dipping sonar, with acoustic processor, and the Eaton APS-128 radar compatible with the Sea Skua missile.

Armament: Standard weapons in the ASW role are one or two AS torpedoes, Mk 46 being due for later replacement by Mk 50 ALWT. Previous versions flew with Sparrow AAMs in the ship defence role, and with a chin turret in the armed SAR mission. Today the versatility of the Seasprite is fully appreciated, and it is possible that further upgraded examples may carry the Penguin anti-ship missile, with the BAe Sea Skua for export customers.

Future: The evergreen nature of the Seasprite has been remarkable. Whereas production terminated at 190 in the 1960s, almost all of these single-engined machines subsequently being upgraded at least once to later versions, the production line reopened in 1972 with new SH-2Fs and then reopened again ten years later. Six new SH-2Fs to the latest (13,500lb, 6124kg) standard have been funded in each of the past three annual defence budgets, and evaluation of a twin-T700 conversion designated YSH-2G is now expected to lead to a major further upgrade programme with these new engines. In any case Active and Reserve LAMPS I Seasprites will remain operational beyond year 2000.

Key to stores:
1 AIM-7E Sparrow AAM (not standard).
2 Rescue hoist.
3 BAe Sea Skua anti-ship missile.
4 Door-mounted M60 7.62mm machine gun.
5 Sidewinder AAM (AIM-9N shown).
6 ASQ-81 MAD towed body.
7 Mk 50 ALWT (advanced lightweight torpedo).
8 Auxiliary fuel tank.
9 ALR-66 radar warning receiver.
10 Marine marker.
11 LN-66HP surveillance radar.
12 GE Universal Turret with 7.62mm Minigun.
13 Mk 46 anti-submarine torpedo (Mk 44 may also be carried).
14 Bendix AQS-13B dipping sonar.
15 Penguin Mk 2 Mod 7 anti-ship missile.
16 DIFAR sonobuoy.
17 Mk 25 smoke marker.
18 DICASS sonobuoy.
19 AN/SSQ-41/47 sonobuoy series.

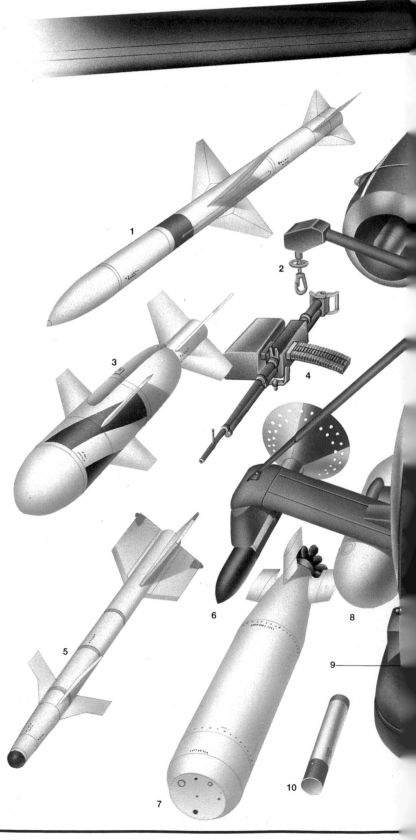

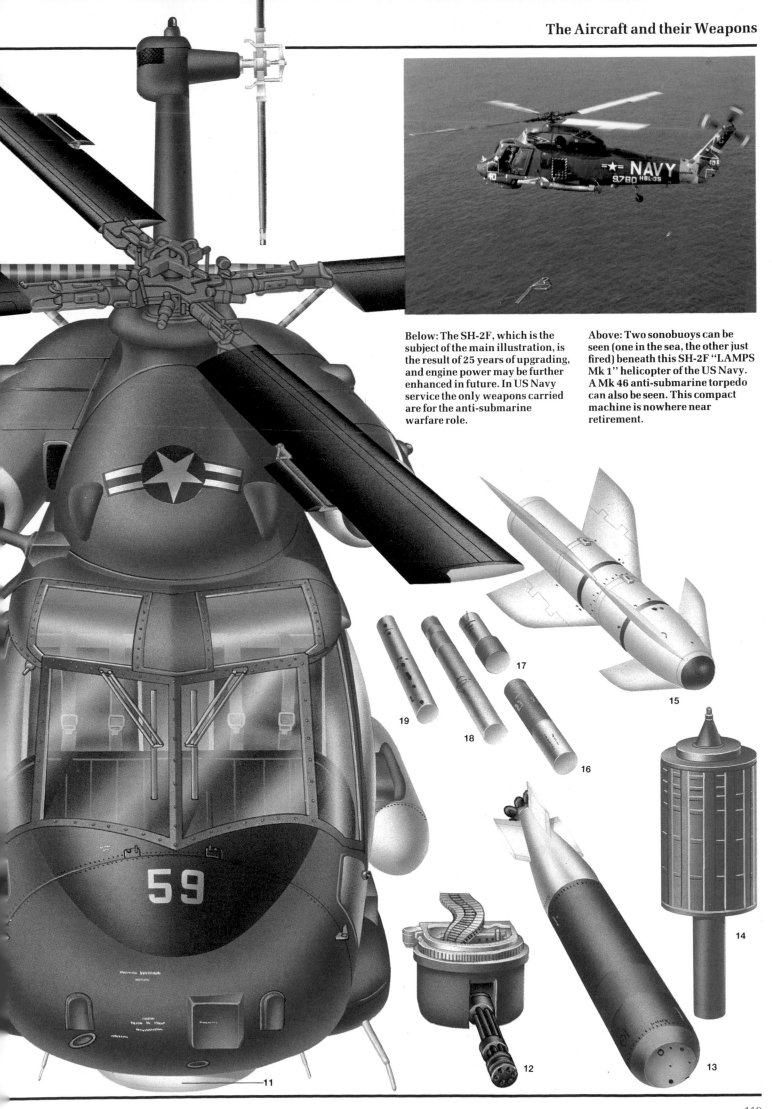

Below: The SH-2F, which is the subject of the main illustration, is the result of 25 years of upgrading, and engine power may be further enhanced in future. In US Navy service the only weapons carried are for the anti-submarine warfare role.

Above: Two sonobuoys can be seen (one in the sea, the other just fired) beneath this SH-2F "LAMPS Mk 1" helicopter of the US Navy. A Mk 46 anti-submarine torpedo can also be seen. This compact machine is nowhere near retirement.

Kamov Ka-25

Origin: Soviet Union, first flight believed 1960.
Type: Multirole shipboard helicopter with ASW, ASST and utility versions.
Engines: Two Glushenkov free-turbine turboshaft engines, (current) 990shp GTD-3BM, (early, being upgraded) 900shp GTD-3F.
Dimensions: Diameter of each three-blade rotor 51ft 7.7in (15.74m); length (ignoring rotors) 32ft 0in (9.75m); height overall 17ft 7.4in (5.37m).
Weights: (approximate) Empty 10,500lb (4765kg); maximum loaded 16,535lb (7500kg).
Performance: Maximum level speed at SL (typical) 137mph (220km/h); cruising speed 120mph (193km/h); hovering ceiling OGE 6,890ft (2100m); range (external tanks, with reserves) 404 miles (650km).
Background: N. I. Kamov was a pioneer of the coaxial helicopter, which because of its compact overall dimensions is especially well suited to shipboard operation. All the early types were piston-engined, but in 1961 the prototype Ka-25 was displayed, with twin-turbine power (and "armed" with two awesome-looking missiles which later transpired to be dummies of a fictitious type). Originally called Harp by NATO, the invented Western name was later changed to Hormone. Three distinct variants have been identified, together accounting for 460 helicopters delivered in 1966-75: Hormone-A for ASW, Hormone-B for ASST, and Hormone-C for SAR/utility duties. All three are equipped for shipboard operation, and serve aboard warships of the Soviet and Indian navies, but in Syria, Vietnam and Yugoslavia the Ka-25 operates from shore bases.
Design: From the start Kamov sought to minimise overall dimensions (though in fact the US Navy SH-2F is smaller and much more powerful, despite having a single rotor). Traditional fully articulated rotors were used, necessitating wide vertical separation, which in turn means a rather clumsy hub with long push/pull rods linking the various clockwise and anticlockwise swashplates and blade roots. All hinges require lubrication. The original blades had aluminium D-spars with nitrogen pressure crack detection, and light honeycomb-filled rear pockets, but it is believed most Ka-25s still in use have new composite blades. Alcohol deicing and automatic cockpit-controlled blade folding are standard. Previous Kamov helicopters had twin fins, but the Ka-25 has upper and lower fixed central fins, horizontal tailplanes with elevators and endplate fins and rudders which are toed inward. The tail is carried on a deep oval tailboom carried on a bulkhead at the rear of the light-alloy fuselage, whose outer skin incorporates bonded sandwich panels. The deep underfloor structure contains tankage and, in

most versions, various sensors and a weapon bay. Above the floor is the side-by-side cockpit and the main cabin which measures 12ft 11.5in (3.95m) long, 59in (1.5m) wide and 49.2in (1.25m) high. There is an aft-sliding door on each side of the cockpit and a large aft-sliding door on the left of the cabin. The latter accommodates the ASW/ASST displays and up to three operators, or in the transport role provision is made for cargo or up to 12 passengers on fold-down seats. To meet the requirements of shipboard operation a special four-legged landing gear is fitted, with long-stroke vertical oleo struts, castoring nose wheels and mainwheels with sprag-type (positive locking) brakes. In the ASW/ASST roles the rear legs can be pivoted out and up out of the field of view of the radar by retracting the main diagonal struts. All four legs can be equipped with rapid-inflating emergency buoyancy bags. The engines are mounted parallel ahead of the gearbox, with plain inlets fitted with electric anti-icing but no filters or particle separators. The plain jetpipes project to each side with no IR suppression. Aft of the gearbox is the fan-blown oil cooler, with rearward-facing outlet.
Avionics: All versions have a chin-mounted radar, which in the ASW version is called Big Bulge by NATO, operating in I/J band. Other equipment of this version includes the A-346Z data link to surface vessels, SRO-2 IFF with aerials above the nose and tail, UHF/VHF/HF with blade and wire aerials, radar altimeter, doppler and associated autohover, Tie Rod electro-optical sensor and, in some examples, a towed MAD as used on the Mi-4 and Mi-14. This version carries sonobuoys (usually three

Size-A class) in an external box on the right side of the fuselage. In the rear of the main fuselage, just ahead of the tail boom, is a standard dipping sonar installation. The Tie Rod installation is vertical and apart from giving night and all-weather vision of the dipped sonar its purpose is uncertain. The SAR/utility version has none of the ASW gear but does have a radar, and features a searchlight, loud hailer, ventral dome amidships and extra sensor in a streamlined nacelle projecting ahead of the ventral fin. The ASST version has no ASW gear but the radar is the fat bulging Short Horn, and a second sensor, said to be a radar, projects in a vertical cylinder under the rear of the cabin. All versions have comprehensive RWR and IRCM with all-round coverage; some have been seen with a Home Guard quad yagi array on the nose.
Armament: The Hormone-A is the only armed version. An internal linear weapons bay houses two 450mm AS torpedoes or depth charges and other stores. Four dye markers can be carried externally in lieu of auxiliary tanks. Some ASW machines have a deep rectangular weapon bay, reportedly for wire-guided torpedoes. "Small fire-and-forget ASMs" have been reported since 1982 but not seen in photographs so far made public.
Future: With the Ka-27 taking over from the Ka-25 in its combat roles the earlier helicopter will probably increasingly be used for mission training and utility duties. No new operational version is expected, and the composite-blade programme is completed.

Left: An excellent photograph of Ka-25 Hormone-A helicopters operating from one of the very formidable *Kiev* class ships. This version has full ASW gear and a radome with a flat underside. Flotation gear is not normally carried, though readily available. IFF is fitted at nose and tail.

2

3

4

6

7

8

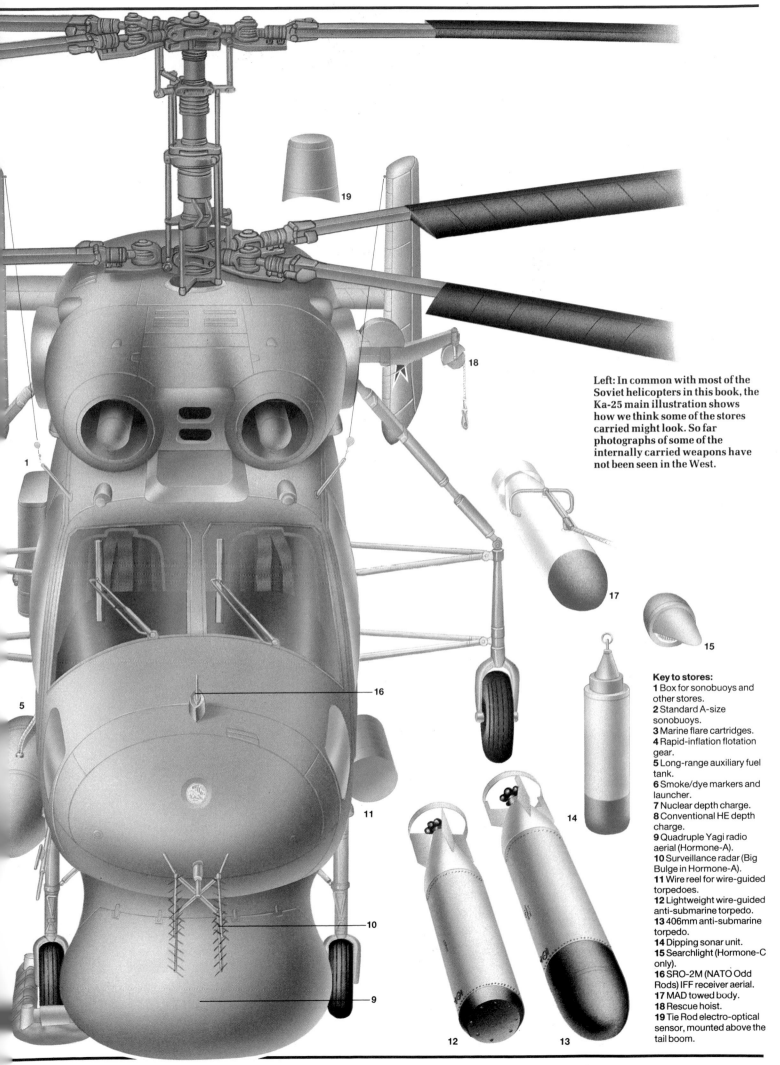

Left: In common with most of the Soviet helicopters in this book, the Ka-25 main illustration shows how we think some of the stores carried might look. So far photographs of some of the internally carried weapons have not been seen in the West.

Key to stores:
1 Box for sonobuoys and other stores.
2 Standard A-size sonobuoys.
3 Marine flare cartridges.
4 Rapid-inflation flotation gear.
5 Long-range auxiliary fuel tank.
6 Smoke/dye markers and launcher.
7 Nuclear depth charge.
8 Conventional HE depth charge.
9 Quadruple Yagi radio aerial (Hormone-A).
10 Surveillance radar (Big Bulge in Hormone-A).
11 Wire reel for wire-guided torpedoes.
12 Lightweight wire-guided anti-submarine torpedo.
13 406mm anti-submarine torpedo.
14 Dipping sonar unit.
15 Searchlight (Hormone-C only).
16 SRO-2M (NATO Odd Rods) IFF receiver aerial.
17 MAD towed body.
18 Rescue hoist.
19 Tie Rod electro-optical sensor, mounted above the tail boom.

Kamov Ka-27

Origin: Soviet Union, first flight 1979-80.

Type: Shipboard helicopter for: (A) ASW, (B) ASST, (C) SAR/utility.

Engines: Two 2,225shp Isotov TV3-117V turboshaft engines.

Dimensions: Diameter of each three-blade rotor 52ft 2in (15.9m); length (blades folded) 40ft 2.3in (12.25m), (ignoring rotors) 37ft 0.9in (11.3m); height (top of rotor head) 17ft 8.6in (5.4m).

Weights: (estimated) Empty about 14,220lb (6450kg); maximum loaded (normal) 24,250lb (11000kg), (with slung load) 27,775lb (12600kg).

Performance: (at normal max weight) Maximum speed 155mph (250km/h); cruising speed 143mph (230km/h); hovering ceiling OGE 11,480ft (3500m); range/endurance (with auxiliary tanks) 497 miles (800km)/4hr 30min.

Background: The Ka-27 and its civil counterpart the Ka-32 are natural successors to the Ka-25, developed under the leadership of S. V. Mikheyev, who has led the bureau since Kamov's death in 1973. It was evident that more capability could be packed into the same overall compact dimensions as the Ka-25, the key being greater engine power. The engine KB of S. P. Isotov was already developing an uprated version of the mass-produced TV2 engine, and there was no difficulty in fitting this into the new Kamov helicopter. With the much greater power available the performance was considerably improved even at much heavier weights, and it was sensible to enlarge the fuselage to take full advantage of the increased payload margins. As in the case of the Ka-25 three versions were planned from the outset for the AV-MF (naval air force), and these have been given the NATO names Helix-A (ASW) and Helix-B (ASST); it would be reasonable to assign Helix-C to the SAR/utility model. The latter closely resembles the civil Ka-32S, used for multiple duties from icebreakers. There is also a basic Ka-32 flying crane and oil-rig support version.

Design: Naturally Mikheyev sought a "minimum change" design, apart from the decision at the outset to lengthen the fuselage. The much greater power did require redesign of the gearbox and transmission, and because new technology had matured in time the opportunity was taken to redesign the blades to use composite materials from the start. The hubs and control system were redesigned in detail, using titanium alloy for the main hub spiders, elastomeric bearings and fully duplicated hydraulic controls without manual reversion. The blades are wholly of composite materials apart from an abrasion-resistant leading edge strip with electric deicing (said to be operative whenever the engines are running, though this would usually waste power). The spar is assembled from plies and filament winding in carbon and glassfibre, with 13 trailing pockets with aramid-fibre (Kevlar type) skins stabilized by a nylon-honeycomb filling. For the first time in a production Soviet helicopter the entire rotor system has been designed to minimise vibration. The helicopter is suspended from four damped straps incorporating tuned balance weights, and the three blades of the lower rotor are fitted with anti-vibration masses bolted across the spar just inboard of the inner end of the lifting aerofoil part of the blade. These blade masses are readily adjustable. As before the blades can be folded manually to the rear to lie within the track of the rear landing gears, when they slightly overhang the tail. Compared with the Ka-25 the fuselage and rotor pylon and engine group are of slightly improved aerodynamic form. Oddly (according to brochures) the interior cabin width has decreased, to 51in (1.3m), though it looks unchanged and the fuselage has the same basic cross section. Indeed the height (which if anything appears more constricted than before) is now given as 52in (1.32m), the new

cabin length being 14ft 10in (4.52m), excluding the side-by-side cockpit. In most Ka-27s dual controls are fitted, but in the Ka-32 the right seat is occupied by a navigator, with a seat behind him for a loadmaster/winchman, and the same is true of the Ka-27 SAR/utility version. Much of the fuselage and tail are of composites, with highly stressed primary structure and joints being titanium. The fuselage is sealed for buoyancy. The tail has just the two outer fins, now with large fixed inboard slats. The engines have electrically heated inlets, the internal tanks are pressure-fuelled and a gas-turbine APU is fitted in the rear of the pylon fairing. Auxiliary external tanks are larger than on the Ka-25 and scabbed flat on each side of the fuselage. Transport versions normally have 16 passenger seats, folding against the cabin side and rear walls.

Avionics: The radar (for which no NATO name had been published in 1986) has a larger but shallower scanner giving a much neater chin radome than on the Ka-25. Other equipment includes a totally new automatic flight-control system, fed by a low-airspeed sensor, radar altimeter and doppler (a close formation photograph has been published of a civil Ka-32 with the crew all looking out of the main cabin door, the cockpit being empty). No Tie Rod EO sensor is fitted, but an upgraded ESM suite is fitted, probably with active dispensers and jammers. Helix-A carries 10 or 12 sonobuoys in boxes on both sides, compared with three in Hormone-A.

Weapons: No details are yet known, but Helix-A carries all its armament internally without needing a projecting bay. The bay length is slightly greater than in the Ka-25, but weapon options are probably the same.

Below: A rare colour photograph, taken aboard *Novorossiysk*, serving with the Soviet Pacific Fleet. Ships of this class carry up to 19 Ka-27 helicopters.

Future: All evidence suggests that the Ka-27 family are outstanding shipboard helicopters. Purchase of 18 by the Indian Navy, which has the very latest version of Sea King, speaks for itself. It is doubtful that any greatly modified Ka-27 variant will be needed. It would have been reasonable to expect the new air-combat helicopter called Hokum by NATO to use a similar engine/rotor system. Oddly, while Hokum's gross weight is put at less than half that of the Ka-27, its rotors are said to be of 59ft 8.5in (18.2m) diameter, giving over 31 per cent greater disc area. These figures do not make sense, in the author's view.

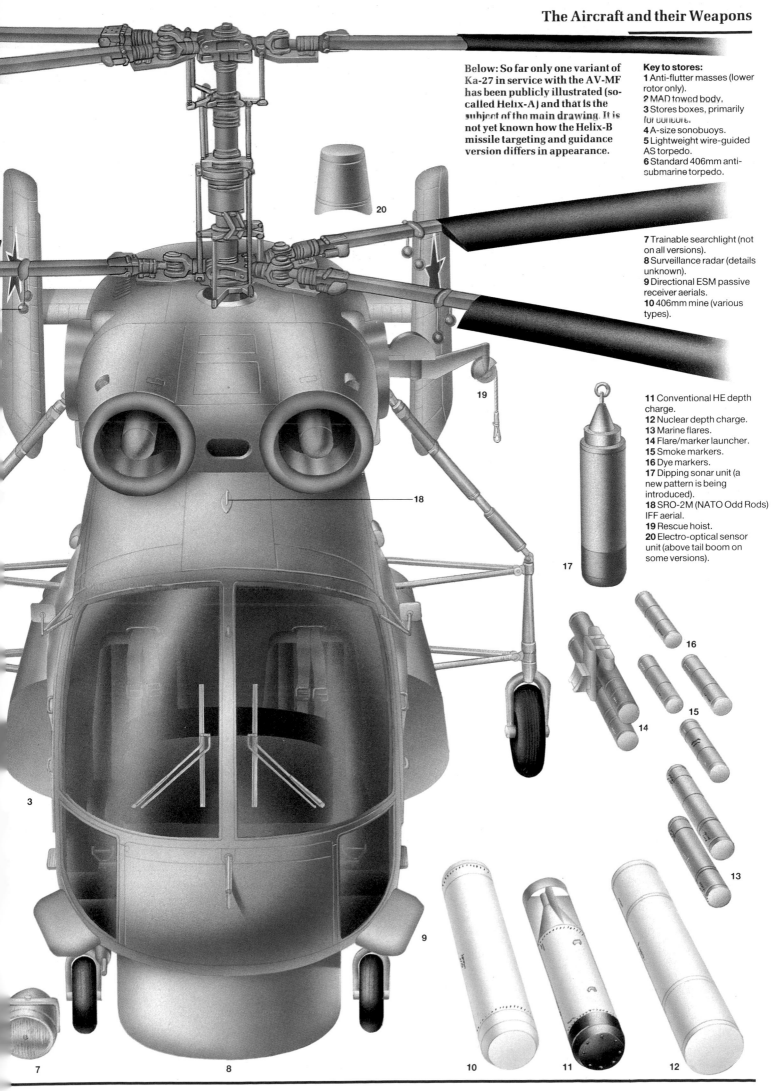

Below: So far only one variant of Ka-27 in service with the AV-MF has been publicly illustrated (so-called Helix-A) and that is the subject of the main drawing. It is not yet known how the Helix-B missile targeting and guidance version differs in appearance.

Key to stores:
1 Anti-flutter masses (lower rotor only).
2 MAD towed body.
3 Stores boxes, primarily for sonobuoys.
4 A-size sonobuoys.
5 Lightweight wire-guided AS torpedo.
6 Standard 406mm anti-submarine torpedo.

7 Trainable searchlight (not on all versions).
8 Surveillance radar (details unknown).
9 Directional ESM passive receiver aerials.
10 406mm mine (various types).

11 Conventional HE depth charge.
12 Nuclear depth charge.
13 Marine flares.
14 Flare/marker launcher.
15 Smoke markers.
16 Dye markers.
17 Dipping sonar unit (a new pattern is being introduced).
18 SRO-2M (NATO Odd Rods) IFF aerial.
19 Rescue hoist.
20 Electro-optical sensor unit (above tail boom on some versions).

MBB BO 105

124

Origin: West Germany, first flight 16 February 1967; also produced in Canada, Indonesia and Spain.
Type: Multirole light helicopter, with versions for anti-tank fighting, liaison, observation and SAR.
Engines: Two 420shp Allison 250-C20B turboshafts (Canadian 105D planned for later use of one Pratt & Whitney Canada PW205B with 1,000shp rating from two 523shp power sections).
Dimensions: Diameter of four-blade main rotor 32ft 3.4in (9.84m); length (rotors turning) 38ft 11in (11.86m), (ignoring rotors 28ft 1in, 8.56m), (CB version, 28ft 11in, 8.81m); height (top of rotor head) 9ft 10in (3.0m).
Weights: Empty (basic CB version) 2,813lb (1276kg); (PAH-1 with crew) 4,217lb (1913kg); loaded (standard) 5,291lb (2400kg), (maximum) 5,511lb (2500kg).
Performance: Maximum sustained speed (CB) 150mph (242km/h), (PAH) 137mph (220km/h); maximum rate of climb (PAH) 1,770ft (540m)/min; hovering ceiling OGE (CB) 5,298ft (1615m), (PAH) 5,184ft (1580m); range (CB, standard fuel, max payload, 5,000ft/1524m) 408 miles (657km).
Background: One of the first major post-war aircraft development programmes to be undertaken in Federal Germany, the BO 105 was launched in 1962 with a government contract for an advanced rotor with a rigid hub and composite blades. This was first tested on an Alouette, while the first BO 105 was ground-tested with a previous articulated rotor. The first flight was made by the No 2 prototype, which was the first to be fitted with the new rotor. From the start the BO 105 was probably the most expensive small five-seater in the world, largely because of the choice of twin turbine engines. In return customers got a machine of the highest quality with extraordinary powers of climb and manoeuvre and, in most versions, with clearance to fly by day or night in any weather (often IFR with a single pilot). After a slow start this helicopter was both sold and licensed all over the world, over 1,200 having been sold by early 1986. These sales include 100 BO 105M and 212 BO 105P for the Heeresflieger (army aviation) and 20 TOW-equipped CBs for the Swedish army.
Design: This helicopter was designed by Bölkow (later merged into MBB) around the advanced rotor schemed in 1960 by Dipl-Ing E. Weiland. Lockheed pioneered the rigid rotor, but Weiland worked independently to create a rotor with feathering hinges only, with several new features. The forged titanium hub holds the four blades in roller bearings, for pitch change, all flexure and torsion being accommodated in the glassfibre spar. A titanium strip protects the leading edge (stainless steel is used on the tail rotor), the rpm being unusually high at 424. Since 1970 blades have had a NACA 23012 "droop snoot"

profile. The rest of the helicopter is relatively conventional, with a light-alloy fuselage and tail boom, with a titanium deck under the engines and glassfibre-reinforced cowling panels. All versions have simple skid landing gear, with heavy landings cushioned by plastic deformation of the legs. Emergency rapid-inflation flotation bags can be attached to the skids. Internally the whole space ahead of and below the engine group is usable. The main cabin measures 55in (1.4m) wide and 49.2in (1.25m) high and seats the pilot and either copilot or passenger in front. To the rear can be either a three-seat bench, or provision for two stretchers or cargo loaded through sliding side doors or clamshell doors at the rear. The rear cargo compartment is slightly narrower than the main cabin and has a height of 22.5in (0.57m). In the armed versions the rear compartment is seldom used, and the cabin is devoted chiefly to mission equipment. All versions have comprehensive night lighting and optional equipment can include a searchlight, loudspeaker, rescue hoist, external load hook, auxiliary tanks (in the cargo compartment), fuel jettison, stability augmentation system, cabin heating, snow skids (large area), anti-icing system and folding main rotor.
Avionics: All versions have comprehensive radio, there usually being two whip aerials above the cabin, one under the tail boom and VOR ring aerials on the sides of the boom. If a radio compass is fitted it makes a small blister under the boom. Many military customers have a large blade aerial above the cabin. The Heeresflieger M (VBH) is a liaison/observation model with uprated dynamic parts and augmented low-level navaids. The same customer's 105P (PAH-1) is missile-armed and has a roof-mounted SFIM APX397 autostabilized sight, as well as an unusual auto-azimuth control which steers the helicopter towards the target (demanding the same uprated gearbox and high-thrust tail rotor as the VBH). Another PAH extra is Singer ASN-129 doppler. Swedish 105CBs have the Saab Helios sight which has Pilkington optics, a night thermal imager and laser receiver/ranger, and can have a laser illuminator module added. Mexican navy 105s have radar and special ship gear.
Armament: Main armament of the two anti-tank versions comprises six HOT (105P) or eight TOW (Swedish 105CB). Many other

weapons hve been fitted, as illustrated, many being used only by the originating country.
Future: MBB will lose no sensible opportunity to develop this extremely successful helicopter, and for several years has been studying a switch to the much more powerful versions of Allison 250 engine, or to the LTS 101 or the French TM 319. More comprehensive warning and ECM/IRCM protection is also another likely possibility, though this depends mainly on the customers.

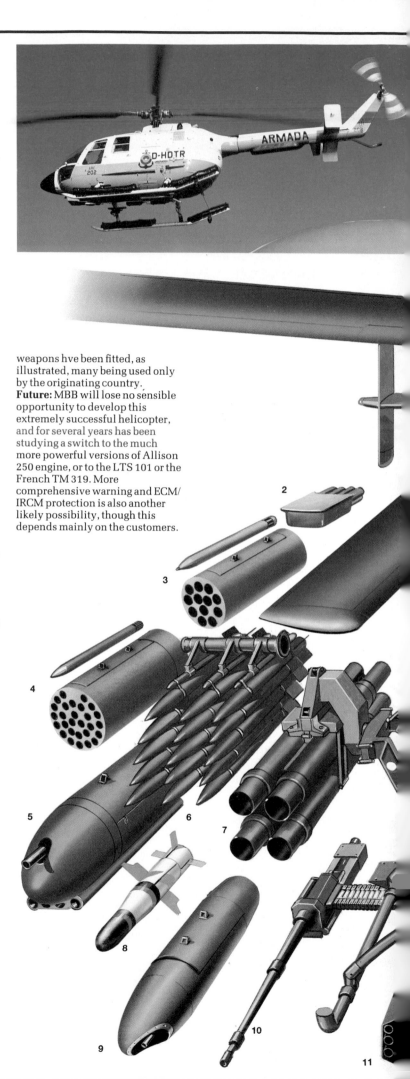

Right: Photographed prior to delivery – on shipboard landing trials, still with German registration – this attractively painted BO 105CB today serves with the Armada de Colombia. Note the black flotation bags attached to the landing skids, the nose radar, and the long box for doppler radar under the tail boom.

Below: The subject of the main illustration is the PAH-1 anti-tank version now used by the Heer (West German army). Most of the other weapon fits are used by export customers.

Key to stores:
1 Anti flutter masses.
2 Chaff/flare dispenser (BOH 300 shown).
3 HL-12-70 launcher and 2.75in rocket.
4 SNIA 28-tube launcher and 80mm rocket.
5 FN ETNA HMP and MRL 70 pod (combined 12.7mm [0.5in] Browning machine gun pod with four 70mm rocket tubes).
6 RWK 051 installation of 15 SURA 81mm rockets.
7 Quadruple TOW tubes.
8 TOW (wings and fins deployed).
9 FFV Uni-Pod 0127 (0.5in Browning gun).
10 Rheinmetall HBS 202 20mm gun.
11 SNEB launcher for 22 rockets of 68mm calibre.
12 Brandt launcher for 12 SNEB 68mm rockets.
13 Oerlikon KAD 20mm cannon.
14 GE 7.62mm Minigun in Emerson FTS.
15 LAU-5002A/A with CRV7 70mm rocket.
16 CASA 04.080 launcher for 80mm Oerlikon rockets.
17 HOT missile.
18 HOT launch tubes.
19 FN ETNA TMP-5 twin 7.62mm machine-gun pod.
20 Twin Stinger tubes, with missile.
21 AEREA Door Gun Post with 0.5in Browning.
22 Stabilized roof sight (APX397 shown).

MBB/Kawasaki BK 117

Origin: Joint programme by West Germany and Japan, first flight 13 June 1979.
Type: Multirole light helicopter with armed military version.
Engines: Two 592shp Avco Lycoming LTS 101-650B-1 turboshaft engines.
Dimensions: Diameter of four-blade main rotor 36ft 1in (11.0m); length (rotors turning) 42ft 8in (13.0m), (ignoring rotors) 32ft 9in (9.98m); height (to top of rotor head) 11ft 0.3in (3.36m).
Weights: Empty equipped (A-3) 3,737lb (1695kg), (A-3M) 5,644lb (2560kg); maximum loaded (both) 7,055lb (3200kg).
Performance: Maximum sustained speed (max weight) 154mph (248km/h); economical cruising speed at SL 132mph (213km/h); maximum rate of climb (max wt) 1,476ft (450m)/min; hovering ceiling OGE (6,614lb, 3000kg) 5,495ft (1675m); range (SL, standard fuel, no reserve, max wt) 306 miles (493km).
Background: In 1974-77 MBB was working on the BK 107, a helicopter in the 7/9-seat class, while Kawasaki designed a very similar machine designated KH-7. Kawasaki picked twin LTS 101 engines and sought a foreign partner. The two companies agreed to collaborate on 25 February 1977. It is a 50/50 programme with MBB responsible for main and tail rotors, control systems, tail and boom, skids, engine compartment and hydraulics, and Kawasaki responsible for the fuselage, transmission, fuel system, electrical system and standard items of equipment. The first flight article flew at MBB, while the first production model flew in Japan in December 1981. The 117A-1, of 6,283lb (2850kg) gross weight, has been largely superseded by the A-3 with a larger tail rotor and increased weight. The armed A-3M was disclosed at the 1985 Paris airshow.
Design: To a great degree the 117 is an enlarged 105, though there is considerable Kawasaki input and the transmission is derived from that of the KH-7. The main rotor is almost identical with the latest 105 standard, though the blades are larger and fitted with prominent anti-vibration weights, and the rotational speed is reduced. The anti-erosion strips are now stainless steel throughout. The engine installations are quite different from those of the 105, the emphasis being on horizontal flow of air into a much shallower compartment which leaves a greater depth underneath for cargo. The engines exhaust through two widely separated pipes, whereas in the 105 there are a close group of four exhaust pipes with sharp curvature. The fuselage has a totally different profile, the usable forward "pod" portion being wider, longer and more streamlined and the tailboom being very much smaller. The tailplane (horizontal stabilizer) carries endplate fins of greater size, delta shape, sharply inclined to

give a sideways thrust to the right in cruising flight and thus reduce power absorbed by the tail rotor (which is of the semi-rigid teetering type). Most of the airframe is conventional light alloy, but most compound-curvature panels are of sandwich construction and many parts have Kevlar composite skins. Standard fuel, housed in four flexible cells under the floor, is only fractionally more than in the 105, but the total can be almost doubled by adding optional internal auxiliary tanks. As in the 105 there are forward-hinged doors on each side of the side-by-side cockpit, aft-sliding jettisonable doors on each side of the cabin and clamshell rear doors giving rear access for cargo or stretchers. The shallower engine compartment has enabled the cargo/stretcher bay to be of more useful depth of 39in (0.99m). Overall cabin length is 9ft 11in (3.02m), maximum width 58.7in (1.49m) and height 50.4in (1.28m). Dual controls are a customer option in all versions, and in the passenger role up to ten people can be carried in addition to the pilot. The military A-3M can carry 11 troops, when stripped of most of the weapons and heavier sensors.
Avionics: All versions offer such customer options as VHF/AM, VHF/FM, HF and UHF, ADF, R-Nav systems, Omega VLF/Navstar, Decca, Loran, LDNS (laser/doppler navigation system), AHRS (attitude/heading reference system), radar altimeter, ATC/IFF transponder, VOR/DME, encoding altimeter, IFR instruments and a pitch/roll SAS (stability augmentation system). The A-3M additionally is offered with either a roof-mounted SFIM APX M397 stabilized sight (for HOT missiles) or an MMS of up to 264lb (120kg) weight, Racal RAMS 3000 series management system with 1553B databus and cockpit MFDs (multifunction displays), Racal Prophet RWS, digital weapon control avionics, chaff/flare dispensers and an IRCM pulsing jammer.
Armament: Weapons are unlikely to be carried except by the dedicated A-3M version. This has

been displayed with an underfuselage Lucas turret armed with a Browning 0.5in (12.7mm) gun with 450 rounds, controlled by an HMS (helmet-mounted sight). The primary anti-armour weapons would probably be two quad installations of HOT or TOW missiles, though alternative weapons can include air-to-air missiles, rocket launchers, gun pods, a fixed forward-firing cannon and a door installation of a 0.5in Browning or later guns.
Future: At the time of writing the BK 117A-3M had not been ordered, though interest in it is strong in

many countries. PT Nurtanio of Indonesia, a long-time licence-builder of the BO 105, began producing the BK 117A-3 in 1985 and is likely in due course to build the armed version. It is obvious that the very high equipped empty weight of the A-3M leaves little margin for useful load, and it would seem logical for more powerful engines (of which several are available) to be installed eventually to enable loaded weight to rise to about 8,500lb (3856kg).

Left: The prototype BK 117A-3M was hurried to completion for display at the 1985 Paris airshow. It appeared with Lucas turret, quad HOT anti-tank missiles and two sights.

Below: The main drawing is of necessity based upon the only example so far built of the A-3M military version, combined with the published schedule of armament.

Key to stores:
1 Anti-flutter masses.
2 FN ETNA HMP and MRL 70 pod (combined 12.7mm [0.5in] gun pod with four 70mm rocket tubes).
3 12-tube launcher (various) and 2.75in rocket.
4 RWK 051 launcher for 15 SURA 81mm rockets.
5 Brandt 68-22 launcher for SNEB 68mm rockets.
6 Quad TOW launcher.
7 SNIA launcher for 28 rockets of 50mm calibre.
8 FFV Uni-Pod 0127 for 0.5in gun.
9 TOW missile.
10 Rheinmetall HBS 202 20mm gun.
11 PEAB (Philips Sweden) chaff/flare dispenser.
12 Lucas Aerospace turret (0.5in gun).
13 GE 7.62mm Minigun in FTS installation.
14 Oerlikon KAD 20mm axial gun.
15 LAU-5002A/A launcher and CRV7 rocket.
16 HOT missile.
17 FN ETNA TMP-5 twin 7.62mm machine-gun pod.
18 Quad HOT launcher.
19 CASA 04.080 launcher for 80mm rockets.
20 Twin Stinger tubes, with missile.
21 Racal Prophet RWS (radar warning system).
22 AEREA Door Gun Post with 0.5in Browning.
23 SFIM APX M397 roof sight (alternative to 25).
24 IRCM pulsed jammer (ALQ-144 shown).
25 Mast-mounted sight (alternative to 23).

McDonnell Douglas 500/530 Defender (OH-6 Cayuse)

Origin: USA, first flight 27 February 1963; Defender licensed to Korean Air (S. Korea).

Type: Multirole light military helicopter, (OH-6A) observation, (Defender) can be equipped for virtually all military/naval helicopter roles.

Engine: One Allison T63/250 turboshaft engine, (OH-6A) 317shp T63-5A derated to 252shp, (500M series) usually 420shp 250-C20B derated to 375shp, (530MG) 650shp 250-C30 derated to 425shp.

Dimensions: Diameter of main rotor, (OH, 500M) four blades, 26ft 4in (8.03m), (500MD, MG and 530) five blades, 27ft 4in (8.33m); length (rotors turning, OH) 30ft 3.8in (9.24m), (500MD) 30ft 10in (9.4m), (MG, 530) 32ft 1in (9.78m), (ignoring rotors, OH) 23ft 0in (7.01m), (500MD) 25ft 0in (7.62m), (MG, 530) 23ft 11in (7.29m); height (top of rotor head, OH) 8ft 1.6in (2.48m), (500, 530) 8ft 8in (2.64m), (with MMS) 11ft 2.3in (3.41m).

Weights: Empty (OH) 1,229lb (557kg), (500MD) 1,976lb (896kg); maximum loaded (OH) 2,400lb (1089kg) (overload 2,700lb, 1225kg), (500MD) 3,000lb (1361kg), (530MG) 3,550lb (1610kg).

Performance: Maximum cruising speed at SL (OH) 150mph (241km/h), (500, 530) 137mph (221km/h); maximum rate of climb (OH) 1,840ft (561m)/min, (500MD) 1,650ft (503m)/min, (530MG) 2,070ft (631m)/min; hovering ceiling OGE (OH) 7,300ft (2225m), (500MD) 5,800ft (1768m), (530MG) 14,100ft (4298m); range (standard fuel, SL, no reserves, OH) 370 miles (595km), (500MD) 242 miles (389km), (530MG) 207 miles (333km).

Background: The former Hughes Helicopters won the 1961 US Army LOH (Light Observation Helicopter) competition with the OH-6A Cayuse, first flown on the date given above, which flew rings round its rivals. This tadpole-like machine scored by being amazingly small, which in turn made it fast and agile. By August 1970 Hughes had delivered 1,434, most of which saw violent action in Vietnam. Subsequently Hughes developed research helicopters for quiet operation, for higher harmonic control to give smooth flight and for Notar (no tail rotor) operation, using aerodynamic circulation around the tail boom instead of a tail rotor. In 1968 Hughes went into production with the civil Model 500, from which stemmed the military 500M, 500MD Defender (built in TOW, Scout and ASW versions) and uprated 500MG and more powerful 530MG Defenders which are important products of today's McDonnell Douglas Helicopter Co.

Design: Remarkably, these attractive and seemingly very modern helicopters are actually quite traditional in design, with a fully articulated main rotor, metal blades and a light-alloy airframe. The main-rotor blades have aluminium skins wrapped round and hot-bonded to an extruded aluminium spar which is retained via a laminated strap and quick-disconnect pins which allow the blades to fold. The two-blade tail rotor has a steel-tube spar and metal (OH-6A, glassfibre) skin. The engine is installed diagonally in the rear fuselage, accessed by clamshell doors. All versions have a cabin with two doors on each side. Side-by-side front seats can have dual controls. The OH-6A seated two passengers behind, or four troops squatting on the floor; current Defenders can seat seven, or take two stretchers and attendants (unless weapons are carried).

Avionics: No helicopter offers a greater range of avionics. The OH-6A seldom carries more than communications radio, ADF, gyrocompass, heading/bearing indicator and IFF. This package has been adapted for the various Defender versions, but current models offer a totally new range of digital equipments linked to a 1553B bus. Basic system management in the latest (530MG) is provided by a Racal RAMS 3000 giving integrated control of all onboard systems and avionics for safe NOE flight in all weather. MDHC claim to have the "most advanced helicopter crew station in the world" enabling a total crew of two to fly almost every kind of mission in the most adverse conditions. Two displays are used, one an MFD with alphanumeric and symbolic data and the other a CDU (control display unit) for flight planning, navigation, frequency selection and subsystem management. Mission avionics include autopilot, Decca doppler integrated with Racal doppler sensor, Ferranti inertial AHRS, ADF/VOR and such options as TOW MMS (mounted on the nose in earlier versions), IFF, FLIR, RWR (usually APR-39), GPWS (ground proximity warning system) and laser ranger. Another option is Black Hole engine exhaust suppression. The 500MD/ASW is equipped with lightweight surveillance radar and an ASQ-81 MAD extended on a cable from the right side (it also has popout floats and ship hauldown gear). All current Defenders can have chaff/flare dispensers fired automatically by threat detection systems.

Armament: The main illustration shows the wealth of equipment fits currently cleared for use on different Defender versions. All have provision for forward-firing weapons, usually hung on standard NATO 14in ejector racks on a tubular mount passing through the rear fuselage. Basic armament of anti-armour versions is two pairs of TOW missiles, with the sight on the left side of the nose for the gunner and a steering indicator for the pilot, or (likely to become standard) the MMS. Both cyclic sticks have triggers for firing guns, rockets or other weapons. The ASW Defender normally carries two Mk 44 or 46 torpedoes.

Future: Development and marketing are now concentrated on the 500MG, the new Paramilitary MG (for low-cost police, border patrol, SAR etc) and the very advanced 530MG. The latter embodies many of the new technologies expected to be used in the US Army LHX.

In addition, Hughes and now McDonnell Douglas Helicopter are using related aircraft to develop the NOTAR and HHC systems, both described in the opening chapters.

Below: Though they share a broadly common airframe, the original OH-6A and today's 530MG are in reality totally different helicopters. The main illustration shows a basic Model 500MD with TOW missiles and the nose-mounted TOW sight. As is often the case, most of the armament fits are used by a minority of export customers, and some are merely tested and available, or applicable to licensed Defender versions.

Key to stores:
1 ASQ-81 towed MAD sensor.
2 12-tube FZ launcher with two 2.75in rockets.
3 7-tube launcher for 2.75in rockets.
4 Twin TOW launcher.
5 TOW missile (wings and fins deployed for use).
6 Martin Pescador attack missile (Argentina).
7 Hughes (McDD Helicopter Co) M230 Chain Gun, 30mm.
8 Mathogo anti-tank missile (Argentina).
9 Spectrolab SX-16 Nightsun searchlight.
10 TOW sight unit (only with TOW installation).
11 XM8 launcher for 40mm grenades.
12 EX-34 Chain Gun in 7.62mm calibre.
13 Twin Stinger installation, with missile.
14 Mk 44 torpedo.
15 Mk 46 torpedo.
16 GE 7.62mm Minigun, in Emerson FTS installation.
17 FN ETNA TMP-5 twin 7.62mm machine-gun pod.
18 Hydra 70 19-tube launcher, with 2.75in rockets (upper, shaped-charge anti-tank; lower, flechette).
19 FN ETNA HMP pod for 0.5in M3P HMG.
20 ALE-39 chaff and flare dispenser.
21 Hughes mast-mounted sight for TOW firing, alternative to 10.

Above: The civil registration N530MG proclaims the identity of this McDonnell Douglas demonstrator, which first flew in May 1984. It carries an exceptional amount of combat equipment including TOW missiles, chin-mounted FLIR and mast-mounted sight. Note tinted windscreen.

McDonnell Douglas AH-64A Apache

Origin: USA, first flight 30 September 1975.

Type: Two-seat anti-armour attack helicopter.

Engines: Two 1,696shp General Electric T700-701 turboshaft engines.

Dimensions: main-rotor diameter 48ft 0in (14.63m); length over tail rotor (ignoring main rotor) 48ft 2in (14.68m); height overall (to tip of air-data sensor) 16ft 9.5in (5.12m).

Weights: Empty (brochure figure) 11,015lb (4996kg); primary-mission gross weight 14,694lb (6665kg); MTO 17,650lb (8006kg).

Performance: Maximum speed (Vne) 227mph (365km/h), (on level) 186mph (300km/h); max cruise 182mph (293km/h); max VROC at SL 2,500ft (762m)/min; hover ceiling (IGE) 13,400ft (4084m), (OGE) 10,200ft (3109m); max range (internal fuel) 428 miles (689km).

Background: The US Army recognized the potential and the need for a dedicated armed helicopter in the early 1960s, but the first attempt to buy one was a failure. The Lockheed AH-56A Cheyenne was a large, complex and expensive machine which in many ways was ahead of its time. Bell managed to meet the immediate need with the smaller and simpler AH-1 HueyCobra series, but the requirement remained for a machine in the class of the Cheyenne, able to fly all front-line attack missions day or night in all weather. The Army grasped the nettle again and in 1972-73 Bell and Hughes designed "clean sheet of paper" rivals, the Hughes being picked in December 1976. Subsequent development was protracted, hundreds of small and large changes being introduced before production was authorized in March 1982. Apart from the rotors most of each Apache is made by Teledyne Ryan, and Hughes (since 1984 a subsidiary of McDonnell Douglas) assembles the helicopters at a new plant at Mesa, Arizona.

Design: Compared with the Cheyenne of 20 years earlier, the Apache is roughly the same size, rather less powerful (though it has two engines instead of one) and somewhat slower. Avionics are in many ways similar, and in fact in some respects the earlier machine was more versatile. The biggest advances are in survivability, the Apache having IR-suppressed engines, comprehensive EW installations (described later) and, above all, an airframe and systems designed to survive strikes from fire of up to 12.7 and 23mm calibre. In general the whole helicopter is conventional, with an all-metal semi-monocoque fuselage and stainless-steel/glassfibre rotor blades. Main blades are attached by multi-laminate straps with quickly removed pins for folding. The hub is articulated, with offset flapping hinges and elastomeric lead/lag dampers. As in the Cobras the pilot sits above and behind the copilot/gunner. Whereas the Cheyenne had retractable landing gear, and the Cobra fixed skids, the Apache has non-retracting tailwheel gear with long-stroke main units designed to cushion crash descents. The tailplane (horizontal stabilizer), originally at the top of the fin, is a powered control surface.

Avionics: The Apache's eyes are TADS/PNVS (target acquisition/ designation sight and pilot's night vision sensor). Though independent the two systems are physically linked and work in parallel. The complete installation was competed for by Martin Marietta and Northrop, the former being selected in April 1982 after prolonged flyoff testing. TADS comprises direct-view optics (wide-field 18° and magnified 4° FOV), a TV camera (NFOV 0.9°, WFOV 4°), a laser spot tracker, and an International Laser Systems laser rangefinder/designator. These are all mounted in a turret (rotating ±120° in azimuth, +30° up and −60° down) and there are extensive fuselage boxes, as well as a primary display for the CPG (copilot/gunner). The TADS can also be switched to provide back-up night vision to the pilot in the event of PNVS failure. The PNVS is simply a FLIR, gyrostabilized and mounted in its own turret above the nose (±90° in azimuth, +20°/ −45° vertically). The FLIR has narrow, medium and wide FOV, respectively 3.1°, 10.1° and 50.0° FOV. The FLIR information is normally presented on a monocle sight (part of the Honeywell IHADSS described elsewhere), on which is superimposed key flight data such as airspeed, radar altitude and heading. In emergency either crew-member can receive video from either the TADS or the PNVS, and both wear IHADSS. NOE flight is assisted by the Litton ASN-143 strapdown AHRS, a simplified inertial system which can store exact target locations, and the Singer-Kearfott lightweight doppler navigation system. Sperry provide the digital autostabilization system, as well as the all-raster (line-by-line, as in TV) generator which processes video signals from TADS/PNVS and feeds them to the cockpit display(s) and IHADSS monocle(s). Other equipment includes ADF, UHF/VHF/AM/FM secure communications, IFF with secure encoding, an omnidirectional air-data system, passive RWR, IR jammer, radar jammer and chaff dispensers.

Armament: Weapons comprise a remotely aimed gun and stores carried under fixed wings. The gun, contracted for along with the helicopter, is the Hughes 30mm M230A1 Chain Gun, a unique single-barrel weapon with external power and a rotating bolt driven by a chain which permits a simplified cycle. In the Apache it is normally controlled to 625rpm, the magazine capacity being 1,200 rounds. Lear Siegler provide the electronic control system, with aiming possible anywhere in the area covered by the sighting systems. In a crash the complete gun mount collapses upwards between the cockpits. The weapon wings, of 17ft 2in (5.23m) span, can carry four pylons each supporting either a quadruple group of Hellfire anti-tank missiles (maximum, 16) or a 19-tube 2.75in rocket launcher (maximum 76 rockets); or up to four 192 gal (871lit) external fuel tanks. The artwork also shows the armament proposed for the naval version, which would carry AAMs (initially AIM-9L Sidewinders) on the wingtips, and various attack missiles up to the size of the AGM-84 Harpoon cruise anti-ship missile.

Future: The Apache production programme has fluctuated in size but since 1984 has stabilized at a planned 675 for the US Army alone, notwithstanding a price much more than double the original ceiling figure (a rise caused mainly by inflation). There is the immediate prospect of export sales, the chief visible customer being Israel. The Navy/Marines had not completed project definition as this was written.

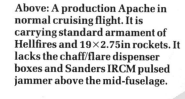

Above: A production Apache in normal cruising flight. It is carrying standard armament of Hellfires and 19×2.75in rockets. It lacks the chaff/flare dispenser boxes and Sanders IRCM pulsed jammer above the mid-fuselage.

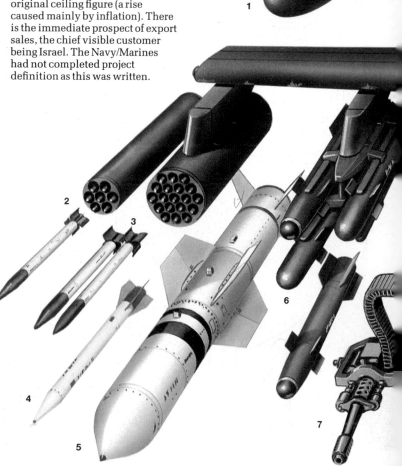

Below: Despite its advanced nature and great complexity, currently the Apache is in production in only one version. The main artwork, however, has to take into account the proposed Marine Corps model (shipboard, Sidewinders but no gun), and the Navy Sea Apache (probably with radar and anti-ship missiles). Both could in theory perform many useful sea and amphibious combat roles, but the situation is still fluid.

Key to stores:
1 Long-range tank, 192 Imp gal (871 lit).
2 Hughes XM260 or other launcher with 2.75in rocket.
3 Standard 19-tube launcher with 2.75in rockets.
4 Zuni heavy rocket, 5in (127mm) calibre.
5 AGM-84 Harpoon (proposed Sea Apache only).
6 Quad Hellfire installation, one missile detached.
7 M230 30mm Chain Gun shown detached.
8 Chain Gun in position under fuselage.
9 TADS sensor group.
10 Aerospace radar-warning receivers.
11 PNVS.
12 Quad TOW launcher, with one missile.
13 Penguin Mk2 Mod 7 missile (Sea Apache).
14 AGM-122A Sidearm anti-radar missile.
15 Twin Stinger box, with missile.
16 AIM-9L Sidewinder (Marine Corps and Sea Apache).
17 M130 chaff/flare dispenser on rear fuselage.
18 ALQ-144 IRCM pulsed jammer.
19 Black Hole IR-suppressed exhaust.
20 Air-data sensors on rotor mast.

Mil Mi-2

Origin: Soviet Union, manufactured only in Poland, first flight September 1961.
Type: Multirole light helicopter, with armed versions.
Engines: Two PZL (Isotov) turboshafts, (most) 400shp GTD-350, (1986) 444shp GTD-350P.
Dimensions: Diameter of three-blade main rotor 47ft 6.9in (14.5m); length (rotors turning) 57ft 2in (17.42m), (ignoring rotors) 37ft 4.8in (11.4m); height (to top of rotor head) 12ft 3.6in (3.75m).
Weights: Empty (cargo) 5,229lb (2372kg); maximum loaded (normal) 7,826lb (3550kg), (special versions) 8,157lb (3700kg).
Performance: Maximum sustained speed 124mph (200km/h); speed for best range (low level) 118mph (190km/h); maximum rate of climb 886ft (270m)/min; hovering ceiling OGE about 3,280ft (1000m); range (low level, max payload, 5 per cent reserve) 105 miles (170km).
Background: The Mi-2 (also designated V-2, short for "helicopter type 2") was designed in the Soviet Union by the experimental bureau of M.I.Mil. A natural successor to Mil's original production helicopter, the Mi-1, the Mi-2 actually came after the much larger Mi-4 and Mi-6, being designed at the end of the 1950s. Instead of a single piston engine behind the short cabin, as in the Mi-1, the Mi-2 has two small turboshafts above the fuselage. This enabled the cabin to be much larger. After its flight-test programme the Mi-1 (called Hoplite by NATO) was transferred to the Polish industry for production, as is normally the case with all light and general-aviation machines. Since 1965 the factory of PZL-Swidnik has delivered well over 4,500 Mi-2 helicopters in many versions. The 24 customers include the air forces of the Soviet Union, Poland, Cuba, Czechoslovakia and Romania.
Design: In all respects the Mi-2 is conventional. Its performance,

especially in the climb, is unimpressive and it has gained so many orders for the valid reasons that it is very highly developed, is very keenly priced and is available in many versions with equipment for almost every conceivable role. The main rotor has a fully articulated hub carrying three blades of a common NACA section (230-13M, slightly thicker than the 230-12 used by the MBB BO 105). The D-spar is a duralumin extrusion, and the lifting part of the blade is completed by bonding on 20 light honeycomb-filled trailing-edge pockets which can be either aluminium or glassfibre. Anti-flutter masses are built into the leading edges, while the trailing edges are fitted with ground-adjustable balance tabs. Hydraulic dampers are fitted, and unduplicated boosters assist the pilot on all cyclic axes. Electric deicing is fitted for both main and tail rotors, as well as a rotor brake, but the blades do not fold. The engines are spaced wide apart, with hot bleed-air deicing and twin exhaust pipes on each side. Between the engines are inlets for air-conditioning and for the fan-assisted oil cooler. The fuselage is light-alloy with steel used at major joints. In front is the cockpit, seating the pilot alone on the left. The cabin behind is 7ft 5.4in (2.27m) long (13ft 4.2in, 4.07m, including the cockpit), 4ft (1.2m) wide and 4ft 7in (1.4m) high. Seating can be provided for eight passengers, or up to 1,543lb (700kg) of cargo can be loaded through two forward-hinged doors

on the right and one on the left. In the ambulance role four stretchers can be carried, with an attendant. Optional equipment includes an under-fuselage hook rated at 1,764lb (800kg) for slung loads and a 264lb (120kg) electric rescue hoist. The horizontal stabilizer (tailplane) is pivoted and controlled by the collective circuit to maintain trim. The fixed landing gear includes a twin-wheel nose unit, pneumatically braked main wheels and a tailskid, and skis are an option. A single 131gal (600lit) rubber fuel tank under the floor can be supplemented by a 52.4gal (238lit) external tank on each side.
Avionics: All Mi-2 versions include HF and VHF radio, gyro compass, radio compass, radar altimeter, blind-flying instruments

and intercom. The windscreen has a wiper and is electrically heated. So far as is known no special sensors are fitted to military versions other than nose and tail RWR, with an option of IR warning also, and an operator sight for guiding anti-tank missiles. For survey and mapping purposes various cameras can be installed in the floor. No dedicated military reconnaissance version has been seen to date.

Below: The Mi-2 is a standard light helicopter throughout the Warsaw Pact forces. This example is serving with the Soviet ground forces, and is seen fulfilling the battlefield reconnaissance and communications task. Newly printed battle situation maps are being delivered to the crew of a PT-76 amphibious tank.

Above: Most Mi-2 helicopters are devoid of advanced combat equipment and are used for liaison and communications. This example in service with the PWL (Polish air force) has a passenger interior, and like most Mi-2s is fitted with a 238lit auxiliary fuel tank on each side. The airframe has provision for weapons.

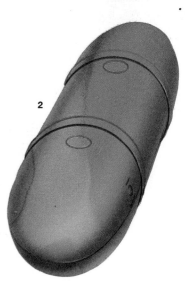

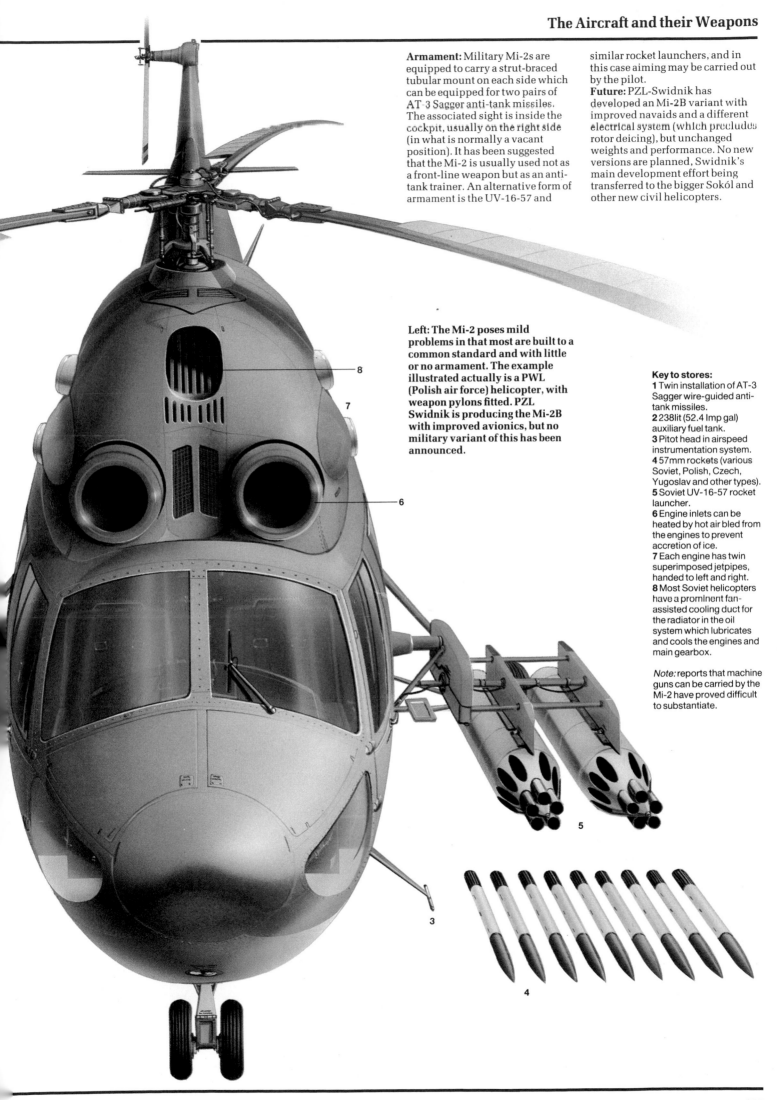

Armament: Military Mi-2s are equipped to carry a strut-braced tubular mount on each side which can be equipped for two pairs of AT-3 Sagger anti-tank missiles. The associated sight is inside the cockpit, usually on the right side (in what is normally a vacant position). It has been suggested that the Mi-2 is usually used not as a front-line weapon but as an anti-tank trainer. An alternative form of armament is the UV-16-57 and similar rocket launchers, and in this case aiming may be carried out by the pilot.

Future: PZL-Swidnik has developed an Mi-2B variant with improved navaids and a different electrical system (which precludes rotor deicing), but unchanged weights and performance. No new versions are planned, Swidnik's main development effort being transferred to the bigger Sokól and other new civil helicopters.

Left: The Mi-2 poses mild problems in that most are built to a common standard and with little or no armament. The example illustrated actually is a PWL (Polish air force) helicopter, with weapon pylons fitted. PZL Swidnik is producing the Mi-2B with improved avionics, but no military variant of this has been announced.

Key to stores:
1 Twin installation of AT-3 Sagger wire-guided anti-tank missiles.
2 238lit (52.4 Imp gal) auxiliary fuel tank.
3 Pitot head in airspeed instrumentation system.
4 57mm rockets (various Soviet, Polish, Czech, Yugoslav and other types).
5 Soviet UV-16-57 rocket launcher.
6 Engine inlets can be heated by hot air bled from the engines to prevent accretion of ice.
7 Each engine has twin superimposed jetpipes, handed to left and right.
8 Most Soviet helicopters have a prominent fan-assisted cooling duct for the radiator in the oil system which lubricates and cools the engines and main gearbox.

Note: reports that machine guns can be carried by the Mi-2 have proved difficult to substantiate.

Mil Mi-4, Harbin Z-5

Origin: Soviet Union, first flight May 1952; Z-5 built in China (see Background).

Type: Assault transport, ASW and SAR helicopter.

Engine: Originally one 1,700hp Shvetsov ASh-82V (Chinese HS-5A) 14-cylinder radial piston engine, (Z-5 derivative) one 1,875shp Pratt & Whitney Canada PT6T-6 twin-turboshaft.

Dimensions: Diameter of four-blade rotor 68ft 11in (21.0m); length (rotors turning) 82ft 1in (25.02m), (ignoring rotors) 55ft 1in (16.79m); height (overall) 17ft 0in (5.18m).

Weights: Empty (typical of utility Mi-4 and Z-5) 11,883lb (5390kg); maximum loaded (Mi-4 military and ASW) 17,196lb (7800kg).

Performance: Maximum sustained speed at SL 130mph (210km/h); normal cruising speed 99mph (160km/h) (Z-5 with PT6T, same as maximum); hovering ceiling OGE (at 15,983lb, 7250kg) 2,280ft (695m); range (11 passengers and baggage) 155 miles (250km).

Background: In September 1951 Soviet designers were summoned to the Kremlin and ordered by Stalin to build larger and more capable helicopters. All found excuses except Mil and Yakovlev. Eventually it was agreed Mil would build a large helicopter with an ASh-82 engine and single rotor, while the Yak bureau would build a heavier tandem-rotor machine using the same engine and rotors. Despite intense pressure to complete development within a year (which was accomplished) the Mi-4 emerged as a thoroughly successful machine. Assessed in the West as "a copy of the S-55" it was in fact more than three times as powerful. It sustained a major production programme, over 3,500 being built (in batches separated by intervals) by 1966. In addition about 1,000 were built in China from 1959, with licensed engines incorporating small differences.

Design: In 1951 the bulk and weight of large piston engines limited the number of ways a transport helicopter could be designed. Mil followed the layout of the S-55, with the engine mounted in the nose, in a fireproof compartment normally enclosed by large left/right clamshell doors. The engine was mounted diagonally, the crankshaft axis being at an angle of 25° to drive straight up via clutch and cooling fan to the main gearbox. As in the S-55 the shaft passes up between the seats on the high cockpit, which usually has dual controls. Pilots climb aboard via kick-in steps up the side of the fuselage, entering via a sliding window on each side, or they can enter the main cabin via the door at the rear on the left or the full-width rear clamshell doors which can admit bulky cargo or small vehicles up to a maximum weight of 3,836lb (1740kg). Maximum slung load is 2,866lb (1300kg). Early Mi-4s had tapered blades with wood/fabric aerofoils on a steel-tube spar. These vibrated and had very short life, and from 1954 were replaced by much longer untapered all-metal blades with bonded honeycomb rear pockets. Alcohol deicing is used for the blades of both rotors and cockpit windscreens. Hydraulic boosters are used in the flight controls, and the collective circuit controls the angle of the horizontal stabilizer. Most versions have fixed landing gears, with optional skis or pontoon floats, but some Z-5s appear to have only a single nose gear. Civil and VIP versions have three large square windows each side, but the mass-produced military versions have smaller circular windows. All Soviet (but not Chinese) military variants have a ventral gondola for a navigator/observer whose task is to guide the pilots into restricted landing zones or other sites. The Chinese found the view ahead and down from the open sides of the cockpit fully adequate and omit the gondola. In the assault role the usual troop load is 16, while in the casevac mission eight stretchers can be carried with a seated attendant. There are specialized ASW and EW tactical jamming versions.

Avionics: All versions have full night and winter equipment, but are not cleared for blind low-level flight. Standard equipment includes VHF and HF communications, radar altimeter, radio compass and directional gyros. Many have SRO-2 IFF, and other options include Tacan/DME and Sirena RWRs covering both to front and rear. The ASW model has a chin-mounted radar, side-mounted sonobuoys and rear-mounted MAD normally recessed into the clamshell doors. The special EW version, called Hound-C by NATO, is distinguished by front and rear pairs of enormous projecting rods carrying Yagi arrays of dipole aerials. These are strongly directional arrays thought to be used for transmitting jamming signals to blot out enemy communications.

Armament: Most Soviet assault Mi-4 transports were equipped for firing infantry weapons from the windows. Some had a heavy machine gun aimed ahead from the navigator's gondola, while in

Above: One of the better-known recipients of the Mi-4 was Finland's Ilmavoimat, which purchased three for use in a transport squadron based at Utti. They had the standard gondola and were equipped for heavy slung loads, while a rescue hoist was installed inside the side door. These machines have been replaced by Mi-8s.

exercises in the 1960s small groups carried forward-firing rocket launchers and gun pods. The ASW version carried a single AS torpedo or other store. Chinese Z-5s are unarmed and used for assault transport or, by the Navy, in the SAR role.

Future: No decision had been taken in 1985 on whether to re-engine existing Z-5s with the coupled PT6T turboshaft. It is considered more likely that the Chinese will use this engine in a new helicopter.

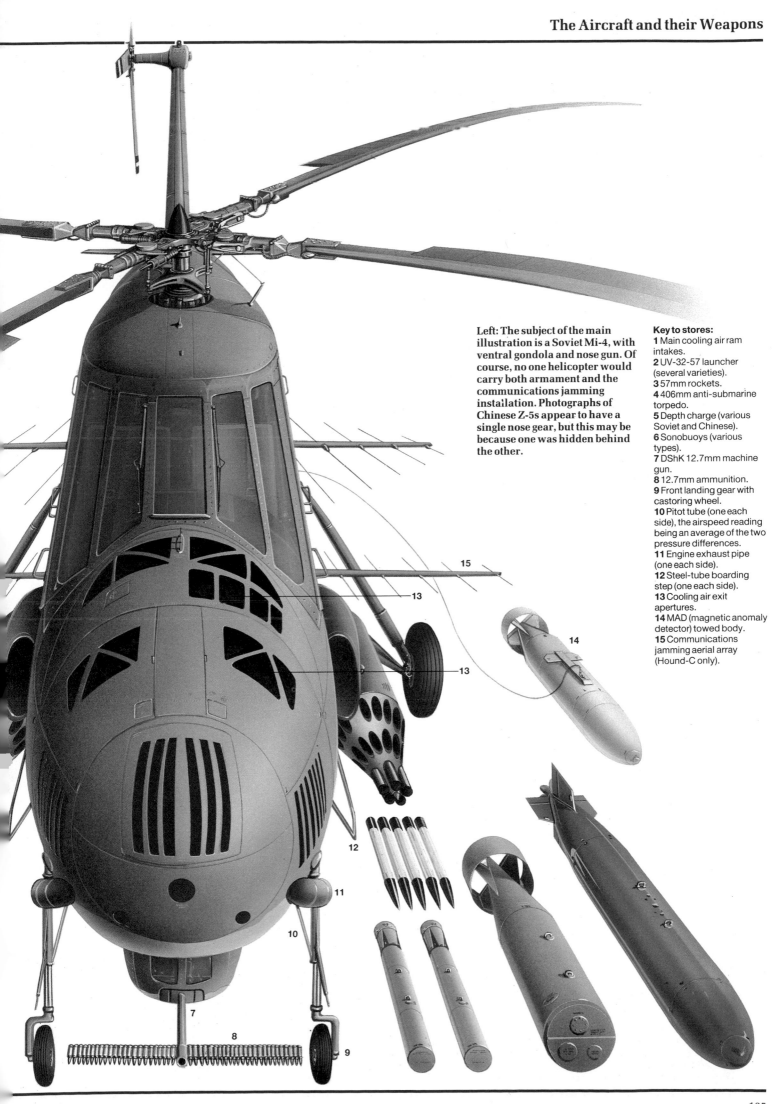

Left: The subject of the main illustration is a Soviet Mi-4, with ventral gondola and nose gun. Of course, no one helicopter would carry both armament and the communications jamming installation. Photographs of Chinese Z-5s appear to have a single nose gear, but this may be because one was hidden behind the other.

Key to stores:
1 Main cooling air ram intakes.
2 UV-32-57 launcher (several varieties).
3 57mm rockets.
4 406mm anti-submarine torpedo.
5 Depth charge (various Soviet and Chinese).
6 Sonobuoys (various types).
7 DShK 12.7mm machine gun.
8 12.7mm ammunition.
9 Front landing gear with castoring wheel.
10 Pitot tube (one each side), the airspeed reading being an average of the two pressure differences.
11 Engine exhaust pipe (one each side).
12 Steel-tube boarding step (one each side).
13 Cooling air exit apertures.
14 MAD (magnetic anomaly detector) towed body.
15 Communications jamming aerial array (Hound-C only).

Mil Mi-6

Origin: Soviet Union, first flight September 1957.

Type: Heavy transport helicopter.

Engines: Two 5,500shp Soloviev D-25V (TV-2BM) free-turbine turboshafts.

Dimensions: Diameter of five-blade main rotor 114ft 10in (35.0m): length (rotors turning) 136ft 11.3in (41.739m), (ignoring rotors) 108ft 10.3in (33.179m); height (rotor head) 22ft 0in (6.71m), (over tail rotor) 32ft 4in (9.86m).

Weights: Empty 60,053lb (27240kg); maximum loaded 93,695lb (42500kg).

Performance: Maximum level speed 186mph (300km/h); maximum cruising speed 155mph (250km/h); climb at 89,285lb (40500kg) time 9.7min to 9,843ft (3000m); hovering ceiling OGE not published (IGE at 88,183lb/ 40000kg is 8,202ft/2500m); range (17,637lb/8000kg payload, internal fuel) 373 miles (600km).

Background: Originally known as the V-6, and dubbed Hook by NATO, the Mi-6 was by a very wide margin the largest helicopter in the world when it appeared in 1957. It was also the fastest, despite its completely conventional design, the only unusual feature being the optional addition of wings (of 50ft 2.5in, 15.3m span) to unload the main rotor slightly in cruising flight. Built to meet a 1954 joint civil/military requirement, the Mi-6 was intended for heavy military assault, with the capability of landing heavy rockets on their launch vehicles, or any other loads up to 12 tonnes, and also of serving in the heavy crane and short-haul airlift role with Aeroflot, for example in opening up previously unexplored regions in mountains, deserts and, especially, in Siberia. It proved remarkably successful, over 800 being delivered to many customers. Over 400 still serve in the military role in the Soviet Union, Algeria, Egypt, Iraq, Peru and Vietnam.

Design: The Mi-6 was the world's first helicopter of modern configuration with twin turbine engines mounted above the fuselage adjacent to the main gearbox, thus leaving the cabin completely unobstructed. An indication of the size of this

helicopter is given by the statistics for the main R-7 gearbox, which accepts the front drive from the two parallel engines, reduces speed by 69.2:1 to the rotor shaft and also drives the oil-cooler fan (served by the third front ram inlet) and tail rotor. This box is about 79in (2.0m) square and 10ft (3m) high, and weighs 7,055lb (3200kg) exclusive of oil. Everything else about the Mi-6 is on the same grand scale, but based on the technology of the mid-1950s. The enormous main hub is fully articulated and fabricated in steel, with coincident flapping and drag hings and control via welded swashplates moved by triple hydraulic boosters, one in each independent system. The blades are of TsAGI-modified NACA 23011 section (11 per cent thickness) with an extruded spar of high-tensile steel tube with sections of aerofoil attached by bonding and countersunk screws. The tail rotor has "bakelite ply" (a plastic-impregnated wood veneer) blades with steel spars. Early Mi-6s had electrothermal deicing of all blades, later changed to alcohol. The fuselage, tailboom and wing are all flush-riveted in light alloy, the wing (which is removed in the crane role) being set at 15.75° incidence to provide one-fifth of the gross lift in cruising flight. The flight deck has four jettisonable doors and seats two pilots, navigator, radio operator and flight

engineer. The main cabin is about 39ft 4in (12.0m) long, measured from the flight-deck rear bulkhead, 8ft 8.3in (2.65m) wide at the floor (about 10ft, 3m, higher up) and from 6ft 7in (2.01m) high at the front to heights from 8ft 6in (2.59m) to 8ft 8in (2.64m) over most of the length. Full-width rear clamshell doors and vehicle ramps are moved hydraulically, ground power being provided by a 100hp gas-turbine APU mounted on a trolley and used for main-engine starting. Maximum payload is 26,455lb (12000kg) internal or 19,841lb (9000kg) as a slung load. Normally tip-up wall seats are provided for 70 equipped troops, but 20 additional seats can be attached down the centre of the cargo floor. In the casevac role 41 stretcher casualties can be carried, with two seated attendants. Standard equipment includes a 1,764lb (800kg) cargo loading and positioning winch, with pulley blocks to multiply the force. There are three cabin side doors, two on the left and one on the right. Maximum fuel capacity of 3,794gal (17250lit) is accommodated in 11 fuselage cells and four auxiliary (ferry) drums, two internal and two slung externally. Other features

include fixed landing gear (no ski or pontoon options) and a pivoted horizontal stabilizer connected to the collective circuit for trim.

Avionics: Standard equipment includes three-axis autopilot, blind-flying and night instrumentation, VHF and HF radio, intercom, radio compass, directional gyro, marker beacon

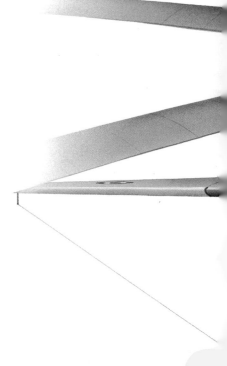

Below: Bearing the serial number 21874, this civilian Mi-6 was photographed whilst operating in the Yamalo-Nenets autonomous *okrug* (district), in typical tundra.

Below: A relatively rare recent view (July 1985) of military Mi-6As seen during Exercise Caucasus '85. Note the 12.7mm nose guns. In the background are Mi-24 Hind-Ds.

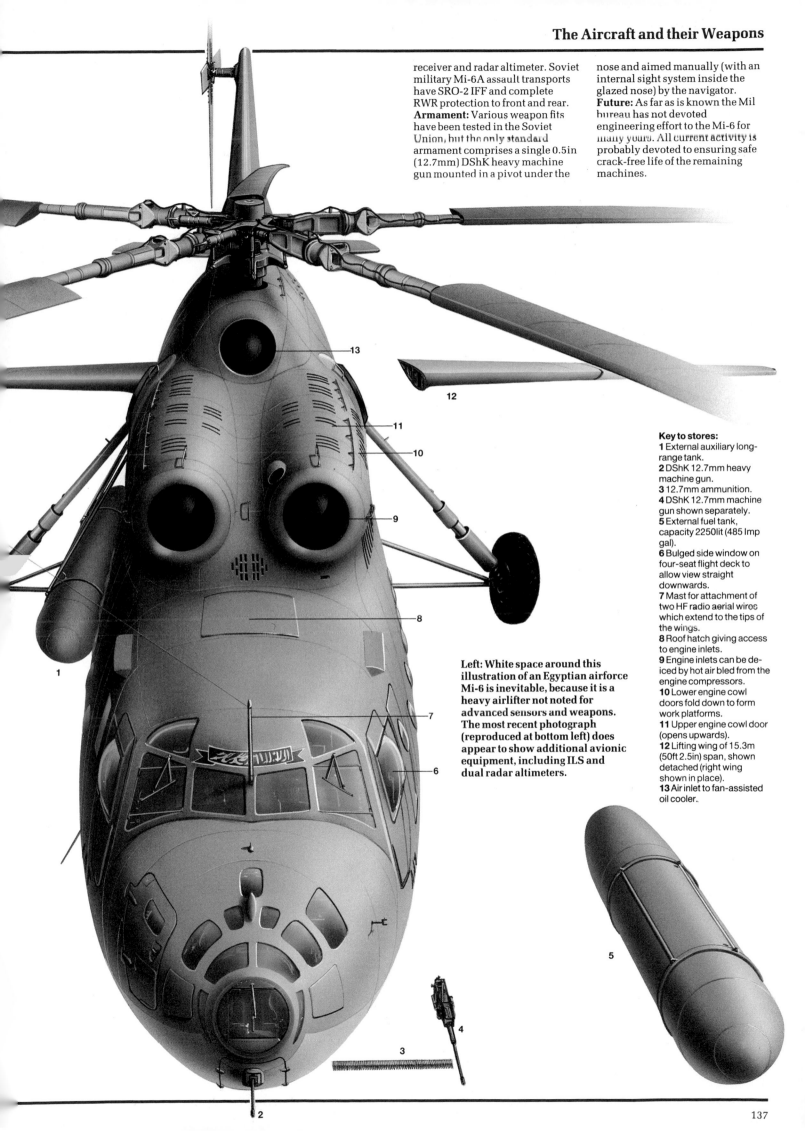

receiver and radar altimeter. Soviet military Mi-6A assault transports have SRO-2 IFF and complete RWR protection to front and rear.
Armament: Various weapon fits have been tested in the Soviet Union, but the only standard armament comprises a single 0.5in (12.7mm) DShK heavy machine gun mounted in a pivot under the nose and aimed manually (with an internal sight system inside the glazed nose) by the navigator.
Future: As far as is known the Mil bureau has not devoted engineering effort to the Mi-6 for many years. All current activity is probably devoted to ensuring safe crack-free life of the remaining machines.

Left: White space around this illustration of an Egyptian airforce Mi-6 is inevitable, because it is a heavy airlifter not noted for advanced sensors and weapons. The most recent photograph (reproduced at bottom left) does appear to show additional avionic equipment, including ILS and dual radar altimeters.

Key to stores:
1 External auxiliary long-range tank.
2 DShK 12.7mm heavy machine gun.
3 12.7mm ammunition.
4 DShK 12.7mm machine gun shown separately.
5 External fuel tank, capacity 2250lit (485 Imp gal).
6 Bulged side window on four-seat flight deck to allow view straight downwards.
7 Mast for attachment of two HF radio aerial wires which extend to the tips of the wings.
8 Roof hatch giving access to engine inlets.
9 Engine inlets can be de-iced by hot air bled from the engine compressors.
10 Lower engine cowl doors fold down to form work platforms.
11 Upper engine cowl door (opens upwards).
12 Lifting wing of 15.3m (50ft 2.5in) span, shown detached (right wing shown in place).
13 Air inlet to fan-assisted oil cooler.

Mil Mi-8 and Mi-17

Origin: Soviet Union, first flight see Background.

Type: Multirole transport helicopter.

Engines: Two Isotov free-turbine turboshafts, (8) 1,700shp TV2-117A, (17) TV3-117MT each rated at 1,900shp and with 2,200shp emergency single-engine rating.

Dimensions: Diameter of five-blade main rotor 69ft 10.2in (21.29m); length (rotors turning, 8) 82ft 9.7in (25.24m), (rotors turning, 17) 83ft 2in (25.352m), (ignoring rotors, 8) 59ft 7.4in (18.17m), (ignoring rotors, 17) 60ft 5.4in (18.424m); height (rotor head) 15ft 7.2in (4.755m), (overall) 18ft 6.5in (5.65m).

Weights: Empty (8 cargo) 14,603lb (6624kg), (8 military) 16,005lb (7260kg), (17) 15,653lb (7100kg); maximum loaded (8) 26,455lb (12000kg), (17) 28,660lb (13000kg).

Performance: Maximum speed at SL at max wt (8) 143mph (230km/h), (17) 155mph (250km/h); maximum cruising speed at max wt (8) 112mph (180km/h), (17) 149mph (240km/h); hovering ceiling OGE at normal gross wt of 24,470lb/11100kg for both, (8) 2,625ft (800m), (17) 5,774ft (1760m); range (standard fuel, max wt, 5 per cent reserve, 8) 276 miles (445km), (17) 289 miles (465km).

Background: The need to find a modern twin-turbine successor to the Mi-4 was obvious by the late 1950s, but nobody could reasonably have predicted the scale on which this outstanding transport helicopter would be built. Though considerably bigger, more powerful and more capacious than a Sea King the Mi-8 has rolled off the production lines at two plants (at Kazan and Ulan Ude) at such a sustained tempo that deliveries exceed 10,000, and production has now transferred to the more powerful Mi-17. The new TV2 engine was not ready in time for the first prototype, which flew in early 1961 with a derated Soloviev D-25 engine and an interim four-blade (modified Mi-4) main rotor. This machine, designated V-8 and dubbed Hip-A by NATO, was soon followed by the second V-8 fitted with early TV2 engines and an interim five-blade rotor, flown on 17 September 1962. Rather protracted development, with new main rotor hub and blades introduced in 1964, delayed production to 1966. Subsequently many versions, by far the most numerous being the basic (civil/military) Mi-8T, were produced.

Design: The configuration is similar to that pioneered with the Mi-6, with an unobstructed cabin and nose cockpit hung under left/right handed engines mounted parallel ahead of the main gearbox, with the tail and anti-torque rotor carried on a slim boom and with fixed tricycle landing gear with twin nosewheels. The main hub is machined from high-strength steel and carries the five blades in conventional oil-lubricated hinges, those for flapping and drag being a few inches apart. Each blade has an extruded D-spar with gas-pressure warning of cracks, and with the NACA 230 profile completed by screwing on 21 honeycomb-filled trailing pockets, structure being light alloy throughout. Flight control forces are applied by duplicated hydraulic boosters, and automatic controls link collective to engine power, synchronize the two engine speeds and torques and, in the Mi-17, open up either engine to its contingency rating following failure of the other. The Mi-17 can be identified by the shorter engine cowlings, similar to those of the Mi-14 and Mi-24. It also has the tail rotor on the left. Both have a side-by-side cockpit with dual controls and an engineer seat behind, with access via the huge bulged side windows which both slide to the rear. Both helicopters are equipped for icing conditions, with electrically heated windscreens and rotor blades and with bleed-air heating of the engine inlets. The main cabin measures 7ft 8in (2.34m) wide, 5ft 10.9in (1.8m) high and a length varying from 17ft 6.2in (5.34m) in the cargo role (with full-section rear clamshell doors and vehicle ramps) to 20ft 10.4in (6.36m) in the passenger role. The main aft-sliding door on the left side can be equipped with a 331lb (150kg) electric rescue hoist. Maximum cargo load in the Mi-8T and Mi-17 is 8,818lb (4000kg) internal and 6,614lb (3000kg) on a sling; in the troop or passenger role up to 32 cabin seats can be installed, and the casevac version carries 12 stretcher patients and an attendant. Up to 814gal (3700lit) of fuel can be carried in the main tank, two external drums and two ferry tanks strapped in the cabin; the right external tank has reduced capacity because ahead of it is a long fairing for optional air-conditioning as an alternative to the standard cabin heating.

Avionics: Standard equipment on the military 8T includes HF and VHF, intercom, radio compass, radar altimeter with GPWS, 4-axis autopilot with autohover, and doppler (in box under tailboom). Soviet machines have SRO-2M IFF, Tacan/DME, Sirena RWR (360°), chaff/flare dispenser, IR jammer and IR suppressed engines.

Armament: The most common Soviet assault variant, NATO Hip-E, is described as the world's most heavily armed helicopter with a 0.5in (12.7mm) DShK gun aimed from the cockpit, 192 rockets of 57mm calibre and four AT-2 Swatter missiles for use against armour or fortifications. Other known weapon fits are illustrated. So far no military Mi-17 has been seen, though production for foreign air forces has been announced and it is certain that this helicopter is replacing the Mi-8 in production. New weapon fits may be expected.

Future: As predicted immediately above, future armed versions of the Mi-17 (called Hip-H by NATO) are to be expected, and these may differ from versions of the Mi-8. The basic design is so satisfactory that it may be some time before a completely new helicopter in the 13-tonne class makes its appearance, despite the fact that by most standards the technology is obsolescent (see comments under Background in next entry, Mi-14).

Below: The helicopter depicted as the subject of the main artwork is a Soviet Hip-E, but additionally showing the communications jamming aerials of the specialized Hip-K. The Mk 46 torpedo shown is used on export versions of the Mi-8. Further upgrades and conversions are bound to appear in the next few years.

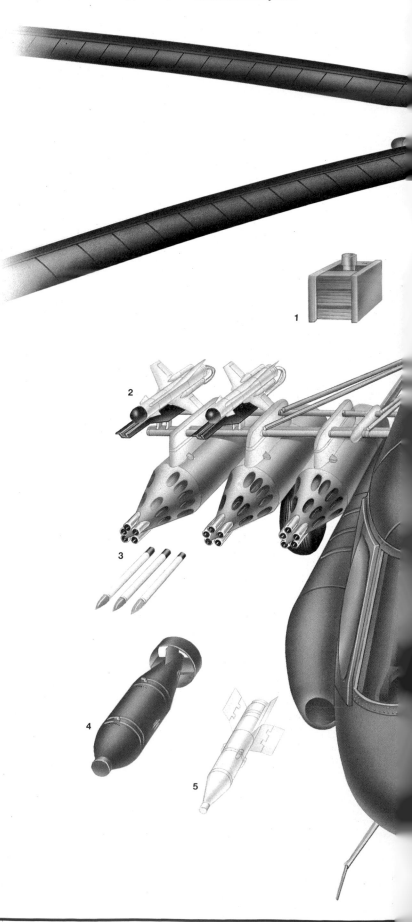

Right: Photographed during Exercise Bright Star in 1980, this Egyptian Mi-8 (basic Hip-C) carries the number 1420. A standard fit is a twin rack for stores on each side; though much less than the weapons capability of the Hip-E version, the basic machine can still carry 128 rockets of 57mm calibre.

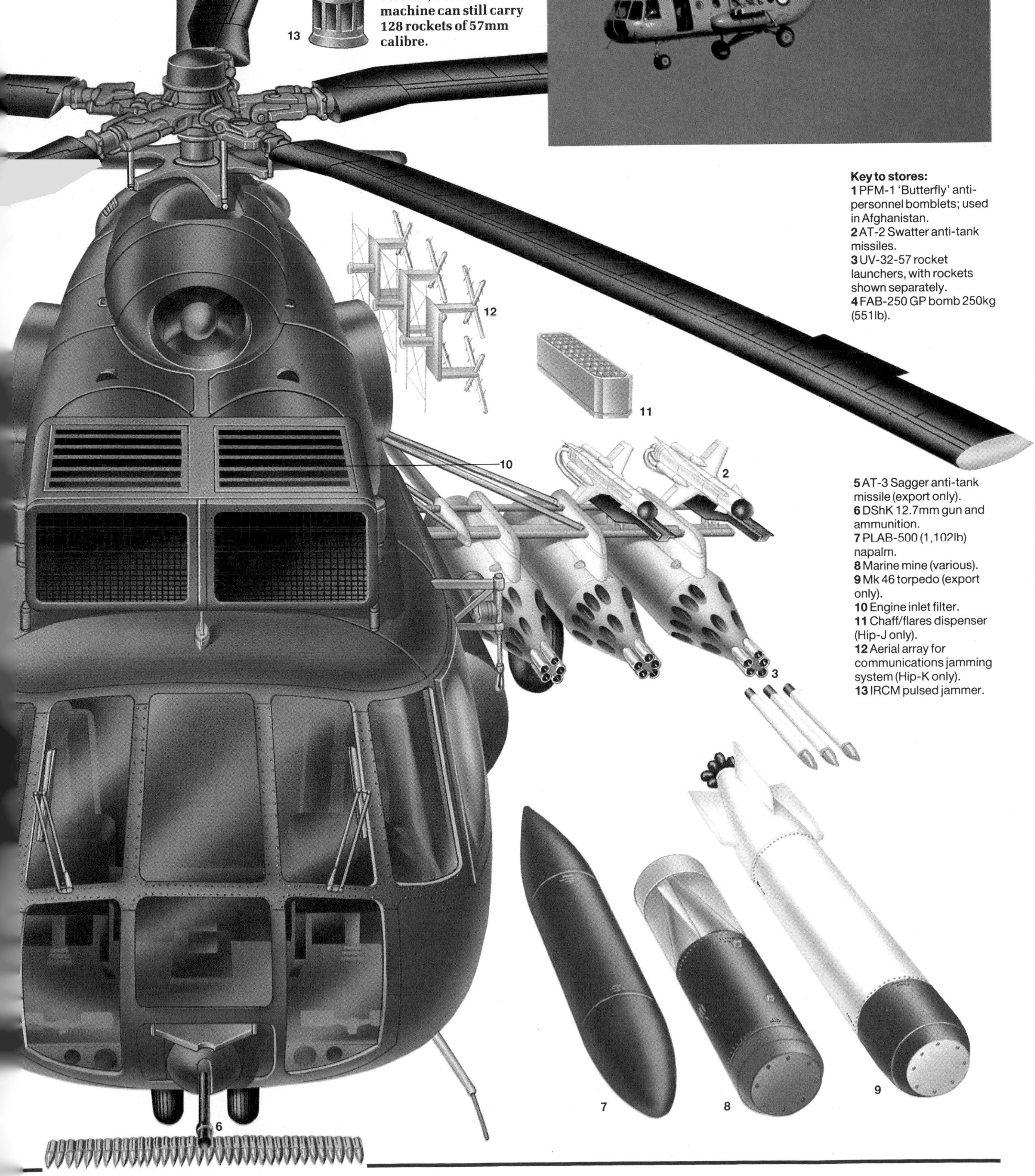

13

Key to stores:
1 PFM-1 'Butterfly' anti-personnel bomblets; used in Afghanistan.
2 AT-2 Swatter anti-tank missiles.
3 UV-32-57 rocket launchers, with rockets shown separately.
4 FAB-250 GP bomb 250kg (551lb).

12

11

10

2

5 AT-3 Sagger anti-tank missile (export only).
6 DShK 12.7mm gun and ammunition.
7 PLAB-500 (1,102lb) napalm.
8 Marine mine (various).
9 Mk 46 torpedo (export only).
10 Engine inlet filter.
11 Chaff/flares dispenser (Hip-J only).
12 Aerial array for communications jamming system (Hip-K only).
13 IRCM pulsed jammer.

3

6

7   **8**   **9**

Mil Mi-14

Origin: Soviet Union, first flight 1973.

Type: Shore-based ASW helicopter.

Engines: Two 2,200shp Isotov TV3-117 turboshafts.

Dimensions: Diameter of five-blade main rotor 69ft 10.2in (21.29m); length (rotors turning) 83ft 0in (25.3m), (ignoring rotors) 60ft 5.4in (18.424m); height overall 22ft 7.7in (6.9m).

Weights: Empty equipped, about 19,400lb (8800kg); maximum loaded 30,864lb (14000kg).

Performance: Maximum speed (max wt, SL) 143mph (230km/h); maximum cruising speed 124mph (200km/h); hovering ceilings, not published but very low at max wt; range (maximum fuel) 497 miles (800km).

Background: During the 1970s the Mil design bureau proposed several advanced derivatives of the Mi-8 with TV3-117 engines, amphibious boat hulls, fully retractable landing gear and a full-section rear ramp door resembling that of the American S-61R. None of these went ahead, though the TV3 engine was adopted for the Mi-17, a minimum-change Mi-8. It was also adopted for the almost completely new Mi-24 family, which flew initially with TV2 engines, and also for the V-14 prototype of a new ASW helicopter for operation from shore bases. In most respects the V-14 used exactly the same engine installations and dynamic parts as the Mi-17, but it introduced a new fuselage and landing gear as already studied for Mi-8 versions. The new helicopter, designated Mi-14 and called Haze by NATO, was needed to replace the Mi-4 ASW version in operations from shore bases of the AV-MF. It has also been widely exported and developed into an MCM version.

Design: Most of this helicopter is common to at least one other Mil production type, the engines and rotors being the same as the Mi-17, though the variable-incidence horizontal stabilizer is apparently larger and of less-tapered shape and the fin (rotor pylon) is of a new design. The obviously new area concerns the lower half of the fuselage, which despite incorporating two large side-by-side weapon bays is sealed for amphibious operation from calm water. Stability on the sea is provided by two rear sponson floats and a third small float under the tail. The new landing gear comprises left and right single-wheel nose units spaced as far apart as possible (as on the Mi-4), retracting hydraulically into open bays on each side of the fore-part of the planing bottom of the hull, and twin-wheel main gears which retract backwards to be housed in open bays in the undersides of the sponsons. Along the side of each sponson is a rounded fairing which at the rear becomes a deep vertical fin, the lower part of which is submerged when the helicopter is waterborne. No external fuel tanks are carried by the Mi-14 and it has been suggested, probably correctly, that fuel is carried in the rear and outer parts of the sponsons. Apart from the important addition of ASW sensors, and, in a version called Haze-B, MCM (mine countermeasures) gear, the rest of the fuselage and boom structure is little changed from that of the Mi-17. The cockpit, doors and windows are externally unchanged, though at the rear the main cabin is sealed off. Instead of clamshell rear loading doors the main pod section of fuselage is cut short and terminates in a bluff rounded fairing containing the MAD cable reel and winch and, lower down, various other sensors. Grouping sensors, and possibly the internal displays, as far aft as possible helps to balance the extra mass of the radar under the nose. The two pilots also act as visual observers, and in the tactical compartment are three sensor operators.

Avionics: Not very much is known about the Mi-14, despite service since 1976 with six export customers. Clearly basic communications and navigation equipment is at least as good as in other Soviet large helicopters, and the Mi-14 is equipped for day and night operation in icing conditions. Its autopilot and autostabilization system enables the pilots to translate automatically from forwards flight to a hover at any given height for dipping sonar, irrespective (within limits) of wind and sea state. The dipping sonar is extended from a recess in the right underside of the rear of the fuselage. Immediately to the rear of it are two large chutes for sonobuoys, of which a reported 32 can be carried internally. In the centre of the rear fuselage is the MAD "bird", which appears to be of the same pattern as carried since the 1960s by the ASW version of the Mi-4. Centred under the rear of the fuselage are two projecting cylinders which are too large to be RWR or ESM installations (though the Mi-14 is very fully equipped with defensive electronic systems). Under the nose is the main surveillance radar, which may be similar to that carried by the Ka-27 though the radome is more bulged underneath. Doppler is carried under the tail boom. The MCM variant has no ASW sensors, retaining only the main radar and doppler, but has an additional small pod fairing high on the forward right side of the fuselage, as well as an unidentified strip or strake along the fuselage beneath the cabin windows. MCM gear replaces the MAD installation.

Armament: The ASW version, Haze-A, has left and right weapon

bays running the full length of the planing bottom, each closed by left and right downward-hinged doors made in three sections. The weapons certainly include AS torpedoes, depth bombs and probably mines and other stores.

Future: Over 100 of the Haze-A version were serving with the AV-MF by early 1986, and low-rate production of both models was continuing. New variants, including possibly transport and AEW versions, may appear in due course.

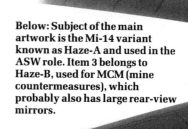

Below: Subject of the main artwork is the Mi-14 variant known as Haze-A and used in the ASW role. Item 3 belongs to Haze-B, used for MCM (mine countermeasures), which probably also has large rear-view mirrors.

Below: This Mi-14 – seen here with all four units of its landing gear extended – was co-operating with a *Kashin*-Mod class BRK (large rocket ship). The location was probably the Black Sea; Mi-14s seldom go far from the shore.

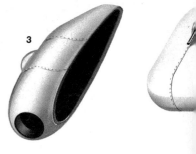

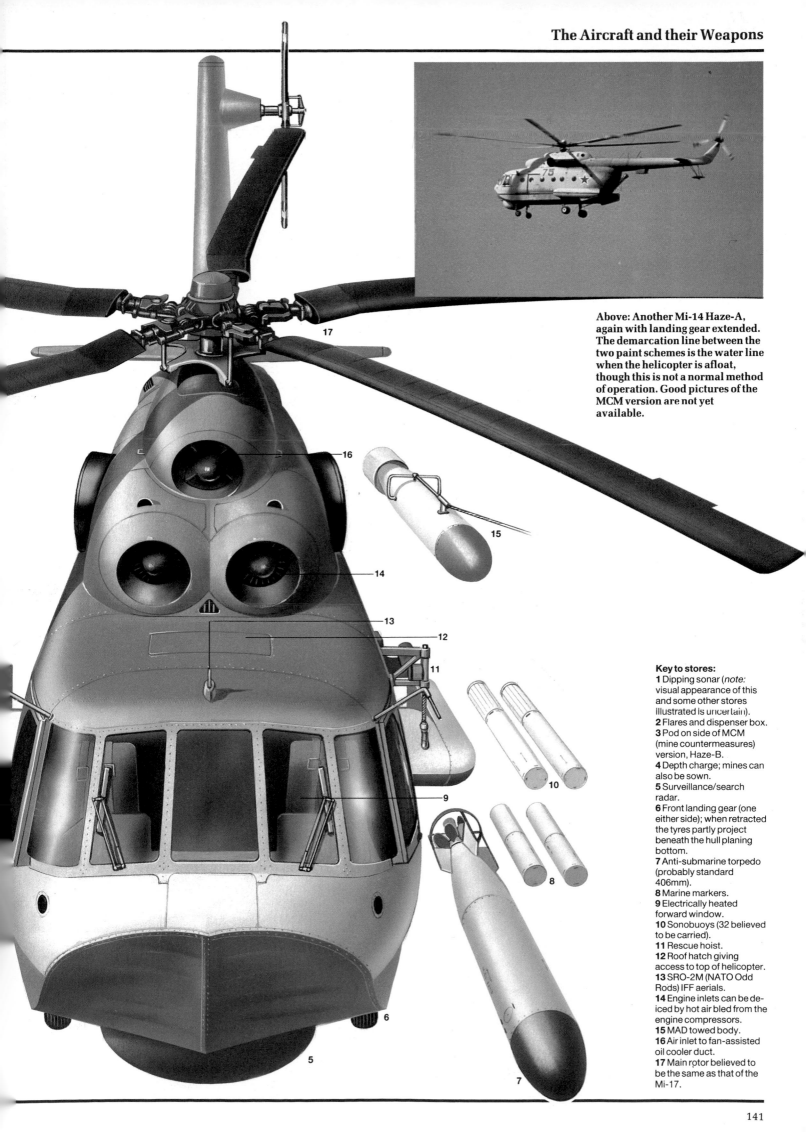

Above: Another Mi-14 Haze-A, again with landing gear extended. The demarcation line between the two paint schemes is the water line when the helicopter is afloat, though this is not a normal method of operation. Good pictures of the MCM version are not yet available.

Key to stores:
1 Dipping sonar (*note:* visual appearance of this and some other stores illustrated is uncertain).
2 Flares and dispenser box.
3 Pod on side of MCM (mine countermeasures) version, Haze-B.
4 Depth charge; mines can also be sown.
5 Surveillance/search radar.
6 Front landing gear (one either side); when retracted the tyres partly project beneath the hull planing bottom.
7 Anti-submarine torpedo (probably standard 406mm).
8 Marine markers.
9 Electrically heated forward window.
10 Sonobuoys (32 believed to be carried).
11 Rescue hoist.
12 Roof hatch giving access to top of helicopter.
13 SRO-2M (NATO Odd Rods) IFF aerials.
14 Engine inlets can be de-iced by hot air bled from the engine compressors.
15 MAD towed body.
16 Air inlet to fan-assisted oil cooler duct.
17 Main rotor believed to be the same as that of the Mi-17.

Mil Mi-24 and Mi-25

Origin: Soviet Union, first flight not later than late 1972.
Type: Multirole combat helicopter; all specification figures estimated.
Engines: Two 2,200shp Isotov TV3-117 turboshafts
Dimensions: Diameter of five-blade main rotor 55ft 9in (17.0m); length (rotors turning) 68ft 11in (21m), (ignoring rotors and nose projections) 60ft 8in (18.5m); height (rotors turning) 21ft 4in (6.5m).
Weights: Empty (all versions) 16,534lb (7500kg) (official Western estimate is 18,520lb/8400kg); normal loaded 24,250lb (11000kg).
Performance: Maximum level speed in service about 199mph (320km/h), but A-10 (the Mil OKB designation) helicopters of Hind-C type, without modification, have set speed records at up to 228.9mph (368.4km/h); cruising speed (full weapon load) 183mph (295km/h); maximum rate of climb 2,953ft (900m)/min; hovering ceiling OGE 7,218ft (2200m); official Western estimate of combat radius is 99 miles (160km), but A-10 has set record at full throttle round 621-mile (1000km) course.
Background: The Soviet Union has always shown itself willing to finance totally new weapons, to meet specific requirements, even when it would be simpler and cheaper to modify an existing design. This family of helicopters was regarded as so important that it is based on a completely new design despite the fact that – especially at the outset – it bears a very close resemblance to the Mi-8. Compared with the Mi-8 the Mi-24 is slightly smaller, and has a much smaller main rotor, and it was originally sized to carry a unique mixture of eight troops in a cabin as well as heavy loads of attack weapons including missiles. New versions introduced greater power, new rotors and a new tandem-seat forward fuselage. For ten years production at two plants, at Arsenyev and Rostov, has exceeded 15 per month. Over 300 have been exported outside the Warsaw Pact.
Design: No other helicopter combines the weapons, sensors, armour and flight performance of this family, to say nothing of adding a cabin for eight troops, or four stretcher casualties, or urgent front-line cargo (including reloads for the helicopter's own weapon launchers). The main rotor has a fully articulated hub of machined steel, with the usual hydraulic lead/lag dampers, and retains the blades by unusually short coupling links. These are bolted to the extruded multiple spars of titanium alloy, around which are bonded the honeycomb-filled glassfibre skins. The leading edge of each blade has an anti-erosion strip and electrothermal deicing, and a balance tab is fitted to the outer trailing edge. The tail rotor has three aluminium-alloy blades and except for the first Mi-24 version is on the left of the fin (this considerably reduced rotor "slap" and tail-rotor noise). The metal

fuselage is not of the pod-and-boom form but is quite streamlined, and the tricycle landing gears are fully retractable. The main gears fold straight back, up and in to stow the wheels transversely. The twin-wheel nose unit is longer in current versions to provide ground clearance for the chin-mounted sensors. The large wings, always fitted, are set a high angle of incidence and provide about one-quarter of the lift in cruising flight, thereby unloading the rotor and increasing attainable speeds. They also have pronounced anhedral, which enables rockets and missiles to be loaded easily from ground level. The engines are close together ahead of the gearbox, and usually have hemispherical inlet protectors to deflect ice and other matter. Above and between the engines is the oil cooler, and aft of the rotor is an APU mounted transversely. The first production versions, called Hind-A, -B and -C, had a large four-seat cockpit (pilot, copilot, navigator/gunner and forward observer) with access via the two giant left-side windows, the forward one hinging up and the bulged rear one sliding aft. The main cabin has a large door on each side which opens above and below, the lower section having integral steps. Current Hind-D and -E (called Mi-25 at least in export versions) have a flight crew of only two, the weapon operator in front having a canopy hinged to the right and the pilot, above and behind, having a door on the right. All versions have extensive armour.
Avionics: All versions have extremely comprehensive electronic flight-control and engine-management systems, communications and all-weather navaids including a projected map display. The long nose probe is a sensitive low-airspeed system. Most versions have an electro-optical (LLTV) sensor on the tip of the left wing (Hind-A, top of left inboard pylon). Under the nose on Hind-A is an optical gunsight. Hind-D and -E have an impressive group of sensors including radar and LLTV and, since 1982, a FLIR. All feed the integrated front cockpit sight system. Outstandingly complete ECM/IRCM warning and jamming systems are installed.
Armament: Hind-A carries a manually aimed 0.5in (12.7mm) nose gun and six pylons, usually loaded with four UV-16-57s and two pairs of AT-2 Swatters. Many other stores can be carried up to an external weight of 3,307lb (1500kg). Hind-D has a four-barrel 12.7mm gun turret under the nose. Hind-E replaces this with a GSh-23L cannon fixed on the right side, and can fire AT-6 Spiral laser-homing missiles instead of AT-3s.
Future: Despite the appearance of the Mi-28 Havoc the versatile Mi-24/25 remains in full-scale production for WP forces and export, and is almost certainly being continually developed and updated.

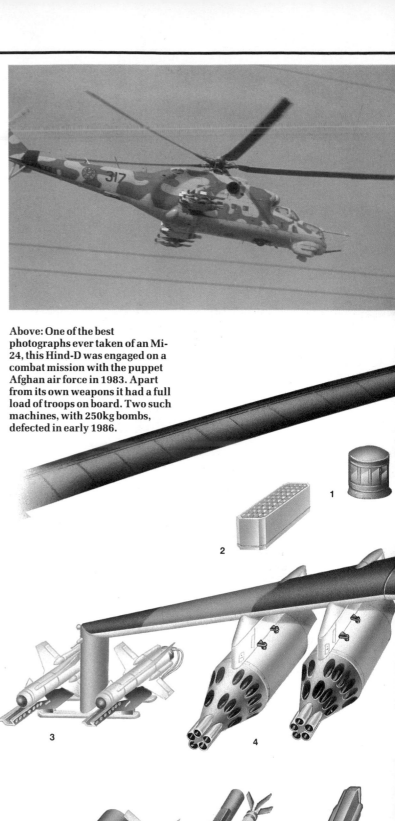

Above: One of the best photographs ever taken of an Mi-24, this Hind-D was engaged on a combat mission with the puppet Afghan air force in 1983. Apart from its own weapons it had a full load of troops on board. Two such machines, with 250kg bombs, defected in early 1986.

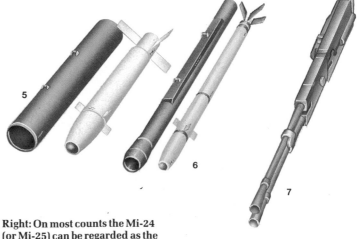

Right: On most counts the Mi-24 (or Mi-25) can be regarded as the world's No 1 combat helicopter, which is surprising because its combination of sensors, weapons and passengers is unique. A Soviet Hind-D is depicted.

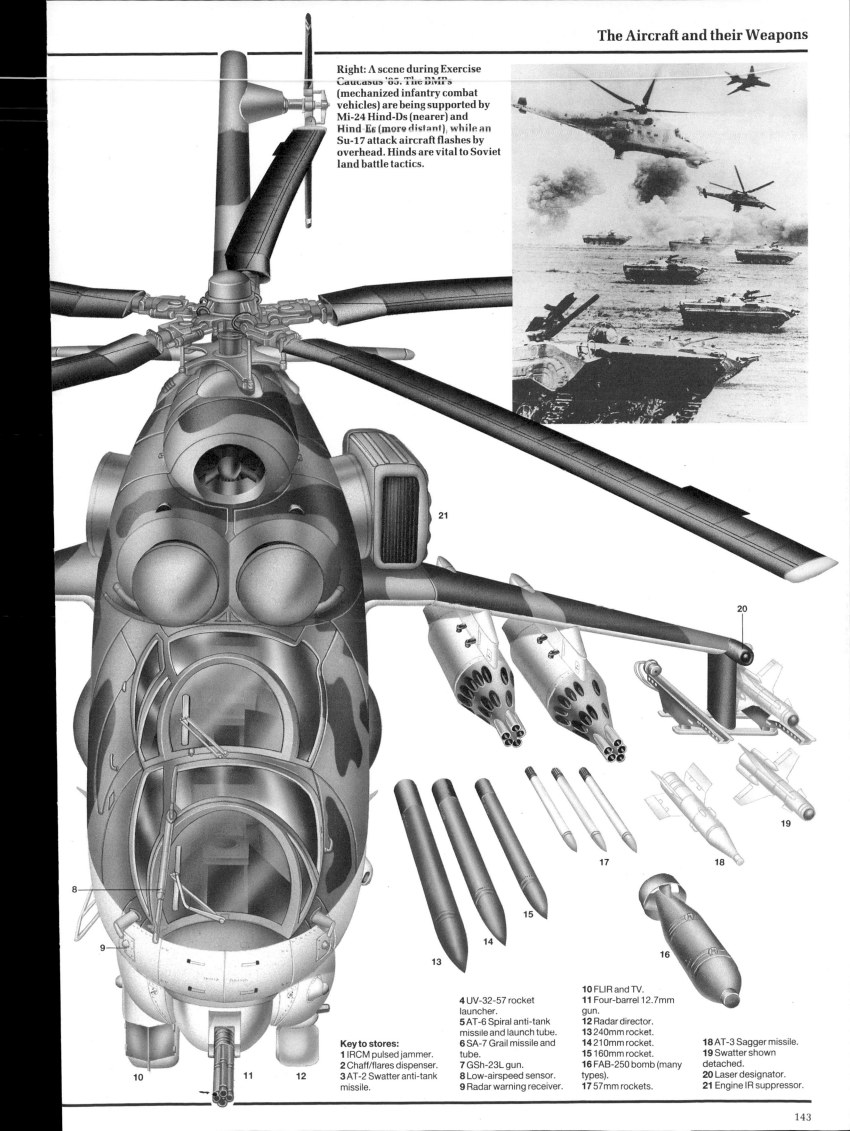

Right: A scene during Exercise Caucasus '85. The BMPs (mechanized infantry combat vehicles) are being supported by Mi-24 Hind-Ds (nearer) and Hind-Es (more distant), while an Su-17 attack aircraft flashes by overhead. Hinds are vital to Soviet land battle tactics.

Key to stores:
1 IRCM pulsed jammer.
2 Chaff/flares dispenser.
3 AT-2 Swatter anti-tank missile.
4 UV-32-57 rocket launcher.
5 AT-6 Spiral anti-tank missile and launch tube.
6 SA-7 Grail missile and tube.
7 GSh-23L gun.
8 Low-airspeed sensor.
9 Radar warning receiver.
10 FLIR and TV.
11 Four-barrel 12.7mm gun.
12 Radar director.
13 240mm rocket.
14 210mm rocket.
15 160mm rocket.
16 FAB-250 bomb (many types).
17 57mm rockets.
18 AT-3 Sagger missile.
19 Swatter shown detached.
20 Laser designator.
21 Engine IR suppressor.

Mil Mi-26

Origin: Soviet Union, first flight 1979.

Type: Heavy transport helicopter.

Engines: Two 11,400shp Lotarev D-136 free-turbine turboshafts.

Dimensions: Diameter of eight-blade main rotor 104ft 11.8in (32.0m); length (rotors turning) 131ft 3.8in (40.025m), (ignoring rotors) 110ft 7.8in (33.727m); height (top of main rotor head) 26ft 8.7in (8.145m).

Weights: Empty 62,169lb (28200kg); loaded (normal) 109,127lb (49500kg), (max) 123,457lb (56000kg).

Performance: Maximum level speed at SL 183mph (295km/h); normal cruising speed 158mph (255km/h); hovering ceiling OGE 5,906ft (1800m); service ceiling 15,092ft (4600m) but has (among many other world records) lifted a 22,046lb (10000kg) payload to 20,997ft (6400m); range (internal fuel, max wt, 5 per cent reserve) 497 miles (800km).

Background: The Soviet Union's need for battlefield heavy-lift helicopters is equalled only by its need for giant helicopters to open up undeveloped regions, especially the Tyumen region of Siberia. To succeed the Mi-6 M. I. Mil masterminded the world's biggest helicopter, the gigantic V-12 (Mi-12) with reverse-tapered braced "wings" carrying on their tips complete Mi-6 engine/rotor groups. With a "span" across the rotors of 219ft 10in (67m) the V-12 was unwieldy, and it missed by a large margin meeting the GUGVF (civil air fleet) requirement that the empty and loaded weights should be in the ratio 1:2. It flew in 1968 but by 1970 development was abandoned. Mil died in that year and was succeeded by M. N. Tishchyenko, who promptly asked for a new engine of double the power of the D-25V. Promised this, Tishchyenko designed a completely conventional "penny farthing" helicopter which just happens to be bigger, and in almost every respect more capable, than any other in existence.

Design: To meet the severe empty/loaded weight ratio Tishchyenko had to pack more helicopter than ever before into a space actually smaller than an Mi-6. The wish to use advanced technology was curbed by the over-riding demand for reliability in the harshest and most remote areas of the world. This demanded robust simplicity, and the result is an excellent compromise. The main hub is not steel but forged in high-strength titanium alloy, saving over 2,205lb (1000kg). The hub is fully articulated, and secures eight blades each with a steel-tube spar and 26 bonded aerofoil sections of Nomex-filled glassfibre. Leading edges have a titanium anti-erosion strip and electric deicer. The tail rotor, on the right, has five glassfibre blades. The Mil bureau designed the main gearbox. The engines have particle-protected inlets with bleed-air deicing, and an oil cooler at the upper level. Fuel is housed in eight integral underfloor tanks. Surprisingly, the APU is under the floor of the flight deck, which is pressurized and air-conditioned and seats pilot and copilot, navigator and engineer. Windscreens have wipers and electric deicing. The four big side windows are bulged, the front pair swinging open. Access is via three downward-hinged doors (two left, one right) each with integral steps, and full-section hydraulically driven rear clamshell doors and vehicle ramp. Aft of the flight deck is a four-seat compartment. The unpressurized main cargo hold, with loadmaster seat and two 5,511lb (2500kg) electric winches on full-length ceiling rails, measures 39ft 4in (12m) long (49ft 2in, 15m, including ramp), 10ft 8in (3.25m) wide and 10ft 4.8in (3.17m) high (slightly less at the front). A flight-deck indicator reads gross weight, fed by the main landing-gear legs whch can be adjusted to suit the desired loading height of the rear doors. Normal payload is 44,092lb (20000kg), internal or as a slung load, which enables a wide range of important weapon systems and other military loads to be carried. If necessary heavier loads can be carried; for example on 3 February 1982 a prototype lifted 55,115lb (25 tonnes) to 13,451ft (4100m). There are normally 40 fold-down seats along the walls, and about 60 more can be attached to the floor, which is of very strong titanium. A ladder gives access to the tail boom, and there are steps up the outside of the fuselage. In this helicopter the horizonal stabilizer is fixed in flight, but adjustable on the ground. The Mi-26 sets a very good level of smooth flight, vibration being "one-tenth that of the Mi-6".

Avionics: Standard equipment includes a multimode mapping and weather radar, managed by the navigator at the rear on the right. The pilots have doppler-driven moving map displays, as well as TV screens on which they can switch pictures from cameras looking back under the nose, forward from under the fin and vertically down through a floor hatch. The advanced multichannel flight-control system has powerful autostabilization and autohover capability at any desired height. Rather poor photographs of VVS (air force) Mi-26 helicopters (which are dubbed Halo by NATO) show various RWR and other installations, as well as HF wire aerials. This version has small openable windows in the rear clamshell doors, and has been seen disgorging pairs of BMD armoured vehicles; the big ASU-85 airborne SP gun can also be carried. On the ground the APU supplies power for the hydraulic, electric and air-conditioning systems.

Armament: There is no armament visible on military Mi-26 helicopters, but the small windows in the rear clamshell doors could be used for firing infantry weapons, and the various side and flight-deck windows might be also.

Future: This outstanding helicopter will certainly remain in production for many years, and the production total of 800 Mi-6s shows what might be expected. The first export customer was the Indian Air Force. Tishchyenko is now engaged in a long-term study of an even more capable successor.

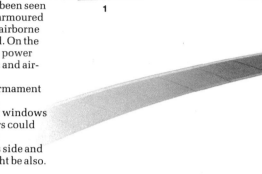

1

Above: No other helicopter has an interior anything like as capacious (dimensions at left). This view was taken from the cockpit rear bulkhead, the rear cargo doors being closed and ramps stowed. Tip-up seats are standard equipment.

Below: In early 1985 this was one of five Mi-26s then flying. Nos 06141 and 06118 were used for publicity pictures, while 06173 went to the Paris airshow. Several others have since appeared in military camouflage.

3

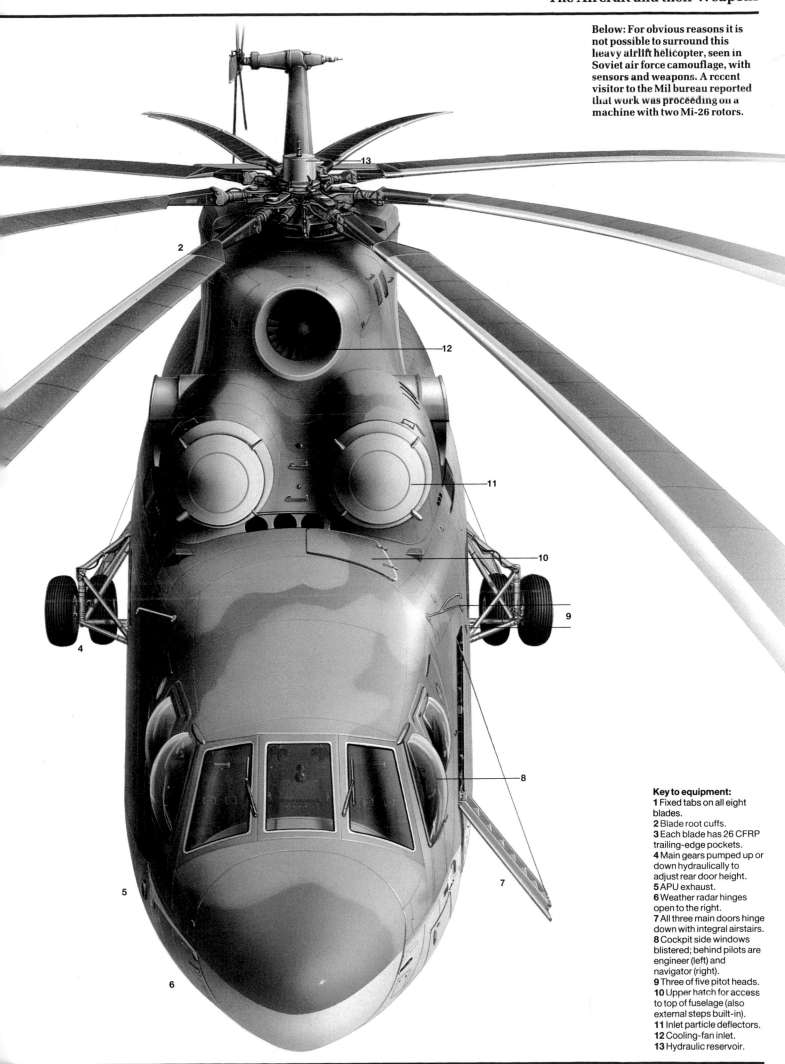

Below: For obvious reasons it is not possible to surround this heavy airlift helicopter, seen in Soviet air force camouflage, with sensors and weapons. A recent visitor to the Mil bureau reported that work was proceeding on a machine with two Mi-26 rotors.

Key to equipment:
1 Fixed tabs on all eight blades.
2 Blade root cuffs.
3 Each blade has 26 CFRP trailing-edge pockets.
4 Main gears pumped up or down hydraulically to adjust rear door height.
5 APU exhaust.
6 Weather radar hinges open to the right.
7 All three main doors hinge down with integral airstairs.
8 Cockpit side windows blistered; behind pilots are engineer (left) and navigator (right).
9 Three of five pitot heads.
10 Upper hatch for access to top of fuselage (also external steps built-in).
11 Inlet particle deflectors.
12 Cooling-fan inlet.
13 Hydraulic reservoir.

Mil Mi-28

Origin: Soviet Union, first flight probably 1982-3.
Type: Anti-armour and anti-air combat helicopter; all data estimated.
Engines: Probably two 2,200shp Isotov TV3-117 turboshafts.
Dimensions: Diameter of five-blade main rotor 55ft 9in (17m); length (rotors turning) 59ft 1in (18m), (ignoring rotors) 57ft 1in (17.4m); height overall 15ft 3in (4.6m).
Weights: Empty 14,990lb (6800kg); maximum loaded 20,060lb (9100kg).
Performance: Maximum speed probably about 230mph (370km/h) see text (Design) for comment; mission radius 149 miles (240km).
Background: Western observers have persistently commented on the unique design of the Mi-24/25, which is virtually a "gunship" attack helicopter with an added cabin. Clearly both the Mil OKB and the Soviet customer authorities have from the 1960s been carefully studying the alternative of a true armed helicopter without a cabin, and in the Mi-28, called Havoc by NATO, they have at last bought it. It is reasonable to assume that everything so far published about this helicopter has been gleaned from interpretation of satellite imagery. Thus, while the appearance from above may be well known, the underside (and to a lesser degree the side elevation) is probably still an enigma. The US Defense Department predicted Havoc in 1984, and the first regiment will probably be equipped in about 1987-88.
Design: It would have seemed reasonable for this helicopter to retain the proven engine installation and other dynamic parts of the Mi-24. According to the DoD this is not the case. The rotors may be unchanged, but the engine installation is completely new and more nearly resembles that of the US Army AH-64 Apache. The two turboshaft engines, which may well be the same as those fitted to the Mi-24, are mounted far apart on the sides of the fuselage. Why this major change should be made is obscure, especially as the DoD artists who have produced paintings of the Mi-28 have left nowhere where the big oil cooler duct could be installed, neither have they indicated the existence of an APU (there is no room for an APU to be mounted transversely behind the rotor as in the Mi-24). Yet a further odd feature is that the engines are shown as being faired into the wings, whereas it is normal practice to make the wings removable. The wings are also shown without anhedral, but as this helicopter may sit lower on the ground than the Mi-24 this may be correct, the governing factor being the ease with which the pylons and rails can be reloaded. Certainly there is very little Mi-24 left in this helicopter, which is designed for air combat as well as surface attack. It seems obvious that flight performance should handsomely

exceed that of the Mi-24, yet DoD estimate of maximum speed is 186mph (300km/h), which is 43.5mph (70km/h) *slower* than speeds already achieved by the bigger machine. The DoD has depicted the Mi-28 as having a slim but amazingly deep fuselage, with a vast bulged nose almost destroying the view from the front cockpit; this is discussed later under Avionics. With no cabin to bother about there is no evident reason why the fuselage should have such depth and such a huge opaque nose. The crew, presumably gunner in front and pilot behind, are drawn inside deeply stepped cockpits each with an angular flat-plate canopy which must hinge open forwards together with the windscreen. The landing gear is shown as being a fixed tailwheel type with no oleo strut up the side of the fuselage. Thus the rear fuselage lies close along the ground, there being no pod/boom shape, and terminates in a swept fin with the tail rotor on the right and a half-tailplane (horizontal stabilizer) on the left. The engine inlets are shown with remarkably small foreign-object deflectors on the front, and the jetpipes are curved upward but are not depicted with any obvious IR suppressing device. Such a fitment would seem essential, to back up the extensive armour and redundant structural and systems design needed for survival on future battlefields.
Avionics: The DoD has said that, naturally, the Mi-28 is fitted with IR suppressors and IR decoy devices, the former presumably being a pulsed jammer. On the high tip of the nose is drawn a black blob said to be a radar (clearly of millimetric proportions) which faces ahead only. Most curious of all is the so-called "observer station" in the underside of the nose. According to the DoD the underside of the nose contains windows for visual observation. Thus, either there is a third crew-member squatting or lying in the nose or the gunner has optics linking him to something looking out through these windows. The one thing the crew need is the best possible view throughout the forward hemisphere. Battle helicopters of the 1990s cannot be managed by pilots relying on directions relayed from an observer looking through "chin" windows. The only plausible interpretation is that the pilot flies by looking out of his rear cockpit and the gunner does his aiming of the gun(s) and missiles by means of a sight system which looks out through the underside of the nose. According to several published Soviet articles this is the worst possible place to put the sight, because to use it necessitates exposing the whole helicopter.
Armament: Obviously, the weapon wings can carry a wide range of stores including missiles for use against armour and other aircraft, especially helicopters. Sergei Sikorsky has guessed that

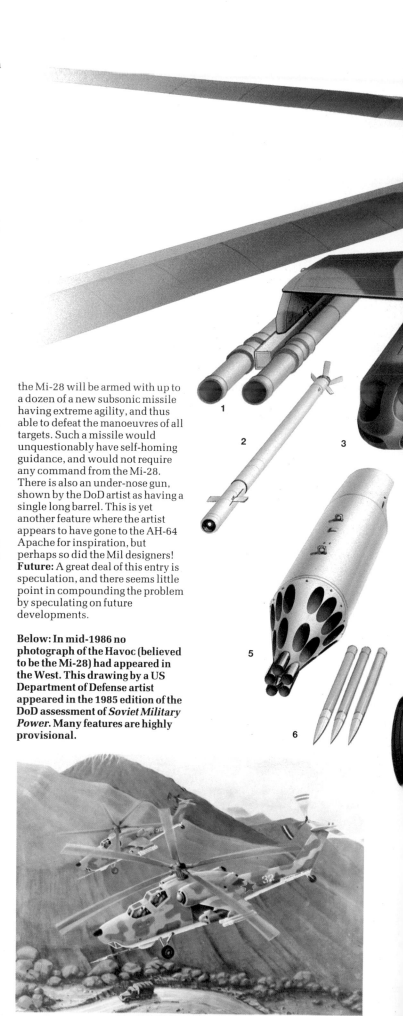

the Mi-28 will be armed with up to a dozen of a new subsonic missile having extreme agility, and thus able to defeat the manoeuvres of all targets. Such a missile would unquestionably have self-homing guidance, and would not require any command from the Mi-28. There is also an under-nose gun, shown by the DoD artist as having a single long barrel. This is yet another feature where the artist appears to have gone to the AH-64 Apache for inspiration, but perhaps so did the Mil designers!
Future: A great deal of this entry is speculation, and there seems little point in compounding the problem by speculating on future developments.

Below: In mid-1986 no photograph of the Havoc (believed to be the Mi-28) had appeared in the West. This drawing by a US Department of Defense artist appeared in the 1985 edition of the DoD assessment of *Soviet Military Power*. Many features are highly provisional.

Below: The main illustration is even more speculative than the painting on the facing page. This is because virtually all the detail, as well as some of the major features are, by necessity, guesswork. The same applies to some of the weapons, notably the 30mm gun. The rotors are copied from the Mi-24 Hind.

Key to stores:
1 Twin launcher for SA-14 modified AAM.
2 SA-14 mod AAM (provisional).
3 Quad launcher for ''AT-6 Spiral Mod''.
4 AT-6 Spiral Mod anti-tank missile (provisional).
5 UV-32-57 rocket launcher.
6 57mm rockets.
7 New 30mm gun with ammunition.
8 Cylindrical radome.
9 SRO-2M (NATO Odd Rods) IFF aerials.
10 FAB-250 bomb.
11 Chaff/flares dispenser.
12 GSh-23L 23mm gun (may not be fitted).
13 30mm ammunition drum.
14 Inlet shields (anti-debris, noise and radar).
15 IRCM beacon jammer.
16 Upturned IR-suppressed jetpipes.

Sikorsky S-61 (CH/HH-3, SH-3/ASH-3 Sea King)

Origin: USA, first flight 11 March 1959.

Type: ASW/SAR helicopter (S-61R, transport/SAR).

Engines: Two General Electric T58 turboshafts, (A and derivatives) 1,250shp T58-8D, (D and derivatives) 1,400shp T58-10, (R) 1,500shp T58-5.

Dimensions: Diameter of five-blade main rotor 62ft 0in (18.9m); length (rotors turning, SH-3D) 72ft 8in (22.15m), (ignoring rotors, SH-3D) 54ft 9in (16.69m), (ignoring rotors, CH-3E) 57ft 3in (17.45m); height (3D, top of main rotor head) 15ft 6in (4.72m).

Weights: Empty (basic S-61A transport/SAR) 9,763lb (4428kg), (SH-3D) 11,865lb (5382kg), (CH-3E) 13,255lb (6012kg); maximum loaded (A) 21,500lb (9752kg), (SH-3D) 20,500lb (9299kg), (CH) 22,050lb (10002kg).

Performance: (typical of all at 20,500lb) Maximum speed at SL 166mph (267km/h); cruising speed 136mph (219km/h); maximum rate of climb 2,200ft (671m)/min; hovering ceiling OGE 8,200ft (2499m); range (max fuel, 10 per cent reserve) 625 miles (1,006km).

Background: The first practical ASW helicopter was the HSS-1 version for the US Navy of the Sikorsky S-58. By 1955 it was clear that turbine engines, and especially the Navy-funded GE T58, would make possible a dramatic improvement in performance. The result was the S-61, first funded by the Navy as the HSS-2 (redesignated SH-3 after 1962) and flown in 1959. Perhaps not even Sikorsky quite appreciated that the same rather specialized basic helicopter would be developed not only in SAR/transport versions using the same airframe but also in stretched non-amphibious airline versions and as the very different S-61R, built for the USAF as the CH-3 and HH-3. Sikorsky built over 750, and some 400 were built by licensees Westland (see pages 164-165), Agusta, Mitsubishi and P&W Canada.

Design: With only minor penalties Sikorsky designed this helicopter to have an amphibious flying-boat hull, water stability being provided by left and right strut-mounted floats fitted with pop-out buoyancy bags. At the time of its design the use of twin engines mounted entirely above the cabin adjacent to the gearbox was novel, and the S-61 also broke new ground in having five-blade rotors, automatic blade folding and a complete folding tail, an advanced flight-control system with autopilot and autostabilization linked to a doppler and radar altimeter for autohovering control over a fixed point in the ocean regardless of wind, and perhaps above all in combining both sensors and weapons in order to perform both the ASW search mission and the ASW strike mission. This required a large tactical compartment amidships which automatically provided sufficient room for useful transport versions. Nevertheless the S-61

had been designed for the SH-3 ASW role, and while it was not difficult to produce the HH-3 armed SAR/utility model, the VH-3 executive version for the White House and the airline versions, there was also the possibility of redesigning the machine as a multirole transport. This was flown as the S-61R on 17 June 1963. It led to the CH-3E transport and HH-3E Jolly Green Giant armed SAR version used in Vietnam. The S-61R, today made only by Agusta, introduced a pod-and-boom fuselage with a full-section hydraulically driven rear ramp door for loading vehicles and other bulky cargo. The cabin of this version is 25ft 10.6in (7.89m) long, 78in (1.98m) wide and 75in (1.91m) maximum height. The interior can accommodate 25 armed troops, 30 passengers, 15 stretcher casualties or 5,000lb (2268kg) of cargo. S-61R versions have tricycle landing gear with twin nosewheels remaining largely visible when retracted and twin-wheel main units retracting forwards into large sponsons which provide water stability. All other variants have twin-wheel main units retracting rearwards into the floats and a single fixed tailwheel. All models have a similar two-pilot cockpit. The main rotor has a steel spider and fully articulated blades with oil lubrication.

Avionics: All ASW versions have dipping sonar, usually the Bendix AQS-13B, F, or AQS-18, doppler, radar altimeter and active/passive sonobuoys, markers and smoke floats. US Navy SH-3H Sea Kings have Texas Instruments ASQ-81(V) MAD, carried on the right side, while the Agusta-Sikorsky ASH-3D has a chin-mounted SMA APS-707 surveillance radar. Many variants have RWR/ESM/IRCM and similar defensive electronic and IR warning systems, the chief installation in the SH-3H being the General Instrument ALR-66(V)1 crystal video RWR.

Armament: The original armament of the SH-3 family was "up to 840lb (381kg) of weapons including homing torpedoes". This is strange, because the Mk 44 and 46 torpedoes used weigh about 515lb (234kg) each, meaning that only one could be carried. Yet today's Agusta-Sikorsky ASH-3D can carry four of these torpedoes, and in fact has an external load limit of 8,000lb (3629kg). Alternatives for the ASH-3D include four AS.12 ASMs, or two AM.39 Exocet, Marte 2 or Harpoon anti-ship missiles, none of which are normally carried by the SH-3H. The main illustration shows the many other customer options.

Future: With nearly 1,200 in service worldwide, the S-61 represents one of the biggest and most diverse prospects for future updating. These helicopters have no announced fatigue problem, and their basic design will remain competitive until the end of the century. GE have studied fitting the T700 engine.

Above: US Navy BuNo 148974 was built as an SH-3A but upgraded later to SH-3G standard. Assigned to training unit HS-1 at NAS Jacksonville, Florida, it is seen recovering a practice torpedo.

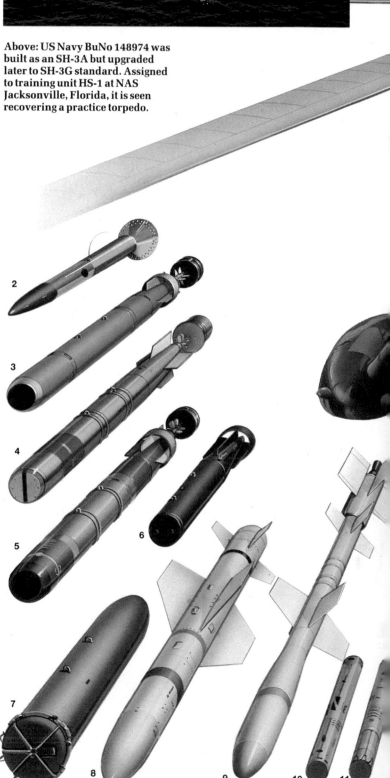

Key to stores:
1 Rescue hoist.
2 MAD towed body, TB-623/ASQ-81(V).
3 Whitehead Motofides A244/S torpedo, with parachute.
4 Mk 46 torpedo with parachute.
5 Mk 44 homing torpedo with parachute.
6 Mk 11 Mod 3 depth charge.
7 MISAR MR-80 mine and parachute pack.
8 AGM-84 Harpoon cruise missile.
9 Marte (Sea Killer Mk 2) anti-ship missile.
10 Q-41 passive (Sparton) sonobuoy.
11 Q-47 active buoy.
12 Radar warning (ESM) receivers.
13 Q-53 DIFAR passive sonobuoys.
14 Smoke/float/flame 3.5lb-type No 2 markers.
15 Schermuly combined day/night marker.
16 Dwarf size sonobuoy.
17 Q-62 DICASS active buoy.
18 Q-77 active buoy.
19 BAe Sea Skua anti-ship missile.
20 AM.39 Exocet anti-ship missile.
21 Matra/Oto Melara Otomat cruise missile.
22 Penguin Mk 2 Mod 7 anti-ship missile.
23 Mk 104 minesweeping gear.
24 AS.12 missiles.
25 Bendix AQS-13B dunking sonar.
26 Pitots.
27 Inlet particle deflector.

Left: The principal illustration is based on an Agusta-Sikorsky ASH-3H multirole naval version, as operated by the Italian navy, though many of the items arrayed around it are carried only by US-built machines.

Sikorsky S-65 (CH/HH-53 Super Jolly, RH/MH-53 Sea Stallion)

Origin: USA, first flight 14 October 1964.

Type: Assault transport helicopter with MCM and SAR versions, data for CH-53D Sea Stallion.

Engines: Two General Electric T64 turboshafts, (A) 2,850shp T64-6, (B) 3,080shp T64-3, (C, D, G) 3,925shp T64-7 or -413, (MH-53D) 4,380shp T64-415.

Dimensions: Diameter of six-blade main rotor 72ft 3in (22.02m); length (rotors turning) 88ft 3in (26.9m), (ignoring rotors and FR probe) 67ft 2in (20.47m); height (top of rotor head) 17ft 1.5in (5.22m), (over tail rotor) 24ft 11in (7.6m).

Weights: Empty 23,485lb (10653kg); mission takeoff 36,400lb (16511kg), (maximum) 42,000lb (19051kg).

Performance: Maximum speed at SL 196mph (315km/h); cruising speed 173mph (278km/h); maximum rate of climb 2,180ft (664m)/min; hovering ceiling OGE 6,500ft (1981m); range (no external fuel, 10 per cent reserve) 257 miles (414km).

Background: The existence of this extremely important family of transport helicopters is owed to the US Marine Corps, which was pushing for such a helicopter when the S-61 first flew in 1959. The requirement included the ability to fly day or night in adverse (not blind) weather and load vehicles and other bulky loads through a rear ramp door. Another requirement was a sealed fuselage for water landings. Development was speeded by using the rotors and transmission already developed for the US Army CH-54 Tarhe (S-64) crane helicopter.

Design: Using an existing rotor was no problem, though the main gearbox was driven by different engines and the main hub was redesigned to be made partly in titanium and to have power-folding blades. The blades were identical to those of the Tarhe, being traditional aluminium alloy throughout. Likewise the fuselage and tail were conventional riveted light alloy, and Sikorsky did extensive tunnel testing to try to combine a streamlined shape with the inevitable pod-and-boom arrangement necessitated by the rear cargo door. Steel and titanium are used in certain areas of high stress or (cargo floor) subject to impact loads. The cockpit in the bluff nose seats pilot (on the right) and copilot in armoured seats, with a folding seat for the Flight Leader or other supernumerary behind. The main cabin is some 30ft (9.14m) long, and has a maximum cross section of 90in (2.29m) wide by 78in (1.98m) high. The normal load is 37 armed troops on fold-down wall seats, or 24 stretcher casualties and four attendants or 8,000lb (3629kg) of cargo. When operating at maximum weight much greater loads are possible, and in 1968 an uprated CH-53A flew a payload/fuel mass of 28,500lb (12928kg). The rear door is a single-piece ramp, and when a water dam is fitted it can be opened when afloat. Water stability is provided by two large sponsons, the forward part of which houses the fuel (525gal, 2384lit) and the rear section the retracted twin-wheel main landing gears, which pivot forwards. The castoring twin-wheel nose gear retracts rearwards. The tail, which folds downwards to the right for shipboard stowage, has a tall fixed fin, four-blade rotor on the left and fixed horizontal stabilizer on the right. Apart from the power of the engines most of this first generation of Sea Stallion helicopters were generally similar. The most modified machines were a succession of HH-53 special armed SAR helicopters for the USAF Aerospace Rescue and Recovery Service, which had a rescue hoist, flight-refuelling probe, armour, various complex defensive armament schemes, jettisonable long-range tanks on sponson extensions, and a wealth of mission avionics which in Pave Low 3 aircraft included INS, doppler, FLIR and TFR! Some CH-53Ds were modified for

minesweeping, leading to the purpose-built RH-53D (later MH-53D) with greater power and special MCM gear. Unmarked RH-53Ds flew the abortive mission to rescue US hostages from Tehran in April 1980.

Avionics: All versions have communications, navaids, lighting and advanced flight-control systems to fly the mission in day or night visual conditions. The specially equipped Pave Low 3 (HH-53H) is no longer in service. The special MCM versions have equipment for indicating tow-cable yaw angle and tension, and for automatically linking yaw angle to the desired heading and aircraft attitude. The towboom is rated at 20,000lb (9072kg),

compared with 25,000lb (11340kg) for the normal vertical cargo sling, and can handle the Mk 103 mechanical minesweeping gear, Mk 104 acoustic, Mk 105 magnetic and Mk 106 combined magnetic/acoustic. Little has been published on defensive electronics fits but it is clear that most CH-53s now carry passive receivers, one type being the APR-39(V). Sea Stallions of the US Marine Corps, and probably of other operators, can also protect themselves with chaff/flare dispensers. Standard avionics include Tacan/DME, VOR and ILS.

Armament: So far as is known no member of the twin-engine Sea Stallion family in regular inventory service is armed. The equipments illustrated have all been recently associated with different variants.

Future: Apparently all CH/HH/MH-53 helicopters of this family retain their metal blades, though the IMRB (improved main rotor blade) was developed in 1971. This blade is fitted to the CH-53E featured on the next two pages.

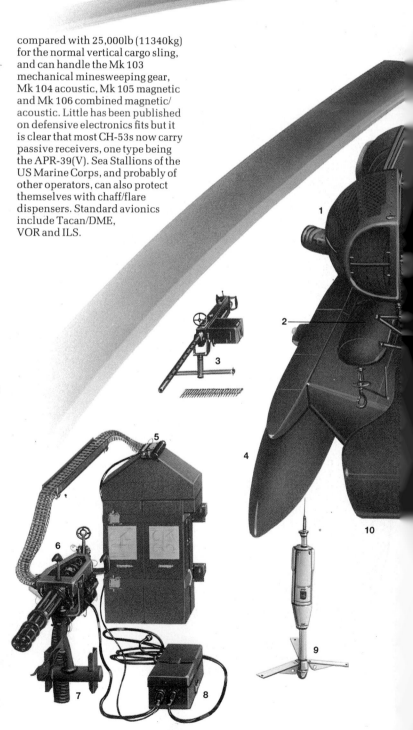

Below: The US Navy's RH-53D Sea Stallion is the specialized MCM (mine countermeasures) version. This example from squadron HM-14 has the MCM gear deployed, the sled being towed through the water astern. The crew watch via rear-view mirrors.

Right: The HH-53H (Pave Low 3) was a very special USAF version, eight of which were packed with sensors for night rescue missions. Equipment included extra navigation aids, AAQ-10 FLIR, APQ-158 terrain-following radar and a flight-refuelling probe.

Key to stores:
1 Inlet particle separators.
2 Rescue hoist.
3 Browning MG3 0.5in heavy machine gun.
4 1703lit (450 US gal) auxiliary fuel tanks.
5 Booster unit at top of four-can ammunition storage.
6 M134 (GAU-28/A) 7.62mm Minigun, with MAU-56A delinking feed and electric drive.
7 Pintle mount with case/link disposal.
8 Control box, 600 to 6,000spm.
9 Jungle Penetrator with three fold-down seats for jungle rescue.
10 Fuel-filled sponsons.
11 Retractable inflight refuelling probe.
12 AAQ-10 FLIR installation.
13 7.62mm Browning or FN GPMG on side-door pintle.
14 Westinghouse AQS-14 towed minehunting sonar vehicle. (For other minesweeping gear that may be carried see next spread, items 2 and 3.)
15 Chaff/flare cartridge dispenser (ALE-39, M130 or similar).
16 Xerox/Loral ALQ-157 IRCM jammer.

Above: Though some of the most interesting items are carried only by other versions, such as the MCM RH-53D (which can also use other MCM gear depicted on p.152) the main drawing shows an HH-53E Super Jolly of USAF No 601 TASS, from Sembach AB. The later CH-53E is the next entry.

Sikorsky S-80 (CH-53E Super Stallion and MH-53E Sea Dragon)

Origin: USA, first flight 1 March 1974.

Type: (CH) Heavy transport, (MH) mine countermeasures helicopter. Data for CH-53E.

Engines: Three 4,380shp General Electric T64-416 turboshafts.

Dimensions: Diameter of seven-blade main rotor 79ft 0in (24.08m); length (rotors turning) 99ft 0.6in (30.19m), (ignoring rotors, FR probe and tail folded) 60ft 6in (18.44m); height (over tail rotor) 28ft 5in (8.66m), (rotor and tail folded) 18ft 7in (5.66m).

Weights: Empty (CH) 33,226lb (15071kg); maximum takeoff (internal payload) 69,750lb (31639kg), (external slung load) 73,500lb (33340kg).

Performance: (all at 56,000lb, 25401kg) Maximum level speed at SL 196mph (315km/h); cruising speed 173mph (278km/h); maximum rate of climb (payload of 25,000lb, 11340kg) 2,500ft (762m)/min; hovering ceiling OGE 9,500ft (2896m); self-ferry range at weight given above 1,290 miles (2076km).

Background: At first glance this appears to be just another version of the original CH-53A Sea Stallion. So it is, but the degree of transformation is shown by the fact that installed power has risen from 5,700 to 13,140shp and maximum payload from 8,000lb (3629kg) to 36,000lb (16330kg)! Development of a growth version of the Stallion series began in 1971 to meet an urgent need for increased assault-transport and heavy-lift capability for the Vietnam war. That it took just ten more years to get the first CH-53E into the hands of the Marine Corps merely underlines how hard this outstanding helicopter had to fight for funding for every stage of development. As of spring 1986 107 had been delivered, and Navy/Marines requirements are expected to exceed 300 by year 2000.

Design: The main rotor blades are geometrically similar to those of the earlier CH-53s, though they are attached via extension straps which increase rotor diameter. Blade construction is of a type intended for use on earlier versions with a titanium spar and Nomex-filled glassfibre/epoxy skin. With the added seventh blade this roughly doubles maximum lifting power. The hub had to be modified with a new steel and titanium structure and elastomeric bearings which need little maintenance. Sikorsky BIM (blade inspection method) is used, with a pressurized gas filling to warn of any cracks, and all blades fold hydraulically. The gearbox had to be upgraded to 13,500shp, and the third engine is mounted aft on the left side driving straight into the box, unlike the original engines which drive bevel boxes well forward near the cockpit from which shafts run back diagonally across the fuselage. The third jetpipe faces left, the same position on the right side being occupied by the fan-assisted oil cooler. Ahead of the totally redesigned upper fairing (which improves

appearance) is a Solar turbine APU. This is started by an hydraulic accumulator, no batteries being carried, and it provides ground power and starts the main engines hydraulically. The fuselage is little altered, though the front end is now a separate glassfibre structure, but the tail is entirely new. The enlarged fin slopes 20° to the left, as does the much bigger aluminium tail rotor, while the fixed tailplane on the right has a gull-wing form to bring the main strut-braced section horizontal. The CH-53E has additional sponson tanks raising internal capacity to 1,017 US gal (3850lit), augmented by two 650 US gal (2460lit) optional drop tanks. The Navy MH-53 MCM (mine countermeasures) version has gigantic sponsons increasing internal fuel to 3,200 US gal (12113lit), giving an endurance on internal fuel of over 20hrs. Both versions can be refuelled by ship hose or via a retractable FR probe. The CH-53E carries 55 troops, or seven standard cargo pallets or a 36,000lb (16330kg) slung load. The MH-53E has uprated hydraulic and electrical systems, special navigational and minefield guidance systems and an even more advanced flight-control system with automatic tow couplers and automatic approach to hover at any desired height whilst towing any available MCM sweeping equipment. The MH weighs 36,336lb (16482kg) empty, has composite tail-rotor blades and various minor changes. The US Navy is receiving 75 from 1986.

Avionics: All versions have advanced Hamilton Standard digital flight controls, with two computers and a four-axis autopilot. Standard equipment includes VHF/UHF, Tacan, VOR and ILS. See Future, below.

Armament: No weapons are carried, though CH-53Es have successfully fired self-defence AIM-9 Sidewinders (see below).

Stinger is another self-defence option.

Future: Addition of self-defence AAMs is one of numerous planned upgrades. Others include: an all-composite rotor hub with all-composite blades (spar, carbon fibre) with swept anhedral tips, all-composite tail rotor (as on MH-53E), electric blade folding, uprated T64-418 engines, Omega navigation, ground-proximity warning, full crew night-vision systems, exhaust IR suppression, missile alert system, chaff/flare dispensers, nitrogen fuel-tank inerting, the ability to top up

the hydraulics from the cargo hold and improvements to the cargo-handling system. The improved rotor blades will increase useful load by at least 3,000lb (1361kg). The S-80E (cargo) and S-80M (MCM) are export versions, offered with a wide range of customer options.

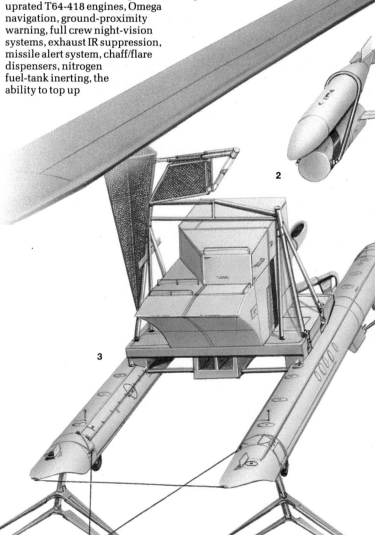

Left: Few publicity pictures can equal this shot of a Marine Corps KC-130F refuelling two CH-53E Super Stallions which are each carrying an LAV-25 armoured vehicle.

Key to stores:
1 Engine inlet particle separators.
2 Mk 104 acoustic minesweeping gear.
3 Edo Mk 105 hydrofoil towed anti-magnetic mine vehicle.
4 Giant (3850lit, 1,017 US gal) sponson tank (MH-53E).
5 Rescue hoist.
6 Minesweeping mirrors.
7 Air-data probe.
8 Browning MG3 0.5in HMG on pintle mount.
9 Twin MLMS Stinger box with missile.
10 Standard 1925lit (508.5 US gal) sponson tank (CH-53E).
11 2460lit (650 US gal) auxiliary tank.
12 AIM-9L self-defence Sidewinder.

13 Chaff/flare dispenser.
14 ALQ-157 IRCM jammer.

Note: for AQS-14 minehunting sonar, which may also be carried, see item 14 on page 151.

Above: Unquestionably the most impressive-looking helicopter in this book, the main artwork depicts a CH-53E Super Stallion, but fitted with the right-hand enlarged tank sponson of the Navy MH-53E Sea Dragon AMCM (airborne mine countermeasures) version. Most of the weapons shown are not standard at present.

153

Sikorsky S-70 (UH/EH-60A Black Hawk and HH-60A Night Hawk)

Origin: USA, first flight 17 October 1974.

Type: (UH) multirole utility transport, (EH) Comint and jamming, (HH) combat SAR.

Engines: Two General Electric T700 turboshafts, (UH) 1,560shp T700-700, (EH) probably as UH, (HH) 1,690shp T700-401, (S-70A export) option of 1,725shp T700-701A.

Dimensions: Diameter of four-blade main rotor 53ft 8in (16.36m); length (rotors turning) 64ft 10in (19.76m), (rotors and tail folded) 41ft 4in (12.6m); height (over tail rotor) 16ft 10in (5.13m), (to top of main rotor head) 12ft 4in (3.76m).

Weights: Empty (UH) 10,624lb (4819kg), (HH) 12,642lb (5734kg); mission takeoff (UH) 16,260lb (7376kg), (HH) 20,413lb (9259kg); maximum alternative takeoff (UH) 20,250lb (9185kg), (HH) 22,000lb (9979kg).

Performance: (at mission TO weight) Maximum speed at SL (UH) 184mph (296km/h), (HH) 167mph (269km/h); maximum cruising speed (UH) 167mph (269km/h), (HH) 147mph (237km/h); hovering ceiling OGE (UH) 10,400ft (3170m); range (UH, max internal fuel) 373 miles (600km); endurance (UH) 2h 18min, (HH) 4h 51min.

Background: In the late 1960s the US Army received approval for an UTTAS (utility tactical transport aircraft system) to replace the UH-1H "in the late 1970s". Today the UH-1Hs are being refurbished for service beyond year 2000, but UTTAS not only exists, as the UH-60A, but is a giant programme which has enabled Sikorsky to develop a whole family of military, naval and commercial helicopters in the 10-ton class. Three prototypes were built, and the UH-60A was declared winner of a contest against a Boeing Vertol rival in December 1976. At the time of writing in 1986 Sikorsky had delivered 760 to the US Army and 11 to the USAF as SAR machines. From 1986 the Army expects to receive 132 EH-60A communications jamming versions, the Marines nine VH-60A for the Presidential Executive Flight and, from 1988, the USAF will buy 90 grossly modified HH-60 Night Hawk combat rescue helicopters. The S-70A is an export version. The US Navy's SH-60B Seahawk is described on the following pages.

Design: The S-70 was a judicious blend of proven and new technology, with major constraints on overall dimensions imposed by the requirement that the helicopter should fit inside a C-130. For this purpose Sikorsky not only made the design compact and able to fold but also developed special air-transportability kits. As finally cleared for production, the main rotor has a hub machined from a single titanium forging, with elastomeric bearings and bifilar self-tuning vibration dampers. The blades have a titanium oval tubular spar, Nomex-filled graphite rear section with glassfibre/epoxy skin,

glassfibre leading-edge counterweight, titanium leading-edge sheath and backswept Kevlar tip. Sikorsky BIM pressurization crack-detection is used, but – amazingly – there is no brake. The tail rotor comprises two crossed two-blade units entirely of composite materials and without hub bearings, tilted over to the left at 20°. The tail includes a large electrically driven tailplane whose angle is determined by airspeed, collective demand, pitch rate and lateral acceleration. The tail permits roll-on landings to be made following loss of the tail rotor, and the entire unit folds to the right. The fuselage, which only in plan has a pod/boom configuration, is mainly light alloy but incorporates various composites in the cockpit, floors and cowls. It is designed to withstand severe crashes from any direction. The cabin is typically 12ft 7in (3.84m) long and 92in (2.34m) wide but only 54in (1.37m) high, and has an aft-sliding door on each side. Loads include 11 equipped troops (14 high-density), six stretchers or four stretchers and three seats. The external slung-load hook is rated at 8,000lb (3629kg), and an option (standard on HH) is a 600lb (272kg) rescue hoist. The tailwheel-type landing gear is fixed. Main tanks are behind the cabin; auxiliary fuel can be carried on the ESSS (see Armament) or, in the HH, on special upswept wings which bring total capacity of this probe-equipped machine to 780gal (3545lit).

Avionics: Basic UH equipment includes doppler, ADF, VOR/marker/glideslope, radar altimeter, secure voice radio, RWR and the ALQ-144 IRCM. The HH-60A has a 1553B data bus, cockpit MFDs, new doppler, INS, GPS, special ADF for locating survivors, FLIR, NVGs, APR-39 RWR, chaff/flare dispenser and auto approach/hover coupler. The EH-60A has Quick Fix II communications interception and monitoring and ALQ-151 jamming, all major installations. There are no plans to fit any Black Hawk with a Hellfire-compatible laser.

Armament: One 7.62mm M60 machine-gun can be aimed from each forward cabin window, one by crew chief (third member of flight crew) and the other by one of the troops. The General Electric Black Hawk Weapon System provides either two 7.62mm Miniguns or two GECAL .50 Gatling guns which are pintle-mounted. An option (not used by the US Army) adds the ESSS (external stores support system), anhedralled wings attached above the cabin with four pylons plumbed for tanks giving range of 1,380 miles (2221km) for staged deployment to Europe. The ESSS can carry 16 Hellfires, M56 mine dispensers, gun or rocket pods, self-defence Stingers, ECM or even motorcycles. The EH is unarmed but the HH has provision for the side-firing M60s.

Future: Tremendous efforts have long been made to increase worldwide sales of all members of the S-70 family. A deal with Shorts is promoting an RTM 322-powered version to meet the UK's AST.404 requirement. An IR suppressor over the jetpipes which works in hovering flight has been tested, as have many new weapon fits and an all-composite rear fuselage. The HH-60G is a proposal to the US Coast Guard, and many other versions are planned.

Above: A standard US Army UH-60A seen about to uplift a light utility carrier. Note the large angle of incidence of the horizontal stabilizer (tailplane).

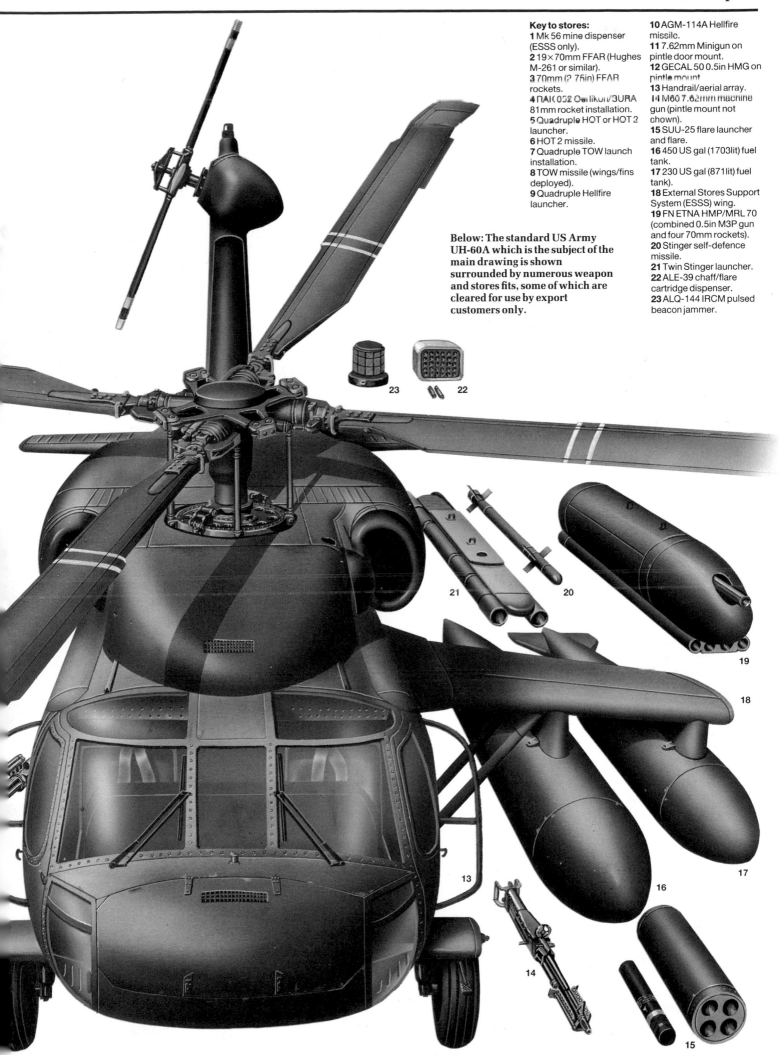

Key to stores:
1 Mk 56 mine dispenser (ESSS only).
2 19×70mm FFAR (Hughes M-261 or similar).
3 70mm (2.75in) FFAR rockets.
4 RAK 052 Oerlikon/SURA 81mm rocket installation.
5 Quadruple HOT or HOT 2 launcher.
6 HOT 2 missile.
7 Quadruple TOW launch installation.
8 TOW missile (wings/fins deployed).
9 Quadruple Hellfire launcher.
10 AGM-114A Hellfire missile.
11 7.62mm Minigun on pintle door mount.
12 GECAL 50 0.5in HMG on pintle mount.
13 Handrail/aerial array.
14 M60 7.62mm machine gun (pintle mount not shown).
15 SUU-25 flare launcher and flare.
16 450 US gal (1703lit) fuel tank.
17 230 US gal (871lit) fuel tank.
18 External Stores Support System (ESSS) wing.
19 FN ETNA HMP/MRL 70 (combined 0.5in M3P gun and four 70mm rockets).
20 Stinger self-defence missile.
21 Twin Stinger launcher.
22 ALE-39 chaff/flare cartridge dispenser.
23 ALQ-144 IRCM pulsed beacon jammer.

Below: The standard US Army UH-60A which is the subject of the main drawing is shown surrounded by numerous weapon and stores fits, some of which are cleared for use by export customers only.

Sikorsky S-70L (SH-60B and SH-60F Seahawk)

Origin: USA, first flight 12 December 1979.
Type: Multirole shipboard helicopter.
Engines: Two 1,690shp General Electric T700-401 turboshaft engines
Dimensions: Main-rotor diameter 53ft 8in (16.36m); length overall (rotors turning) 64ft 10in (19.76m), (main rotor and tail folded) 40ft 11in (12.47m); height (over tail rotor) 17ft 0in (5.18m).
Weights: Empty (ASW mission) 13,648lb (6191kg); gross (ASW mission) 20,244lb (9183kg), (max) 21,884lb (9927kg).
Performance: maximum speed (5,000ft/1524m, tropical) 145mph (233km/h); VROC (SL, 32.2C) 700ft (213m)/min; hover IGE/OGE, range, not released.
Background: In 1970 the US Navy issued a requirement for a LAMPS (light airborne multi-purpose system) helicopter to operate from the platforms of major surface combatants in both the ASW (anti-submarine warfare) and ASST (anti-ship surveillance and targeting) missions. This was won by the Kaman SH-2 described elsewhere. Seeking to update the demand the LAMPS II was issued, but in 1974 this was supplanted by a LAMPS III, for which the prime contract was placed with IBM Federal Systems, as manager of the vital avionics systems. The helicopter thus became secondary; Boeing Vertol and Sikorsky each submitted developed versions of their existing UTTAS utility machines (YUH-61 and 60, respectively), the Sikorsky S-70L being selected after a 1977 fly-off.
Design: Though it uses an airframe basically similar to the Army UH-60A the SH-60B is a far more complicated helicopter. Compared with other machines in the same class, it is bigger and several times more expensive, and it is compatible with very few ships outside the US Navy. The rotors and transmission are as on the UH-60 except for the addition of a rotor brake and electric power folding of the main rotor. The tailplane is larger and rectangular. The landing gear differs in having a much shorter wheelbase to improve deck spotting, the new tail gear having twin wheels on a long-stroke extensible vertical leg which is raised for normal flight. The main gears are, surprisingly, designed to a lower energy requirement and so are simpler and have shorter stroke, but multi-disc brakes are added. The engines and all systems are marinized against salt-water operation, and other features include an inflight-refuelling probe (used with tankers or, hovering, in refuelling from ships), a Rast (recovery assist, secure and traversing) for safe recovery on deck in bad weather, buoyancy devices, rescue hoist and, of course, a totally redesigned fuselage packed with avionics and mission equipment. Almost the only parts simpler than the UH-60, apart from main legs, are the two unarmoured front cockpit seats.

Avionics: Largest of the sensors, the Texas Instruments APS-124 radar occupies almost the entire space under the forward fuselage, the large rectangular aerial (antenna) rotating inside a shallow circular radome. Fast scanning is claimed to give good detection of targets in high sea states, with a digital scan converter to give scan-to-scan integration. The radar supplies an on-board MPD (multipurpose display) and also, via the ARQ-44 data link, displays on LAMPS-equipped ships. The US Navy has always regarded its seagoing helicopters as extensions of the ship, rather than as totally independent platforms like those of the Royal Navy. Texas Instruments also supply the MAD, with the ASQ-81(V)2 towed "bird" carried on a winch-equipped pylon well aft on the right side. The section of cabin under the rotor is filled by a large rack with 25 sonobuoy launch tubes, arranged 5×5, each tube having five buoys fired pneumatically (a total of 125). The SO (sensor operator) station is on the left; he has to monitor the radar, MAD, acoustics (including control of active sonobuoys) and ESM systems. The ESM installation is the Raytheon ALQ-142, with four square aerials facing to four diagonally opposite points of the compass, two on the nose and two on the tapered flanks of the fuselage. It provides identification and bearing of hostile surveillance radars, using sorting techniques to analyse the emissions. Though the belly contains attachments for the Rast hauldown and a 6,000lb (2722kg) cargo hook, there is no provision for dipping sonar. Other avionics include doppler, Tacan, UHF/DF, radar altimeter, various processors and comprehensive secure communications and IFF.
Armament: Normal armament comprises two Mk 46 torpedoes, though the later British Sting Ray is an alternative offering much higher lethality. In due course it is expected that the EX-50 ALWT (advanced lightweight torpedo) will become available. So far no attempt has been made to fit anti-ship weapons, but the US Navy is known to have studied plans to deploy the Kongsberg Penguin Mk 2 Mod 7.

Future: The main new variant in prospect is the SH-60F, the "CV-helo" which is expected to replace the Sea King SH-3H in the dedicated ASW role operating from aircraft carriers. This would be visibly different, with a simple nose resembling the UH-60, the radar, ESM, MAD, sonobuoy launcher, acoustic processor, data link and cargo hook all deleted. Instead it would have the Bendix AQS-13F dipping sonar, the latest version of the long-established AQS-13 family, on a hydraulically driven 1,500ft (457m) cable. On the left an extended folding sponson carries a 100gal (454lit) long-range tank inboard of the torpedo to give up to 4.25h mission endurance. Of course, the basic Seahawk is being continually updated, Lot 4 (Fiscal 1985) having an increased-capacity main transmission rated at 3,400shp and later batches being planned eventually to have composite main-rotor blades to eliminate the current titanium spars.

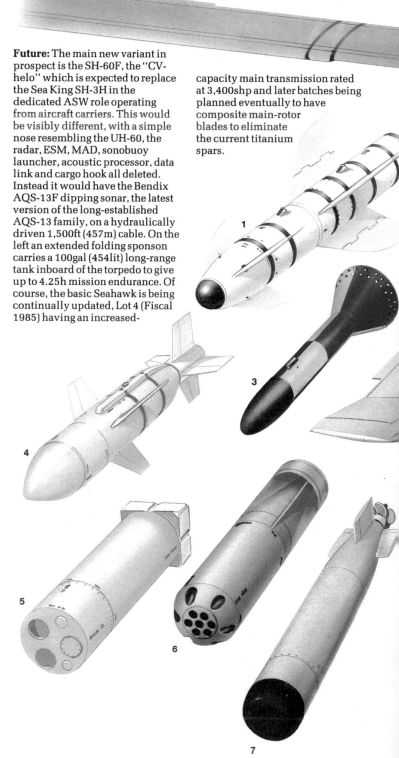

Left: Here seen operating from an FFG of the *Oliver Hazard Perry* class, the SH-60B is relatively big and very expensive, but meets the severe requirements of the US Navy. This machine is assigned to HSL-41 (home base, NAS North Island, at San Diego), but the modern camouflage makes identification much more difficult than formerly. In contrast, the MAD "bird" is brightly painted.

Below: All SH-60Bs so far delivered for combat duty are to a common standard, as illustrated here. Item 12, the dipping sonar, would be carried only by the proposed SH-60F (CV-Helo), which would have other differences outlined in the text.

Key to stores:
1 Penguin Mk 2 Mod 7 anti-ship missile.
2 Rescue hoist.
3 ASQ-81 MAD towed "bird".
4 BAe Sea Skua anti-ship missile.
5 Mk 36 mine.
6 Mk 53 depth bomb.
7 Mk 46 anti-submarine torpedo.
8 ALQ-142 ESM passive receiver aerials (two at front, two at rear).
9 Forward data-link aerial.
10 APS-124 radar (under fuselage).
11 Mk 50 advanced lightweight torpedo.
12 Bendix AQS-13F dipping sonar sensor.
13 Sparton dwarf DIFAR sonobuoys.
14 A-class sonobuoys (many species).
15 AGM-84 Harpoon cruise missile.

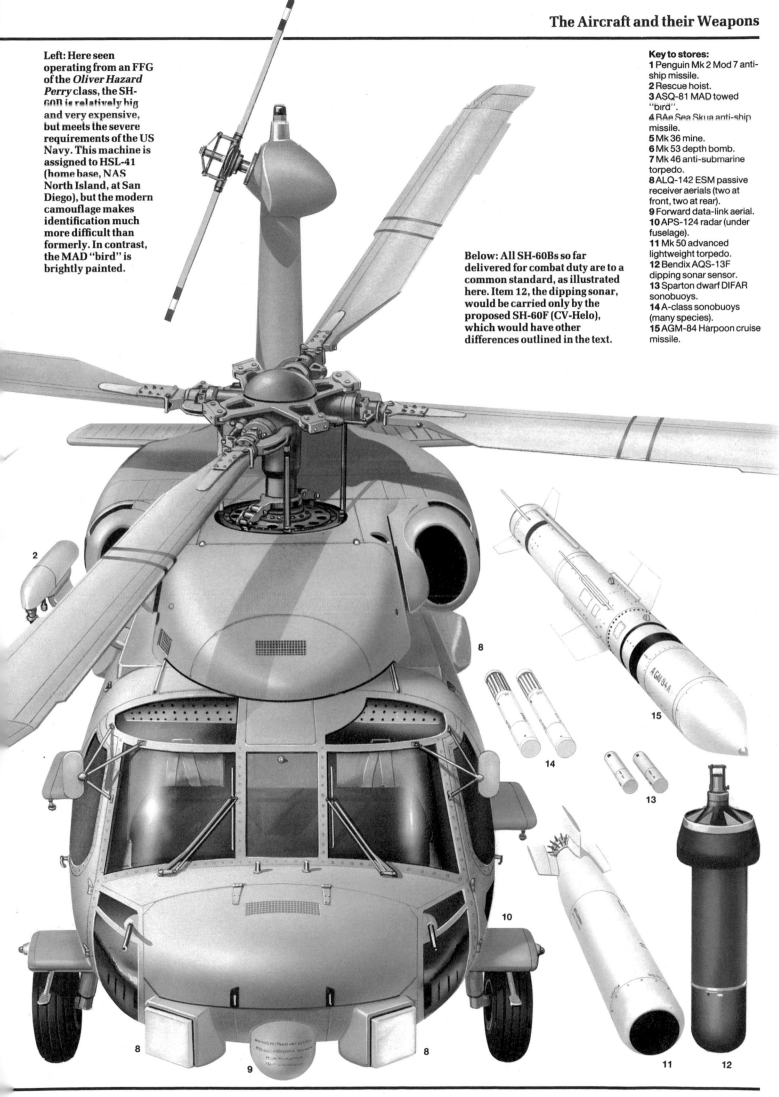

Sikorsky H-76 Eagle

Origin: USA, first flight (S-76) 13 March 1977.

Type: Multirole armed utility helicopter, (N) multirole naval helicopter.

Engines: Two turboshaft engines, customer choice of 960shp Pratt & Whitney Canada PT6B-36 or 735shp Allison 250-C34.

Dimensions: Diameter of four-blade main rotor 44ft 0in (13.41m); length overall (rotors turning) 52ft 6in (16.0m) (N slightly longer); fuselage length 43ft 4.5in (13.22m); height over tail rotor (MMS being slightly lower), 14ft 9.7in (4.52m).

Weights: Empty (H-76) 5,610lb (2545kg), (N) about 6,200lb (2812kg); max (H-76) 10,300lb (4672kg), (N, ASW mission) 10,953lb (4968kg).

Performance (H-76, PT6 engines, clean, no MMS): maximum speed 178mph (286km/h); maximum cruising speed 167mph (269km/h); maximum rate of climb at SL 1,700ft (518m)/min; hover ceiling IGE 8,700ft (2652m), OGE 5,900ft (1798m); range (standard fuel) about 335 miles (539km), but highly variable.

Background: The S-76 was designed purely as a civil helicopter to give Sikorsky a bigger share of the executive, offshore and GA market. The result is one of the best-sellers in the 12-seat (max) class, and an unmodified Mk II with 650shp Allison engines set 12 world records including speeds up to 213mph (343km/h). Some features stem from S-70 (Hawk family) research, the main rotor being a scaled version of that of the UH-60A. With such a firm basis, Sikorsky eventually judged that, despite the absence of any immediate home market, there would be little risk in funding a multirole military version, with numerous customer options. Casevac and initial military models were offered in 1981, and by late 1983 the decision had been taken to develop advanced anti-armour and naval models.

Design: As it was based on the existing S-76 the military and naval versions have a similar airframe. This shows no trace of the erstwhile pod-and-boom layout, nor does it have an amphibious hull. Instead the fuselage is almost perfectly streamlined, the nose being mainly glassfibre composite, the main cabin section light-alloy honeycomb sandwich and the rear section and tail a conventional light-alloy semi-monocoque, access doors mainly being Kevlar composite. The main rotor has a forged aluminium head, articulated elastomeric bearings needing no maintenance, and blades with an extruded titanium spar of oval section, Nomex honeycomb core, glassfibre skin and leading edges of abrasion-resistant nickel or titanium. The tailplane is an all-moving slab, which on the ground helps to keep people away from the four-blade tail rotor mounted on the left of the fin. All three units of the landing gear have single wheels and are

fully retractable. The engines are neatly installed on each side aft of the rotor gearbox (Allison and PWC engines having visibly different installations) with options including inlet particle separators and IR suppression of the jetpipes. Fuel is housed in high-strength tanks below the rear cabin, another option being self-sealing coverings. The cockpit seats pilot and copilot. The main cabin can seat ten troops with weapons and equipment; alternatively an MPPS (multi-purpose pylon system) can be installed, plus seats for seven troops. Naval versions normally have reduced cabin seating depending on mission, equipment and weapons.

Avionics: Basic equipment fit normally includes VHF transceiver, VHF, FM/AM, UHF com, UHF/DF, ADF, VOR/ILS, DME, transponder and dual RMI, course-deviation indicator, ELT (emergency locator transmitter), intercom, cabin speaker and external loudhailer. Normal equipment would also include full blind and night-flying lights and instruments, radar altimeter, stability-augmentation system, and 3,307lb (1500kg) cargo hoist, 600lb (272kg) rescue hoist and emergency flotation gear. Targeting equipment can include a Hughes Aircraft MMS, TOW roof sight, FLIR or Saab-Scania reticle sight. The naval H-76N can be fitted with Ferranti Seaspray 3 or MEL Super Searcher radar in a chin pod, as well as dual digital auto flight controls with many auto functions, AFCS-coupled hover, doppler, tactical nav system, tactical data-link, hover-inflight refuelling, roof or mast-mounted FLIR, strengthened landing gear giving greater ground/deck clearance, hauldown and securing system and power-folding blades.

Armament: All H-76 versions can have a 7.62mm or other machine gun pintle-mounted in each doorway. The MPPS can carry all standard rocket pods, machine-gun pods, Hellfire, TOW, Sea Skua and Stinger missiles and various other weapons. The H-76N can carry two Sea Skuas, or two Mk 46 or Sting Ray torpedoes. All versions can be comprehensively equipped with EW installations including chaff/flare dispensers, and the H-76N can carry a 300lb (136kg) ECM pod to fly versatile jamming missions.

Future: In the basic S-76 Sikorsky has an excellent helicopter with high speed, great versatility and fairly low signatures. To most of the world's helicopter builders the lack of a home market, and failure to sell to one's own government, would prove severe if not insuperable marketing handicaps. This is not likely to be the case with Sikorsky, and indeed customers (led by the Philippines) have shown no sales resistance to this attractive machine. At the same time, Sikorsky are so eager to penetrate the market that the company could be accused

of making certain claims that are rather exaggerated. To describe the H-76 as "the most cost/effective multimission helicopter in the world" is extremely hard to disprove, but to add that it is "the only helicopter designed for troop transport and assault, armed escort, anti-armor, search and rescue, and air ambulance" appears to be a claim that would be

disputed by rival manufacturers in the USA, France, Britain and West Germany, quite apart from the Soviet Union. Though developed from a helicopter designed solely as a General Aviation passenger transport, the H-76 and the proposed H-76N naval versions promise to be worthy rivals to the established machines in this class.

Left: This demonstrator was in mid-1986 still the only example of what Sikorsky hope to be a worldwide bestseller. Sikorsky's aggressive marketing is backed up by political and financial penetration but it needs to be supported by superior products. The H-76 Eagle is in many ways genuinely superior, but the sales picture has so far been disappointing.

Key to stores:
1 Stinger or POST (passive optical Stinger) missile.
2 Twin Stinger launch tubes.
3 General Electric GPU-2/A lightweight 20mm gun pod (with 300 rounds).
4 Rescue hoist.
5 TOW anti-armour missile (fins deployed).
6 Quadruple TOW launch tubes.
7 FN ETNA HMP and MRL 70 multi-purpose pod, (combined 12.7mm M3P gun and four 70mm rockets).
8 FN ETNA TMP-5 twin 7.62mm gun pod.
9 FN 7.62mm machine gun.
10 FFV Uni-Pod 0127 (0.50in Browning gun).
11 Mk 46 torpedo.
12 Marconi Sting Ray torpedo.
13 General Electric 7.62mm Minigun.
14 BAe Dynamics Sea Skua anti-ship missile.
15 Hellfire missile.
16 Standard 2.75in rockets.
17 Rocket launcher, 19 x 2.75 in.
18 Hellfire missiles (quadruple).
19 Oerlikon SNORA 81mm rocket.
20 Oerlikon SNORA SAL 12-80 launcher.
21 Oerlikon HL-7-80 launcher.
22 2.75 in rocket (fins deployed), typically BEI Hydra 70.
23 Roof-mounted sight (Hughes TOW type but GEC Avionics MonoHUD also qualified).
24 Oerlikon KAD B-12 20mm gun and ammunition.
25 M130 chaff/flare dispenser.
26 ALQ-144 pulsed IRCM jammer.
27 Mast-mounted sight (Hughes TOW type).

Note: The H-76N naval version may be qualified to carry a MAD, dipping sonar and 360° search radar.

Above: Arrayed around the proposed definitive H-76 are all the stores at present envisaged for both it and for the H-76N naval version. Further development naturally hinges upon winning orders from customers.

Westland Wessex

Origin: Great Britain, based on US S-58 design, first flight 17 May 1957.
Type: (HC.2, HU.5) multirole utility and assault transport, (HAS.3) ASW.
Engine: (HC.2, HU.5) one Rolls-Royce Coupled Gnome 110/111 rated at 1,550shp, but with two power sections of 1,250shp each, (HAS.3) one 1,600shp Rolls-Royce (formerly Napier) Gazelle 165 turboshaft.
Dimensions: Diameter of four-blade main rotor 56ft 0in (17.07m); length (rotors turning) 65ft 9in (20.04m), (main rotor and tail folded) 38ft 6in (11.73m); height (to top of main rotor head) 14ft 5in (4.39m).
Weights: Equipped empty (3) 7,850lb (3561kg), (5) 8,657lb (3927kg); maximum loaded 13,500lb (6124kg).
Performance: Maximum speed (max wt at SL, all) 132mph (212km/h); cruising speed 121mph (195km/h); maximum rate of climb (5) 1,650ft (503m)/min; hovering ceiling OGE (3) 3,100ft (945m), (5) 4,000ft (1219m); range (standard fuel, HAS.3) 302 miles (486km), (HU.5) 330 miles (531km).
Background: Throughout the early 1950s the Royal Navy sought an effective hunter/killer ASW helicopter, and for eight years contracted with Bristol for what became the Type 191 twin-turbine tandem-rotor machine. This made such poor progress that in 1956 the Admiralty cut its losses and decided the best way out was by the proven Sikorsky S-58 (HSS-1) but fitted with a turbine engine. The S-58 was added to Westland's existing Sikorsky licence, Napier was already developing the Gazelle free-turbine engine for the Bristol 191, and the Wessex HAS.1 reached the Royal Navy in April 1960 (first squadron, No 815, July 1961). By this time the twin-engine safety of the Coupled Gnome engine had led to its substitution in the HC.2 transport (73 for RAF), HCC.4 (two for The Queen's Flight) and HU.5 (101 for Commando assault). The original 140 HAS.1s were upgraded to HAS.3 standard by adding radar and much other new equipment, and uprating the Gazelle; three HAS.3s were built as attrition replacements. The RAN bought 27 Gazelle-engined Mk 31s.
Design: As far as possible the Wessex retains to this day the original aerodynamics and structure of the S-58, typical of the 1950-51 era. The main rotor has a fully articulated oil-lubricated hub, with manual blade folding and hydrauic control, carrying blades with a hollow extruded aluminium D-spar and 20 trailing-edge pockets with aluminium ribs and sheet covering. Heavy balance weights and a tracking weight are fixed inside each tip. The fuselage was unusual for its day in having normal (not pod-and-boom) shape, with the bottom horizontal and close to the deck or ground, supported by conventional fixed tailwheel type landing gears with the main shock strut long enough to be pivoted to the fuselage top

longeron. This attachment is just below the cockpit windows, the cockpit being completely above the front of the cabin to leave the nose free for the engine. The latter is installed at an angle of 39°, driving via a diagonal shaft passing up between the pilot seats to the main gearbox immediately behind the cockpit. This arrangement enabled the payload to be distributed fore and aft of the main rotor and enabled the engine to be accessible from ground level. Except for the VIP-furnished CC.4, still the only helicopters in The Queen's Flight, most Wessex are used mainly in overwater operations and have rapid-inflation popout buoyancy bags carried outboard of the main wheels. The tail rotor, together with the swept pylon fin and fixed tailplane, pivot round to the right for shipboard stowage. Even the fully equipped ASW marks are jacks of all trades and have a rescue hoist and provisions for rapid conversion to the assault transport role with 16 troop seats or attachments for eight (RAF, seven) stretchers or internal or slung cargo up to a weight of 4,000lb (1814kg) (RAF, 3,600lb, 1633kg). Normal crew of the HAS.3 comprises two pilots, sonar operator and anti-submarine control officer; that of the HC.2 and HU.5 is usually two pilots plus a winchman or loadmaster.
Avionics: The HAS.3 has a duplicated flight-control and Newmark autostabilization system for day/night and adverse overwater navigation and auto approach to the hover for dipping sonar operations. The usual sonar is the Plessey Type 195; HISOS 1 has been developed using Wessex assistance but will not be retrofitted to these helicopters. Other equipment includes UHF (with standby and homer), HF with wire aerials along both sides of the fuselage, Ryan APN-97A doppler, upper and lower IFF and rear ventral rod transponder and, in the HAS.3, the MEL AW.391 search radar mounted dorsally behind the rotor (giving rise to the common name of "Camel" for this version).
Armament: Normally the HC.2, CC.4 and HU.5 are unarmed, even in Northern Ireland and the Falklands. The HAS.3 has side attachments for up to two AS torpedoes, usually of Mk 46 type though other weapons can be carried. Alternatives to torpedoes include GPMG or rocket pods or, earlier in their career, four AS.11 or AS.12 wire-guided missiles (the HAS.3 in the Fleet Air Arm Museum, riddled with bullet holes, disabled the Argentine submarine *Santa Fe* with two 250lb/113kg depth charges and subsequently attacked with a door-mounted GPMG).
Future: Upgrading of all marks of Wessex continued into the 1980s, but the effort has now eased because, though most will remain in service for about another five years, it is not cost/effective to fund further improvements.

Above: A Wessex HU.5 of the Royal Navy firing an AS.12 heavy wire-guided missile during exercises from RNAS Yeovilton. The HU.5 is normally an unarmed transport, used for many tasks including Royal Marine Commando assault.

Key to stores:
1 FN 7.62mm GPMG on doorway pintle mounting.
2 7.62mm ammunition.
3 External long-range tank, 100gal (161lit)
4 Aérospatiale missile mounting.
5 Rescue hoist.

6 Twin Aérospatiale AS.11 wire-guided missiles.
7 Mk 44 anti-submarine torpedo.
8 Mk 46 anti-submarine torpedo (both torpedoes with parachutes).
9 Rapid-inflation flotation bags.

10 Twin jetpipes on each side from single engine.
11 SNIA BPD 51mm (2in) rockets.
12 SNIA BPD 14-tube 51mm rocket launcher.
13 BAe Mk 11 depth charge.
14 Twin Aérospatiale AS.12 heavy wire-guided missiles.
15 Plessey Type 194 dipping sonar (Wessex HAS.1 only).

16 Plessey Type 195 dipping sonar.
17 HF communications aerial masts and wires (both sides of helicopter).
18 Top of radome of AW.391 search radar ("Camel hump").

Above: The large drawing shows stores cleared for use by all types of Wessex, though the HAS.3 illustrated operates only in the ASW role, with torpedoes, and is devoid of sensors except a sonar.

Westland Scout and Wasp

Origin: Great Britain, first flights see below (Background).
Type: (S) Multirole tactical army helicopter, (W) shipboard ASW, SAR and utility helicopter.
Engine: One Rolls-Royce Nimbus turboshaft, (S) Nimbus 102 flat-rated at 685shp, (W) Nimbus 503 flat-rated at 710shp.
Dimensions: Diameter of four-blade main rotor 32ft 3in (9.83m); length (rotors turning) 40ft 4in (12.29m); (ignoring rotors) 30ft 4in (9.24m); height (over tail rotor) 11ft 8in (3.56m), (to top of main-rotor head) 8ft 11in (2.72m).
Weights: Empty (S) 3,185lb (1445kg), (W) 3,480lb (1579kg).
Performance: (At max wt) Maximum speed at SL (S) 131mph (211km/h), (W) 120mph (193km/h); cruising speed (S) 122mph (196km/h), (W) 110mph (177km/h); maximum rate of climb (S) 1,670ft (509m)/min, (W) 1,440ft (439m)/min; hovering ceiling OGE (W) 8,800ft (2682m); range with four passengers and full allowances (S) 315 miles (507km), (W) 270 miles (435km).
Background: Design of a new turbine-engined helicopter, the P.531, was started by Saunders-Roe Ltd at Eastleigh in November 1957, the design team being that taken over by Saro from the former Cierva company. Powered by a Blackburn (Anglicised Turboméca) Turmo engine of 325hp, it first flew on 20 July 1958. The Turmo was developed into the Bristol Siddeley Nimbus, fitted to the "production prototype" P.531-2 flown on 9 August 1959. This was further developed into the Scout AH.1 for the British Army and the Wasp HAS.1 for the Royal Navy, the first examples of each type respectively flying on 4 August 1960 and 28 October 1962. In 1960 Saro was taken over by Westland and these helicopters were transferred to the Hayes factory of the former Fairey Aviation company, also taken over by Westland. Subsequently 160 Scout AH.1s (plus small export orders) were built, as well as 98 Wasp HAS.1 and exports of this version to South Africa, Brazil, the Netherlands and New Zealand.
Design: In all major respects the Scout and Wasp are conventional machines, designed before what might be called "new technology" came on the scene. The main rotor has a fully articulated hub holding the metal blades by inner torsion bars. The tail rotor has four blades, wood on the Scout and metal on the Wasp, and is carried on a swept fin. On the Scout there is a fixed tailplane (horizontal stabilizer) with endplate fins mounted under the tailboom. The Wasp has a different half-tailplane on the right side at the top of the fin, and the entire tail section folds to the right for shipboard stowage. The most obvious difference between the two helicopters is that, while the Scout has simple tubular skids, with recoil-damper shock absorption and removable ground-manoeuvring wheels, the Wasp has a very sophisticated landing

gear specially designed for operations from small warships. The "four-poster" gear has long-stroke Lockheed shock struts able to absorb very high rates between a sinking helicopter and an upcoming deck. The wheels are carried on short vertical struts which swing on upper and lower V-struts pivoted to the fuselage, the shock strut being mounted diagonally. The front wheels, with the same 8ft (2.44m) track as those at the rear, are normally aligned fore/aft. The rear wheels are usually splayed out at 45° to prevent unwanted movement on a violently oscillating deck; in any case in RN service it is standard procedure, on deck recovery, to go immediately into reverse pitch, pressing the helicopter downwards, while deck "lashers" attach straps to the legs and pull them taut. A unique and prominent feature is the flotation gear, large flat boxes held high on each side at roof level to ensure that the floating helicopter cannot capsize. Scouts and Wasps have four hinged doors. There are two front seats, dual controls being an option. At the rear is a triple seat, removable for cargo or (Scout) armament. Maximum slung payload is 1,500lb (680kg), and a customer option is a Lucas air-driven rescue hoist and provision for four stretcher casualties, two of them in external panniers.
Avionics: All versions have blind-flying instruments and full night equipment. Scouts were delivered with VHF and an Army (B.47/48) radio but have since been upgraded. Wasps have duplicated UHF and a UHF homer, radar altimeter, and autopilot/autostabilization system to facilitate low-altitude hovering in the wake of ships. The need for precise position information in Northern Ireland led to the installation of Dectrac, linked with the Decca hyperbolic navaid, formerly used. Another add-on equipment is the SX-16 Nightsun 30 million candlepower switchable white/IR Xenon swivelling searchlight with variable-width beam.
Armament: Originally the Scout was unarmed, but it soon carried two pairs of SS.11 wire-guided missiles, aimed via a Ferranti AF120 or AF530 stabilized sight in the cockpit roof. In Northern Ireland standard kit includes either a door-mounted GPMG (at a pinch one can be mounted on each side, though there is not much room for the two gunners) or twin forward-firing GPMGs mounted on the skids, converging at a selected distance ahead and aimed by a Chinagraph mark made on the windscreen. The Wasp HAS.1 was originally intended to drop AS torpedoes at a point directed by the parent ship, no ASW sensors being carried. Later this role was exchanged for general missile attack, the front-seat observer being trained to guide SS.11 or AS.12 missiles. Wasps of the Brazilian navy are armed with the

Avibras LM-70/7 rocket launchers and the same manufacturer's Helicopter Armament System in which an LM-70/7 rocket launcher is combined with a pivoted FN MAG 7.62mm machine gun.
Future: Little effort is being applied to further upgrades of these popular machines, which have been steadily reduced in numbers serving with the British Army and Royal Navy, some finding buyers abroad. Both, however, will remain in British service until 1990.

Above: A recent formation of Royal Navy Wasps operating from the shore base HMS *Osprey*, at Portland, Dorset, where crews are trained for the embarked ships' flights.

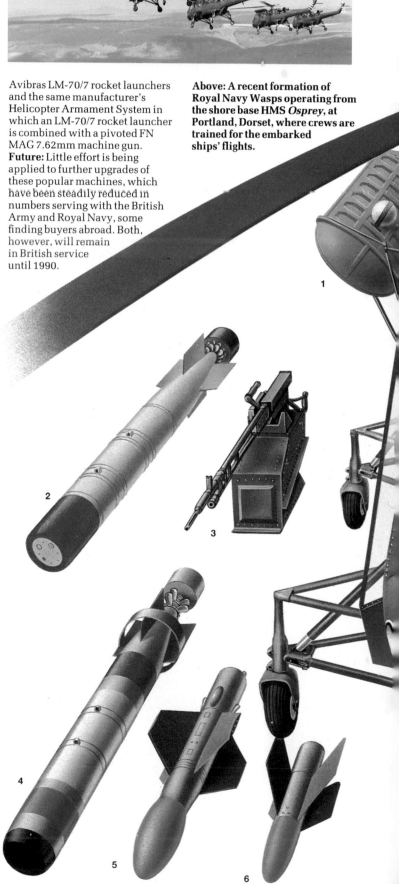

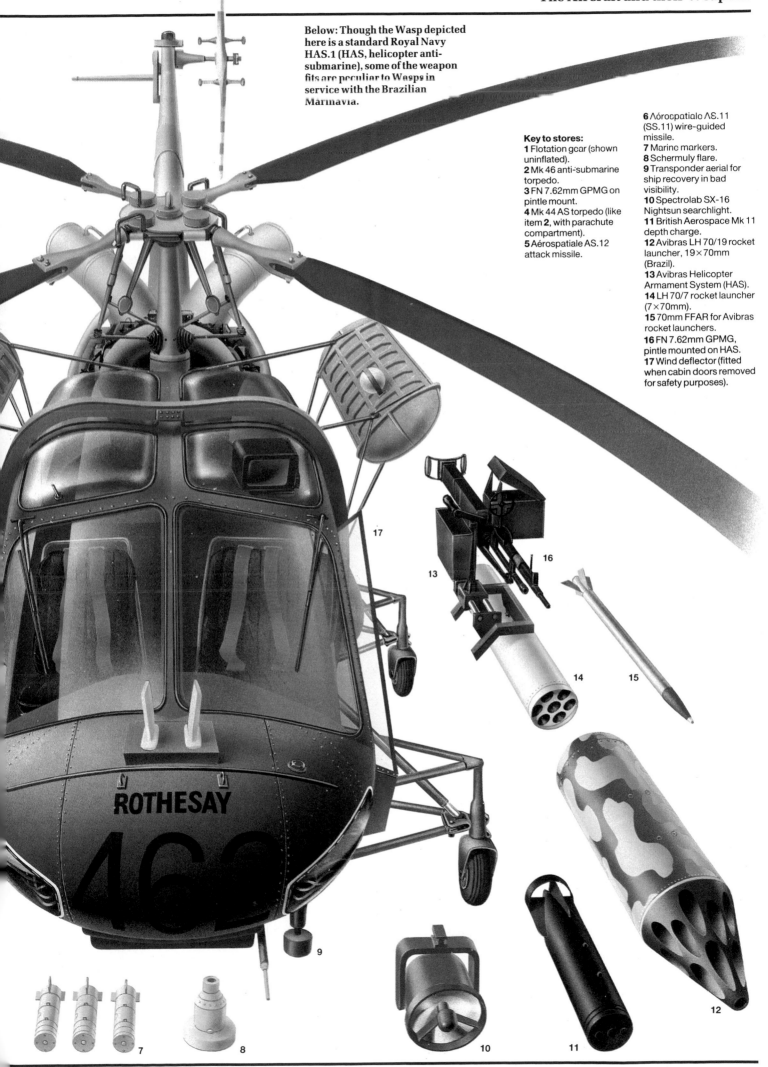

Below: Though the Wasp depicted here is a standard Royal Navy HAS.1 (HAS, helicopter anti-submarine), some of the weapon fits are peculiar to Wasps in service with the Brazilian Marinavia.

Key to stores:
1 Flotation gear (shown uninflated).
2 Mk 46 anti-submarine torpedo.
3 FN 7.62mm GPMG on pintle mount.
4 Mk 44 AS torpedo (like item 2, with parachute compartment).
5 Aérospatiale AS.12 attack missile.
6 Aérospatiale AS.11 (SS.11) wire-guided missile.
7 Marine markers.
8 Schermuly flare.
9 Transponder aerial for ship recovery in bad visibility.
10 Spectrolab SX-16 Nightsun searchlight.
11 British Aerospace Mk 11 depth charge.
12 Avibras LH 70/19 rocket launcher, 19×70mm (Brazil).
13 Avibras Helicopter Armament System (HAS).
14 LH 70/7 rocket launcher (7×70mm).
15 70mm FFAR for Avibras rocket launchers.
16 FN 7.62mm GPMG, pintle mounted on HAS.
17 Wind deflector (fitted when cabin doors removed for safety purposes).

ROTHESAY

Westland Sea King and Commando

Origin: Great Britain, based on US S-61 design, first flight 7 May 1969 (Commando 12 September 1973).
Type: (Sea King 2, 5 and derivatives) ASW, (Sea King 3) SAR, (Mk 2AEW) AEW, (Mk 4 and Commando) multirole transport.
Engines: Two Rolls-Royce Gnome (T58-derived) turboshafts, (all current versions) 1,660shp Gnome H.1400-1.
Dimensions: Diameter of five-blade main rotor 62ft 0in (18.9m); length (rotors turning) 72ft 8in (22.15m), (main rotor and tail folded) 47ft 3in (14.4m); height (overall) 16ft 10in (5.13m), (to top of rotor head) 15ft 6in (4.72m).
Weights: Empty (ASW) 13,672lb (6202kg), (transport) 12,253lb (5558kg); maximum loaded (most) 21,000lb (9526kg), (AEW) 21,400lb (9707kg), (Advanced) 21,500lb (9752kg).
Performance: (all at 21,000lb, 9526kg) Maximum speed 143mph (230km/h); normal cruising speed 129mph (208km/h); maximum rate of climb 2,020ft (616m)/min; hovering ceiling OGE 3,200ft (975m); range (standard fuel) 764 miles (1230km), (max payload 28 troops plus 30min reserve) 276 miles (444km).
Background: In 1959 Westland extended its existing Sikorsky licence to include the HSS-2 (S-61), but it was to be more than eight years before the first order was placed by the Royal Navy. Though the original Sea King HAS.1 was based on the HSS-2 (SH-3A), important differences were incorporated, as noted under Design. One change was fitting the 1,500shp Gnome H.1400 engine with full-authority electronic control. Power was uprated in the HAS.2, which was the basis for many export versions. Subsequent British marks are the HAS.3 for SAR, HC.4 for assault transport and logistic support, the HAS.5 for ASW and (conversions) the Mk 2AEW. The Advanced Sea King now in production for export becomes the HAS.6 as Royal Navy conversions. The export Commando is basically the HC.4
Design: Naturally the minimum of changes were introduced in the original Sea King HAS.1 of 1969. The Gnome installation did not differ significantly from that of the T58s, but internally the British machine was totally new. Whereas the US Navy helicopter had been a remote sensor/weapon carrier

working in close conjunction with its parent ship, the Sea King HAS.1 was from the start designed for total independence. The Newmark Mk 31 flight-control was arranged to provide attitude/heading/height hold, three-axis stabilization in manoeuvres, auto approach to or from the hover at any height (with position hold in any wind) and an auxiliary trim facility. The main cabin was arranged as a tactical compartment with two operators able to manage a complete tactical plot and kill without external assistance. All amphibious Sea Kings (ie, not HC.4 and Commando) have the ability to carry out such diverse roles as ASW (if equipped), SAR, troop and cargo transport (with slung load), casevac and (Advanced Sea King) anti-ship missile attack. Again except for the HC.4 and Commando, which are distinguished by having simple fixed landing gear without floats, all versions have automatic folding and spreading of the main rotor. The complete tail folds on all versions. Current Advanced Sea Kings, starting with the Mk 42B for India, have an uprated transmission and completely new all-composite main-rotor blades produced by computer-controlled filament winding. All models have tankage arranged in two wholly separate systems, with a customer option of additional underfloor tank raising capacity to 818gal (3719lit). Self-ferry cabin and external tanks give a range of 1,105 miles (1778km). Customer options include a rear cabin bulkhead moved 71in (1.8m) aft to give more room for mission equipment (such as LAPADS), all-weather deicing of inlets and blades, and a choice of a flat-plate engine inlet deflector (mainly for sea spray and snow) or large box inlet filters for sandy deserts.
Avionics: Various VHF/UHF radios are usually backed up by HF with wire aerials. Normal equipment includes doppler, Gyrosyn compass, radar altimeter and Mk 31 flight control system. ASW Sea Kings have MEL AW.391 or (current) MEL ARI.5991 Sea Searcher radar, Plessey Type 195

or Bendix AQS-13B dipping sonar, Ultra mini-sonobuoys with passive dropping equipment and LAPADS acoustic processing and display system. Very comprehensive IFF/EW systems are usually installed. Non-ASW versions usually have VOR, ILS, and integrated Decca 71 doppler and TANS. The Indian Mk 42B Advanced Sea King has the GEC Avionics AQS-902 sonics/tactical processing system. This version, like the HAS.5, can use signals from buoys dropped by other friendly aircraft. Today Royal Navy Sea Kings have Racal MIR-2 Orange Crop ESM on the nose, and the Egyptian air force has Commandos equipped with

Selenia IHS.6 ESM/ECM. The radar carried by the Mk 2AEW is the Thorn EMI Searchwater with Cossor Jubilee Guardsman IFF using the same scanner in a pressurized kettledrum radome extended down hydraulically when on station.
Armament: Normal load for ASW versions comprises up to four Mk 46 (or other) torpedoes or four Mk 11 depth charges or a Clevite

simulator. Auxiliary stores include Mini-sonobuoys, marine markers and smoke floats. The Indian Mk 42B carries two Sea Eagle anti-ship missiles (helicopter version with rocket boost). The Sea King HC.4 has a cabin-mounted 7.62mm GPMG and most of the customer options of guns, rockets and missiles are illustrated.
Future: All future production will have composite blades, and if funds were available these would be retrofitted to all British Sea Kings. Westland had delivered 234 Sea Kings and 79 Commandos when this was written, and many are the subject of update programmes. All RN HAS.1 and

HAS.2 helicopters have been brought to HAS.5 standard, and these in turn will be upgraded as HAS.6s with MEL Super Searcher radar, with integrated processor giving MAD and sonic inputs on one display.

Below: Among the more colourful Sea Kings are the Mk 43 SAR machines of the Royal Norwegian AF. They are similar in equipment to the British (RAF) HAR. Mk 3.

Key to stores:
1 Rescue hoist.
2 Searchwater radar in pressurized kettledrum radome (Mk 2 AEW only).
3 Bendix AQS-13B dipping sonar.
4 FN 7.62mm GPMG on pintle mount, with ammunition.
5 Inflatable flotation gear (just visible).
6 Advanced Sting Ray torpedo.
7 A244/S torpedo and parachute pack.

8 Mk 46 torpedo and parachute.
9 Mk 44 homing torpedo and parachute.
10 Mk 11 depth charge.
11 Twin MLMS (Stinger) launcher.
12 Stinger missile.
13 Sparton sonobuoys: Q-41 passive type.
14 Q-47 active buoy.
15 Q-53 DIFAR passive buoy.
16 Q-62 DICASS active buoy.
17 Q-77 active type buoy.

18 Dwarf Sparton buoy.
19 Vinten VIPA reconnaissance pod.
20 Orange Crop ESM passive receivers (and at rear).
21 Spectrolab SX-16 Nightsun searchlight.
22 Penguin Mk 2 Mod 7 anti ship missile.
23 Three 3.5lb No 2 smoke/flame float markers.
24 Schermuly day/night marker.
25 BAe Sea Eagle anti-ship missile.

26 TB-623/ASQ-81 MAD towed body.
27 AM.39 Exocet anti-ship missile.
28 BAe Sea Skuas (four).
29 GE SUU-11B/A Minigun 7.62mm pod.
30 Plessey Cormorant (HISOS) dipping sonar (array shown deployed).
31 Plessey Type 195 dipping sonar.
32 Inlet particle shield.
33 Reprofiled carbon-fibre composite blades.
34 Unbraced tailplane.

Left: The subject of the main artwork is an Advanced Sea King, with composite blades, shown in the low-visibility colours of the Mk 2 AEW. Note that all the Westland variants have unbraced tailplanes (horizontal stabilizer).

Westland Lynx (army)

Origin: Great Britain (original version shared 70/30 with Aérospatiale), first flight 21 March 1971.

Type: General-purpose multirole tactical helicopter.

Engines: Two Rolls-Royce Gem turboshafts, (most) 900shp Gem 2, (AH.5, 7) 1,120shp Gem 41-1, (Lynx-3) 1,346shp Gem 60.

Dimensions: Diameter of four-blade main rotor 42ft 0in (12.8m); length (rotors turning) (most) 49ft 9in (15.16m), (-3) 50ft 9in (15.47m), (main blades folded) (most) 43ft 2.3in (13.16m), (-3) 45ft 3in (13.79m); height (over rotors) (most) 12ft 0in (3.66m), (-3, MMS not fitted) 10ft 10in (3.3m).

Weights: Empty (AH.1) 5,683lb (2578kg), (-3, estimate) 7,114lb (3227kg); maximum takeoff (1) 10,000lb (4536kg), (-3) 13,000lb (5897kg).

Performance: (maximum weight) Maximum speed (clean, SL, both) 190mph (306km/h); cruising speed (1) 161mph (259km/h), (-3) 172mph (277km/h); maximum rate of climb (1) 2,480ft (756m)/min; hovering ceiling OGE (1) 10,600ft (3231m); typical range with troops, 20min reserve (1) 336 miles (541km), (-3) 385 miles (620km).

Background: Originally designated WG.13, the Lynx is the only helicopter to have been designed by Westland; it was also the first metric British design. Planned as a multirole military, naval and civil machine in the 4.5ton class, it quickly proved outstanding in such matters as flight performance, agility (including aerobatics) and mission versatility, and in the Falklands its toughness was also apparent (in contrast to some other helicopters). As part of the Anglo-French Helicopter Agreement of 1967 Aérospatiale were awarded 30 per cent of the manufacturing task, this being the intended French proportion of purchases. In fact France has so far bought 12 per cent, and competed with the Lynx wherever possible. Despite this the British machine has sold to 11 air forces and navies on sheer merit. First-generation Lynx are all broadly similar, being divided into skid-equipped army versions and wheel-equipped naval marks, each group having appropriate avionics and weapons. In 1984 Westland flew the first second-generation Lynx-3 (not to be confused with the earlier Lynx HAS.3 of the Royal Navy). The Lynx-3 is a larger, heavier and more powerful machine being developed in army and navy versions. The army version is the subject of the main illustration; the navy Lynx on the following pages is a first-generation machine.

Design: Like all parts of the Lynx the engines, gearboxes and rotors were designed to the very latest technology in 1968-9. The compact three-shaft engines have electrically deiced inlets and are fed from bag tanks totalling 1,616lb (733kg) (-3, 2,205lb, 1000kg) with every conceivable arrangement for front-line fuelling/defuelling. The main gearbox has conformal gears and set new standards in compact design with few parts. The main rotor hub is machined from a single titanium forging and its four extension arms are attached direct to tubular ties whose end-fittings are bolted to the blade root. Each blade has a stainless-steel two-spar box to which is bonded a Nomex-filled glassfibre rear section. The Lynx-3 blades are entirely of filament-wound composite construction with advanced BERP tips. The tail rotor has a light-alloy spar (all-composites in the Lynx AH.7 and Lynx-3, with rotation reversed to reduce noise). Current Lynx have a fixed half-tailplane at the top on the right side of the swept fin. The Lynx-3 has a large symmetric tailplane of inverted aerofoil profile at the bottom of the tailboom, the army variant also having end-plate fins; all these tail surfaces are fixed. The fuselage is a streamlined pod-and-boom, mainly light alloy but with much glassfibre. The two hinged cockpit doors and large sliding cabin doors are all jettisonable. Behind the pilots' seats the minimum cabin length is 81in (2.06m), width 70in (1.78m) and height 56in (1.42m). The Lynx-3 cabin is 12in (0.3m) longer. Normal loads in the Lynx AH.1 include 10 armed troops, three stretchers and attendant or a cargo load of 2,000lb (907kg) internal or 3,000lb (1361kg) external. Lynx-3 internal payload is 3,400lb (1542kg).

Avionics: Westland offer a tremendous variety of customer options, but standard kit includes GEC Avionics autopilot/autostab system, Decca 71 doppler and TANS, Gyrosyn GM9 compass and radio compass. Options include VOR/DME, ILS, IFF, RWR, and radar altimeter. Missile-armed versions have various choices, the British Army AH.1 and 7 have the Hughes TOW sight (made by BAe) on the cockpit roof. In 1986 BAe received a £60m contract to add a full night-vision capability. Standard ECM dispenser is ALE-39. The Lynx-3 can have TADS/PNVS or other sensors in the nose, on the roof or in an MMS, and an IRCM jammer will be carried. All data will be digital, via 1553B bus.

Armament: The main illustration gives an idea of what is available! The 60 anti-tank AH.1s of the British Army carry eight TOW, plus eight reloads in the cabin, or a team of three gunners with their own launchers and missiles. All weapons depicted have been cleared for use. The Lynx-3 is expected to carry eight or 16 Hellfire plus Stinger AAMs.

Future: Almost all future development is concentrated on the formidable Lynx-3, which though initially a dedicated anti-armour helicopter is also the obvious starting point for an important new generation of multirole tactical helicopters. It is very much to be hoped that part-acquisition of the company by UTC, parent of Sikorsky, will not adversely affect this.

Key to stores:
1 Twin-finned tail.
2 ALE-39 chaff/flare dispenser.
3 DAT mine dispenser (two types loaded).
4 Engine particle jets.
5 SURA 12×80mm rocket installation.
6 Standard E2 rocket launcher, 19×2.75in, with rockets shown separately.
7 SNORA launcher for 6×81mm rockets, with rocket shown separately.
8 Quadruple RBS.70, with missile in front.
9 Quadruple HOT launchers.
10 HOT missile, fins deployed.
11 SNEB 68mm rockets.
12 Brandt 22×68 (SNEB) launcher.
13 Brandt 12×68 (SNEB) launcher.
14 BAe Alarm anti-radar missile.
15 Smoke markers.
16 Spectrolab SX-16 Nightsun searchlight.
17 TADS sight system.
18 AS.12 attack missile.
19 Matra SATCP Mistral missile.
20 Stinger (MLMS) missile.
21 Oerlikon KAD B-12 20mm cannon.
22 Oerlikon KBA 25mm cannon.
23 7.62mm Minigun in Emerson FTS installation.
24 Twin MLMS (Stinger) launcher.
25 Quadruple AGM-114A Hellfire missiles.

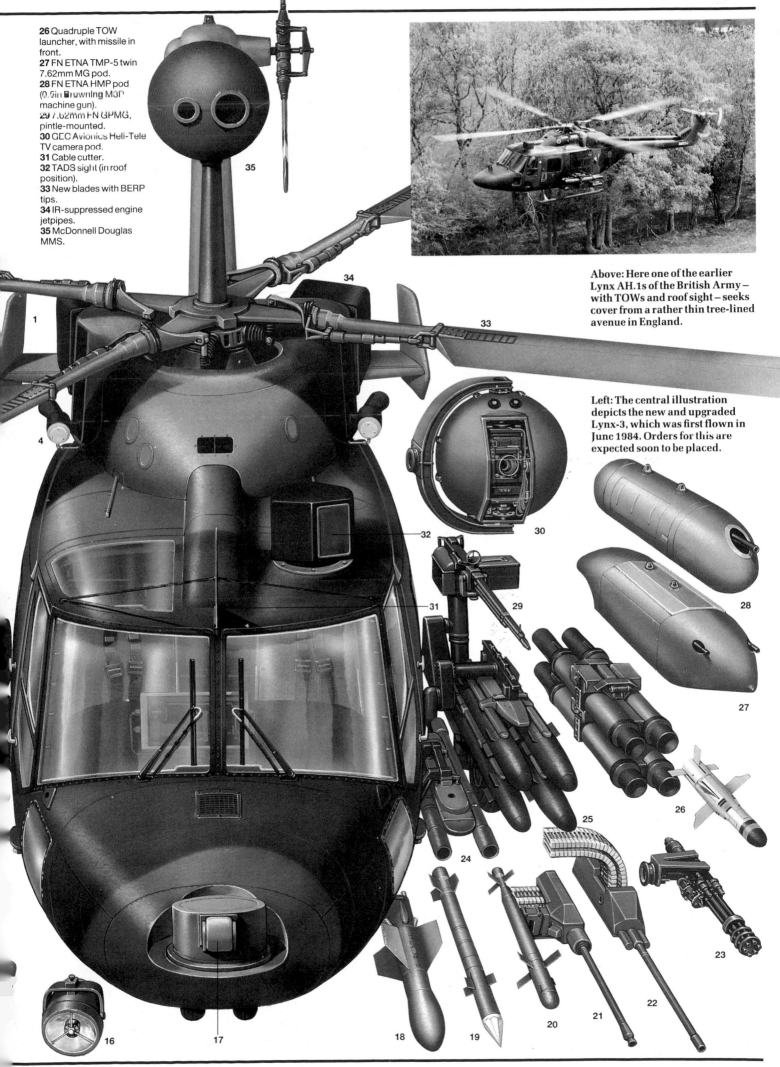

26 Quadruple TOW launcher, with missile in front.
27 FN ETNA TMP-5 twin 7.62mm MG pod.
28 FN ETNA HMP pod (0.5in Browning M3P machine gun).
29 7.62mm FN GPMG, pintle-mounted.
30 GEC Avionics Heli-Tele TV camera pod.
31 Cable cutter.
32 TADS sight (in roof position).
33 New blades with BERP tips.
34 IR-suppressed engine jetpipes.
35 McDonnell Douglas MMS.

Above: Here one of the earlier Lynx AH.1s of the British Army – with TOWs and roof sight – seeks cover from a rather thin tree-lined avenue in England.

Left: The central illustration depicts the new and upgraded Lynx-3, which was first flown in June 1984. Orders for this are expected soon to be placed.

Westland Lynx (navy)

Origin: Great Britain, first flight 25 May 1972.

Type: Multirole shipboard helicopter, for ASW, ASST, ASM attack, SAR, reconnaissance, vertrep transport etc.

Engines: Two Rolls-Royce Gem turboshafts, (2) 900shp Gem 2, (3, 4 and exports) 1,120shp Gem 41-1, (Lynx-3) 1,346shp Gem 60.

Dimensions: Diameter of four-blade main rotor (most) 42ft 0in (12.8m), (-3) may be slightly increased; length (rotors turning) 49ft 9in (15.16m), (main rotor and tail folded) 34ft 10in (10.62m), (-3 figures respectively 50ft 9in, 15.47m, and 45ft 3in, 13.79m); height (rotors turning) 11ft 9.7in (3.6m), (-3) 10ft 10in (3.3m).

Weights: Empty (2,3) 6,040lb (2740kg), (-3) about 7,500lb (3400kg); maximum loaded (2) 10,000lb (4536kg), (3, 4 and exports) 10,500lb (4763kg), (-3) 13,000lb (5897kg).

Performance: Maximum cruising speed 144mph (232km/h); (-3) 172mph (277km/h); cruising speed on one engine 140mph (225km/h); maximum rate of climb 2,170ft (661m)/min; hovering ceiling OGE (3, 4) 8,450ft (2575m); radius (SAR, max speed, three crew and seven rescuees, full allowances) 111 miles (179km); time on station (ASW, full sensors and weapons, max speed transits to station at 58 miles/93km radius) 2h 29min; range (normal fuel) 368 miles (592km), (-3) 385 miles (620km).

Background: At the start of the Lynx programme in 1967 it was agreed with France that one version of this versatile helicopter would be developed for naval roles. The first five development Lynx were of Army configuration, the first naval (HAS.2) prototype being the sixth. Subsequently the naval Lynx was produced not only for the two original customers but also for eight export customers, with progressive upgrading in power and equipment. A mock-up has been built of the new-generation naval Lynx-3 but no order has yet been placed.

Design: The basic design of the Lynx has already been outlined in the preceding entry. The existing naval versions are virtually identical in engine installation, rotors and dynamic parts, and in most parts of the airframe and on-board systems. The main differences are found in the landing gear, shipboard features, and in the cockpit, avionics and weapons. The original HAS.2 for the Royal Navy entered service at a weight of 9,500lb (4309kg) but was upgraded later to the figure given above. This introduced all the naval features, most prominent of which is the use of wheeled landing gear. The main gears have vertical shock struts mounted on short rear-fuselage sponsons. Each carries a single wheel toed out at 27° for deck operations. After landing these wheels are manually rotated fore/aft and locked in that position for movement into and out of the hangar. The nose gear has twin wheels and is hydraulically

steerable to 90° left/right. All four wheels have sprag (positive locking) brakes to prevent motion on deck in a heavy sea. The brakes engage automatically following hydraulic failure. Customer options include pop-out flotation bags and a hydraulically powered harpoon deck lock and haul-down system. For shipboard stowage the main rotor can be folded manually and the complete tail folds down to the right. Early HAS.2s had a slimmer tailboom than the main production, three windows in each of the large cabin sliding doors, a different nose profile and other changes. The main dropped stores are attached to pylons on the sides of the fuselage under the main doors. A third hydraulic system, at the same 2,050lb/sq in (144kg/cm²) as the others, is installed in naval Lynx to operate such mission equipment as dipping sonar, MAD, deck-lock harpoon and rescue winch (in most Lynx the winch is a clip-on electric installation). The 3,000lb (1361kg) external load cable normally has electric emergency release (not fitted on army Lynx). In the late 1970s the requirement of the Royal Netherlands Navy for an ASW helicopter led to an upgraded Lynx with Gem 41-1 engines driving through a new three-pinion gearbox, and this became standard on all later Lynx including the HAS.3 (RN) and Mk 4 (French Aéronavale).

Avionics: Naval Lynx have full night and (almost) all-weather capability. Navaids include VOR/DME, ILS, Tacan, ADF and I-band ship transponder. Mission equipment includes surveillance radar (Ferranti Seaspray or Héraclès ORB 31W), IFF and ESM, the latter usually being Racal Orange Crop (MIR-2). ASW gear includes Texas Instruments or Crouzet MAD, Bendix or Alcatel dipping sonar (not in the RN yet) and marine markers. For wire-guided missiles an AF.530 or APX.334 roof-mounted sight can be fitted.

Armament: Standard AS armament comprises two torpedoes, of the types depicted. Standard anti-ship missile is Sea Skua, four of which can be carried (in the South Atlantic war in 1982 the Lynx/Skua combination scored four out of four in blizzard conditions, the missile then not having been cleared for use). Other compatible sensors and stores are shown in the main artwork.

Future: Royal Navy Lynx flights, currently numbering over 50, are being upgraded with Seaspray Mk 3, Gem 42 engines, Racal RAMS and new avionics. Westland hope that, despite part-ownership by competitor Sikorsky, it will also be possible to develop the Lynx-3 in its naval form (HAS.6 and 8 for the RN). This would have the BERP rotor (with negative-thrust capability for recovery on pitching decks), low tailplane without fins, nose-mounted 360° radar and FLIR, MAD, dipping sonar and active/passive sonobuoys.

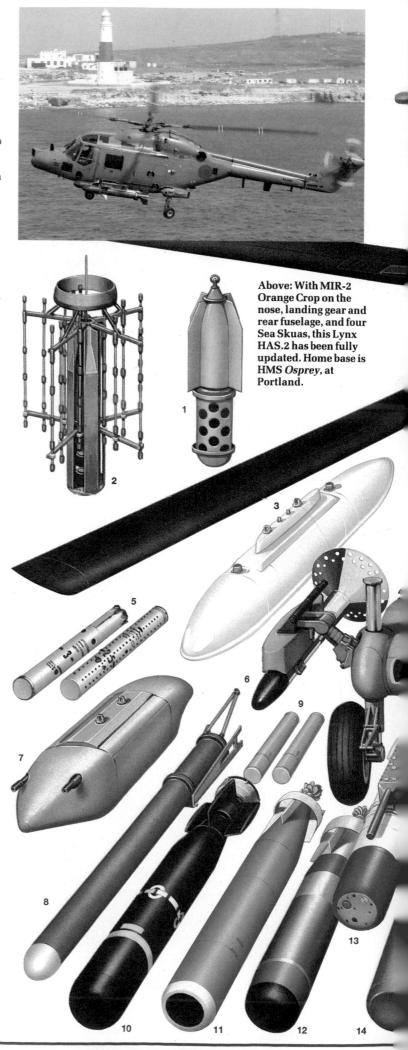

Above: With MIR-2 Orange Crop on the nose, landing gear and rear fuselage, and four Sea Skuas, this Lynx HAS.2 has been fully updated. Home base is HMS *Osprey*, at Portland.

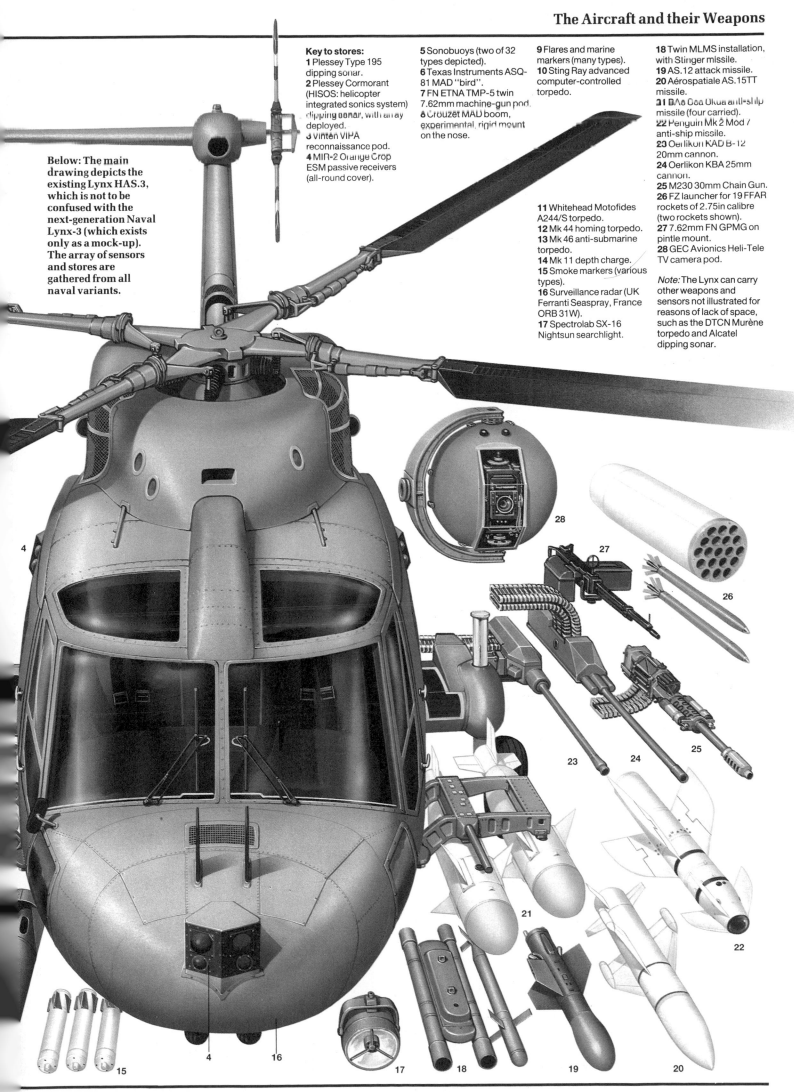

Key to stores:
1 Plessey Type 195 dipping sonar.
2 Plessey Cormorant (HISOS: helicopter integrated sonics system) dipping sonar, with array deployed.
3 Vinten VIPA reconnaissance pod.
4 MIR-2 Orange Crop ESM passive receivers (all-round cover).

5 Sonobuoys (two of 32 types depicted).
6 Texas Instruments ASQ-81 MAD "bird".
7 FN ETNA TMP-5 twin 7.62mm machine-gun pod.
8 Crouzet MAD boom, experimental, rigid mount on the nose.

9 Flares and marine markers (many types).
10 Sting Ray advanced computer-controlled torpedo.

11 Whitehead Motofides A244/S torpedo.
12 Mk 44 homing torpedo.
13 Mk 46 anti-submarine torpedo.
14 Mk 11 depth charge.
15 Smoke markers (various types).
16 Surveillance radar (UK Ferranti Seaspray, France ORB 31W).
17 Spectrolab SX-16 Nightsun searchlight.

18 Twin MLMS installation, with Stinger missile.
19 AS.12 attack missile.
20 Aérospatiale AS.15TT missile.
21 BAe Sea Skua anti-ship missile (four carried).
22 Penguin Mk 2 Mod 7 anti-ship missile.
23 Oerlikon KAD B-12 20mm cannon.
24 Oerlikon KBA 25mm cannon.
25 M230 30mm Chain Gun.
26 FZ launcher for 19 FFAR rockets of 2.75in calibre (two rockets shown).
27 7.62mm FN GPMG on pintle mount.
28 GEC Avionics Heli-Tele TV camera pod.

Note: The Lynx can carry other weapons and sensors not illustrated for reasons of lack of space, such as the DTCN Murène torpedo and Alcatel dipping sonar.

Below: The main drawing depicts the existing Lynx HAS.3, which is not to be confused with the next-generation Naval Lynx-3 (which exists only as a mock-up). The array of sensors and stores are gathered from all naval variants.

Missions and Tactics

It is easy to regard the helicopter as the poor relation of military aviation. Compared with its fixed wing contemporaries it lacks performance. It cannot fly as fast, as high, or as far. Its load-carrying capacity is relatively small. It does not possess the sleek glamour of the fast jets, the imposing presence of the large transports. It is noisy, uncomfortable, and generally unspectacular. It is fatiguing to fly, and mechanically complex. Considering the performance and capabilities of other flying machines, it is not particularly cheap for what it does. Yet it has caused a revolution in almost every branch of warfare, and apart from strategic bombing, looks set to play a part in almost every air warfare role. Within certain limits it is even nibbling at the fringes of air superiority and muscling in on the fast jets. What is so special about the helicopter? Basically, just two things. It is the only vertical takeoff and landing transport machine in service, which furthermore can pick up and unload cargo and personnel while hovering; it does not have to land while doing so. It also has a unique capability of being able to fly very low at relatively slow speeds; the so-called nap of the earth flight, or hover-taxying. This last quality gives it in effect the attributes of a fast surface vehicle with a 100 per cent cross-country capability, one that can scale sheer cliffs and traverse swamps and forests with equal facility.

The early roles undertaken by the helicopter were search and rescue, and communications. For many years it was considered too vulnerable for use on the battlefield, being easy to detect, and slow and easy to hit once detected. It gave sterling service in the Korean War, 1950 to 1953, and not only picked many downed pilots out of the sea, but also rescued a considerable number from behind enemy lines. Casualty evacuation (CASEVAC) from just behind the front lines direct to the field hospitals also saved many lives that might otherwise have been lost. Helicopters were also used on occasion to carry supplies to the front line. They were extensively employed in counter-insurgency operations in Malaya from 1950 onwards, giving the ground forces a hitherto unknown degree of mobility. At sea, the helicopter took on its first offensive role – anti-submarine warfare (ASW) – with the arrival of a machine large enough to carry both the detection gear and the weapons. This offensive role was possible because a submerged submarine was in no position to bite back.

The helicopter gunship was born of necessity. A great proportion of the Vietnam War was a gigantic counter-insurgency operation. Troops had to be placed very rapidly in close proximity to the enemy, and defence suppression was essential. This was provided by the gunships which preceded and supported the troop carriers into the landing zone. Many valuable lessons were learned, but the cost was fearful. US helicopter losses to enemy action totalled 2,589 during the war.

Two main factors influenced the development of the helicopter into a front line weapon. The first was increasing lethality of surface-to-air fire; the second was the advent of guided missiles suitable for helicopter use against tanks and ships. The first cast doubts on the effectiveness of fast jets over the battlefield; survival and accuracy are opposing rather than complementary factors. Fast jets needed to fly low at speed to survive; the helicopter can use stealth and fly even lower to the same end. The second factor meant that at last the helicopter had the offensive capability that hitherto it had lacked. At sea, this meant that quite small ships could carry their own offensive air power which would enable them to strike at an opponent both from long range and from an unexpected direction. A further role undertaken by Navy helicopters was that of airborne early warning, enabling this capability to be added to the organic air power of ships too small to carry suitable fixed-wing aircraft. Minesweeping has also been added to the tally. Overland, air mobility has been added to air portability, giving greatly enhanced flexibility to the ground forces, and improving both their reaction time and their effectiveness.

The following section deals first with techniques of flying a military helicopter, and then examines in turn the naval missions, the battlefield missions, and helicopter air combat.

Below: Combat troops sprint away from a UH-60A Black Hawk which has just set down on the desert. Although it is not inherently a very efficient flying machine, the versatility of the helicopter and its ability to do things fixed-wing aircraft cannot attempt, means that it has a vital role to play in any conventional conflict.

Helicopter Flying

From its rather humble origins in the 1940s and early 1950s, the helicopter has progressed out of all recognition. It now fulfils nearly every aerial function that does not demand long range, high speed, and high altitude, and it even looks as though it might encroach into the air superiority arena, marginally to be sure, but where it will all end no-one knows. Given man's propensity for armed conflict, the helicopter ace is sure to emerge sooner or later.

Like any other flying machine, the helicopter has its advantages and its limitations. As a pure flying machine it is not very efficient, and these defects manifest themselves in the form of short range, lack of altitude performance, low maximum speed – the practical limit is about 180kt (205mph, 330km/h) – little g tolerance, the limit being about 3g, and inherent instability, which makes it a difficult machine to fly. Offsetting these shortcomings is the fact that it can perform a wide variety of tasks; its ability to hover allows it to do things that no fixed-wing aircraft could attempt, not even the Harrier, while its ability to hug the contours of the terrain is unsurpassed. In essence it is the total fast moving amphibious surface vehicle with 100 per cent cross-country capability; a surface skimmer with the ability to climb vertical cliffs and to leapfrog obstacles. It is more versatile than the fixed-wing aircraft, and it is

Above: Battlefield helicopters are essentially fast moving surface vehicles with a 100 per cent cross country capability. This BO 105P anti-armour helicopter in German army service, armed with HOT missiles, is shown down in the weeds, its natural habitat.

also cheaper, by quite a wide margin. It would be true to say that over the last few decades the helicopter has altered the face of warfare.

Helicopter flying breaks down into three main categories: over-water operations, over-land operations, and combined operations. These in turn break

down into many different roles, which we shall examine as we go. But first we must consider the problems of flying over water and also over land, in order to avoid undue repetition later in this section. Having covered these, there will be no need to repeat them when considering specific missions in subsequent sections on specific military operations.

OVER-WATER FLYING

Flying over a calm sea on a sunny day in peace time is, barring mechanical failures, a pleasant occupation, and presents few problems. In wartime it is rather

Left: A Bell AH-1 HueyCobra fires a pair of 2.75in FFARs. From this angle the HueyCobra looks almost prehistoric, but it is a modern battlefield weapon. The menacing appearance and ability to pop up suddenly where least expected can adversely affect enemy morale.

more fraught if there is a possible threat from enemy action. Then the priority is to fly low, close to the surface in order to avoid radar detection. If this does not square with the particular needs of the mission, a compromise altitude must be found. Low flying over a glassy, mill pond surface on a hazy day, when no horizon is apparent, can make life a little difficult, and reliance must be placed on the radar altimeter. Out at sea, the enemy air threat will probably only be from one sector, and this will narrow down the area of visual search. Much the same factors apply as in fixed-wing combat: never fly with your back to the Sun, and try to establish cross-Sun patrol lines, making all turns into the Sun. If any cloud cover exists, be ready to use it, in terms of placing it between the attacker and your own helicopter. Sunlight strobing on the blades of the rotor and glinting on the canopy are dead giveaways, so flying in areas where clouds cast their shadow has its advantages. But only where a direct threat exists can these detection avoidance measures be taken, as they may compromise the main mission.

Left: Apart from ships, oil rigs, and the occasional island, the sea has no obstacles, but over-water flying still presents problems. Visually judging altitude can be tricky, and often there is no horizon. This is a Royal Navy Lynx of 815 Squadron, carrying Sea Skua missiles on its left pylon, MAD bird and Mk 46 torpedo on right.

Above: Last light, and a Sikorsky UH-60 hovers low over the water with landing lights on to assist the pilot in judging his height. In moonlight it is trickier, in full darkness even worse, and in fog very difficult. Nevertheless it must be done when circumstances dictate. A high level of precision flying is called for.

Flying at night is obviously more difficult than flying by day, and a combination of night and bad weather is the worst of all. This last is, however, a mixed blessing, as it minimizes the enemy air threat. Missions such as anti-submarine patrols must be flown around the clock, unless the weather is so bad as to make flying totally impossible.

The helicopter pilot is given a comprehensive instrument flying course. In the Royal Navy, this consists of 11 to 12 hours instruction, plus theory, at the end of which he is tested. He is expected to fly blind to a high degree of accuracy, and to be able to make a precision approach to the landing deck on a ship, to a tolerance of plus or minus 10 degrees of heading, plus or minus 10kt (11.5mph, 18.5km/h) of speed, and plus or minus 100ft (30m) of altitude, although of course at the bottom end of the approach there can be no minus figure; a bit high is the only alternative. Having achieved this basic minimum, he is then

expected to progress to the point where these figures are halved, to five degrees, 5kt (5.75mph, 9.25km/h) and 50ft (15m). This is very hard work, but it must be achieved.

On large ships, such as aircraft carriers, there are meteorological officers, who are responsible for weather forecasting, but many helicopter pilots operate from small ships, and are thus responsible for their own forecasts. A weather chart is received in the form of a signal, and the pilot has to plot his own from that, drawing in the isobars and weather fronts. From this he produces his own forecast.

In the Falklands campaign in 1982, a considerable amount of flying was done in thick fog. Radio traffic had to be kept to a minimum, and radar, which is also an emission and thus detectable by the enemy, used sparingly. The radar-equipped helicopters could afford a quick scan to avoid bumping into the ships of the Task Force. For the non-radar equipped helicopters, life was more difficult;

as Lt-Cdr Nick Foster, who flew a Wessex of No. 845 Squadron recalls:

"We flew in absolutely appalling conditions. We were not flying on instruments; we flew at low level, close to the sea . . . Sometimes we were just hover-taxying at 40 to 50kt (46 to 58mph, 74 to 93km/h), at a height of 20 to 30ft (6 to 9m). We had to have a very good idea of where the other ships were before we got airborne. I remember that on one occasion I had to go to *Invincible*. I just groped along for 20 to 30 miles (37 to 56km), and another ship gave me a heading to steer for a certain distance. When I was in the right vicinity, I slowed right down, and she suddenly came boring through the mist, about 40 to 50 yards (37-46m) away. I landed on the back end, and was unable to see the bridge."

One of the more exciting moments of a young helicopter pilot's life is landing on the pad of a small ship in high seas and strong winds. Soviet helicopter pilot N. Bezdetnov addressed this problem in an article in *Aviatsiya i kosmonavtika* in 1983:

"Even experienced pilots . . . unconsciously maintain a glide path that is geometrically motionless relative to the ship. This inevitably leads to cyclic

displacements of the helicopter in the terrestrial co-ordinate system at a frequency equal to the ship's natural oscillation . . . it seems to the pilot that the ship stops pitching and rolling. The danger is that the resulting perceived line of total glide path displacement in the terrestrial system may extend to the water, and if the pilot, while visually maintaining the glide path, begins tracking its deviations, (the illusion of pitch cessation), the helicopter may hit the water. For this reason, in spite of good visibility at night, the pilot must continue instrument flying until he is within 100m (328ft) of the ship . . . When the deck is pitching and rolling, the touchdown point . . . is continuously displacing in both the vertical and horizontal planes . . . Lateral displacements cause much more difficulty (than vertical displacements) . . . If while hovering above the deck the pilot loses his picture of the pitch and roll dynamics, he will unconsciously conform to the ship's co-ordinate motion . . . when the ship rolls, the helicopter will roll to an equal degree. Intent on orienting himself with the deck, the pilot will not see this roll, but will notice an apparent displacement of the landing pad

(relative to his machine), and control accordingly to conform." Bezdetnov's solution to this problem is to come into a high hover above the pad at an altitude of between 100 and 130ft (30 and 40m) before letting down vertically until one wheel touches, then maintain the hover until the other wheel touches before cutting the power.

Landing a helicopter on a heaving deck at night is undoubtedly a difficult operation,

but the Soviets are fond of such things as "logical-mathematical methods", and the foregoing was an example of this, although it does illustrate the problem graphically. Oddly it makes no mention of either the prevailing wind, nor the turbulence caused by the ship's superstructure, both of which are strong factors affecting the landing. But different nations, different methods. How does the Royal Navy do it?

In as many as half the night

Left: An everyday scene in the life of a Navy helicopter pilot as a Lynx approaches the landing pad of the Leander class frigate HMS *Danae*. The Lynx, making a standard approach from the port side, is decelerating. Ideally the wind should be blowing from the port side, minimising turbulence from the ship's superstructure.

Right: One solution to the problem of landing a helicopter on the heaving deck of a small ship in bad weather is RAS (Recovery Assist and Secure). A cable from the ship is connected to the helicopter prior to landing. The helicopter is then reeled in like a kite on a piece of string. The pilot can always break contact in the event of an emergency.

landings made on small ships, there is no natural horizon. The instrument panel contains an artificial horizon, but this is of little use as, in complete contrast to the Soviet recommendation, the approach is flown with the pilot looking out of the window and not in at the dials. On the ship is a glidepath indicator down which the helicopter flies. A green light denotes "on the glidepath", amber means too high, and red too low. This is gyro-stabilized to some

Left: Deck operations from small ships are not always carried out on calm seas under blue skies. Here a Lynx, anchored to the grid by the Harpoon securing system, is readied for flight. The roll angle of the ship can clearly be seen. What is less apparent is the pitch; this deck could rise and fall equally dramatically.

extent, but if the ship is moving a lot in the water, the pilot can be taken out of the beam. The glidepath is flown to a point about quarter of a mile (400m) from the ship. In the British service, the approach is always made from the left side, partly because, unlike fixed-wing aircraft, the pilot sits in the right-hand seat. At this point, the horizon bar, a line of lights along the top of the hangar, is turned on. This gives the pilot the roll of the ship. He moves in close, establishes a hover, judges the deck motion, then moves across it and lands. Ideally as the landing is made from the port side, a wind from this side should be blowing. If it is not, then turbulence will ensue from the ship's superstructure. If this is particularly severe, or there are other factors, a cross-deck landing may have to be carried out, while in the worst possible

situation the pilot has to land facing the stern; this is very difficult at night but there are times when it is unavoidable.

The United States Navy operates differently again. A landing signal officer using lighted wands directs the pilot rather in the manner of the oldtime "bats" with fixed-wing aircraft, and they have adopted a system of shipboard recovery in which a cable is attached to the helicopter prior to landing, so that it may then be "reeled in".

OVER-LAND FLYING

Large waves notwithstanding, the sea is relatively flat, and apart from the odd ship, has no obstructions. Not so the land, which varies from flat plains to undulating hills to full scale mountains. In many places the terrain is liberally obstructed with buildings, tall trees, power lines, and radio masts, contact with which can quite spoil a helicopter pilot's day. Climate also plays a part, varying between hot dusty deserts and snow-covered terrain experiencing sub-zero temperatures, all of which affect the helicopter's performance. The terrain and its obstructions are both good and bad news. They can be utilized by the low-flying helicopter to give cover;

Deck Landings in Heavy Seas

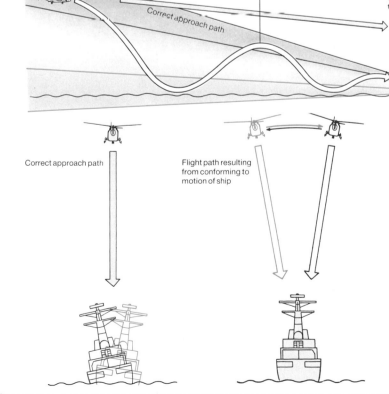

Above and left: A pitching and rolling deck can easily disorient a pilot if he is not careful. As the upper diagram shows, he must follow the indicated glide path to land safely on the flight deck. Watching the pitch of the deck may lead him into a switchback course as he tries to make the helicopter conform to the motion of the ship. In extreme cases this can cause him to fly into the water. The Soviet approach is to establish a high hover over the ship, and then to let down vertically. However, this can also be problematic if the ship is rolling severely (as the lower diagrams show). If the pilot loses his picture of the roll dynamics, he may unconsciously try to correct for the roll motion, with the consequences seen at lower right.

on the other hand they can conceal enemy ground forces lying in ambush.

The route that the helicopter flies is carefully planned to avoid high risk areas where possible, while obstructions like high tension cables are carefully noted. In rear areas, helicopters may fly at altitudes well above any ground obstacles, but in areas where a threat, either ground or air, may exist, the survival of the helicopter depends in the main on remaining undetected. Detection may be accomplished in four ways: by radar, by infra-red, visually, and in some cases, aurally. It is impossible to guard against all of these, but a high degree of protection is obtained by the simple expedient of flying at very low altitudes, and using terrain masking. This very low flying is referred to as "nap of the earth" flying, or NOE. It requires a high degree of skill, and a trade-off with speed is necessary. However fast the helicopter can fly, the pilot will have his hands full at 100kt (115mph, 185km/h) over cluttered terrain, and sometimes not even this speed will be possible.

Terrain masking is the art of using whatever cover exists. If there is rising ground between the flight path and the enemy positions, the helicopter can stay below it and remain out of sight. Woods or even buildings may serve to screen it, wholly or partially, from visual or other forms of observation. Staying below the skyline is also important. Hills may have to be crossed, but it may be possible to skirt round them rather than having to go over the top. Avoiding detection from the air is rather more difficult, although dead ground can often be utilised for concealment, dead ground being defined as areas from which there is no direct line of sight. This is more useful against an adversary at low level than one higher up. But this apart, there is still plenty that can be done to aid concealment. Cloud shadow can be utilised as explained in the over-sea section. A green helicopter flying over wooded areas is much harder to pick out than one flying over open fields. A well camouflaged helicopter is difficult to spot over a background into which it merges, but on a sunny day its shadow will show up clear and black against a lighter background. This can be partially negated by flying *very* low, so that the machine partly masks its own shadow, although in, for example, desert conditions, this can be counter-productive if the slipstream kicks up a trail of dust. If broken ground exists, rocks, boulders etc, these plus the shadows that they cast will tend to break up the outline of the helicopter's shadow so that it presents less of a hard image, and is thus more difficult to see. Overflying lakes and other bodies of water should be avoided; not only do they contrast the helicopter beautifully, but they

make it easier to detect on radar. The procedure is to fly around the edge of them.

Both bad weather and night flying pose problems, although they are great aids to concealment. The development of night vision goggles (NVG), forward looking infra-red (FLIR), and low light television (LLTV) will make the task easier, as will radar to detect obstacles. Ground mapping radar is not carried at present; the speeds do not really warrant its use. The radar altimeter will give warning of rising ground; the route must be

planned to avoid cliffs. Instrument flying can be used to get from one point to another at moderate altitudes, but at low level there is not a lot of future in it. Low flying at night must be done visually. Night vision goggles are a great help, turning a starlit night into something approaching dusk vision, although "flash" can be a drawback if a bright light comes into the range of vision.

As at sea, weather can be a dangerous enemy, and visibility minima for over-land operations tend to be rather wider than for

Compromise, Speed v. Security

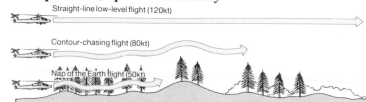

Straight-line low-level flight (120kt)

Contour-chasing flight (80kt)

Nap of the Earth flight (50kt)

Left: Straight line flight at an altitude just sufficient to clear all obstacles is fastest by a good margin, but is most liable to be detected. NOE flight, making the maximum use of cover, is slower, but offers the best chance of avoiding detection, while contour chasing offers a compromise. The tactical situation decides which.

Top: A McDonnell Douglas AH-64 Apache peeps shyly through the trees in this excellent example of how to use natural cover. In fact the background has been carefully selected in order to make the Apache visible to the camera.

Above: Sikorsky UH-60 Black Hawks traverse desert terrain in a first class example of how not to remain undetected. Suitably camouflaged, they might have merged with the background, but their hard black shadows show up perfectly.

over-sea flying. The two greatest hazards to the helicopter pilot are icing and whiteout. As these are often encountered in mountain flying, we will consider them closely in the next section.

MOUNTAIN FLYING

Flying in mountainous terrain is an art form on its own. The pilot has to be able to assess the wind. Weather forecasts are not sufficient as valleys, bowls and ridges can all alter the direction of the prevailing wind by up to 180 degrees. They also cause severe turbulence. All this has to be anticipated. In areas where opposition may be encountered, the pilot flies tactically, keeping below the skyline and picking the areas which offer the best cover. Often it is necessary to follow the line of a valley, and in this case it is standard procedure to fly at an altitude that is about halfway up the hillside. There are two reasons for this. The first stems from the air threat. A fighter pilot looking down into a valley tends to look down the middle; his vision is funnelled in by the sloping sides and the natural tendency is to look past the helicopter creeping along about halfway up. The second is a result of a combination of enemy air threat and flight safety. If the fighter does spot the helicopter, or

Tactical Mountain Flying

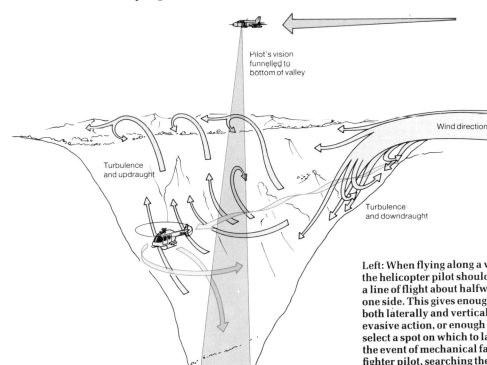

Left: When flying along a valley, the helicopter pilot should choose a line of flight about halfway up one side. This gives enough space both laterally and vertically for evasive action, or enough time to select a spot on which to land in the event of mechanical failure. A fighter pilot, searching the ground below, tends to allow his vision to funnel to the bottom of the valley, missing the helicopter flying halfway up. The updraught side of the valley gives free lift but sometimes the threat makes it necessary to seek the best cover.

Below: An AH-64 Apache in "hot and high" mountain terrain is seen flying along what is presumably the updraught side of a valley. Under "hot and high" conditions power is at a premium, and every bit of extra aid is welcome.

if a mechanical failure occurs, it gives maximum air space on one side in which to evade in the first case, and select a suitable spot on which to free wheel (auto-rotate) down. The question arises, which side of the valley to fly? In a threat area, the answer is always the side that gives the best cover, even if the difference is merely the shady side against the sunny side. All else being equal, if the prevailing wind is blowing strongly across the ridges on either side of the valley, it will result in turbulence, with a strong downdraught on the upwind side and an updraught on the downwind side. The updraught gives free lift and is thus an aid to flying, especially if the aircraft is heavily laden. The updraught side can be thus considered distinctly preferable.

The Soviet helicopter forces in Afghanistan have gained a great deal of experience of mountain flying in extreme conditions; snow and freezing temperatures, and heat and dust. The following has been extracted from an article in *Aviatsiya i kosmonavtika* by Lt-Col B. Budnikov.

"Turbulence . . . intensifies as one approaches a ridge. It is felt earlier when crossing a ridge into a headwind than crossing it with a following wind. In the presence of downdraughts one should fly at least 600m (2,000ft) above a mountain range less than 2000m (6,500ft) high, and at least 1000m (3,250ft) when the range is over 2000m high. Before flying over a ridge or through a pass, one should reduce speed to 160km/h (86kt, 99mph) in order to keep power in

reserve . . . If the pilot has been unable to gain a safe altitude he must . . . cross the ridge at such an acute angle that it would allow him to turn rapidly away from peaks should a downdraught be encountered . . . Special caution should be exercised when flying near a slope which is poorly visible due to the Sun shining on the cockpit canopy, also in narrowing or box canyons. In such cases the speed maintained should allow for 180 degree turns. In a bank of up to 30 degrees at an indicated air speed of 80km/h (43kt, 50mph) at normal takeoff weight, or a bank of up to 15 degrees at speeds of 100km/h (54kt, 62mph), the turning radii (of the Mi-8 Hip) are 87.5 and 295m (287 and 968ft) respectively. The width of the gorge should therefore be twice the radius plus a safety factor of 100m (328ft).

"When landing crosswise to an irregularity in the terrain on swampy or snow-covered ground, the collective rotor pitch should not be reduced to the minimum, so that if the helicopter begins to tip over it can be lifted away again . . . It is far more difficult than usual to land or take off from a dusty site. After hovering, the helicopter should be lowered in such a way that by the time horizontal visibility deteriorates, there is reliable vertical visibility up to the point of touchdown. At a dusty site, if conditions permit, the helicopter can be landed like a fixed wing aircraft . . . one must land the Mi-8 at a speed of 50 to 60km/h (27 to 32kt, 31 to 37mph), disengage the pitch control, reduce rotor speed, and brake the wheels.

"On takeoff it is possible, at minimum pitch and with full throttle, to disperse the dust and then accelerate upwards to leave the dust rapidly behind."

These were the mountain flying lessons learned in Afghanistan by Soviet helicopter pilots. One exploit that aroused considerable attention took place on the cliffs overlooking the Panjsher Gorge, which the "dushmans", or rebels, were using as a route to infiltrate the country. Army observation posts were set up on the cliffs, which in many cases could only be reached by helicopter. One of these was situated on a knife-edged ridge, sheer on one side, very steep on the other, and about 4,920ft (1,500m) high. A call for help was received from this post and answered by Military Pilot First Class Major Anatoly Surtsukov. There was no area on which to land and the wind was gusting strongly. Major Surtsukov succeeded in evacuating the post by hooking the nose wheel and one main wheel on the ridge, and balancing, with a combination of power and wheel braking, long enough for the evacuation to be carried out.

While this was undoubtedly a fine piece of flying, capabilities of this order are not unique to the Soviet Union. The Royal Navy helicopter squadrons are expected as a standard part of their training to be able to fly out to a mountain, and place one wheel on top of a trig point. It needs careful training, but it is not regarded as being terribly difficult, although it is obviously an example of extreme precision flying.

Above: A Royal Marines Lynx AH.1 in winter conditions on a mountain top. The blowing snow is a clear indication of the turbulence that is encountered in mountain flying. Mountain flying in winter calls for high training standards, both in flying, and in being able to "read" the weather.

Below: One of the greatest hazards to helicopter safety in winter is icing, which can form very rapidly and with little or no warning. An AH-64A Apache is seen undergoing de-icing tests near Minneapolis, while carrying a full warload. The build-up of ice (yellow) can be seen on the front.

Icing and whiteout are weather conditions encountered in many areas, but they are most frequently encountered during mountain flying. In unfavourable conditions, ice can build up very fast, and it only takes three or four minutes for sufficient to accumulate on the leading edge of the rotor, to destroy the lift to such a degree that the helicopter descends uncontrollably. To avoid this, the most important thing is for the pilot to be able to recognize the onset of icing at a very early stage. The increased atmospheric density in cold weather improves the performance of both the engine and the rotor, consequently the helicopter handles in a more sprightly manner than in hot weather. Warning that icing has commenced can be given by even small changes in such things as engine temperatures, cruising revs, torque settings etc, and the pilot should check these immediately after takeoff. If the ice starts to build up, it causes increased vibration. Once it has been recognized, the only solution is to run out of the icing zone as quickly as possible, either by a direct route or by climbing or descending.

Whiteout is caused by heavy snow accompanied by high winds which cause visibility to drop to zero. If whiteout conditions are forecast, the mission must be cancelled. If the helicopter is already airborne, the mission is aborted and it returns to base. If caught unexpectedly, or the urgent nature of the mission demands that it must be attempted, the pilot must either abort or try to fly on instruments to a clear area, possibly by climbing to a safe height if navigational aids are available to ensure that a return can be made.

A classic operation carried out in appalling weather was the recovery of a small SAS force from Fortune Glacier, South Georgia, in April 1982. Conditions were terrible, with winds gusting up to hurricane force. Three Wessex helicopters of the Royal Navy were assigned to the task, and they landed successfully and picked up the SAS men. As the first Wessex took off, it immediately entered whiteout conditions, was caught by a gust, and tipped on its side. By some miracle there were no injuries, and the survivors boarded the remaining two helicopters, which then took off. Flying in extreme turbulence, a second Wessex also ran into whiteout conditions. Flying entirely on instruments, the pilot headed for a clear area ahead, only for his aircraft to be caught by a severe downdraught, and it failed to clear the top of a ridge by a matter of feet. The third Wessex, brilliantly handled by its pilot, Lt-Cdr Ian Stanley, successfully returned to HMS *Antrim*. After refuelling he made two abortive attempts to return to the scene. At the third attempt he made it, and evacuated the survivors, some of whom had been in both incidents. For his courage, skill, and determination in this exploit he was later decorated.

Below: Royal Navy Wessex HU.5s of 845 Squadron exercising in Norway. The downwash from the rotor blows snow into the air on takeoff and landing, often seriously impairing the pilot's vision, both downwards and horizontally, as seen here.

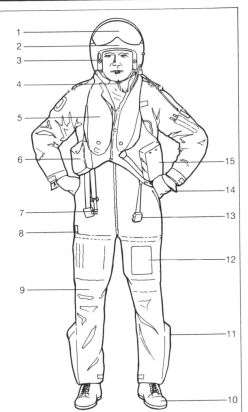

The Royal Navy Helicopter Pilot

1 Double visor system for the protective helmet – clear inner visor, tinted outer.
2 Mk 3C aircrew protective helmet.
3 Oxygen mask attachment hooks.
4 Throat microphone (boom microphones are also used)
5 Mk 25 lifepreserver.
6 Survival aids pocket containing miniflares (×8), first aid kit, strobe light, and a heliograph.
7 Liferaft attachment lanyard.
8 Aircrew knife Mk 3.
9 Nomex aircrew coverall Mk 14.
10 Aircrew boots.
11 Lower leg pockets.
12 Acetate knee boards.
13 Personal survival pack attachment lanyard.
14 Cape leather gloves.
15 Pye personal locator beacon pocket.

A Typical Helicopter Pilot

Lt-Cdr G.R.N. (Nick) Foster was born in London in 1952. He discovered an interest in ships at an early age, which was encouraged by his father. At school (Bristol Grammar and Rugby), he was a member of the Naval Section of the CCF. His ambition was to join the Royal Navy; nothing else was ever considered; and he entered the Royal Naval College, Dartmouth, straight from school in 1970. It was there that he took his first flight, in a Wasp helicopter, and in his own words, "that was it". He applied to become an aviator. After five years in the Service, including two spent in Hongkong, he commenced flying training in 1975. Six months on Bulldogs with the Royal Air Force at Leeming was followed by a further six months at Royal Naval Air Station Culdrose flying Gazelles, where he gained his wings. His first appointment was to fly Wasps, based at RNAS Portland, but was often away at sea operating from small ships. In 1979 he was selected for commando training; six months at RNAS Yeovilton with 707 Naval Air Squadron, followed by an appointment to an operational naval squadron, 845, flying the Wessex V, where much of his time was spent in Northern Ireland. Just as his tour was about to expire, the expedition to the South Atlantic was mounted, and Nick with his Wessex helicopter were attached to the Royal Fleet Auxiliary *Fort Austin*. Intensive flying followed, much of it in foul weather and thick fog. Nick and his crew also participated in the rescue of survivors from HMS *Sheffield*. Shortly after, they were transferred to the *Atlantic Conveyor*, which was hit by an Exocet on 25 May.

Nick was aboard at the time, and deciding that the water looked cold, coolly donned his survival gear before abandoning ship. Returned to RNAS Yeovilton, he attended the Helicopter Warfare Instructor's Course between September and December 1982, and was then posted to 707 Squadron as the helicopter warfare instructor. A year later he was promoted to become Senior Pilot of the squadron, a job that he held until December 1985. He is currently a Staff Officer at BRNC Dartmouth, training embryo naval officers. Married for twelve years, with daughters aged eight and ten, Lt-Cdr Foster carries an air of authority lightly. The impression he gives is that of a dedicated professional, an excellent communicator, and a man devoted to the Royal Navy and to flying with the Fleet Air Arm.

The Naval Missions

Naval helicopter missions break down into two main categories; over-water, and amphibious operations. The over-water missions are anti-submarine warfare (ASW), anti-surface vessel operations (ASV), over-the-horizon (OTH) missile targeting, maritime patrol, search and rescue (SAR), minesweeping, airborne early warning (AEW), naval gunfire support (NGS), electronic support measures (ESM), and chaff screening. Amphibious operations are mainly concerned with landing and supporting Marines, and coastal reconnaissance. Rescue and casualty evacuation overlap the two. The way in which all these missions are carried out will to a degree depend on the available hardware, to which the larger portion of this book is devoted. Other factors affecting mission procedures are the tactical situation, including relative strengths, the nature of the threat, and the available force size,

combined with the operational philosophy of whichever nation is conducting them. We shall begin by considering ASW missions.

ANTI-SUBMARINE OPERATIONS

Anti-submarine warfare is an all-embracing activity carried out not only by helicopters, but by fixed-wing aircraft, both land- and carrier-based, by surface and sub-surface vessels. Helicopters have certain advantages over fixed-wing aircraft, among which their hovering and vertical landing capability are the most important. They can use "dunking" sonar, which the fixed-wing aircraft certainly cannot; they can be based on quite small ships, which means that a surface force can carry its own organic air power even without having an aircraft carrier along, and they are many times cheaper both to purchase and to operate than a dedicated fixed-

Above: Winner of a competition for the Light Airborne Multi-purpose System III (LAMPS III) for the US Navy was the SH-60B Seahawk, seen here displaying the radome of its APS-124 search radar mounted on the underside, as it lands on USS *Crommelin*.

Left: A Sea King Mk. 5 hovers as it retrieves its Plessey Type 195 dunking sonar. Dunking sonar has certain advantages over expendable sonobuoys, not the least of which is that the depth can be varied. Dunking sonar helicopters usually hunt in pairs for greatest effect.

wing sub-hunter, which means that many more of them can be acquired. They can also operate in weather too marginal for conventional fixed-wing aircraft. Not all the advantages are one way of course. The fixed-wing sub-hunter can patrol a greater area and cover the ground in a much shorter time. It has a longer range, the space for more sophisticated electronics, and a greater weapons load. But however capable the fixed-wing aircraft is, the facts remain that there are never enough aircraft carriers to go round. There will be times when the weather will be too bad for fixed-wing types to operate, while the land-based, long-range sub-hunters are less effective in direct proportion to the distance out over the sea that they are called upon to operate; the time taken to reach the patrol area increases, while (without in-flight refuelling) the time on station progressively diminishes. But having said that, ASW operations are essentially a combined and integrated effort, with fixed-wing aircraft utilizing their superior speed and range to sweep the seas far out from the surface force, while the rotary-wing craft maintain a barrier closer in.

The purpose of ASW operations is to protect the surface vessels. If the hostile submarine(s) can be sunk at the same time, this is a

Above: A fairly recent role for helicopters is minesweeping. This is the Sikorsky MH-53E Sea Dragon with a Mk 105 hydrofoil for sweeping magnetic mines in tow. Helicopters were used to sweep the harbour of Haiphong in 1973, and the Suez canal in 1984.

Right: The Kaman SH-2F Seasprite was the original LAMPS helicopter for the USN. It is seen here with a basic ASW fit of ASQ-81 MAD on the starboard side, with an auxiliary fuel tank alongside, and a Mk 46 acoustically homing torpedo on the port side.

bonus, but the "safe and timely arrival" of the surface vessels is paramount. Back in World War II, many submarines were sunk by aircraft, but the true value of air ASW operations lay in the fact that patrolling aircraft forced the submarines (or submersibles as they then were) to break off their attack and lose contact. The number of ships saved in this way is incalculable. Although the undersea threat is now the true submarine, armed with longer-range weapons of much greater sophistication, and faster under the water than the old Mk VII U-Boat was on the surface, the principles of such operations remain the same.

As in any other form of warfare, the first priority is to detect the enemy. This is closely followed by the need for positive identification. Three basic methods are used. They are radar, magnetic anomaly detection (MAD), and, most important, sonar. There are others: interception and radio fixing of messages (highly unlikely these days), and visual contact, which is also highly unlikely, but not impossible.

Radar detection of a submarine takes two forms; active and passive. Passive detection will only occur if the submarine is emitting, which it will do for two reasons. The first is if it is checking

for an air threat, the second is if it is seeking a target at which to launch a missile. Either way, it will be surfaced, probably hull down, a position in which it will be vulnerable to active radar detection. It is practically impossible to detect underwater targets by radar, so unless the submarine is wholly or partially surfaced, or, in the case of a diesel electric boat, is using its schnorkel which can be picked up by radar at remarkably long ranges, there is

little or no chance of detecting it by radar. Even if the submarine meets one of these conditions, much is dependent on the helicopter being in the right place at the right time.

Being in the right place at the right time is even more essential for visual detection. A surfaced submarine is a small target in the vastness of the ocean, while a schnorkel is even smaller. Compared with radar, the human eye is limited by both distance and weather, although, in the right

conditions, the schnorkel leaves a wake which can be seen from a considerable distance. Despite this, however remote the chances of spotting something may seem, visual search cannot be entirely discounted. On rare occasions it is possible to see a submerged submarine from the air, although only in clear water and when the angle of the light is just right.

A submarine is a large metal object, of sufficient size to distort marginally the earth's magnetic

Left: Dunking sonars come in all shapes and sizes; this is the Thomson HS.12, slung beneath a huge French 321G Super Frelon of the Aéronavale. Like the Plessey sonar shown on page 180, HS.12 operates in both active and passive modes.

own climate and weather, and any one of these factors will influence the performance of a sonar.

The problems are further aggravated by the presence of man. The sounds of surface vessels going about their lawful business, coupled with offshore drilling rigs, dredging, and other activities, make the sea a very noisy place. In some regions, rocks being dragged across the sea bed by the current, or icebergs grinding together produce a noisy background. When it is understood that low frequency sounds can travel many thousands of miles through the water, it can be seen that listening for a submarine is not quite the pushover that it first appears.

possible, and this means slowly. It also means that when crossing a patrol line, it is at risk for longer from both MAD and active detectors. A further disadvantage of silent running is that the target vessel will almost certainly be moving faster than the submarine, which will be dropping farther and farther back. It was mentioned earlier that some submarines carry a long-range missile armament, but of course the traditional submarine weapon is the torpedo, and the use of this weapon means that the submarine needs to close to within quite a short range of the target.

Operationally, the difference between active and passive sonar is that active sonar can be considered to be a form of underwater radar, emitting sound instead of an electronic impulse, and listening for the echo, whereas the passive sonar is a pure listening device. In the first case, the submarine captain will know, or be pretty certain that he has been detected, while in the second case

field. This distortion can be detected by extremely sensitive devices called magnetic anomaly detectors, or MADs. The actual field distortion decreases in direct proportion to the cube root of the distance from the object causing it, which makes MAD an extremely short range detection instrument. To avoid distortion caused by the helicopter itself, a MAD bird is normally streamed behind it over the surface of the water. This considerably reduces the helicopter's speed and manoeuvrability; it is also extremely difficult to achieve a position directly over the submarine because of the distance between the helicopter and the instrument. It is normally used in the attack phase rather than as a detection instrument, but it can be very useful when patrolling confined waterways, for instance the Straits of Gibraltar.

The most widely used means of submarine detection is acoustic, in the form of sonar. This can be either active or passive, using disposable sonobuoys, or a dunking instrument suspended below the helicopter. Yet a third method is possible; many ships carry sonar equipment, the range of which is greater than the range of their anti-submarine weapons. The range and accuracy of detection is such that small helicopters, such as the Lynx, can carry homing torpedoes to the required area and launch an attack guided from the ship. On the other hand, the ever increasing range of anti-shipping weapons carried by submarines, especially of the sea-skimming missile type, makes it essential to try to force them back out of range. As modern surface-to-surface anti-ship missiles have a range of up to 150nm (173 miles, 278km), this is easier said than done, as a single ship will need surveillance of a perimeter some 942nm (1,085 miles, 1747km) in circumference, to give 100 per cent coverage.

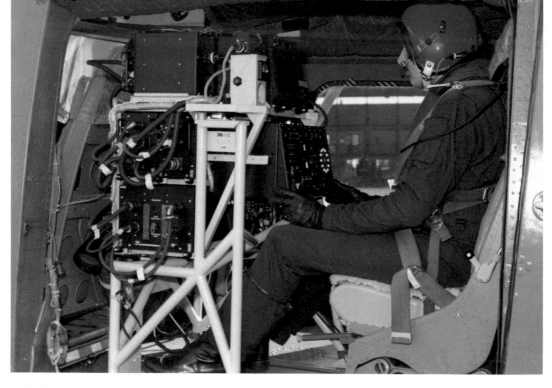

Ideally the anti-submarine hunt will be a combined operation using both fixed-wing aircraft, with their high relative speed, long range, and greater mobility, with helicopters supporting closer in. The type of listening and detection device used will depend on the tactical situation; the nature of the perceived threat and the means available, and perhaps surprisingly, the geographic location. The oceans are not a homogeneous mass of water. The sea bed has its own topography, with mountains and valleys, muddy plains, sandy deserts, and even forests of kelp and coral. It has currents which often travel in different directions at different depths, sharply defined changes of temperature, and storms. In fact, the oceans can be said to have their

Apart from remaining submerged, submarines have two main ways of avoiding detection: speed and stealth. Fortunately for the ASW helicopter these two qualities are contradictory. Speed would enable the submarine to cross the helicopter's patrol line in the shortest time, thus giving the helicopter less time to detect it. But speed causes noise. Apart from the engines, pumps etc, travelling at more than 6kt (7mph, 11km/h) causes cavitation from the propellors, and passive acoustic detectors can pick this up from a considerable distance. In passing, perhaps we should mention that nuclear powered submarines tend to be more noisy than the conventional boats. To avoid the attentions of passive detectors, the boat must run as silently as

Above: The rather cramped sonar operator's position in the Super Frelon, showing the Thomson Sintra HS.12 installation, at the top of which can be seen a visual display. One sonar-equipped Super Frelon is used to direct up to three torpedo-armed hunters.

he will have no such indication. There are advantages and disadvantages in both situations for the hunting helicopters. The captain aware of having been detected will take evasive action and become a much more difficult target. On the other hand, in most cases he will be more intent on survival than on pursuing his attack. Active sonar tends, therefore, to be a defensive measure in its own right. The captain unaware of having been

The Anti-Submarine Screen

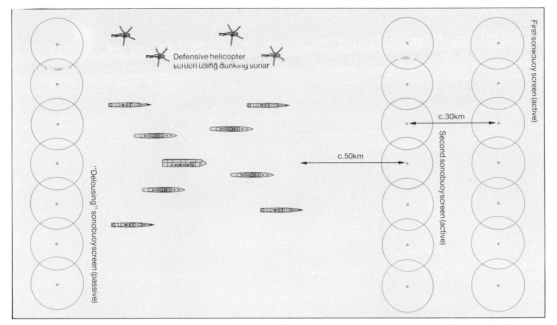

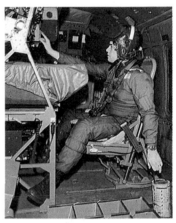

Left: To defeat a submarine attack on a surface force, the fleet must be surrounded by a "tripwire" that warns when an intruder penetrates it. A combination of both active and passive sonar devices is used to form a screen. The spacings involved are determined by enemy weapon ranges and the speed of the fleet. A rear screen of passive sonobuoys is laid, plus a forward screen of active sonobuoys, while the threat flank is guarded by a screen of helicopters with dunking sonar. As the fleet closes the forward screen, a further area is deloused and a second screen laid.

Below: The Sea King is much larger than the Seasprite and carries both dunking sonar and sonobuoys. Mechanical dispensers are not used and the sonobuoy, in this case apparently a Dowty Jezebel F, is released down a chute while the operator records its position. Jezebel F has selectable depth settings.

Left: Loading a sonobuoy into a Kaman SH-2F Seasprite, where it is carried in a dispenser panel. The Seasprite is a bit on the small side to carry dunking sonar as well as the other ASW kit and thus is generally reliant on sonobuoys for detecting submerged submarines. These are ejected in preplanned positions and patterns to give an excellent probability of detection. The Seasprite then patrols the sonobuoy barrier.

detected will pursue his objective, and if the ASW helicopters can maintain the element of surprise, he becomes a much easier target for them.

The sea is much too large a place to sow liberally with expendable sonobuoys, which are, after all, rather expensive. Nevertheless, they have their uses. With fixed-wing aircraft providing the outer layer of ASW defence, the helicopters can lay a screen of sonobuoys across the path of the surface force, renewing it as the force progresses. It seems likely that this screen will consist of active buoys, as a submarine seeking to close from head-on can afford the luxury of silent running, letting the surface force close him rather than vice versa, and it thus might succeed in penetrating a screen of passive detectors. As the surface force nears the first detection screen, the helicopters need carefully to search the area beyond with dunking sonars before laying the second screen.

Much the same applies to the rear of the surface force, except that in this region passive detectors can be advantageously used. The necessity for the submarine to close the surface force denies it the comparative safety of silent running. This rear screen would be laid immediately astern of the surface vessels, and remaining active for the next few hours, would act as a de-lousing net.

Sonobuoys could also be used to screen the flanks, but this would really need a double screen of both active and passive sensors. Helicopters with dunking sonars can carry out this function far more effectively. Many occasions will arise where the threat is from one flank only, and so they can concentrate on this sector.

Both sonobuoy patterns and helicopter patrol patterns are determined by the capability of the detectors in the prevailing conditions. For example, sonobuoys would not be spaced at their maximum detection distance, but would be allowed a considerable amount of overlap, otherwise a narrow "gate" might exist, through which an uninvited guest might fortuitously slip undetected.

When using dunking sonar, it is preferable for ASW helicopters to work in pairs. The helicopter has certain restrictions when using this device, whether in the active or passive modes. When in the hover, it uses fuel at a greatly increased rate; it should also ideally face into the wind, so that there is no tendency to weathercock. When the sonar is lowered into the water, the helicopter is immobilised; when it moves to a new search position the sonar has to be retracted and the helicopter is then blind, contact has to be broken. Such a situation is avoided when two helicopters work as a team; one always has its sonar in the water, holding contact. The other, using its MAD, and guided by the aircraft in contact, can establish an exact course for the submarine, and with a series of passes lay a line of smoke floats by day, or flares by night. Having done this, an attack can be launched, either with depth charges or with homing acoustic torpedoes.

The same principles that govern the use of active or passive sonobuoys also hold good for the use of active or passive dunking sonar. Obviously passive detection is preferable as it does not alert the submarine commander, and there is consequently little or no evasive action to contend with. However, against a silent runner, or in certain tactical circumstances such as when the submarine has or is rapidly approaching torpedo range of the surface force, there is little choice. A silent runner may demand the use of active sonar to

hold contact, while in the latter instance the submarine commander is being deliberately warned that he is being tracked and at any moment may be attacked. This should be sufficient to take his mind off attack and concentrate it on survival. If the attack can be thwarted, the helicopter has won the engagement. Being tracked by a pair of helicopters using dunking sonar is a bewildering experience for a submarine commander, never quite knowing whether they are still in contact, whether they are using a combination of active and passive detectors, and being totally unable to predict the direction

from which the next set of "pings" will come. In the case of a diesel electric submarine, he also knows that a prolonged hunt may well exhaust his batteries. In addition he realises that in a "worst case" situation, he is being hunted by a combination of fixed-wing aircraft, helicopters, and a hunter-killer submarine. It is an unenviable situation in which to be.

Sonobuoys are useful in that they can be laid to form a defensive screen, but dunking sonar also has certain specific advantages. In some areas, notably the Mediterranean, there are layers of water of differing temperatures.

There is little mixing between the layers, and the interface, called the thermocline, can act as a barrier to sound signals. The dunking sonar can often be lowered through these layers and is thus less subject to inteference; the depth of the sonar can also be varied to meet the prevailing conditions.

ASV OPERATIONS

Anti-surface vessel operations are conducted on the same general principles as ASW; search, detect, and attack. Radar is the primary search tool; both active and passive detection are used, although visual

Dunking Sonar Search Pattern

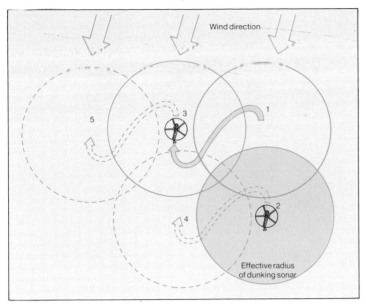

The Submarine Hunt

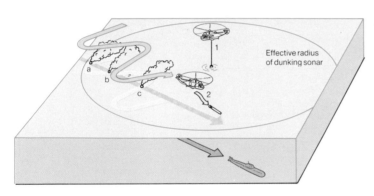

Top: Two helicopters using dunking sonar can set up a search pattern that is very hard to evade. The first dunking position is at 1. The second helo dunks at 2, which frees the first to move on to 3. The second helo then moves to 4. The serpentine tracks allow the helos to station into the wind when deploying the sonar.

Left: The downwash from the rotor lashes the sea into foam as this Royal Navy Sea King retrieves its dunking sonar. The helicopter is immobilised when using the sonar and is forced to hover facing into wind to avoid weathercocking. To change position it winds the sonar up and loses contact, which is why such helicopters work in pairs.

Above: Helicopter No 1 holds sonar contact on an enemy submarine and directs No 2 towards it. Using MAD, No 2 makes contact and drops smoke floats at a, b and c. This fixes the course and approximate speed of the submarine, and allows No 2 to launch an acoustic torpedo from an optimum position.

Right: Submarines are not the only adversary for naval helicopters. Here a BO 105CB launches a pair of FZ 2.75in rockets at a smoke float scoring what looks like a direct hit with one of them. Apart from counter-insurgency operations, it is difficult to imagine waterborne targets for this weapon.

Top: A Royal Navy Lynx launches a Mk 46 acoustic torpedo. A braking parachute is deployed to lessen the impact with the water. This in turn is deployed by a small drogue chute. The acoustic torpedo is preferred to the depth charge as an anti-submarine weapon because it offers a much higher chance of scoring a kill.

Above: Before launching a torpedo attack, even with a homing weapon, it is desirable to establish the speed and course of the target. This is done by using MAD combined with smoke and flame floats, three of which are shown here on the bomb carrier of a Royal Navy Lynx. These floats are dropped to mark the target's course.

detection cannot be entirely discounted. As with ASW, helicopters can hunt alone, in pairs, or in conjunction with fixed-wing aircraft. Again, much will depend on the tactical circumstances, one of the most vital of which is whether the opposing force has any organic air support, either fixed- or rotary-wing. Unlike ASW, avoiding detection by the surface force is of prime importance. There is less room for an element of bluff.

At very low altitudes, radar has a very short range; as the impulses travel in straight lines, the horizon is very limited. For effective search

the helicopter must gain height. Once the target is detected, much will depend on the type of anti-shipping missile carried, and its homing system. The range is always sufficient, with modern weapons at any rate, to allow the helicopter to stand off out of range of the ship's defensive systems. Typical homing systems are semi-active radar as in the Sea Skua; inertial guidance with active radar terminal homing as in the Sea Eagle and Harpoon; and inertial guidance with infra-red terminal homing as in Penguin. In most systems with inertial mid-course guidance, it is possible to

Left: The Agusta-Sikorsky ASH-3D carries the Marte Mk 2 anti-ship weapon system. The missile, seen here at launch, is a subsonic sea skimmer with a range of roughly 12 miles (20km). The target is acquired by radar and data is then processed and fed to the missile, which is a fire and forget weapon. After firing, the helicopter can evade immediately.

preprogramme the missile to fly a dogleg course to the target, so that it approaches from an unexpected direction.

SARH has the disadvantage that it requires the helicopter to illuminate the target by radar during the missile's time of flight. This may easily warn the target that it is being attacked, and give it time to deploy countermeasures. With the guidance systems that use inertial midcourse navigation, once the helicopter has acquired the target, it can switch the radar to standby, drop below the radar horizon where it is invisible to the target's radar, and feed attack data to the missile's autopilot via the attack computer. Alternatively, if two helicopters are working as a team, the detecting machine can transmit data for launch to its partner. If the two are widely separated, this, coupled with a dogleg approach by the missile, enables the attack to be made through the back door, so to speak. A further alternative is to allow friendly surface vessels to launch missiles on target data provided by the helicopter. Such a system allows surface ships to attack targets that are "over-the-horizon", the target data being supplied to the ship by an airborne helicopter.

Helicopters have vital roles to play even after the missiles are launched, both in defence and attack. Defensively they can deploy chaff and flares to decoy the missiles away from the ships. Offensively it would be possible for them to assist in defence suppression by launching anti-radiation missiles to home on the target vessel's radars, which will be vital to the defence. In this connection, the British Aerospace Alarm looks an absolute winner, as it can be launched before the defensive radars are switched on, and will loiter above the enemy force at high altitude, ready to activate as soon as a hostile emission comes on the air.

The Dogleg Attack

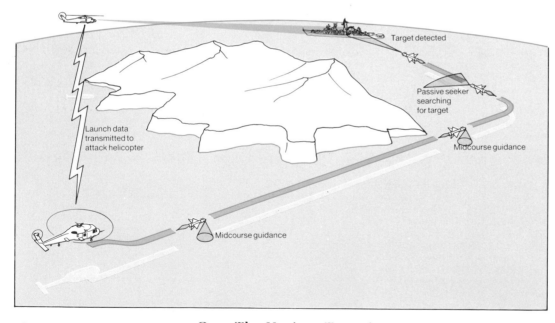

Target detected

Passive seeker searching for target

Launch data transmitted to attack helicopter

Midcourse guidance

Midcourse guidance

Above: A helicopter acquires the target on radar, and transmits data to its companion, lurking in the radar shadow of the island. It launches a Penguin, its midcourse guidance preprogrammed to fly a dog-leg course, so attacking from an unexpected direction.

Right: The helicopter can also be used to supply over-the-horizon targeting data for its own ship's missiles. The target would have little idea whether its attacker was ship, aircraft, submarine, or another helicopter, and little clue as to its position.

Over-The-Horizon Targeting

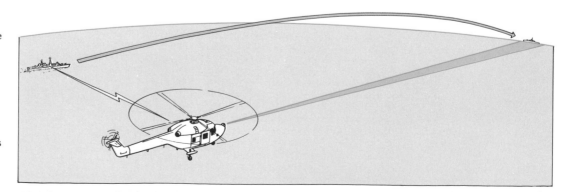

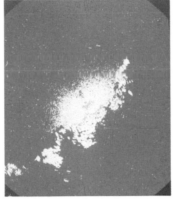

Above: The SA 365F Dauphin carries the Thomson-CSF Agrion 15 radar, the antenna of which is seen here looking like the business end of a vacuum cleaner. Four AS.15TT anti-shipping missiles are carried for which the radar provides semi-automatic command guidance.

Below: Helicopters are always likely to come under attack, and need countermeasures as much as any fixed-wing aircraft. A Boeing Vertol CH-46 Sea Knight puts on a great firework display using IRCM (infra-red countermeasures) flares which offer a confusing choice of targets to a heat-seeking missile.

Above: Radar processing has made giant strides in recent years. On the left is an unprocessed MEL Super Searcher display showing clutter. The processed picture (right) clearly shows the coastline, the helicopter in the centre, and just above it a previously undetected fighter.

Below: Different search patterns have been evolved to suit varying circumstances. This is the area search pattern. The length of leg flown is slightly less than half the time that the vessel sought will take to cross the scan width at full speed, while the spacing between legs is slightly less than the full scan width, to give an overlap that should ensure that nothing slips through undetected. If longer search legs are needed, the overlap can be increased or two helicopters may be used.

Area Search

Decoying missiles away from the ships sounds distinctly risky. Against sea-skimming missiles there is little danger, however, as the radar altimeters keep them at a pre-set height above the water, and provided that the helicopter keeps above this altitude, the missile will pass harmlessly beneath it. Some missiles, such as Penguin, have a terminal pop-up and dive trajectory. This presents more of a risk, but unless the helicopter gets in the way at the pop-up point, it should come to no harm.

Sea Skua Attack Profile

MARITIME PATROL

Patrolling may either be undertaken as a mission in its own right, or it may be an integral part of many other missions. It is a feature of any flight which does not involve a direct journey to a known destination. Searching is implied; and it does not matter whether this is for a target, or an object, or simply to check that no targets or objects exist in a certain area. The objective of the patrol is to sweep

the area in the most efficient manner, rapidly, but not so quickly that a chance exists that the object of the search will be missed. Fixed- and rotary-wing aircraft are complementary for maritime patrolling. The fixed-wing aircraft can cover a greater area than the helicopter in a given time by virtue of its speed, and possibly by virtue of the greater sophistication of its sensors. But in some circumstances, its speed is a handicap. It will have less time to see a man in the water as it sweeps

past; it is more limited in poor visibility; and if urgent assistance is needed on the surface, it cannot stop to help, as a rotor-craft can do immediately.

Various search patterns have emerged to suit different sets of situations. The dunking sonar search has been covered earlier, but there are many others. If the objective is to establish that no large ships are in a given area, a straight pass at medium altitude using radar will generally suffice. More complex patterns are derived from the need to search a wide area, and they are based on a combination of the width of scan in a single pass coupled with the cruising speed of the helicopter, modified by the maximum speed of the object being sought. Scan in this context can be defined as the width of vision by whatever means, reduced by a certain amount to give sufficient overlap to compensate for errors or unexpected events. The length of leg flown will be slightly less than half the time that the object sought would take to cross the scan width at full speed. If it is desirable to have longer search legs than this,

Left: A typical Sea Skua attack sequence. Flying a search mission, the helicopter detects a hostile vessel (1). Turning the radar off, it drops below the radar horizon and closes the target (2). When in range, it climbs, re-acquires the target, and launches a Sea Skua.

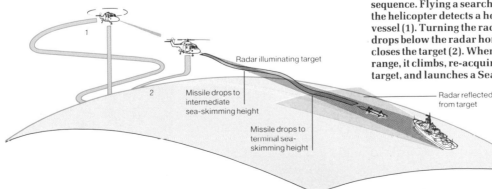

then two helicopters should be employed. The leg is flown, then the helicopter reverses its course and flies back on a reciprocal heading at just less than one scan width away from its original track. In this way the search area is gradually widened.

When searching for stationary objects, a disabled ship for instance, the procedure is somewhat different. The helicopter flies to the last known, or perhaps projected position, from where it begins a square search. This involves flying away from the position for a distance of just under a scan width, reversing course just under one scan width away, flying back to just under one scan width past the original position, then turning at right angles. For every stretch of water that has been scanned, the helicopter turns at 90 degrees, gradually enlarging the pattern at each turning point.

Very small objects demand a different pattern. In this case it might be a man in a dinghy, and visual search would be necessary. The search is started at the target's last known position, and the helicopter flies downwind, (the most likely direction) for a relatively short distance as determined by the prevailing conditions. Turning, he then flies at roughly a 72 degree angle to his previous course for a short time before turning yet again and heading in to cross the starting point once again. In this way, always turning in the same direction, a search pattern shaped like a five bladed fan emerges, with the most intense search taking place at the centre.

Patrol patterns are at the heart of most operations from search and rescue to fleet defence, and they also take in such diverse activities as monitoring fishing areas and anti-contraband operations.

Other activities related to maritime patrol are electronic support and intelligence gathering missions, the reconnaissance of a sparsely inhabited coastline,

The Square Search

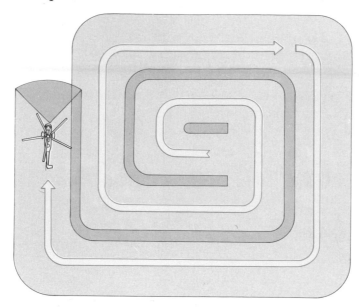

The Small Object Search

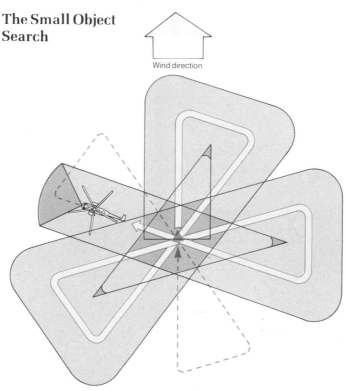

Wind direction

Left: The square search is used to find stationary objects. It starts from the calculated, last known, or projected position of the object sought. The first leg, often down wind, is flown for a distance of just under one scan width before reversing to just under a scan width off the original track. At the end of this leg, the helo expands the search pattern making a series of 90° turns.

Below left: A small object, such as a dinghy, or a man in the water is singularly difficult to find even in good weather. The small object search is designed to cross the most likely area many times, to produce the highest probability of success. The pattern is started at the last known position and is flown downwind for the first leg, turning for a short distance then turning again to cross the centre position and search upwind. So the pattern continues.

where the ability of the helicopter to investigate closely such features as small coves and inlets is invaluable, and naval gunfire support missions, where an observer spotting for the guns is carried, or in some instances, actually deposited in an advantageous position on shore, then lifted off again after the bombardment.

AIRBORNE EARLY WARNING

British experience in the Falklands conflict in 1982 clearly underlined the need for AEW as an organic part of the fleet. Prior to this it had been thought that operations would always be carried out within range of ground-based air support. By contrast the giant American carriers are equipped with their own fixed-wing AEW aircraft, but bearing in mind their size and the amount of power that such carriers represent, they are probably the world's highest value single targets, and as such, no expense has been spared to defend

Left: Bell AH-1S HueyCobras of the Japanese Ground Self Defence Force patrol a rugged coastline. They are armed with a universally mounted 20mm cannon in the chin position, eight TOW wire-guided anti-tank missiles, and two unguided rocket packs. This gives a healthy punch against both tanks and small ships.

Below: A Royal Navy Sea King Mk 4 airlifts a Snowcat tracked vehicle over the inhospitable wastes of northern Norway, while the crewman in the open door monitors progress. Helicopters permit very rapid deployment of troops and their equipment across rugged country.

Bottom: US Marines double across the deck of an amphibious assault ship to board a CH-46 Sea Knight. The helicopter gives rapid ship to shore deployment and can set down the troops accurately

them. But few if any carriers other than those of the United States Navy are large enough to accommodate aircraft like the Grumman E-2C Hawkeye.

An AEW helicopter was the obvious answer, and this duly emerged in the shape of the ubiquitous Sea King fitted with an adapted Searchwater surveillance radar with the antenna housed in an inflatable dome on the right hand side, which retracts through 90 degrees for takeoff and landing. The Sea King AEW can patrol the fleet at a moderate altitude at typically 20nm (23 miles, 37km) range for 3¾ hours. The radar has a full 360 degree scan and it is reported that it can detect bomber-sized targets at medium altitude out to a distance of 170nm (199 miles, 320km), and a low level cruise missile type target at some 40nm (46 miles, 74km). As one would expect bearing in mind its sea surveillance origins, Searchwater has good look-down qualities, and in fact, with little more than a bit of switchology, it can convert back into its sea surveillance role, in which it retains its air-to-air capability against low-flying aircraft. It can also exert an indirect influence on ASW and ASV operations. Long-range cruise missiles could be launched against the fleet either from surface vessels or from

Far left and left: The lack of organic airborne early warning cost the British forces dearly in the South Atlantic conflict in 1982. The result was the AEW helicopter, the ubiquitous Sea King fitted with a modified Searchwater radar carried in an inflatable radome which swivels aft through 90° when not in use. This example is from 849 Naval Air Squadron, based at Culdrose. The nearer picture shows the avionics compartment in the Sea King, with the Searchwater displays. It has quite a respectable performance and can easily convert back to an ASV function.

submarines using targeting guidance data provided by Soviet Tu-20 Bear D aircraft. This form of attack would be negated by interception using Sea Harriers controlled with the aid of information provided by the AEW Sea King.

COMBINED OPERATIONS

The role of the helicopter in combined operations is to get the marines ashore as quickly and safely as possible, together with all their equipment, artillery, vehicles, and first line ammunition. Once there they must be kept supplied, reinforced, and moved from place to place as the tactical situation demands. Support must also be given in the shape of artillery spotting, general airborne observation, and unit co-ordination, if necessary directly from the helicopter. Anti-tank helicopters will give added firepower, and in the case of the USMC, gunships are routinely carried on their amphibious assault craft, for defence suppression. The task of the main force of helicopters is to land the "boots" in the right place in the space of a few minutes so that they can immediately start to act as a co-ordinated force. To do this, the transport helicopters will utilize evasion and concealment measures as previously described. In the South Atlantic in 1982, helicopters proved invaluable for rapidly transferring troops and materiel from ship to shore, and then maintaining the pace of the advance across the island, particularly in carrying artillery pieces, ammunition and general supplies. Casualties were carried on the return trip, enabling them to reach medical attention very quickly. As a direct result, very few succumbed to wounds that might otherwise have proved fatal.

The British 3 Commando Brigade is assigned to the protection of the Northern Flank of NATO, operating in the far north of

Norway. The country is inhospitable and the surface communications poor. The helicopter gives them mobility and keeps them supplied in the very worst Arctic conditions. Normally the helicopters will operate in ones or twos, but on a raiding mission, six or even twelve may be used. The largest scenario envisaged is the two company lift; 240 marines together with artillery, vehicles and supplies. This will take up to two dozen helicopters, all flying in the confined space of a Norwegian valley. They would fly tactically, taking advantage of all

concealment that the terrain offers, in a long corridor. In winter the helicopters wear white camouflage to decrease their visibility. If they have to spend any time on the ground in an area where an enemy air threat exists, a parachute draped over the canopy prevents the Sun from glinting on the perspex, which is one of the surest giveaways.

To sum up, in combined operations the helicopter is the greatest force multiplier for the Marines on the ground, acting in both the mobility and logistical roles.

The Battlefield Missions

Tactics can be fairly defined as the art of combining firepower and movement. The unique qualities of the helicopter have revolutionized the modern battlefield: they can bring firepower to bear at the critical point with great rapidity, put down troops complete with their equipment with great precision, and keep them supplied. All this is coupled with the ability to cross difficult or impassable obstacles with ease, and to turn flanks where previously no flank had existed. Air mobility and vertical envelopment are the new buzzwords. Furthermore it is not beyond the bounds of possibility that in the next ten or twenty years the helicopter may supersede the tank, which is looking increasingly vulnerable to modern weapons.

AIR MOBILITY

Air mobility must not be confused with air portability. History shows that small, well trained, and extremely mobile forces can affect the battle, or even the campaign, to an extent completely disproportionate to their numerical strength. Air portability is a valuable asset, let there be no doubt about that. It allows troops and equipment to be moved rapidly to a threatened area to execute a blocking movement, and to reinforce and resupply an advance in double quick time. But air mobility is something else again. Basically it calls for specially trained and equipped units capable of carrying out hard hitting and flexible operations, often behind enemy front lines. For this role the helicopter is invaluable. It can take the troops in, set them down pretty well exactly in the place that they need to be, give them fire and anti-armour support, keep them supplied, and at the end of the day, either extract them, or redeploy them as the situation demands.

It is a truism of war that battles are often won or lost in the minds of the field commanders. The battlefield has always been a confusing place and the fog of war is hard to dispel. The mobility of modern armies using fast-moving armour and motorized infantry will only add to the confusion, and for long periods commanders will be uncertain of the true situation. Helicopter-borne cross-FLOT (Forward Line Of Troops) operations will add greatly to the confusion and may well give rise to doubt or hesitation in the minds of the commanders of the forces against whom they are directed.

Left: A HueyCobra skims low over broken country at sunset. A close support and attack helicopter, the AH-1 has a two man crew seated in tandem, with the pilot behind the gunner, and carries a wide variety of weapons. This dramatic picture captures the atmosphere of the hunter about to stalk its prey.

Units attacked from an unexpected direction, especially from the rear, will be disorganized, while no unit can proceed very far with a blocking force across its POL (Petrol, Oil, Lubricants) supply lines. Chaos can equally result from a cross-FLOT raid on a command unit, if this can be identified and hit. Specific operations by the main forces can be aided, such as an opposed river crossing, by dropping formations in the rear of the enemy defences. Quite apart from tactical considerations, morale tends to suffer in a unit threatened from both front and rear. On the other hand, an airmobile unit operating behind enemy lines can act both as an objective for a friendly armoured thrust, and a relatively safe area in which it can regroup.

Crossing the FLOT obviously presents problems. A spot must be selected where there is a gap between enemy formations, and this depends on good intelligence. Failing this, a weak sector or link must be chosen through which a corridor can be blasted, probably by a combination of artillery and air strikes backed up by helicopter gunships. Crossing the FLOT by night is a possibility, as this gives a measure of protection against enemy optically-guided weapons, but as the helicopter needs to fly rather higher by night than by day it will be more vulnerable to radar-laid weapons. In daylight conditions it will use terrain masking and all other concealment measures as described earlier. Speed is of course an advantage, so long as it does not compromise the necessity of remaining undetected. It is always better to arrive a few minutes late than end as a smoking heap on the ground on the way to the objective.

Air mobility, while it depends on the speed and cross-country capability of the helicopter, also relies on speed of reaction. Mission planning must be meticulous; each helicopter must know exactly where on the landing site to set down its load, whether troops or weapons or vehicles, so that they are best placed for instant use, and command contingencies must be catered for in the event of casualties or radio failure.

Left: Abseiling from a hovering helicopter, in this case a UH-60 Black Hawk, enables troops to be set down in otherwise inaccessible places, such as a mountain ridge or a jungle clearing. The key to the battlefield is mobility, and the air mobility provided by the helicopter force can influence events out of all proportion to its numerical strength.

Generally of course, radio silence will be observed; where it is absolutely necessary single code words are used to modify previous instructions. If pick up is required, the timing of the operation will be even more critical than that of the landing. The last thing the troops or the helicopter force can afford is to hang around waiting for one another. But while a high level of precise planning is required, it must not take so long as to prejudice the speed of reaction, or the vital opportunity may be missed. This is where an air-mobile force differs from an air-portable unit, which is not specially trained for the task.

THE BATTLEFIELD HELICOPTER

The battlefield helicopter carries out many roles, anti-armour, infantry fire support, scouting and general reconnaissance, forward air control, artillery spotting, acting as an elevated command post, and mine sowing, quite apart from logistic support, CASEVAC etc. Although not yet used in a major conflict, the helicopter is now regarded as an important battlefield weapon in its own right. How it is used will depend on the specific role for which it is tasked, the weapons fit, the tactical situation, and the operational doctrine of the user nation. Essentially it is an offensive weapon, even though at times used in a defensive situation. Its first task on the battlefield is often thought to be the suppression of anti-air weapons, which are its main enemy. This achieved, it can get on with the job in hand, that of defeating the enemy forces. To the man in the street, the helicopter is a slow and noisy, rather oddly-shaped flying machine. It is relevant to ask how it appears to the other side. Just for interest,

Above: The Boeing Vertol CH-47 Chinook is a medium lift machine and is used by many nations in the logistics support, troop and cargo carrying roles. This example is airlifting an M198 howitzer which is carried as an underslung load. The Chinook gave sterling service in the Vietnam war.

Below: UH-60 Black Hawks seen here transporting light vehicles across desert terrain. The Black Hawk can carry an 8,000lb (3628kg) cargo load or 11 fully equipped troops. This variant is primarily used by the US Army Airborne Divisions. Performance is remarkable for its size.

what is the Soviet soldier's impression of a battlefield helicopter? And how does he propose to deal with it? Tank commander Guards Senior Sergeant A. Bespalov addressed the problem in Znamenosets in 1982.

"Helicopter gunships were the most impressive sight for both me and other novice tank crewmen. Now that's a really formidable weapon, I thought to myself. Can anybody stand up to it? . . . As a rule, helicopters appear suddenly over the battlefield, utilizing various kinds of cover . . . Anyone spotting helicopters should immediately radio the threat in the clear . . . As soon as I am alerted by radio that a helicopter has been sighted, or if I have spotted a helicopter I at once order the driver: 'Stop!' I pick up the target and take accurate aim. I fire a short (3 to 4 rounds) ranging burst. Since the gunner is permitted to determine the distribution of tracer rounds in the belt, I put most of these rounds at the very beginning. This way it is easier to range, especially on a sunny day. If the first burst is off target, I quickly adjust my aim and fire a long burst for effect . . . An opportune moment to open fire is when a helicopter hovers for several seconds to take precise aim at its selected armoured target . . . if I have missed a hovering helicopter I immediately order the driver 'Advance!' Staying put means becoming a good target for the helicopter. The driver must be completely competent in his manoeuvres, advancing to the next stopping point at high speed, sharply changing direction right and left.

"Now let's assume that the helicopter has fired an anti-tank missile from a range of say 3000m (9,843ft). There is no need to panic, for the missile will be in flight from between 15 and 20 seconds. This is plenty of time for the driver to execute an evasive manoeuvre."

Finally Sergeant Bespalov delivers his verdict, "No matter how potent a modern helicopter with its formidable weapons may be, it can successfully be engaged by a tank crew with high proficiency and excellent morale."

The foregoing may be accounted unduly optimistic and not terribly realistic, but it probably reflects the view of tank men of all nations that they are going to fight back to the best of their ability. Nor should it be over-looked that tank guns acounted for some two dozen helicopters in Lebanon in 1982. Much the same attitude is evident in the infantry, as the following extract from a 1984 article in *Voyennye Vestnik*, by Major-General M. Belov shows.

"Success in combating enemy helicopters depends to a large extent on the personnel's psychological stability, and their readiness to fight in the immediate vicinity of the ground enemy and under the effects of his rifle, machine gun, and artillery fire . . . In order to develop the soldier's mental readiness to combat enemy helicopters, it is important for them to picture this combat clearly and to be sure of their own weapons and equipment. The most important conditions for preventing a 'fear of helicopters' in the privates and NCOs of the motorized rifle *podrazdeleniye* [squads] is a clear impression of the picture of real combat, a

Above: The beam gun position is not of the best. The arc of fire is restricted, and the problems of target precession, bullet drop and vibration all reduce accuracy.

Left: Military Exercise Caucasus 85, and Soviet Mi-24 Hind gunships make a simulated missile attack on a tank force. The Hind is not well suited to NOE flight and would appear vulnerable to ground fire.

knowledge of the strong and weak points of enemy helicopters, a conviction as to the possibility of effective struggle against them (on some days South Vietnamese patriots shot down five or six helicopters of the American interventionists with the organic weapons of the rifle squad), and an ability to handle one's weapon expertly."

One would expect that training the infantry to fight back with rifles was more of a morale booster than anything else, and the exhortation to emulate the Viet Cong in a war that ended a decade and a half ago seems a bit slim. But not a bit of it! General Belov continues: "It is advisable to give trainees practice in conducting concentrated fire . . . It is advantageous to conduct this fire with small arms in bursts

of five to eight rounds, with an overall expenditure of up to a magazine of cartridges per sub-machine gun or machine gun. Experience indicates that this density of fire provides reliable destruction of unarmoured targets . . . at distances up to 500m (1,640ft).

Soviet riflemen not only shoot at helicopters, they are sometimes in the helicopters, being shot at. Naturally they prefer to shoot back, adding their fire power to that of the helicopter when on an assault mission. We have all seen news film of American door gunners over Vietnam blazing away. It looks easy, but the problems are more intractable than most. When a bullet leaves the gun, it first encounters the downwash from the rotor. It is affected by the speed of the helicopter causing a relative wind, lead must be allowed for a fast-moving target, while the relative movement of the helicopter and the target may cause the target to precess. All these must be allowed, plus bullet drop for range. Both rifle and machine gun fire are intensively practised, from moving railway cars and from helicopter mockups suspended from a cableway. Writing in *Znamenosets* in 1978, Senior Sergeant P. Fedorov outlined the basics, "the position of the sighting point depends on the speed of helicopter flight, the direction and speed of target movement, the distance between them, and the direction and velocity of the wind . . . (We used) the simple, easy to remember rule: to determine the lead, divide the speed by ten. It helps the rifleman orient himself quickly and find the amount of lead exactly because 10 per cent of

Target Lead, Air to Ground

All speeds are in km/hr. Distances are in metres. The Soviet rule of thumb is to divide the relative speed of the target by 10 which gives the lead in metres. Here are shown the aim points needed to hit various moving and static targets.

Right: A door gunner blazes away with his M60 machine gun from a UH-1H Huey over Vietnam. His field of fire is better than that shown on the facing page, but he still needs a considerable amount of agility to be effective. More than 1,000 Hueys were lost over Vietnam between 1967 and 1970.

Below: The multi-barrelled M134 7.62 mm Minigun gives new meaning to the term "blaze away" as it spews bullets at a ground target. Close examination shows the empty cases being ejected overboard; this gives a clue to the high rate of fire of this weapon, which is used against soft targets. The helicopter is the UH-60.

the speed in km/h gives the magnitude of the lead in metres with sufficient accuracy, and it is not difficult to translate metres into target lengths in order to read off the magnitude of aiming . . . and not get shot down while tracking." This bare description is however a little misleading. When he talks of "speed", he is referring to the relative speeds over the ground of the helicopter and the target. A helicopter making an air speed of 100kt (115mph, 185km/h) into a 30kt (35mph, 56km/h) headwind, has a ground speed of 70kt (81mph, 130km/h). Therefore, against a static target the lead should be 13m (43ft). If the target is 4m (13ft) long, the lead should be three target lengths. If however the target is moving, its speed will modify the calculation. If it is moving in the same direction as the helicopter, its speed must be deducted from the equation; while if movement is in the opposite direction it must be added. The helicopter ground speed may well be known, but the target speed must be guessed; there will be no time for precise measurement. Add to this the helicopter vibration and the fact that the target is unlikely to be on a parallel course, and it can be seen that a great deal of "Kentucky windage" is involved. "Lead" against a moving target can also be misleading. If the helicopter and a moving target are both heading in the same direction, precession of the target will occur, it will appear

to be moving backwards relative to the helo. Under these circumstances, "lead" will be the distance of aim-off *behind* the target. All in all, it appears that accuracy will be at a premium under these circumstances and is likely to serve little purpose other than keeping the defender's heads down.

THE SCOUTING MISSION

In a confused battlefield situation, it may be necessary for helicopters to reconnoitre in order to establish both the enemy line of thrust and their progress to date. Methods will vary according to circumstances; in Afghanistan for instance, against relatively primitively armed tribesmen, it is possible to stand off at medium altitude and scan the area, or even to try to draw their fire. This would prove an expensive luxury in a central European war against an opponent lavishly equipped with modern weapons. But in either scenario, one rule holds good. A scouting mission must be carried out by a pair of helicopters, partly for mutual support, but mainly so that in the event that one is shot down, it is known instantly what has happened to it. A recce trip flown solo which ends in the helicopter being lost without reporting back is worse than useless; the mission must be reflown, and time is wasted.

Operational Effect of Scout Helos

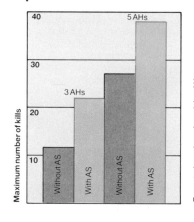

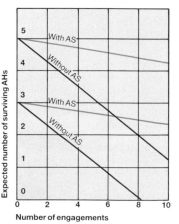

It can be argued that on the modern battlefield the helicopter should not be used for scouting, and that cheaper and less vulnerable RPVs should be used to gather the necessary information. But in some circumstances it cannot be replaced. The helicopter can carry a forward air controller (FAC) to direct strikes, either by fixed-wing aircraft or by attack helicopters. Alternatively it can be used to direct artillery fire. The RPV that can carry out these functions has yet to be invented. The particular value of the FAC is that in most cases air strikes are carried out by reference to specific geographical points which the pilots can identify, for example 1,500ft (457m) north east of the hill

Above left: Scout helicopters to control the attack increase the attack helicopters' effectiveness. Operational analyses (above) show that without scout helicopters co-ordinating the mission, attack helicopter losses will increase.

with the barn on the south side and clump of trees on the summit. The FAC is uniquely able to pass on directions of this nature, calling in cab ranks of aircraft to the attack. Rapid response is the name of the game, and the scout helicopter has a valuable role to play. But in central Europe it would be forced to make full use of all available cover, creeping forward until contact with the enemy was made.

Left: For the scouting mission, helicopters will work in pairs wherever possible, so that if one is lost, the circumstances will be known, and the survivor will take over the mission. They will not however fly the close formation shown here by A 129 Mangustas of the Italian Army, but will spread wide and leapfrog one another from cover to cover when in proximity to enemy forces.

Above left: An MBB BO-105P of the West German Army breaks cover and fires a HOT anti-armour missile. Aiming is done through a roof-mounted sight. Six HOT missiles are normally carried.

Above: A typical ambush position as a West German BO-105P, armed with six HOT missiles, lurks just below the treeline. This picture illustrates just how closely a helicopter can get into cover.

THE ATTACK MISSION

The attack helicopter's weapons vary, but they generally consist of anti-tank guided missiles, optically or laser guided; pods of unguided rockets; and either a cannon or a heavy machine gun facing forward. The gun may be either fixed, or mounted in a traversable barbette. Normally the helicopter will come to the hover in order to aim its weapons, but Soviet Hinds in Afghanistan have been reported as using a high speed diving attack, followed by a hard breakaway at low level. On the modern battlefield, this ploy appears to be positively suicidal, but while the Hind is the fastest military helicopter in service today, its response to control inputs is slow and its transient performance correspondingly poor. It is not suited to Western style NOE flying, and judging by Soviet training missions that have been described in military magazines, it seems to be regarded as a fast tank, used both in conjunction with the armour and to guard the flanks of an armoured thrust, with the accent on speed rather than avoiding detection.

The Western attack helicopter doctrine emphasises the avoidance of detection, using hover-taxying just above the earth, at some sacrifice of speed, and attacking from ambush wherever possible. Where dedicated fixed-wing anti-tank aircraft are available, the attack helicopters will work closely with them, concentrating on suppressing the opposing anti-air weapons while the fixed-wing fliers, probably American A-10s, deal with the tanks.

Defending against an armoured thrust, the ground will be carefully reconnoitred and defensive positions selected. These could be woods, escarpments, buildings or any form of cover that offers. Let us take the British Army Air Corps methods as an example.

The minimum number of helicopters deployed to an ambush will be three, but there will probably be a greater number, depending on the overall situation. If one is lost to any cause, there will still be a pair remaining, which is the smallest tactical unit. They will deploy behind the lines in a position which gives an unobserved run to the selected ambush positions, into which they will only move when there are bare minutes to spare. A tank attack will inevitably be accompanied by self-propelled artillery, and the gunners may decide to give possible helicopter ambush positions a working-over beforehand. If this is the case, moving the helicopter into position at the last possible moment may save unnecessary casualties.

Once in the ambush positions, the helicopters will observe the advancing armour, and select their

Below: Ambush positions are chosen in advance where possible, together with secondary hiding places. The attack helicopters, three is the preferred minimum number, position themselves in the secondary hides, only taking up the ambush position at the last moment.

Ambush Positions

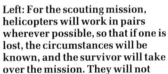

Ambush positions

Secondary hides

The Battlefield Missions

targets. The AAC Lynx has a roof-mounted sight, and this high location enables it to operate with only the sight and the rotor visible to the enemy. To launch its missiles, usually the BGM-71 TOW, the helicopter must break cover, either with a pop-up or pop-sideways manoeuvre. This is performed to allow the missile to clear the cover, although when it is in flight, the helicopter can resume its former position with just the sight exposed, to allow tracking to take place. The operator's task is to keep the sight aligned on the target; TOW, which is wire-guided, is corrected automatically. The accuracy in practice firings exceeds 90 per cent; while this cannot be expected to be achieved in battle, such missiles are nevertheless going to do a great deal of damage to an opposing force. The ambush helicopters remain in position, using their weapons as long as is feasible; when their hides start to come under heavy fire, then is the time to pull back to the next position, ready to repeat the dose. The selection of the ambush sites is a matter for careful consideration. They should not be too obvious; they should not be on the skyline; they should allow the helicopters a concealed approach and retirement; and they should allow the full range of the anti-tank missile to be used.

Springing the Trap

The future of the helicopter in the anti-armour role appears to lie in new technology. The mast-mounted sight will enable the helicopter to keep even its rotor down below cover, while new weapons will be able to be launched in a "fire and forget" mode, allowing simultaneous attacks on multiple targets. It should also be possible for them to be fired from behind cover, popping up and over before lining up on target. To a degree such capabilities are with us in the shape of Hellfire, which uses laser homing, and can be utilized with ground based designators. If these have individual coding, missile launches in very quick succession

Laser Designation and Targeting

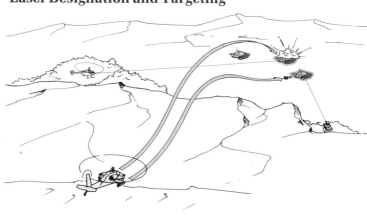

Above: The McDonnell Douglas 530MG is small and compact but it packs a deadly punch. It is seen here launching a TOW optically-tracked wire-guided anti-armour missile. The sight is mast mounted above the rotor which reduces the amount of helicopter exposure.

Left: The helicopter will remain behind cover for as long as it can but when the time comes for it to launch a missile, it is forced to break cover, using either a pop-up or a pop-sideways manoeuvre. Good control transients are needed.

Below left: Laser-guided weapons such as Hellfire can be launched from concealed positions. All that is needed is a designator, either in another helicopter or on the ground, to illuminate the target. Multiple attacks are possible.

become possible. Imaging infra-red (IIR) guidance is yet another possibility. This is not to suggest that simple optical guidance is the only feasible method at the moment. If this were the case, smoke or poor visibility or night conditions would make operational employment of the weapons impossible. This is of course not so, and the reader is referred to "Visionics and Sensors" for a fuller discussion of the available technology.

ANTI-PERSONNEL AREA SUPPRESSION

Although the anti-armour mission is important, it should not be

Multi-Dart Helicopter Anti-Armour System

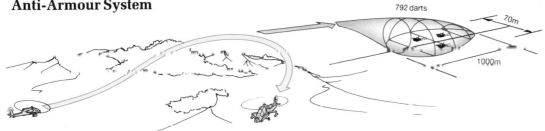

792 darts
70m
1000m

Left: An interesting combination of the anti-personnel fleche of WW I vintage, and the SNEB pod is the Thomson-Brandt Multi-Dart anti-armour system. A battery of 68mm rockets is launched at the target, these burst after a predetermined time, releasing a shower of armour-piercing steel darts at high velocity. A total of 792 darts spreads over an elliptical area of 55,000m². This gives a density of one dart to every 70m².

Right: Unguided rockets are not the most accurate weapons, and it is usual to salvo, or ripple fire (as here) them to saturate the target area. An Army Air Corps Lynx lets fly with a battery of SURA rockets at a range target.

allowed to obscure the fact that the infantry are the most important troops on the battlefield. The attack helicopter must be prepared to deal with them too. This is where pods of unguided rockets, and also the gun, have a vital part to play. To use the rockets effectively, the helicopter must leave the shelter of the ground, execute a rapid climb followed by a brief attack run, aim and launch the rockets, at the same time spraying the general area to keep the defender's heads down, and follow this with a hard downward break. Ideally the climb should be initiated from a concealed position; if there are hills in the background the maximum altitude should not take the helicopter above the skyline, while the direction of the break should be towards cover. The attack should be made by many helicopters in rapid succession, approaching from different directions. Careful planning and timing is essential to prevent a helicopter straying into the path of "friendly" fire. An attack of this nature is designed to reduce the effectiveness of counter air fire by confusing the defenders and diffusing their fire effect.

The Soviet Union has developed a minimum strike element of three machines. Colonel B. Nesterov, writing in *Aviatsiya i kosmonavtika* in 1983, describes its workings.

"The combat formation would consist of a two helicopter search and strike element and a single

helicopter to provide cover. The strike pair would fly in loose formation, parallel to the battle line. The wingman would be positioned slightly to the rear, and somewhat higher than the leader. The third helicopter would bring up the rear at a distance ensuring good visual contact and mutual fire support. They would fly at minimum altitude and at optimum speed. Following the orders of the leader (shown by changes in aircraft altitude), they would from time to time turn towards each

Below: The nose of the Apache is packed full of sensors. Central above the nose is the FLIR, while the pale blue object houses the direct view optics, with day TV below, and laser designator at bottom. On the other side is the night vision sensor. Hellfires are carried.

other at a 15 or 30 degree bank and change positions in the formation. This would make it possible to increase their detection range for camouflaged or concealed point targets, would lessen the accuracy of ground air defence weapons, and improve observation of the rear hemisphere. The flight commander flies the cover helicopter. His prime mission is battlefield command and control. He suppresses defensive fire from the flanks on the front pair, and is the first to attack the ground target if the strike element is late in spotting it."

The weaving as described is interesting. It provides a better chance of spotting a concealed point due to the rapidly changing angles. The weaving might also have the effect of making the formation's course appear

uncertain to the defence, although there is a penalty to be paid in terms of a reduction in the speed of advance over the ground. The cover helicopter also plays a part in guarding against air attack on the search and strike element. On the other hand he is himself very vulnerable, having no cross-cover. Finally, any opponent who has heard of this tactical formation will concentrate their defensive efforts on the rear helicopter, and in the long run this could prove costly in flight commanders.

Below: The front two helicopters patrol in sucked abreast formation with the wingman slightly higher. Every so often they change places, alternately gaining and losing height. The element leader brings up the rear. In a real war, this might prove costly in leaders.

Soviet Three-Ship Element

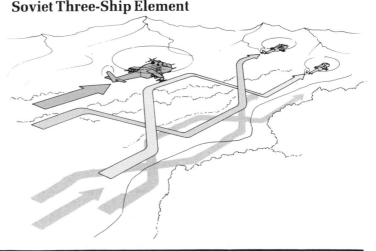

Helicopter Air Combat

The widespread use of helicopters has ensured one thing: they are certain to encounter fixed-wing aircraft over the battlefield. They are also certain to encounter other helicopters. These two are different ball games, and therefore must be considered separately.

The performance disparity between a modern fixed-wing fighter and a modern helicopter is so wide as to make it look, at first glance, a "no contest". In terms of performance alone, it is the equivalent of a modern supersonic fighter of the 1980s versus a flying machine of World War I vintage. The disparity of weaponry also appears to make matters worse, as the fighter will often be carrying radar-homing, beyond-visual-range missiles, and almost certainly close-range, infra-red-homing dogfight weapons. By contrast, the helicopter will most likely be armed with air-to-gound weapons which are not exactly suited to the air-to-air arena. The views from the opposing cockpits are totally different, and we shall examine them in turn.

FIGHTER V. HELICOPTER

The fighter pilot does not see the helicopter as an easy target. The main reason for this is that the

Above: A Sikorsky H-76B Eagle during air-to-air combat trials. It is armed with a BEI Hydra 70 rocket launcher. The role and tactics of the helicopter in air-to-air combat is currently the subject of much intensive research and evaluation.

Left: In the unhappy event of a war in Central Europe, the main fixed-wing air threat to NATO helicopters would be the MiG-23 Flogger, many hundreds of which are allocated to Frontal Aviation, but the main air threat will come from Soviet helicopters.

helicopter pilot is on home ground; he is used to flying at zero feet, hopping over hedges and dodging around trees, and is quite capable of leading the fighter slap into a power line if there is one in the vicinity. By contrast, the fighter pilot is used to moving around the countryside at about 900ft/sec (275m/sec) with about 250ft (76m) clearance. Over flat, bare terrain he can hack it lower than this, but when there are obstacles around, the speed does not give him much time to avoid them. At typical helicopter altitudes, he is not very happy.

NOE flying also negates his superior weaponry to a great extent. His pulse doppler radar enables him to look down at the

Right: This TOW-armed AAC Lynx, flying down among the weeds, makes an almost impossible target for a fighter, which would need to use doppler radar for look-down. The Lynx speed would probably be below the Doppler threshold, but radar returns from the rotor, first from the advancing then the retreating blades would be picked up and be wildly conflicting.

helicopter from a safe height, but if its relative speed is less than 90kt (104mph, 167km/h), the doppler threshold will filter it out in the same way that it would filter out a moving car on a road. Using ordinary pulse radar, the helicopter may well be lost in the ground returns. But even if he can acquire it, illuminating it for a radar-homing missile launch is a very different matter. Radar impulses reflecting off the helicopter's rotor blades will produce a mass of conflicting radar returns, causing either the radar or the missile to break lock. Heat homers are a bit better, although compared with an afterburning jet fighter, the helicopter is not a very strong IR emitter. There are always heat emissions from the ground; the Sun reflecting from snow is a surprisingly strong source of IR radiation, while in a battlefield scenario, a burning tank may confuse the issue. Even assuming a missile can track the helicopter, if launched at a shallow angle (as it is likely to be), it may easily impact the ground as it corrects its course. There is a fair chance also that its proximity fuze may be triggered

prematurely, either by the ground or by obstacles that it passes on its track. To summarize, missiles might work, or they might not. This leaves the gun. There may well be problems with radar ranging, which means that fixed sight must be used. A report from the October War of 1973 credits an Israeli fighter pilot with making no less than eight passes against a helicopter using radar ranging

before switching to fixed sight for the kill. Rarely will there be time even for three passes in a battle situation!

Cannon shells are unaffected by the proximity of the ground, but the fighter pilot is. To make a guns pass against a helicopter, he has to get down low, point down at the target, and get in close. If he has managed to surprise the helo pilot, and approach unobserved from six

o'clock, then all well and good. But a diving attack against an ultra-low target is something else again when it is manoeuvring defensively. Nor can its weaponry be ignored. The fighter totally outperforms the helicopter, but the helicopter can totally outmanoeuvre the fighter at close quarters. The fighter pilot is taught in air combat manoeuvring never to overshoot his opponent, but against a helicopter, overshooting is completely unavoidable. If the rotary-wing craft is armed with air-to-air missiles, it can spin around and launch at the departing fighter's tailpipe before it can get out of range. What can the fixed wing pilot do to avoid becoming a target? The helicopter will be turning as he approaches, and he will also be turning to track it. As he passes it, he can reverse his turn and exit in the other direction, thus giving the helicopter a greater angle of traverse to acquire him, by this means buying a few extra seconds in which to open the range. He can pass as close over the top of the rotor as he dares; his jetwash might just tip the helicopter out of control (flight safety separation distances are quite high), or he can disengage by pulling vertically upwards, although in the proximity of enemy air defences this would be inadvisable; he might find that a SAM was following him upstairs.

Left: Some real NOE flying by an Agusta A 109A, hugging the slope line with just enough clearance to avoid embarrassment if caught by an unexpected downdraught. NOE flying in any but flat and open terrain makes attack by a fixed-wing fighter difficult, if not impossible, unless it is carrying rocket pods. It would take a very mean fighter pilot to dig this A109A out of its hole.

These three methods of overshooting would be fine against a single helicopter, but in a one versus two situation, the second helicopter is almost invariably going to get a shot at him. A single fighter attacking two helicopters should attempt the surprise attack from astern, but failing this, a line of approach that puts both the helicopters in the line of fire at once is probably the best course to follow.

A straw poll of fighter pilots revealed that if they encountered a helicopter by chance, they would have a go at it, but if the first attack failed they would not persevere. Risking a multi-million pound fighter against a comparatively cheap helicopter is not a reasonable proposition in the normal way of things. Only in exceptional circumstances, such as a large scale helicopter raiding force crossing the FLOT and heading for a vulnerable rear area, would fighters be tasked against helicopters. It is equally unlikely that fighters would intervene against a helicopter force over the battlefield. The difficulty of integrating fighters with Army SAMs and anti-aircraft guns would be extreme. While fighter pilots seem generally agreed that the gun is the best weapon to use against a helicopter, it was also suggested, and widely approved, that a pod of SNEB unguided rockets would be effective. They have a reasonably long range, and a pod of them would spread to cover a wide area, giving a high chance of a hit.

HELICOPTER V. FIGHTER

The helicopter does not have the performance to carry the fight to the fixed-wing aircraft, and therefore must always fight on the defensive, during the performance of its main mission. The main mission is of primary importance and so the objective of the

helicopter pilot is to survive the fighter attack. Kills are a bonus, what our American friends would call "frosting".

The best way to survive fighter opposition is to avoid detection. By the nature of things, the helicopter will be flying lower than the fighter, and all else being equal, the odds are greatly in favour of the helicopter pilot sighting the fighter before he himself is seen. Few helicopters have any rearward visibility, and this must be countered by flying in pairs abreast for mutual cross cover. If the helicopter crewman, sometimes referred to as the "talking baggage", is not engaged on essential tasks, he should also be employed on lookout duty. A weaving course should also be adopted to clear the blind spot astern, especially if the Sun is in this quarter.

When a fighter is sighted, the helicopter pilot performs the airborne equivalent of the infantryman's dive into a ditch; he will try to lose himself in dead ground and hide behind hills, trees, or whatever cover presents itself. If caught completely in the open, altering course directly away from the fighter may help, as this will present little or no relative movement, and relative movement is one of the first things to catch the eye. There is an excellent chance of remaining unobserved, as the fighter pilot will be concerned not only with his main task, but also with keeping a lookout for enemy fighters.

Above: A Wessex Mk 5 of the Royal Navy seen contour chasing over Dartmoor during a fighter evasion exercise. Helicopter rear vision is notoriously poor and the Wessex is no exception. If the aircrewman in the back, "the talking baggage", has nothing more urgent to do, he should have his head in the port side blister.

Right: The attack begins when the fighter turns to bring its nose to bear. The helicopter pilot has to spoil the shot by a combination of manoeuvre designed to both reduce the tracking time and change the angle off, and (below) increase the fighter's dive angle and rate of descent. The proximity of the ground is quite a deterrent.

Evasion: Helicopter v. Fighter

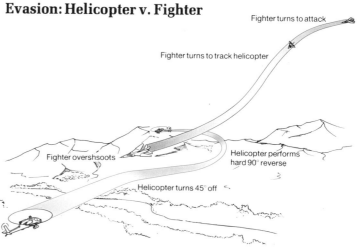

Fighter turns to attack

Fighter turns to track helicopter

Fighter overshoots

Helicopter performs hard 90° reverse

Helicopter turns 45° off

Increasing the Dive Angle

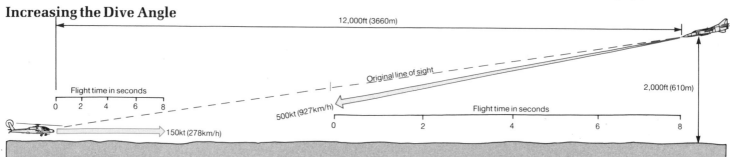

12,000ft (3660m)

Flight time in seconds

0 2 4 6 8

Original line of sight

2,000ft (610m)

Flight time in seconds

0 2 4 6 8

500kt (927km/h)

150kt (278km/h)

Left: A prototype Mirage 2000 lets fly with four SNEB pods. Not an intrinsically accurate weapon, the 68mm unguided rockets spread to give a shotgun type effect. While most fighter pilots questioned favoured the gun to attack low flying helicopters, many advocated using the unguided rocket pod.

If the helicopter has been seen, this will quickly become apparent, because the fighter will manoeuvre to reach an attacking position, usually turning towards the helicopter.

As the fighter turns in to attack, the helicopter should perform the standard air combat manoeuvre and turn into it. At the same time, it should gain 150 to 200ft (45 to 60m) of height. Turning into the attack has two advantages. It increases the rate of closure, which gives the fighter less time to line up his attack. It also brings the helicopter's weapons to bear. In this connecton, it has been claimed that an Iraqi Hind shot down an Iranian Phantom in a head-on pass, although this cannot be regarded as more than a lucky break for the helicopter crew.

As the fighter begins to line up for the attack, the helicopter should offset its course by up to 45 degrees to complicate the tracking solution. The fighter will have started out from a higher altitude in a shallow dive, the rapid closure will ensure that this steepens quite quickly, while the helicopter's course change will ensure that the fighter has to attack from a banked position. The dive angle will be quite shallow, but it will increase the fixed-wing pilot's "pucker factor" by quite a margin. At a speed of 500kt (575mph, 925km/h), a dive angle of just ten degrees will give a vertical rate of descent of almost 150ft/sec (46m/sec). As he closes the helicopter, not only will he be losing altitude fast, but the dive angle will be ever steepening and the vertical rate of descent increasing. Manoeuvring to track the target as well further

compounds the problem. Then when he establishes the correct overlead and rolls his wings level, the helicopter should perform an abrupt 90 degree reversal in the opposite direction, which will force the fighter to roll in the other direction to realign his sights. As the fighter appears to be reaching guns range, inside about 5,000ft (1,524m), the helicopter can get rid of its excess height with a dive or sideslip. This has the effect of making the helicopter appear to drop out of the bottom of the gunsight. If this manoeuvre can be timed to take the helicopter behind cover, then that is perfect, but either way, the fighter pilot has the choice of pushing his nose even further down in order to track, and by this time the ground is coming very close, or breaking off the attack. By these means it is estimated that the helicopter has a 90 to 95 per cent of defeating the attack over land, and at least a 70 per cent chance over water.

Defeating a missile attack is slightly different, but the missile will be launched from a fair

Above right: The disparity in performance and agility between a helicopter and a jet fighter is such that if the fighter attack fails, it risks having the tables turned as he overshoots.

Right: To avoid becoming a target when its attack fails, the fighter should pass close inboard of the helicopter to deny it lateral turning room, then reverse and extend away at low level.

Below right: The Sikorsky H-76 Eagle is a very clean and agile helicopter which is being promoted for military use. This example is engaged in air combat manoeuvring with the camera ship.

Below: Low level manoeuvring is essential in the combat area. This McDonnell Douglas 500MD Defender demonstrates a daisy cutting turn while carrying a full war load.

Turning the Tables

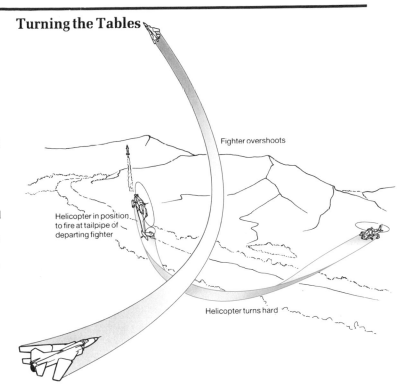

Fighter overshoots

Helicopter in position to fire at tailpipe of departing fighter

Helicopter turns hard

The Correct Fighter Overshoot

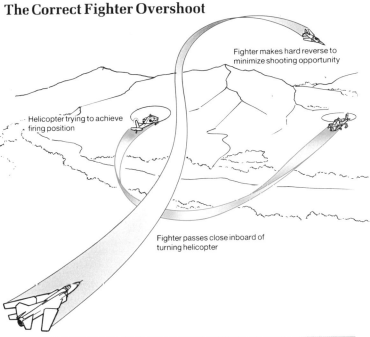

Fighter makes hard reverse to minimize shooting opportunity

Helicopter trying to achieve firing position

Fighter passes close inboard of turning helicopter

Left: A fighter passing close to a helicopter to deny it turning room is all very well, but the pintle-mounted 7.62mm Miniguns in each doorway of this UH-60 Black Hawk make it distinctly risky. Against this adversary, the fixed-wing fighter needs to pull up so that it is shielded by the rotor.

Above: The AH-64A Apache, carrying a full war load, demonstrates a wingover. While this is the most rapid way of changing or reversing course, it involves a pull-up, which means leaving the shelter of the ground. In the presence of a well-armed adversary, this is perilous.

distance, and the launch will be readily apparent to the helicopter pilot. In this event he gets down as low as possible, turning 90 degrees angle off as he does so, and heads for the nearest cover. As we have seen, air-to-air missiles have problems against targets at ground level. The 90 degree angle off is simply to give the missile's homing and tracking system the maximum amount of work to do.

Assuming that the helicopter is armed, no matter how unsuitable the weapons, it should always try for the first shot. This will give the fighter pilot something else to think about other than achieving a firing solution. Air-to-air missiles are nice to have, as quite apart from their probability of kill, they are a very effective deterrent. If the

fighter pilot is aware that his target may be carrying them, he will be much more circumspect in his approach, conscious that he is tangling with an opponent vastly superior in rate of turn. The helicopter may well have a front gun, either fixed or traversing, and this should be used liberally, preferably with tracer, even though this does not show up too well from a close-range target approaching from head-on. Modern multi-barrel cannon are first class, as their bullet drop is very low; they are therefore very accurate, although the sighting system is unlikely to be optimised for air-to-air combat. Even a 7.62mm machine gun should be used if opportunity offers; it will be a slight distraction, and with luck

it might just damage the engine of the fighter. Anti-tank missiles, such as TOW or HOT, can also be used; scoring a hit would be a matter of extreme luck, the fighter pilot almost certainly would not see it coming, but he would be aware that something had been launched at him and be unsure of what it was. In short, anything that distracts the fighter pilot from his attack and uses up units of his mental capacity is of value. A very useful alternative would be to loose off a pod of unguided rockets at the fighter. This would play Hob with the pilot's concentration, and there is a fair chance that he might go look for someone who doesn't play so rough.

The usual outcome of all these situations is that the fighter will overshoot the helicopter, and this is where it might possibly turn the tables. In fixed-wing combat training, fighter pilots are taught to pass close inboard of a better-turning opponent to deny them lateral turning room. If the helicopter carries a beam gunner, this could prove to be a serious mistake. Tracking the fighter would be impossible, but a line of fire across the fighter's track may prove effective. Even small arms can be damaging at close range.

Turning ability is basically a function of velocity, and the low speed of the rotary-winged machine enables it to turn very fast indeed. If the turn is initiated quickly enough, the helicopter will get a shot at the departing fighter's rear end, preferably with a heat missile, but a cannon could prove deadly. A valid alternative at this stage is for the helicopter to disengage; the chances are that the fixed-wing fighter will have lost visual contact, and judicious use of cover will ensure that it is not regained.

If the fighter has not lost contact, this will become apparent as after the run-out, it will be seen to turn and line up for a second pass. It should be clearly visible in the turn as it will be presenting its largest, i.e. planform aspect. The helicopter should then turn towards it, not directly into its line of approach, but roughly towards the centre of the circle that the fighter is turning around. This will hopefully force the fighter to back off and reposition, as while he continues to circle, the helicopter will always be moving towards the centre, with the fighter trying to fly in ever decreasing circles to line him up. Helicopters can do this for as long as need be, fixed-wing aircraft cannot!

HELICOPTER V. HELICOPTER

The previous section made it clear that a contest between fixed-wing jet fighters and helicopters is a mismatch, and that when both are handled correctly and the surprise bounce is absent, they are not, in battlefield terms, very dangerous to one another. A fixed-wing aircraft dedicated to anti-helicopter missions would need to be something like an armed Pitts Special! From this it emerges that the best counter to the helicopter is an air combat helicopter, armed for the task, slightly faster and more agile than most, and with specially trained crews. This would be able to tackle the battlefield helicopter in its own ultra-low level environment.

In some ways, helicopter air-to-air tactics are reminiscent of the biplane era; speeds and turning rates are fairly similar, helicopters will use the basic element of two, flying abreast for mutual cross-cover, and height will constitute a

Thwarting a Second Attack

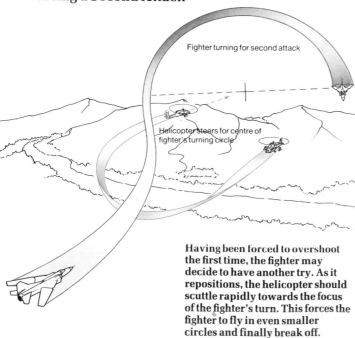

Fighter turning for second attack

Helicopter steers for centre of fighter's turning circle

Having been forced to overshoot the first time, the fighter may decide to have another try. As it repositions, the helicopter should scuttle rapidly towards the focus of the fighter's turn. This forces the fighter to fly in even smaller circles and finally break off.

tactical advantage once battle is joined. It will also be a matter of ambush, and making the most of the factor of surprise. Missiles may be used, but the primary weapon is likely to be the gun.

Disengagement will, however, be more difficult as speed margins will not vary widely, and rarely will there be sufficient height to allow a diving disengagement. This factor is compounded by the long range and great accuracy of modern cannon. Combat will be more two dimensional than is usual with flying machines, and this will place a premium on agility, rate of turn, and transient performance, which is the ability to change flight modes rapidly.

Simulated helicopter combats have generally tended to last only about half a minute and take place

Below: Modern small helicopters are fully aerobatic and some can even take a little negative g. Flown by the incomparable Captain Charley Zimmermann, of German Army Aviation Regiment 16, this MBB BO 105M is put through a loop, as part of a full aerobatic display.

at close range. Like fixed-wing combat, the adversaries strive to achieve a shooting position from which they cannot be shot, which means six o'clock and preferably above. Even door gunners cannot shoot up through their own rotor disc. Once combat is joined, the scramble for position is on, and achieving the high perch while out-turning the opponent to gain a six o'clock position often results in a continuing upward spiral, in the manner of the vertical rolling scissors practised by fixed-wing fighters. But over the battle area, gaining height may not be desirable. Giving the ground gunners target practice is no part of the deal.

At present, helicopter versus helicopter combat is very theoretical. Tactics are being evolved, but these can only be proven on the battlefield, and when real bullets are flying, pilots are less inclined to be fancy. I suspect that in the event, it will be rather similar to tank warfare, albeit faster moving, and consisting of ambushes, raids, and above all, co-ordinated movement and teamwork.

The High Yo-Yo

Attacker pulls high to avoid an overshoot

Attacker manoeuvring for 6 o'clock position

Defender breaks hard

Above: Detecting an attack coming in from astern, the defending helicopter breaks hard into it. To avoid an overshoot the attacker pulls high before dropping in astern.

Opponent forced out in front

The Horizontal Scissors

Attacker increases rate of turn

Helicopter turns hard to reduce forward speed

Above: The scissors consists of a series of hard turns aimed at reducing the forward velocity vector enough to force the opponent out in front into the weapons envelope.

The Side Flare Quick Stop

Deceleration and side flare starts

Attacker climbs and accelerates into 6 o'clock position

Threat overshoots

Above: This manoeuvre was developed by the USMC as a counter to a close range attacker. It involves rapid deceleration combined with out-of-plane manoeuvring.

The Stern Conversion

Below: This consists of a quick offset climb followed by a turning dive into a high six o'clock position. It is countered by a matching climb which ends in an upward spiral.

Attacker accelerates and performs wing-over

Turning dive into attack position

Threat approaching head-on

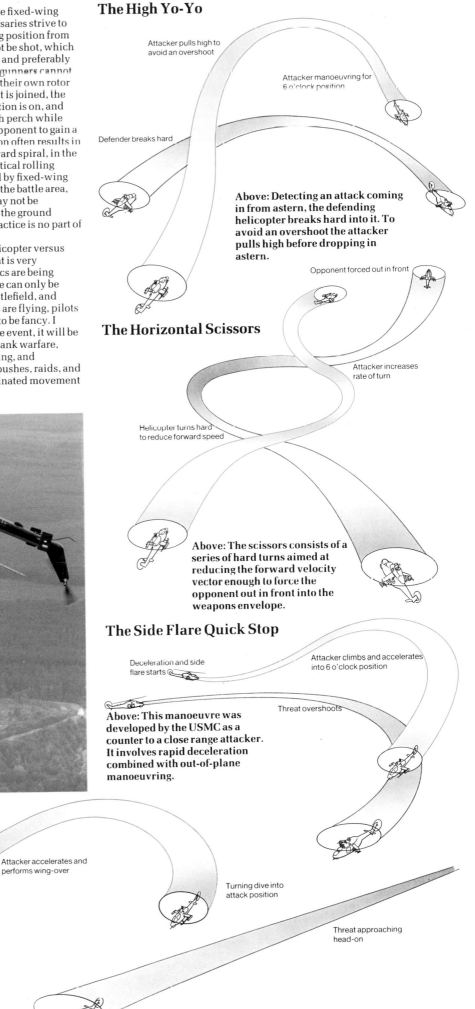

Glossary

A

AAH Advanced attack helicopter.
AAM Air-to-air missile.
ABC Advancing-blade concept, a fundamentally new type of coaxial rotor in which rigid blades are used with all lift coming from the advancing blades.
ACAP Advanced composite airframe program (US).
ACT Active-control(s) technology.
ADF Automatic direction-finding, using radio signal-strength methods.
ADOCS Advanced digital optical control system.
AEW Airborne early warning, using high-flying surveillance radar.
AFCS Automatic flight-control system.
AGM Air-to-ground missile.
AH Attack helicopter(US), Army helicopter (UK).
AHIP Army helicopter improvement program (US).
AHRS Attitude/heading reference system, an avionic device containing precision gyros, usually accelerometers and a microprocessor, and often accepting inputs from Doppler, Omega, GPS Navstar, Tacan or other sensors. The output includes attitude, heading (not necessarily related to true North), and usually rates and accelerations about all axes.
ALH Advanced light helicopter (India).
ALWT Advanced lightweight torpedo.
angle of attack The angle at which a blade meets the air.
Ångström Unit of length, 10^{-10}m.
Anvis Aviator's night-vision (imaging) system.
APDS Armour-piercing discarding sabot, high-velocity gun ammunition.
APU Auxiliary power unit, used mainly on the ground.
ARTI Advanced rotorcraft technology integration.
articulated A rotor hub which provides coning/flapping and lead/lag drag hinges, as well as rotary bearings for pitch change.
ASM Air-to-surface missile.
ASST Anti-ship surveillance and targeting, often to guide missiles fired from friendly ships.
ASV Anti (or air-to) surface vessel.
ASW Anti-submarine warfare.
axial In line with the major axis, thus a gas-turbine compressor in which the air flows parallel to the major axis of the engine, or a gun firing directly ahead.
azimuth Angle in the horizontal plane; bearing or direction.

B

BERP British Experimental Rotor Programme.

C

C³I Command, control, communications and intelligence (I sometimes also said to stand for IFF).
casevac Casualty evacuation.
Cassegrain Optical telescope in which the incoming radiation is reflected by two parabolic mirrors one after the other.
CH Cargo helicopter (US).
chaff Billions of small slivers of metallised plastic which, falling slowly through the sky, form an impervious barrier to radar signals.
chord Distance across a blade or wing, from leading edge to trailing edge.
CKD Component knock-down, new products are despatched from the factory in the form of major assemblies which are put together in a customer's country.
CNI Communications/navigation/ IFF
coaxial Describes upper and lower main rotors turning in opposite directions about the same axis.
collective The flight control channel which increases/ decreases the pitch of all main-rotor blades simultaneously.
composite Material consisting of very strong fibres held together in a matrix of adhesive (usually a resin).
coning angle Angle between the longitudinal axis of a main-rotor blade and the tip-path plane (sometimes inaccurately defined as the vertical angle between the blade root and the axis of rotation).
CPG Copilot/gunner.
CRT Cathode-ray tube.
cyclic The flight-control channel which varies blade pitch cyclically through a maximum and a minimum twice on each revolution.

D

DA Direct acting (fuze).
data bus Main highway along which passes data in the form of electronic signals.
DF Direction-finding, using radio methods
Dicass Directional command-activated sonobuoy system.
Difar Directional acoustic frequency analysis and recording (sonobuoy system).
DME Distance-measuring equipment, using time-of-flight measures of a returned radio signal.
DoD Department of Defense (US).
doppler Form of radar which can measure the difference in frequency between signals reflected from the ground ahead of the aircraft and those reflected from behind, thus giving ground-speed and the drift due to wind.
drag hinge Hinge permitting rotor blade to pivot to front and rear in the plane of rotation.
DVI Direct voice input.

E

Ebsicon Trade name for one type of advanced optical image-intensifier tube.
ECCM Electronic counter-countermeasures, intended to defeat ECM.
ECM Electronic countermeasures, designed to interfere with hostile radars and other sensors.
EH Electronic helicopter, to fly ECM/Elint missions.
elastomeric bearing A bearing in which there is no sliding friction, relative movement between parts being accommodated by elastic distortion of rubber blocks forming the joints.
Elint Electronic intelligence, seeking the fullest knowledge of hostile electronic signals.
ELT Emergency locator transponder.
EM Electromagnetic radiation
ESM Electronic surveillance (USA) or support (UK) measures, typically comprising airborne receivers which measure, analyse and locate the source of enemy radio or radar signals.
ESSS External stores support system (can be attached to Sikorsky UH-60 Black Hawk).
EW Electronic warfare, including ECM, ESM, Elint and many other topics.

F

Facts FLIR-augmented Cobra TOW sight.
FADEC Full-authority digital engine control.
FBL Fly-by-light, use of optical fibres to carry coded light signals to convey main flight-control demands.
FBW Fly-by-wire, use of electric cables, usually in the form of multi-core flat strips, to convey flight-control demands in the form of variable electric currents.
Fenestron Aérospatiale tail rotor with many small blades shrouded in the centre of the tail fin; now adopted in the USA as the fin-mounted rotor.
FFAR Folding-fin aircraft rocket.
flapping hinge Hinge which allows the tip of the blade to pivot upwards.
flechette Small but heavy dart intended to fall on soft targets such as infantry.
FLIR Forward-looking infra-red sensor, seeing objects ahead on a basis of their temperatures.

FOV Field of view
FTS Flexible turret system.

G

GHz Gigahertz, thousands of millions of cycles per second.
GPS Global positioning system.
GPWS Ground-proximity warning system
Ground effect Effect of having a solid flat surface close beneath a hovering helicopter.
gyrostabilized Mounted on gimbals (pivots) and held in a constant attitude, no matter how the helicopter manoeuvres.

H

HACS Helicopter armoured crashworthy seat.
HADS Various meanings, in this context helicopter air-data system.
HAR Helicopter, air rescue (UK).
HAS Helicopter, anti-submarine (UK).
HC Cargo helicopter (UK).
HDD Head-down display, inside the cockpit.
HEI High-explosive incendiary type ammunition.
Helras Helicopter long-range active sonar.
HF High frequency (which is much lower than the VHF and UHF used in most helicopter radios).
HH Search and rescue helicopter (US).
HHC Higher harmonic control.
HIGE Helicopter in ground effect
HISOS Helicopter integrated sonics system.
HLH Heavy-lift helicopter.
HMS Helmet-mounted sight.
HPS Helmet pointing system, in which sensors and/or weapons are slaved to the direction of the wearer's helmet.
hub The centre of a main or tail rotor to which the blades are attached.
HUD Head-up display, cockpit instrument which projects on to a glass screen numbers, symbols and other information all focussed at infinity so that the crew-member can study it while simultaneously watching the ground ahead.
HUM Health and usage monitor(ing).

I

IFF Identification friend or foe, an automatic interrogation/respond radio system which instantly identifies friendly stations (others in peacetime being "unidentified", in wartime being "hostile").
IGE In ground effect, as if the helicopter had the ground immediately beneath it.
IHADSS Integrated helmet and

display sighting system.

II Image intensifier, for use in near-darkness.

ILS Instrument landing system, long-established method of approaching a runway in bad weather.

IMS Integrated multiplex system.

INS Inertial navigation system, completely self-contained and relying on super-accurate gyros and accelerometers.

IR Infra-red, loosely the same as heat.

IRCM Infra-red countermeasures, protecting a vehicle against missiles which fly towards a heat source.

K

kHz Kilohertz, thousands of cycles per second.

L

LAAT Laser-augmented airborne TOW.

LAMPS (Lamps) Light airborne multi-purpose system.

LDNS Laser/doppler navigation system.

lead/lag damper Cushioning buffer to stop blades from being overstressed as they come up against the lead/lag stops.

lead/lag stops Rigid buffers which permit only a limited amount of blade angular movement in the plane of the rotor (trying to catch the blade in front or falling behind).

LED Light-emitting diode.

LHX Light experimental helicopter program (US Army).

LINS Laser inertial navigation system, in which a special laser circuit replaces physical gyros.

LIVE Liquid inertial vibration eliminator.

LL(L)TV Low light (level) TV.

LOAL Lock-on after launch.

Loc Locator beacon.

LOH Light observation helicopter.

LOS Line of sight.

LPI Low probability of intercept, ie an anti-Elint feature.

LRU Line-replaceable unit, a single electronic "black box"

M

MAD Magnetic anomaly detector.

MCM Mine countermeasures, the main element of which is minesweeping.

MCP Microchannel plate.

medevac Medical evacuation; differs from casevac in that patients are typically sick rather than injured.

MFD Multifunction display, a TV-type cockpit display surrounded with buttons with which the user can call up different "menus", or size scales, or many other variables.

MH Multimission helicopter.

MHz Megahertz, millions of cycles per second.

microchannel plate Insulating (dielectric) plate with millions of exceedingly close parallel lines photographed into its surface.

microwave EM radiation of about 1 to 300GHz, falling between far-IR and radio waves.

MLS Microwave landing system, a newer concept than ILS.

MMS Mast-mounted sight which carries sensors high above the rest of the helicopter.

MPPS Multipurpose pylon system.

MTR Main and tail rotor.

N

NFOV Narrow field of view.

Nodamatic Patented form of vibration-damping system in which the connection between the main rotor and the helicopter is flexible and tuned by vibrating masses.

NOE Nap of the Earth, ie at the lowest safe level. In NOE flight speed seldom exceeds 20-25mph (32-40km/h), especially in bad weather.

Nomex Trade name for a particular sandwich structural material with internal "honeycomb" to stabilize the light skin.

Notar No tail rotor (a McDonnell Douglas experimental programme).

NVG Night-vision goggles.

O

OCM Optical countermeasures.

OEI One engine inoperative, a special high-power rating permitted on the remaining engine(s) for short periods.

OGE Out of ground effect, ie with an empty void beneath the helicopter.

OH Observation helicopter.

Omega A navaid having worldwide coverage, using eight ground radio stations; it is especially useful for helicopters as it works down to ground level.

optical fibre Also called a light pipe, a fine fibre consisting of a core of one type of glass surrounded by a sheath of a different type; light is endlessly reflected at the interface and travels to the end of the fibre.

OTH Over the horizon.

P

photon The individual "parcel" of light, that emitted by the transition (from one state to another) of a single electron.

pintle Pivoted mount for a gun aimed by hand.

pitch The angle of a rotor or propeller blade, measured against a fixed setting independent of airflow direction.

PNVS Pilot's night vision sensor.

R

RAM Radar-absorbent material(s).

RAST Recovery assist, securing and traversing (across a ship deck) – a system to help helicopters land on a ship's deck.

RCS Radar cross-section, the apparent size of a target as seen on radar.

RH Reconnaissance helicopter.

rigid rotor One whose blades can flex but have no normal pivoted hinges at the hub.

RLG Ring laser gyro.

RMI Remote magnetic indicator.

ROC Required operational capability.

RSRA Rotor systems research aircraft.

RWR Radar warning receiver, telling a flight crew if their aircraft is being "illuminated" by hostile radar.

S

Saclos Semi-active command to line of sight.

SAM Surface-to-air missile.

SAR Search and rescue; also synthetic-aperture radar.

SCAS Stability and control augmentation system.

SCAT Scout/attack version of LHX.

SFC Specific fuel consumption, rate of fuel consumption for a given power output.

SH Anti-submarine helicopter (US).

Shadow Sikorsky helicopter advanced demonstrator of operator workload.

sidestick Miniature control column at the side of a cockpit through which the pilot can fly the aircraft, using small hand movements.

SIF Selective identification facility (or feature), which enables an aircraft instantly to broadcast its identity on IFF or on ground radar or other distant interrogator.

SL Sea level.

SLAR Side-looking airborne radar.

SOTAS Stand-off target acquisition system.

spm Shots per minute.

sponson A large fairing projecting from the side of the fuselage, looking like a very short thick wing.

SSB Single sideband radio transmission.

SSR Secondary surveillance radar.

Starflex Trade name of Aérospatiale advanced hingeless rotor system.

Steradian Unit of solid angle which, at centre of a sphere, defines an area at sphere's surface equal to square whose side is radius of sphere.

stopped-rotor aircraft Helicopter whose rotor can be slowed down and stopped in flight, its blades thereafter behaving like four wings.

swashplate A disc either fixed or rotating on the main rotor drive shaft, which is tilted in various directions by the pilot's control inputs. Rods from the swashplate control the pitch angles of the blades.

T

Tacan Tactical air navigation system, a simple radio navaid using ground stations.

TADS Target acquisition designation sight.

teetering Balanced at mid-point, like a see-saw.

TFR Terrain-following radar.

TI Thermal imager

tip path The path in space traced out by tips of rotor blades.

torque The turning effect applied to a shaft.

translational flight Flying from one place to another.

triple-A Anti-aircraft artillery (flak).

TWS Track while scan (radar).

U

UH Utility helicopter.

UHF Ultra-high frequency radio.

unmask To let a helicopter come into view of the enemy.

UTS Universal turret system.

V

VCASS Visually coupled airborne systems simulator.

VDU Visual (or video) display unit.

VFR Visual flight rules, ie good weather.

VHF Very high frequency radio.

vidicon A TV camera tube.

visionics Collective term for electronic and electro-optical devices which enhance human vision in darkness, fog or other adverse conditions.

VLF Very low frequency, used for long-range communications, especially with submarines.

VOR VHF omni-directional range, the commonest airline navaid using numerous ground radio stations.

VROC Vertical rate of climb.

VSI Vertical speed (or rate of climb/descent) indicator.

W

WFOV Wide field of view.

Y

yaw Rotation of aircraft about vertical axis, to point in different directions in horizontal plane.

Index

Picture Credits

The publishers wish to thank the many individuals, manufacturers, and defence organisations who have so generously provided illustrations for this book. They are here credited by page number.

Aeronautical Systems Division, USAF: 10/11, 35 lower right, 74 upper.
Aérospatiale: Endpapers, 53 lower, 60 upper, 61 upper, 80, 83, 86, 88, 90, 91, 92
Agusta: 26 upper, 32 centre and both bottom, 64 upper, 95, 96, 98, 194, 199 lower
Aviaexport: 144 upper
Barr & Stroud Ltd: 38 lower left
Paul Beaver: 38 upper, 39 lower, 179 lower left
BEI Defense Systems: 55 (cutaways)
Bell Helicopter Textron: 18 lower, 71 lower, 73 lower, 75 bottom left, 76/7, 77 centre right, 102
Bell-Boeing: 106
Boeing Vertol Company: 8 (upper), 22, 29 bottom, 35 top, 110, 191 upper
British Aerospace: 2/3, 33 centre and bottom left
Austin J. Brown Aviation Picture Library: 116
Decca Navigation Co: 33 top
Department of Defense, Washington D.C.: 4/5, 9 lower, 17 upper, 19 upper, 27 upper, 53 centre, 55 upper, 65 centre and lower right, 67 lower, 68 centre, 68/9, 104, 108, 139, 146, 151, 172 upper, 173, 176 lower, 180 upper, 187 centre, 190 upper, 191 lower, 192 upper
Dowty Electronics: 183 centre right
DTCN: 63 middle
Emerson Electric: 50 upper, 54 top
Euromissile: 37 bottom, 57 cutaway
Ferranti Defence Systems: 46
Ferranti Instrumentation: 45 upper
FFV Ordnance: 70 top, 71 both upper
Fleet Air Arm: 174/5
Fabrique Nationale Herstal S.A.: 201 lower left
Gamma/Frank Spooner Pictures: 122, 143

GEC Avionics: 41 upper right, 43 centre right, 47 top, both centre
General Electric: 50 lower, 52 upper, 54 centre, 193 bottom, 202 top left
Helmets Limited: 65 top right
Mike Hooks: 134
HMS Gannet Photographic Dept: 8 lower
HMS Heron, Yeovilton: 160, 178 upper, 200 centre
HMS Osprey, Portland: 56 upper left, 162, 168, 172/3
Honeywell Inc: 41 bottom
Hughes Aircraft Co: 36, 37 upper left, 42, 43 top right, 56 upper right, 190 upper
Indal Technologies: 175
Institut Lotnictwa: 132
Kaman Aerospace Corporation: 30 lower, 63 top, 119, 181 lower
Kongsberg Vapenfabrikk: 61 cutaway
LHTEC: 28
Link Flight Simulation Division: 9 upper
Loral Electro-Optical: 70 lower right
Lucas Aerospace: 15
Martin-Baker Aircraft Co: 65 lower left
Martin Marietta Aerospace: 31 centre left, 44, 54 lower
Matra: 59 lower
McDonnell Douglas Helicopter Company: 6/7, 16, 23 upper, 24, 29 centre and upper right, 31 upper and lower right, 52 lower, 58 lower, 64 lower, 67 upper, 73 upper, 74 lower, 75 top and centre right, 77 bottom, 79, 123, 130, 176 upper, 177, 178 lower, 189 top, 196, 202 top right
MEL: 66 top and centre, 187 top centre and right
Messerschmitt-Bölkow-Blohm GmbH: 17 lower, 18 upper, 19 lower, 21 right, 30 upper, 35 lower left, 39 upper, 55 lower, 57 both lower, 72 upper right, 114, 124, 126, 172

lower, 185 bottom, 195, 203
NATO: 120
Northrop Corporation: 43 bottom
Oto Melara: 61 lower, 186
Plessey Marine: 48 upper right
Pratt & Whitney: 29 upper left
RNAS, Culdrose: 62, 180 lower, 188 lower left
RNAS, Yeovilton: 21 left
Rolls-Royce: 25 lower left, 26 lower
Sanders: 70 lower left
SFIM: 43 centre left
Sikorsky Aircraft: 20 left, 23 lower, 58 upper, 72 upper left and centre, 75 centre left, 76, 77 centre left, 152, 154, 156, 158, 181 upper, 198 upper, 201 lower right
Smiths Industries: 27 lower
SOPELEM: 40
Mike Spick: 179 centre right
TASS: 136, 142, 144 lower, 192 lower
Thomson Brandt Armements: 200 top
Thomson-CSF: 182, 187 top left
Thorn EMI Electronics Ltd: 188 lower right
T.R.T.: 49
Turboméca: 25 upper and lower left
US Air Force: 14/15
US Army: 1, 105, 193 centre, 197 lower
US Navy: 14, 47 bottom, 48 upper left, 68 left, 100, 109, 140, 141, 148, 150, 183 lower left, 189 bottom
Westinghouse: 48 lower left
Westland Helicopters Ltd: 20 upper right, 32 top, 33 bottom right, 34, 37 upper left, 38 lower right, 41 upper left, 45 lower, 48 lower right, 51, 56 lower, 59 upper, 60 lower, 63 bottom, 66 bottom, 84, 112, 164, 167, 174, 184, 185 top and centre, 189 centre, 197 upper, 199 upper

Landing on a moving deck requires precision flying; this is an SA 365F Dauphin.